Getting It Wrong

Getting It Wrong

How Faulty Monetary Statistics Undermine the Fed, the
Financial System, and the Economy

William A. Barnett

The MIT Press
Cambridge, Massachusetts
London, England

MIT Press books may be purchased at special quantity discounts for business or sales promotional use. For information, please email special_sales@mitpress.mit.edu or write to Special Sales Department, The MIT Press, 55 Hayward Street, Cambridge, MA 02142.

This book was set in Palatino by Graphic Composition, Inc., Bogart, GA. Printed and bound in the United States of America.

Library of Congress Cataloging-in-Publication Data

Barnett, William A.
Getting it wrong : how faulty monetary statistics undermine the Fed, the financial system, and the economy / William A. Barnett ; foreword by Apostolos Serletis.
    p. cm.
Includes bibliographical references and index.
ISBN 978-0-262-01691-9 (hbk. : alk. paper) — ISBN 978-0-262-51688-4 (pbk. : alk. paper)
1. Monetary policy—United States. 2. Finance—Mathematical models. 3. Financial crises. 4. Econometrics. 5. United States—Economic policy—2009– I. Title.
HB139.B3755   2012
332.401'5195—dc23

2011021050

10 9 8 7 6 5 4 3 2 1

Dedicated to the memory of the great econometrician,
Henri Theil, 1924–2000

Contents

Foreword: Macroeconomics as a Science

Apostolos Serletis

There have been dramatic advances in macroeconomics as a science during the past thirty years, but this book's findings nevertheless provide compelling reasons to be cautious about the field's current state of the art, the quality of data on which its conclusions are based, and the central bank policies associated with those conclusions. In this foreword, I provide my own views. In this book, the author, William A. Barnett, wrote part I without mathematics and with minimal use of technical terminology. His reason was to make part I accessible to all readers. His part II is for professionals, and uses both mathematics and professional terminology. While my foreword similarly avoids the use of mathematics, I do use terminology that may be unfamiliar to noneconomists. As a result general readers may find this foreword to be more challenging to read than this book's part I. But I hope that all readers will be able to grasp the general point that I am trying to make in this book's foreword.

Following the powerful critique by Robert E. Lucas Jr. in 1976, the modern core of macroeconomics includes both the real business cycle approach (known as "freshwater economics") and the New Keynesian approach (known as "saltwater economics"). Previously there was a political gap, with the freshwater approach associated mostly with economists having a conservative philosophy, and the saltwater approach associated mostly with economists having a politically liberal philosophy. The current more unified core makes systematic use of the "dynamic stochastic general equilibrium" (DSGE) framework, originally associated with the real business cycle approach. It assumes rational expectations and forward-looking economic agents, relies on market-clearing conditions for households and firms, relies on shocks (or disturbances) and mechanisms that amplify the shocks and propagate them through time, and is designed to be a quantitative mathematical formalization of the aggregate economy.

The real business cycle approach, developed by Finn Kydland and Edward Prescott (1982), is a stochastic formalization of the neoclassical growth model and represents the latest development of the classical approach to business cycles. According to the original real business cycle model, under the classical assumption that wages and prices are fully flexible, most aggregate fluctuations are efficient responses to random technology shocks, and government stabilization policy is inefficient. However, the opposing New Keynesian approach advocates models with sticky prices, consistent with the assumption of sticky nominal wage rates in Keynes's (1936) famous book, *The General Theory*. The New Keynesians point to economic downturns like the Great Depression of the 1930s and the Great Recession that followed the subprime financial crisis, and argue that it is implausible for the efficient level of aggregate output to fluctuate as much as the observed level of output, thereby advocating government stabilization policy.

In recent years, however, the division between the real business cycle approach and the New Keynesian approach has greatly decreased, with the real business cycle approach dominating in terms of its modeling methodology. Thus, the current New Keynesian approach to macroeconomics is based on the methodology originally associated with the real business cycle theory (i.e., the "dynamic stochastic general equilibrium" framework) and combines it with Keynesian features, like imperfect competition and sticky prices, to provide a theoretical framework for macroeconomic policy analysis. Also most recent real business cycle models assume some type of nominal rigidities, so that both technology and demand shocks play a role in determining business cycles. Exceptions include models based on search theory, rather than price rigidities. Both the real business cycle model and the New Keynesian model are largely immune to the Lucas critique, and both recognize that some form of government stabilization policy is actually useful.

How does monetary policy analysis relate to modern macroeconomics? The mainstream approach to monetary policy analysis has primarily become the New Keynesian model. In this New Keynesian modeling approach, monetary policy is often not expressed in terms of money measures (known as monetary aggregates), but in terms of the short-term nominal interest rate. It is to be noted, however, that although monetary policy in those models is not expressed in terms of monetary aggregates, the Fed's adjustments of the nominal interest rate translate into changes in the monetary aggregates. For example, when the Fed conducts open market operations to achieve the desired target for the federal funds rate, it exchanges the "monetary base" (the monetary aggregate directly affected by the Fed's open market operations) for government securities. In New Keynesian models that do not include money directly in the transmission mechanism of monetary policy, money is a derived demand determined in general equilibrium with other important variables. In such models, money remains an important indicator of the state of the economy and of other variables, often a lead indicator.

Within most New Keynesian models, central banks use the short-term nominal interest rate as their operating instrument, but the effects of monetary policy on economic activity stem from how long-term real interest rates respond to the short-term nominal interest rate. In particular, under the assumption of sticky prices, an expansionary monetary policy that lowers the short-term nominal interest rate (e.g., the federal funds rate in the United States) will also lower the short-term real interest rate. Moreover, according to the expectations hypothesis of the term structure of interest rates, the decline in short-term interest rates will also lead to a decline in long-term interest rates and ultimately affect aggregate demand.

This transmission mechanism is intended to work well, even when the short-term nominal interest rate is at or close to zero. With a nominal interest rate of zero, a commitment by the central bank to expansionary monetary policy raises the expected inflation rate, reduces the real interest rate, and leads to a rise in aggregate output. Thus expansionary monetary policy could stimulate spending, even when the short-term nominal interest rate is at zero. This mechanism is in fact a key element in many monetarist discussions of why an expansionary monetary policy could have prevented the sharp decline in output in the United States during the Great Depression of the 1930s, why it would have helped the Japanese economy when nominal interest rates fell to near zero in the late 1990s, and why it could help the United States accelerate the economic recovery in the aftermath of the Great Recession.

However, the collapse of stable relationships in financial markets may be causing the term structure of interest rates relationships, on which the New Keynesian transmission mechanism depends, to loosen. For example, the Federal Open Market Committee in the United States raised the target federal funds rate in 17 consecutive meetings between June 2004 and July 2006, from 1 to 5.25 percent, but long-term interest rates in the United States declined for most of this period. Long-term interest rates throughout the world had in fact exhibited similar declines over that period despite steady increases in short-term interest rates. Similarly, in the aftermath of the financial crisis, the decline in the federal funds rate to (its current range of) between 0 and 0.25 percent, from 5.25 percent in August 2007, has not led to desirable declines in long-term interest rates.

The decoupling of long-term interest rates from short-term interest rates has significant implications for monetary policy. As the federal funds rate has reached the zero lower bound (and cannot become negative), the Federal Reserve has lost its usual ability to signal policy changes via changes in the federal funds rate. Moreover, with the federal funds rate close to zero, the Fed has also lost its ability to lower long-term interest rates by lowering the federal funds rate. For these reasons, in the aftermath of the subprime financial crisis, the Fed and many central banks throughout the world have departed from the traditional interest rate targeting approach to monetary policy and are now focusing on their balance sheet instead, using quantitative measures of monetary policy such as credit easing (the purchase of private sector assets in critical markets) and mostly quantitative easing (the purchase of long-term government securities). Both credit easing and quantitative easing represent expansionary monetary policy designed to reduce long-term nominal interest rates, in the same way that traditional monetary easing reduces short-term nominal interest rates.

A quantitative easing policy in the United States has been the Large-Scale Asset Purchase program. It called for the Federal Reserve to buy $300 billion of long-term Treasury securities, approximately $175 billion of federal agency debt, and up to $1.25 trillion of agency-guaranteed mortgage-backed securities. Most analysts have concluded that this program reduced long-term interest rates (e.g., the yield on ten-year Treasury securities) by as much as 100 basis points below levels that would have otherwise prevailed. Also the second round of quantitative easing (known as QE2), announced on November 3, 2010, will involve the purchase of another $600 billion of long-term US government debt between now and June 2011. There are, however, diminishing returns to quantitative easing, and QE2 is not expected to reduce long-term yields by more than 4 to 5 basis points per $100 billion of Treasuries bought. However, the main objective of quantitative easing is to raise inflationary expectations and reduce real interest rates. Whether this will work remains elusive and is hotly debated. Consider, for

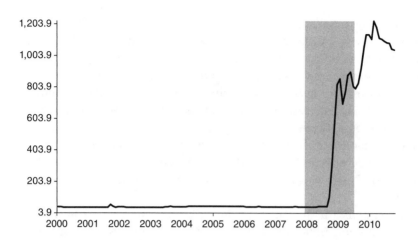

example, the following headlines from *The Economist* (November 27th–December 3rd, 2010): "American Monetary Policy: Fed under Fire" and "The Politics of the Fed: Bernanke in the Crosshairs." If it does, it may create even bigger headaches for the Fed.

In particular, a by-product of the Fed's quantitative easing is the creation of a large quantity of excess reserves, as can be seen in the figure above (where the shaded area represents the Great Recession).

During normal times, when the opportunity cost of holding excess reserves is positive (either because bank reserves earn no interest or if they do, the interest rate that bank reserves earn is less than the market interest rate), banks will increase lending and expand deposits until excess reserves are converted into required (or desired) reserves. The money supply will increase (as the money multiplier will be fully operational), the level of economic activity will rise, and this may lead to inflation. However, to prevent this from happening, and for the first time in its history, the Federal Reserve began paying interest on bank reserves in October 2008, and set that interest rate equal to its target for the federal funds rate. Other central banks took similar actions. In Canada, for example, from April 1, 2009, to June 1, 2010, the Bank of Canada lowered the operating band for the overnight interest rate from (the usual) 50 basis points to 25 basis points (a band with rates between ¼ and ½ percent) and instead of targeting the overnight rate at the midpoint of the band (as it does during normal times), it targeted the overnight rate at the bottom of the operating band. On June 1, 2010, the Bank of Canada re-established the normal operating band of 50 basis points for the overnight interest rate, currently being from ¾ to 1¼ percent.

By paying interest on bank reserves, the Federal Reserve reduces the opportunity cost of holding excess reserves toward zero and removes the incentives on the part of banks to lend out their excess reserves. In this case multiple deposit creation does not come into play (i.e., the money multiplier fails) and the thinking is that the Fed can follow a path for market interest rates that is independent of the quantity of excess reserves in the system. However, as the Fed is searching for new tools to steer the US economy in an environment with the federal funds rate at the zero lower bound and the level of excess reserves in the trillions of dollars (see again the preceding figure), no one is sure how this will unfold!

Recently, in the aftermath of the subprime financial crisis and the Great Recession, policy makers, the media, and a number of economists have raised questions regarding the value and applicability of modern macroeconomics. For example, Narayana Kocherlakota (2010, p. 5) wrote:

I believe that during the last financial crisis, macroeconomists (and I include myself among them) failed the country, and indeed the world. In September 2008, central bankers were in desperate need of a playbook that offered a systemic plan of attack to deal with fast-evolving circumstances. Macroeconomics should have been able to provide that playbook. It could not. Of course, from a longer view, macroeconomists let policy makers down much earlier, because they did not provide policy makers with rules to avoid the circumstances that led to the global financial meltdown.

Also Ricardo Caballero (2010, p. 85) wrote that the dynamic stochastic general equilibrium approach

has become so mesmerized with its own internal logic that it has begun to confuse the precision it has achieved about its own world with the precision that it has about the real one. This is dangerous for both methodological and policy reasons. On the methodology front, macroeconomic research has been in "fine-tuning" mode within the local maximum of the dynamic stochastic general equilibrium world, when we should be in "broad-exploration" mode. We are too far from absolute truth to be so specialized and to make the kind of confident quantitative claims that often emerge from the core. On the policy front, this confused precision creates the illusion that a minor adjustment in the standard policy framework will prevent future crises, and by doing so it leaves us overly exposed to the new and unexpected.

It seems that the inability to predict the subprime financial crisis and the Great Recession, together with the inability to speed up the pace of economic recovery that followed, has damaged the reputation of macroeconomists. This brings me to this unique book by William A. Barnett, a superstar economist who uses mainstream economic theory to explain what happened and why.

For the last thirty years, since the publication of his seminal *Journal of Econometrics* (1980) paper, "Economic Monetary Aggregates: An Application of Index Number and Aggregation Theory," Barnett has taken the scientific approach to macroeconomics, promoting "measurement with theory," as opposed to "theory without measurement" or "measurement without theory." He has been insisting on measurement methods that are internally consistent with the economic theory that is relevant to the use of the data. As Barnett, Diewert, and Zellner (2011) recently put it,

> . . . all of applied econometrics depends on economic data, and if they are poorly constructed, no amount of clever econometric technique can overcome the fact that generally, garbage in will imply garbage out. . . .

Although modern macroeconomics has largely solved the problems associated with the Lucas critique, it has so far failed to address the economic measurement problems associated with the "Barnett critique," to use the phrase coined by Alec Chrystal and Ronald MacDonald (1994).

Barnett (1980a) argued that the monetary aggregates used by the Federal Reserve are problematic, being inconsistent with neoclassical microeconomic theory and therefore should be abandoned. These monetary aggregates are simple-sum indexes, in which all financial assets are assigned a constant and equal (unitary) weight. This summation index implies that all financial assets contribute equally to the money total, and it views all components as dollar for dollar perfect substitutes. This summation index made sense a long time ago, when assets had the same zero yield. It is, however, indefensible today as the data overwhelmingly show that financial assets are far from being perfect substitutes—see, for example, Serletis and Shahmoradi (2007). The summation index completely ignores the complex products and structures of modern financial markets.

Barnett argued that with increasing complexity of financial instruments, there is a need for increasingly extensive data based on best-practice theory. He took the high road and introduced modern economic index-number theory into monetary and financial economics. In doing so, he applied economic aggregation and index-number theory to construct monetary aggregates consistent with the properties of Diewert's (1976) class of superlative quantity index numbers. Barnett's monetary aggregates are Divisia quantity indexes, named after Francois Divisia, who first proposed the index in 1926 for aggregating over goods. Barnett (1980) proved how the formula could be extended to include monetary assets.

Yet, thirty years later, the Federal Reserve and many other central banks around the world continue to ignore the complex structures of modern financial markets and officially produce and supply low-quality monetary statistics, using the severely flawed simple-sum method of aggregation, inconsistent with the relevant aggregation and index-number theory. In doing so, they misled themselves, as well as households and firms, regarding the levels of systemic risk in the economy. Also, unfortunately, thirty years later, the Federal Reserve System does not even include an autonomous data bureau staffed with experts in index-number and aggregation theory, such as the Bureau of Labor Statistics, within the Department of Labor, or the Bureau of Economic Analysis, within the Department of Commerce, to produce and supply high-quality monetary statistics.

In this excellent and research-based book, William A. Barnett departs from the view that the financial crisis and the Great Recession were caused by the failure of mainstream economic theory. He argues the converse: that there was too little use of the relevant economic theory, especially of the literature on economic measurement and on nonlinear dynamics. Barnett argues that rational economic agents make decisions based on conditional expectations and do the best they can with the information they have available. He shows that decisions by private economic agents were not irrational, conditionally upon their information sets and conditionally upon rational nonlinear dynamics. But the contents of their information sets were inadequate and seriously defective.

In providing an explanation of what caused the subprime financial crisis, Barnett also departs from the widely held view by the popular press and most politicians that Wall Street professionals, bankers, and homeowners are to blame for having taken excessive, self-destructive risk out of "greed." He argues instead that many bankers and homeowners are the victims of the financial crisis and that the causes of the crisis were inadequate supervision and regulation of financial firms, inadequate consumer protection regulation, and, most important, low-quality data produced and supplied by the Federal Reserve. Regarding the latter, Barnett argues that poor or inadequate data, originating at the Federal Reserve, produced the misperceptions of superior monetary policy and supported excessive risk-taking by investors and lenders.

The origins of these problems are tracked back to the early 1970s and are shown to have been growing in importance since then, as data production procedures have fallen increasingly far behind the growing public needs from increasingly sophisticated financial markets. The problem is that the Federal Reserve and other central banks have not been producing monetary data consistent with neoclassical microeconomic theory. Under the misperception that the business cycle had permanently ended, economic agents had an incorrect assessment of systemic risk and significantly increased their leverage and risk-taking activities. This led to the credit-driven, asset-price bubble in the US housing market, with prices departing significantly from fundamental values. When the bubble burst, it ended up bringing down the financial system, which not only led to an economic downturn and a rise in unemployment in the United States but also to a global recession.

In this book, in addition to providing evidence that data problems may have caused the subprime financial crisis and the global recession, Barnett also implicitly proposes a *new* business cycle theory, stressing monetary misperceptions due to low-quality data provided by central banks as sources of business fluctuations. This theory could be viewed as an extension of the work originated from Milton Friedman (1968), Edmund Phelps (1970), and Robert Lucas (1981). In their price-misperceptions model, in a rational expectations setting, economic agents have incomplete information about prices in the economy, and monetary shocks (created by the monetary authority) are a principal cause of business cycles. In Barnett's approach, rational economic agents have incomplete information about the economy, because of the unprofessionally produced data by the central bank.

This scholarly book is more timely than ever, after the subprime financial crisis and the wreckage of the Great Recession, written by a maverick in the science of economics. Barnett provides a compelling and fascinating perspective on what happened and why, approaching macroeconomics as a science. He moves orthogonally to the view that the financial crisis and the Great Recession were caused by the failure of mainstream economic theory and the irrationality and greed of private economic agents.

Preface

A foolish faith in authority is the worst enemy of truth.
—Albert Einstein, letter to a friend, 1901

Many books have been written about the Great Recession, precipitated by the financial crisis beginning in 2007 with the breaking of the real estate price bubble.[1] Many explanations have been proposed. In a sense, I agree with them all, since they consist of descriptions of what actually happened.[2] Being descriptions of fact, they need not be viewed as competing. What distinguishes among them is who gets blamed. Just about everyone has been blamed (scapegoated?), including Wall Street firms, bankers, the economics profession, trial attorneys, the medical profession, insurance companies, the media, various governmental agencies, and Congress. What seems to be in common about those blamed is being among the smartest people in the country. Nearly everyone else has also been blamed, by inclusion of homeowners, Democrats, and Republicans. Only those blue collar Independents who are renters are

---

1. The stock market did not crash until 2008, when Lehman Brothers closed.

2. Examples include the astonishingly foresighted books by Shiller (2000, 2005). While I do not disagree with anything in those brilliant books, empirically distinguishing between nonlinear rational-expectations bubbles, nonlinear rational-expectations sunspots, nonlinear rational-expectations chaos, and behavioral-economics explanations are beyond the state of the art of econometrics, especially when the rational decision makers have limited information or are subject to learning, as in state-of-the-art rational-expectations models. For example, no analytical approach yet exists for locating the boundaries of the chaotic subset of the parameter space with a model having more than four parameters. To make matters worse, chaos violates the regularity assumptions of all available sampling-theoretic approaches to statistical inference, since chaos produces a nondifferentiable likelihood function, having an infinite number of singularities. Economic "sunspots" produce even more difficult problems, since the underlying theory assumes incomplete contingent-claims markets. Regarding rational-expectations bubbles, the critically important transversality conditions are notoriously difficult to test.

innocent. But as I argue in this book, all of those explanations are inadequate, if treated as "cause." While there is plenty of blame to spread around, something deeper has happened and needs to be understood to recognize the real source.

As an indication of the problems with the usual explanations, consider the following. It has become common to blame "greed." To my knowledge, the word "greed" has never appeared in a peer-reviewed economics journal. No definition exists within the economics profession, which assumes people do the best they can to pursue their self-interests. How can anyone do better than best? While psychologists, anthropologists, and sociologists may have a rigorous way to define and use that word, economists do not. For example, see Tett (2009) for a social anthropologist's view of greed and its role in the crisis. That point of view usually emphasizes misleading or deceptive behavior. In economic game theory, misleading or deceptive behavior is not necessarily considered to be irrational, but rather a problem for the mathematical literature on "mechanism design," the topic of chapter 3's section 3.7. In media discussions of the financial crisis and the Great Recession, greed is often closely connected with, and sometimes synonymous with, fraud. In economics, fraud is indeed relevant to the fields of law and economics, mechanism design, and institutionalism. But in economic theory, it is hard to see why only fraud should be labeled as "greed," and other crimes not. What about jewel and art thieves and hit men? Are they not "greedy"?

As an economist, I share the usual view of my profession: accusing someone of "greed" is a form of name calling, rather than an adequate explanation of cause. Inadequate regulation is also commonly blamed. Indeed, the weak response of the Federal Reserve ("the Fed") was puzzling, while some banks were sending email messages to random people, including dead people, offering them loans.[3] More effective regulation would have been very helpful to moderate the excesses that grew to ludicrous levels prior to the financial crisis. Certainly there is a colloquial sense in which some sort of "greed" was evident during those years.

But what about the 1920s? Leverage on Wall Street increased to 35:1 prior to the recent Great Recession, but never previously had exceeded 30:1 in US history. Since leverage was lower during the 1920s for many

---

3. For example, my mother, who had died years before and never owned a home, received a mortgage loan offer in a letter sent to my address.

Wall Street firms, some financial firms survived the Great Depression of the 1930s but did not survive the recent financial crisis.[4] Why was leverage lower in the 1920s? Far less regulation existed during the 1920s than prior to the Great Recession, margin requirements were much lower than now, and the "unit investment trusts" of the 1920s were no less capable of facilitating and masking high leverage than the more recent credit default swaps. As explained by Galbraith (1961, p. 52), "The virtue of the investment trust was that it brought about an almost complete divorce of the volume of corporate securities outstanding from the volume of corporate assets in existence. The former could be twice, thrice, or any multiple of the latter." With very low margin requirements, availability of unit investment trusts, and very little regulation, financial firms easily could have matched or exceeded the more recent 35:1 leverage. Were people less "greedy" in the 1920s? That would be a very hard case to make. The common explanations say little more than that people recently made unwise decisions because they did. Certainly something is missing.

---

4. The most widely discussed example is Bear Stearns, which was founded in 1923 and survived the Great Depression. See, for example, *Fortune* magazine, March 10, 2008 online at http://money.cnn.com/2008/03/28/magazines/fortune/boyd_bear.fortune/, by Roddy Boyd. Also see The Wall Street Journal's *Market Watch*, by Alistair Barr, March 13, 2009 online at http://www.marketwatch.com/story/post-bear-stearns-a-chastened-wall, which includes the statement: "In early 2007, Bear Stearns was hooked at record-high levels, sporting a so-called leverage ratio of 35 to 1. For every $1 in equity, it borrowed about $35 to hold a wide array of assets. Around the same time, Goldman, Morgan Stanley, Merrill, and Lehman together averaged leverage ratios of 30 to 1, up from 20 to 1 in 2003, according to Bernstein research." Leverage data were made available to the public in the Form 10-K and 10-Q report filings of the Security and Exchange Commission's (SEC) Consolidated Supervised Entity (CSE) Holding Companies and from General Accountability Office (GAO) leverage statistics.

In *The New York Times*, October 3, 2008, page A1 of the New York Edition, Stephen Labaton imputed the increase in leverage to a 2004 change in rules by the SEC. But why did the SEC change its rules? Perhaps was the SEC convinced that there had been a change in systemic risk, so that increased leverage had become prudent? But in the Wikipedia, you can find the following statement, "financial reports filed by the same companies before 2004 show higher reported leverage ratios for four of the five firms in years before 2004." See http://en.wikipedia.org/wiki/Net_capital_rule#cite_note-7.

Of course, there were no SEC regulations at all during 1920s leading up to the Great Depression, since the SEC was created in 1934. Similarly Lehman Brothers survived the Great Depression. Lehman Brothers was founded as a commodity house in 1850 and entered the underwriting business in a big way in 1906. Merrill Lynch was founded in 1915 and survived the Depression. Goldman Sachs was founded in 1869. One of its closed-end funds, which resembled a Ponzi scheme, failed during the 1929 stock market crash, but Goldman Sachs survived and prospered. Morgan Stanley is a "younger" firm, which was founded during the depths of the Depression.

Although I began as a rocket scientist (a real one), I was subsequently on the economics staff of the elite Special Studies Section of the Board of Governors of the Federal Reserve System in Washington, DC, during the chairmanships of Arthur Burns, William Miller, and Paul Volcker. Unfortunately, the Special Studies research section no longer exists.[5] The kind of intellectual strength and credibility that the Fed had previously centered at that group in the Watergate Building has now been dispersed thinly throughout the Federal Reserve System.[6]

After Arthur Burns left the Federal Reserve Board, he moved to the American Enterprise Institute (AEI) in Washington, DC, to write his memoirs, with the assistance of his ghost writer. I was surprised to receive a phone call from Burns at my Federal Reserve Board office. He asked me to have lunch with him at the AEI. I had never personally met

---

5. Its successor at the Federal Reserve Board in Washington, DC, is the Monetary and Financial Studies (MFS) section. But MFS is not what the Special Studies Section once was, when it was located in the Watergate Building. In fact the Special Studies Section itself was no longer what it once was, when it lost its two miles of distance from the Board Building. That happened when the Martin Building's construction was completed next door to the Board Building, and the economists in the leased Watergate Building space were moved to the Martin Building. The departure of Special Studies economists for academe began soon after that move.

6. Whether the existence of an elite research section, highly visible to the profession, is warranted at public expense in Washington, DC, is debatable, and resentment toward that section by other Federal Reserve economists had much to do with why that section was terminated a few years after it was moved to the Martin Building. But the fact that the Special Studies Section was unique in Washington, DC, government is not debatable.

While I was employed at the Board, I was invited by Arnold Zellner at the University of Chicago to edit a special issue of the *Journal of Econometrics* on the subject of Federal Reserve research. Arnold was an editor and founder of that highly regarded professional journal. I then sent a memorandum inviting submissions from economists in all research sections within the Federal Reserve Board staff and throughout all of the system's regional banks nationwide. Most of the submissions were immediately withdrawn, when I revealed I was going to send the papers out for peer review relative to the journal's normal standards. The exceptions were almost exclusively from within the Special Studies Section and its sister section, Econometrics and Computer Applications (E&CA), which also no longer exists.

At present, long after the termination of the Special Studies Section, Federal Reserve economists' publications in academic journals are thinly spread over all parts of the Federal Reserve System. Many of the associate editors of the Cambridge University Press journal, *Macroeconomic Dynamics*, of which I am founder and editor, are Federal Reserve economists. All of the journal's Federal Reserve associate editors are presently at regional banks, most heavily concentrated at the New York and Chicago Federal Reserve Banks. The journal's advisory editors have only once recommended to me an economist at the Federal Reserve Board for including on the journal's editorial board. She served successfully as an associate editor at the Federal Reserve Board for a few years, but resigned from the Federal Reserve Board staff for a professorship at George Washington University in Washington, DC.

him, while he was the chairman at the Fed. Of course, I agreed to have lunch with him and met him at the AEI. First his ghost writer walked into the room alone. I asked the ghost writer why, during Burns's chairmanship, the rate of growth of the money supply had kept increasing until Burns's second successor, Paul Volcker, stepped in to stop the consequent escalating inflation. Since the days of David Hume (1711–1776), the relationship between money growth and inflation has been well known.[7] Certainly Burns had been aware of the accelerating money growth rate, since the Fed maintained data on an astonishing number of monetary aggregates during his chairmanship. The ghost writer told me it was not Burns's fault, since Burns had to compromise with Congress to retain the independence of the Federal Reserve.

Then Burns walked into the room, and his ghost writer left. Burns told me that he had learned about my work on producing monetary aggregates based on aggregation and index-number theory, and he agreed with me. Encouraged by his favorable comment on my work, I then asked him the same question I had asked his ghost writer. Burns told me to ignore what his ghost writer had said. Burns said he had intentionally been pumping up the money supply to try to lower the unemployment rate, which was growing during the 1970s. He said that he had been educated in the economics of the depression and felt that keeping down unemployment was his primary obligation. He insisted that congressional pressure had nothing to do with it. In retrospect, he said he had been slower than other economists of his generation to recognize that the structural ("natural") rate of unemployment, which cannot be lowered by monetary policy, was rising. All that his accelerating money growth could do was to increase the inflation rate. I believed him to be telling me the truth, and he said something very similar in a speech in Belgrade, Yugoslavia.[8]

Burns's successor as chairman, William Miller, was inadequately qualified for the position and soon was replaced by Paul Volcker. Volcker recognized the source of the problem and instituted the "monetarist experiment" period, during which the rate of growth of the money supply was decreased to bring inflation back under control. But he overdid it, producing a recession. What has been going on since then is heavily documented in this book. In short, the early concept of money, computed by adding up imperfect substitutes, was rendered obsolete

---

7. David Hume, *Political Discourses*, "Of Money," 1752.

8. Arthur F. Burns, "The Anguish of Central Banking," the 1979 Per Jacobsson Lecture, Belgrade, Yugoslavia, September 30, 1979.

by payment of interest on various monetary assets, including checking accounts and checkable money-market deposit accounts. Those interest rates increased to high levels in the late 1970s. When monetary assets yielded no interest, computing monetary aggregates by adding up different kinds of monetary assets was consistent with the relevant economic aggregation theory. Once monetary assets began paying different interest rates, simple-sum monetary aggregation became obsolete, and more complicated formulas became valid. But most of the world's central banks did not fix their severely defective monetary aggregates. As a result monetary data became nearly useless to the public, to the financial industry, to the economics profession, and to the world's central banks. The whole world has recently been paying the price of this fundamental mistake by many of the world's central banks, most conspicuously the Federal Reserve Board in Washington, DC. Monetary data availability and quality from the Federal Reserve Board have been in a steady decline for decades. This book documents the resulting consequences and damage.

During Volcker's chairmanship, Alan Greenspan was on the semiannual panel of advisors to the Federal Reserve Board. I witnessed first-hand the origins of the current economic dysfunctions. Contrary to popular opinion, the origins go back farther than usually believed— to the 1970s—and grew rapidly during the Great Moderation period (1987–2007) of unusually low economic volatility. Following eight years at the Federal Reserve Board, I resigned in December 1982 to accept a position that was too good to refuse: full professor of economics at the University of Texas at Austin, where I was Stuart Centennial Professor of Economics for the next eight years. An "exit interview" is customary upon resignation from the Federal Reserve. I received an exit threat.

A high-ranking Officer of the Board's Staff walked into my office and declared ominously that if I ever became known as a critic of the Fed, its attorneys would harass me for the rest of my life. Not viewing myself as a Fed critic, I viewed the threat as reflecting little more than the intellectual insecurity of that Officer and the weakened state of the Board's staff. Many of the best economists from the Special Studies Section already had left for academic positions. The "exit threat" was unknown to the brilliant Special Studies Section Chief (Peter Tinsley), for whom I worked, until I mentioned it to him 26 years later. He was distressed to learn about it. But maybe the high-ranking officer who delivered the threat was more prescient than I realized at the time. Perhaps he saw this book coming nearly thirty years in advance. I did not.

I have served as an advisor to the Federal Reserve Bank of St. Louis, as a consultant to the European Central Bank, and as an advisor to the Bank of England.[9] Those roles along with my editorship of the Cambridge University Press journal, *Macroeconomic Dynamics*, my editorship of the monograph series, *International Symposia in Economic Theory and Econometrics*, and my own research and extensive publications have kept me close to the thinking of the economics profession's major players. This book uses basic principles of mainstream economic theory to explain what has happened and why. If the economics profession was in any way at fault, it was not from using too much economic theory. It was from using too little.

An objective of this book is to make my conclusions accessible to everyone, including those who have never taken an economics course. As a result the book is divided into two parts. Part I uses no mathematics and is written in a manner accessible to all readers, with the exception of the Foreword by Apostolos Serletis and the book's footnotes. The emphasis is on graphical displays and verbal explanations. But this book connects with a body of very mathematical research developed over a period of more than thirty years. Readers with the necessary level of mathematical preparation can find the underlying mathematics in part II, which serves as appendixes to the chapters in part I. Parts I and II say essentially the same thing, but part I with words and part II with math.[10]

Mathematics is a more rigorous language than English and is inherently important to the economics profession as a means of making clear the logic and internal consistency of analysis. The appendixes may not fully meet the needs of those professionals who might wish to cite the original source publications. Such experts can find the original journal articles collected together and published in three books: Barnett and Serletis (2000), Barnett and Binner (2004), and Barnett and Chauvet (2011b).

---

9. At the St. Louis Federal Reserve Bank, I was a member of the MSI Divisia Advisory Panel during the initial years of construction of that database. MSI stands for "monetary services index," as explained further in section 2.6.3 of chapter 2. My assistance to the European Central Bank included work I did at the bank in Frankfurt, publication of a working paper for the bank, and publication of a resulting journal article. My assistance to the Bank of England was limited to replying to faxed requests for advice about its Divisia monetary aggregates.

10. This division into two parts, one nonmathematical and one mathematical, is unusual in recent economics books. But it is consistent with an earlier tradition, made particularly famous by John Hicks's (1946) classic book, *Value and Capital*.

An unavoidable amount of professional jargon is necessary to make clear the connection between parts I and II. While I am keeping such jargon to a minimum, I define all such words and terms as they are introduced in part I. Exceptions are in some of the footnotes, which are provided for professional economists. Readers who are occasionally distracted by technical terminology can simply skip over such words and phrases. The book is written in a manner that can make its point even to rapid readers who choose to skim over details. *In short, reading this book can be as casual and rapid or as challenging and deep as the reader may choose.*

You will not need to know any of the book's technical results to find previously unrevealed insights into Fed operations. For example, you will learn about a case in which the chairman of the Federal Reserve Board called in the FBI to investigate his entire Washington, DC, staff, including hundreds of economists, to track down the person who provided bank interest rate data to *Consumer Reports*, perhaps in accordance with the Freedom of Information Act. When the person was found, he was fired. Such chilling practices, whether or not justified, are relevant to controversies about the central bank's openness and transparency and to the nature of the Federal Reserve System's incentives, as seen by its employees. You also will learn how faulty monetary aggregate data led Chairman Volcker to overtighten during the period of the "monetarist experiment" in 1979 to 1982 and thereby to induce an unintended recession (chapter 3, section 3.2, table 3.1). You will learn how faulty monetary aggregates more recently led the Fed to be unaware it was fueling the bubbles preceding the financial crisis (chapter 4, section 4.3.1, figure 4.7) and then to be unaware its policy was turning the financial crisis into the Great Recession (chapter 4, section 4.3.3, figure 4.12).

"Fed watchers" routinely obsess about the federal-funds interest rate as an indicator of the stance of monetary policy. Throughout the Great Recession, the federal-funds rate remained stably nearly zero, implying negligible changes in policy for a long period of time. But during those years, Federal Reserve policy was the most volatile in its history (e.g., see figures 4.5, 4.9, and 4.12 of chapter 4), while the federal-funds rate hardly varied at all. As an indicator of Fed policy, the federal-funds rate, contrary to official pronouncements, was a nearly useless indicator of monetary policy. From this book you will learn about the right places to look for policy indicators. The federal-funds rate is among the least important of them.

With growing complexity of financial instruments and institutions, a private-ownership economic system needs increasingly extensive, best-practice information from the central bank. Without such information availability, the second-best alternative is dramatically expanded and costly regulation to constrain poorly informed private decisions. *Increasing financial complexity with decreasing data quality is a toxic mix.*

As in mainstream economic theory, I assume throughout this book that people are rational and do the best they can to pursue their self-interests[11]—*conditionally upon the information that is available to them.* "Ay, there's the rub." (Shakespeare's *Hamlet*)

---

11. The concept of rationality used in economics is weaker than in common usage. To an economist, a person is considered to be "rational," if she does not intentionally act in a manner inconsistent with her own preferences, with full knowledge that the outcome of the decision will be inconsistent with her preferences. Economists are not judgmental about what a person's preferences should be.

Acknowledgments

I have benefited from comments on this book's manuscript from many readers, both inside the government and outside the government, both economists and noneconomists. Those readers include an economist currently inside the Federal Reserve System, two economists formerly inside the Federal Reserve System, a congressional committee staff economist, a Wall Street professional, a currency trader, two attorneys, one physician, one magazine columnist, a few students, many economics professors, and my wife. Since the list is long, I mention below only a few of those to whom I am indebted for valuable comments. They include Apostolos Serletis, Gerald Whitney, Charles Mandell, Richard Anderson, Kurt Schuler, Bruce Rayton, Melinda Barnett, Joshua Hendrickson, Isaac Kanyama, Ryadh Alkhareif, Jing Fu, Kablan Alkahtani, Lili Chen, Febrio Kacaribu, Ibrahima Diallo, Neepa Babulal, Lee Smith, Salah Alsayaary, Mingming Zheng, and Josephine Lugovsky.

I The Facts without the Math

1 Introduction

Central banks in many countries, the venerable Bank of England not excepted, have for decades published deliberately misleading statistics. . . . if the Bank of England lies and hides or falsifies data, then how can one expect minor operators in the financial world always to be truthful, especially when they know that the Bank of England and so many other central banks are not? . . . Inaccuracy as a consequence of privilege is a frequent occurrence. . . . The economist will do well to guard against an interpretation of "data" which are often anything but economic measurements; rather they are tools in the continuing struggle for power.
—Oskar Morgenstern (1965, pp. 20–21, 159, 193), Princeton University

The recent financial crisis that began to mount in 2008 followed the "Great Moderation." Some commentators and economists concluded that the decline in business cycle volatility during the Great Moderation should be credited to central bank countercyclical policy. As more and more economists and media people became convinced the risk of recessions had moderated, lenders and investors became willing to increase their leverage and risk-taking activities. Mortgage lenders, insurance companies, investment banking firms, and home buyers increasingly engaged in activities considered unreasonably risky prior to the Great Moderation. The Great Moderation did not primarily reflect improved monetary policy. The actual sources of the Great Moderation cannot be expected to produce permanent, long-run decreases in economic volatility. The misperception of permanent decrease in volatility was at the core of the financial crisis and recession.

One of this book's objectives is to expand upon the position taken by Barnett and Chauvet (2011a), with inclusion of a systematic unified presentation of the evidence and with documented discussion of the relevancy to current economic problems, but in a manner accessible to all interested readers.[1] In that paper we found most recessions in the past fifty years were preceded by more contractionary monetary policy than was indicated by the official simple-sum monetary aggregates. Monetary aggregates produced in accordance with reputable economic measurement practices grew at rates generally lower than the growth rates of the Fed's official monetary aggregates prior to those recessions, but at higher rates than the official aggregates since the mid-1980s. Monetary policy was more contractionary than likely intended before the 2001 recession and more expansionary than likely intended during the subsequent recovery. This book also shows that monetary liquidity going into the Great Recession of December 2007 to June 2009 was much tighter than indicated by interest rates.

Low-quality and inadequate Federal Reserve data not only fed the risk misperceptions of the public, the financial industry, and the economics profession, but also likely contributed to policy errors by the Federal Reserve itself.

1.1   Whose Greed?

Many commentators have been quick to blame insolvent financial firms, investors, lenders, and borrowers for their "greed" and their presumed self-destructive, reckless risk-taking. Perhaps some of those commentators should look more carefully at their own role in propagating the misperceptions that induced those firms to take such risks.

The following comment from *The Wall Street Journal* (May 12, 2009, p. A16) editorial, "Geithner's Revelation," is informative: "The Washington crowd has tried to place all the blame for the panic on bankers, the better to absolve themselves. But as Mr. Geithner notes, Fed policy flooded the world with dollars that created a boom in asset prices and inspired the credit mania." While I agree the emphasis on expansionary policy is relevant, focusing only on that factor is an oversimplification and does not explain the unprecedented levels of risk exposure. There have been many other periods of comparably expansionary policy, during which financial firms' leverages did not reach such high levels. But I do agree with Geithner that it is time to move beyond scapegoating bankers, Wall Street firms, and just about everyone else, and to look more deeply into what induced rational firms and households to

---

1. Citations, such as this one to Barnett and Chauvet (2011a), refer to references contained at the end of this book in its References section.

believe that such high risk exposure was prudent. Clearly they did not intentionally "underprice" risk.

Then who is to blame for the recent crisis, which is the worst since the Great Depression? A common view is that the troubled firms and households are themselves to blame. According to much of the popular press and many politicians, Wall Street professionals and bankers are especially to blame for having taken excessive risk, as a result of "greed." Homeowners similarly are viewed as having taken excessive risk. But who are the Wall Street professionals, who decided to increase their leverage to 35:1? They include some of the country's most brilliant financial experts. Is it reasonable to assume that such people made foolish, self-destructive decisions out of "greed"? If so, how should we define "greed" in economic theory, so that we can test the hypotheses? What about the mortgage lenders at the country's largest banks? Were their decisions dominated by greed and self-destructive, foolish behavior? If the hypotheses imply irrational behavior, how would we reconcile a model of irrational behavior with the decisions of some of the country's most highly qualified experts in finance? Similarly why did the Supervision and Regulation Division of the Federal Reserve Board's staff close its eyes to the high risk loans being made by banks? Was the Federal Reserve Board's staff simply not doing its job, or perhaps did the Fed too believe systemic risk had declined, so increased risk-taking by banks was prudent? To find the cause of the crisis, we must look carefully at the data that produced the impression Fed policy had improved permanently. That false impression supported the increased risk-taking by investors, homeowners, and lenders.

The federal-funds interest rate has been the instrument of policy in the United States for over a half century. Although no formal targeting procedure has been announced by the Fed, its basic procedure for targeting that interest rate is commonly viewed to be the "Taylor rule," in one form or another. The Taylor rule puts upward pressure on the federal-funds interest rate, when inflation increases, and downward pressure on that interest rate, when unemployment increases. Rather than being an innovation in policy design, the Taylor rule is widely viewed as fitting historic Fed behavior for a half century.[2] The Great Moderation in business cycle volatility was more credibly produced by events unrelated to monetary policy, such as the growth of US

---

2. See, for example, Orphanides (2001). As an illustration of how oversimplified the usual views of that policy are, see Woodford (2003) for an exposition of the complexities of that approach to policy.

productivity, improved technology and communications, financial innovation, and the rise of China as a holder of American debt and sup-
plier of low priced goods. The Great Moderation alternatively could
have resulted from "good luck" in the form of smaller than usual external shocks to the economy. The Great Moderation was widely viewed
as permanent—and was not. This book does not take any position on
what actually did produce the Great Moderation, but does take a position on what did *not* cause the Great Moderation. This book provides
an overview of the data problems that produced the misperceptions
of superior monetary policy and thereby induced the increase in risk-
taking. With the federal-funds rate at near zero, support for the current
approach to monetary policy, which has been dominant for so long, is
now declining.[3]

The focus of this book is on the need for central bank transparency,
and the damage that can be done to transparency, and thereby to the
economy, by poor or inadequate data. Where should we look for the
source of the current economic problems? Should we look at the country's most brilliant financial experts: such as those on Wall Street and
at the biggest banks, where Fed data and information were accepted
and entered into formation of their expectations? Were they irrational,
greedy people who foolishly were self-destructing? No, that does not
get to the root of the problem. How about the stockholders in those
firms, who often lost everything? Did their greed blind them to an outcome that wiped them out, but should have been obvious to them from
the available data? No, I do not think so.

1.1.1 Ponzi Games, Transversality, and the Fraud Explosion

There was extensive fraud in mortgage origination, beginning in 2005,
as is confirmed by the successful Federal Trade Commission (FTC) and
Security and Exchange Commission (SEC) actions against Countrywide
Home Loans, Inc. There also was fraud in the securitization of mortgages. Just about everyone was receiving emailed offers of unwanted
mortgages. The explosion of fraud was associated with the treatment
of risk as an asset class, bought and sold without concern for where it
ended up. But aggregate risk does not disappear by being traded. The
vehicles for the trading of risk were credit default swaps, or CDS. Once
the CDS market collapsed, many assets ceased trading, and asset prices
became difficult to establish. The financial crisis was on. The "players"

---

3. An excellent analysis of the defects of that policy can be found in Cochrane (2007).

in all this were among the world's most sophisticated investors. Is it reasonable to assume that they blindly ignored the risks they were taking out of stupidity? Did credit default swaps appear out of nowhere for no reason? Was fraud a new invention?

An even more extreme case exists: Bernard Madoff. He was perhaps the most sophisticated con man in recent history.[4] He had been president of NASDAQ and was the originator of the computer information technology that produced NASDAQ. His illegal Ponzi game grew for years.[5] At the risk of sounding pretentious, I'd like to introduce a technical term from formal mathematical economics: the "transversality condition." Dynamic mathematical models of the economy have an initial condition, explaining where the economy starts, and a terminal condition, called the transversality condition, toward which the economy approaches in the distant future. Satisfaction of the transversality condition is critical for success of an economy. Violation of the transversality condition produces bubbles and other damaging phenomena, undermining the success of a market economy. The transversality condition is normally a constraint on the growth of debt over very long periods of time. A critical transversality condition in dynamical macroeconomic models is, in fact, called the "no–Ponzi game condition," ruling out the explosion of debt produced by Ponzi game behavior. Madoff must have known he was violating the most fundamental of all transversality conditions in economic dynamics: the no–Ponzi game condition. Had his calculations told him he would end up broke, disgraced, and in prison? I don't think so. Then why did he do it?

Consider Social Security. It is not invested but is backed by an intergenerational social contract. What guarantees the contract will remain

---

4. In the 1700s there were perhaps more extreme confidence schemes, including John Law's Mississippi Bubble and the South Sea Bubble, while in the early 1900s there was the Ivar Kreuger pyramid scheme, which collapsed in the Depression. In explaining his famous match business bubble, Kreuger once said: "I've built my enterprise on the firmest ground that can be found—the foolishness of people" (Robert Shaplen 1960, p. 128).
5. "Ponzi game" is the technical term used in mathematics. In popular terminology, this fraudulent scam is called "Ponzi scheme," named after the famous American swindler, Charles Ponzi (1882–1949), who died in poverty in Rio de Janeiro 15 years following his release from prison in the United States. He did not originate that pyramid scheme, which carries his infamous name. He was inspired by a similar scam 20 years earlier by William F. Miller in Brooklyn, and in fact the same scheme is described in Charles Dickens' 1857 novel, *Little Dorrit*. Funds provided by unsuspecting investors are not invested but rather used to pay returns to prior investors. A "Ponzi game" pyramid, if it absorbs much of a country's wealth, can devastate the economy of an entire country, as nearly happened in Albania after its sudden privatization following the collapse of communism.

acceptable to all future generations? The system's rules prevent early withdrawal. Social Security is a Ponzi game; it does not violate the transversality condition, because of the social contract imposed across generations. But that is not enough. To be a good "investment," the pool of funds from the Social Security tax must grow at a rate faster than the rate of interest. Then future generations will receive pensions from a fund that is growing at a rate exceeding the alternative investment rate-of-return. In short, the population must grow faster than the rate of interest, as was very dramatically the case when immigration to the United States was rapid.

Analogously, Madoff screened his "investors" to accept only long-term investors, who would not withdraw early. He also must have expected available funds to grow at an adequate rate to permit him to continue paying the moderate rate of return he provided. Clearly he had all that figured out. He was too sophisticated not to have known. What he had not counted on during his lifetime was a serious recession producing net withdraws from his pool. Could the SEC have suspected what Madoff was doing, but perhaps had a similar view of the future, so was willing to close its eyes? Madoff's strategy was illegal, while the strategies in the banking industry and on Wall Street were not. But the misperception producing the failures of their plans was the same. They all believed there would never again be a major recession, and the steady economic growth that continued for many years during the Great Moderation would extend far into the future. They were wrong. All of them were wrong.

1.1.2 Conditional Expectations

In mainstream economic theory, consumers and firms are considered to be rational and to do the best they can to pursue their self-interests. But to make their economic decisions rationally, they need to form expectations about the future. Here I need to introduce more technical jargon: "conditional expectations." Conditional expectations are formed, while making use of the information available to the decision maker. To ignore relevant available information in forming expectations is not consistent with pursuit of self-interests. Why would someone intentionally ignore relevant information in forming expectations? The information available to an economic agent is called the "information set."

This is elementary in economic theory: if economic decisions seem misguided—look at the information set. That is the *first place* to look. Should we assume that the information set is just fine, but the decision makers are irrational, greedy fools, not intelligently pursuing their self-interests? To make that assumption flies in the face of a century of mainstream economic research. I must admit to being entirely mystified by the emphasis in the popular press on the converse representation of heavily established economic theory. This book will not fall into that trap. Instead of throwing out a century of economic research, while scapegoating just about everyone in sight, this book will focus on the information set and its role in distorting expectations throughout the economy: some with well-meaning intent, and some not (e.g., Bernard Madoff).

Many considerations are relevant to the misguided actions of private firms, individuals, and central banks during the years leading up to the recent financial crisis. But one common thread applies to all of them: misperceptions induced by low quality monetary statistics, disconnected from the relevant economic aggregation theory. As has been emphasized by the theoretical literature in economics, information shocks can do much economic damage. This book documents the fact that Fed financial data do not meet the standards of best practice methodology and have been declining in quality for decades. The efficacy of economic decentralization, as is central to a private ownership economy, depends heavily upon information availability to individual decision makers. This fact is well established in a highly technical area of mathematical economics called "system design." With financial instruments growing in complexity and increased decentralization from deregulation, what was needed was more and better data and information. *The growth of financial complexity and decentralization with simultaneous decline in data quality was a toxic mix leading up to the misperceptions about systemic risk that were the root cause of the financial crisis and recession.*

1.1.3 Regulation in History and in Theory
In addition to blaming "greed," commentators also often blame deregulation. There is much truth to this point of view, but we must think more deeply to recognize the role of that problem. In economic theory, two kinds of solutions exist to the decisions of consumers and firms: "interior solutions" and "corner solutions." Interior solutions are voluntary solutions constrained only by market prices, incomes, tastes of consumers, and technologies of firms. Under idealized assumptions, a market economy can be proved mathematically to attain a form of optimal allocation of goods and services, called "Pareto optimality" in the field of "welfare economics." This fundamental mathematical proof is widely

known to economists and is used as a justification for "laissez faire" policy prescriptions by some. In contrast, regulation produces corner solutions, with binding quantity constraints on consumers and firms. Those rationing constraints are in addition to the economic system's constraints from market prices, incomes, tastes, and technology. When there are violations to the perfect-markets assumptions, used in the famous, welfare-optimality proofs, regulation can increase welfare. But otherwise the imposition of governmental constraints on private economic decisions decreases welfare. As a result the design of regulation is not a trivial matter, since poorly designed or unnecessary regulation can do damage. Examples of suboptimal economic outcomes are not hard to find in economies subject to excessive or badly designed regulation. Consider, for example, Cuba, North Korea, or recently Greece. All three have large governments and much regulation.

Indeed corner solutions might have been better in the United States than the interior solutions that produced the recent economic problems. As this book argues, the voluntary interior solutions, produced using poor information, were not consistent with the assumptions of classical optimality proofs. Regulations, constraining the economy from drifting far off course along bubbles, would have been advantageous. But far less regulation existed during much of the past century, especially prior to the Great Depression, which was survived by many of the underwriting firms that recently failed on Wall Street. During the 1920s, with less regulation, lower margin requirements, and no shortage of "greed," Wall Street leverage never reached the levels attained prior to the recent financial crisis. In the 1920s, the SEC, the Federal Deposit Insurance Corporation (FDIC), and Regulation Q, permitting the Fed to regulate saving account interest rates—didn't even exist.[6] Deregulation does not force the resulting voluntary interior solutions to incorporate excessive risk-taking exposure.

Leading up to the Great Depression of the 1930s, the "unit trusts" of the 1920s provided a vehicle to create leverage and mask growing risk exposures. See Galbraith's (1961) chapter, "In Goldman, Sachs We

---

6. The Glass–Steagall Banking Act was passed in 1933. The SEC was created in 1934. Other relevant congressional laws passed following the 1929 stock-market crash included the Securities Act of 1933, the Trust Indenture Act of 1939, the Investment Company Act of 1940, the Investment Advisers Act of 1940, and the Sarbanes–Oxley Act of 2002. Regulation by the Federal Reserve, which had been created in 1913, expanded in the 1930s, not just through the availability of the new Regulation Q, but in many other ways. The Gramm–Leach–Bliley Act, enacted in 1999, decreased regulation but left in place far more regulation than existed prior to the Depression. See Patrick (1993) and Meltzer (2002).

Trust." Credit default swaps, or CDSs, and especially the more fiend-ishly complex collateralized debt obligations, or CDOs, were similarly central to the recent crisis. Rather than decreasing risk, by permitting risk to be priced and traded in markets, the complexity of CDSs and CDOs increased the information burden on decision makers. With inad-equate and distorted information within decision makers' information sets, the need existed for increased regulation, especially of the CDS and CDO markets, as poorly understood insurance markets. Instead, we incredibly got both deregulation and decreasing information avail-ability—simultaneously. While more and better regulation could have helped, deregulation alone cannot explain what happened. Again, the place to look is the "information sets," upon which firms and consum-ers conditioned in making their decisions. Somewhere within those information sets lies the explanation of why private sector decisions drifted so far off the economy's optimal course.

1.2   The Great Moderation

As mentioned earlier, those who believed the Great Moderation would last forever included some of the most sophisticated people in the coun-try. But what about the world's leading economists? In my opinion, the greatest living macroeconomist is Robert Lucas, a Nobel laureate in economics at the University of Chicago. In terms of influence on the macroeconomics profession, another great macroeconomist is a more recent Nobel Prize winner: Edward Prescott. Let's see what the two of them were saying during the Great Moderation.

In his 2003 presidential address to the American Economic Associa-tion, Lucas declared that the "central problem of depression-prevention [has] been solved, for all practical purposes." Lucas, who had become a major authority on the business cycle through his path-breaking pub-lications in that area (e.g., see Lucas 1987), had concluded economists should redirect their efforts toward long-term fiscal policy aimed at in-creasing economic growth. Since central banks were presumed to have become very good at controlling the business cycle, he concluded few gains remained available from further improved countercyclical policy. In particular, he concluded that the welfare gains from further modera-tions in the business cycle would be small and not worth the cost of the research.

Edward Prescott, with his coauthor Ellen McGrattan, published an article in the fall 2000 *Minneapolis Federal Reserve Bulletin*, "Is the Stock

Market Overvalued?" They concluded that the stock market was properly valued. On January 1, 2001, the Dow Jones Average was at 10,788. By October 9, 2002, the Dow was 7,286, a decline of 32 percent. Lucas and Prescott are giants of the macroeconomics profession and rightfully so.[7] Were Lucas and Prescott at fault for what happened to the economy? No way. Could we accuse Lucas and Prescott of bad motives and "greed"? Of course not. But if Prescott believed the stock market was valued properly in 2000, and Lucas in 2003 concluded that the Great Moderation's decrease in volatility was permanent, why should we be throwing stones at Wall Street professionals, bankers, and homeowners for having similar views? Ben Bernanke spoke on the Great Moderation at the meetings of the Eastern Economic Association, in Washington, DC, on February 20, 2004. He argued the primary cause was improved monetary policy. Of course, Ben Bernanke is now the chairman of the Federal Reserve Board and is one of the best qualified chairmen the Fed has ever had. But the business cycle is not dead, and the Great Moderation cannot convincingly be explained in terms of superior monetary policy.

Given the views of some of the world's greatest macroeconomists at the time, the widespread misperceptions about systemic risk leading up to the financial crisis are far from surprising. The remaining question, addressed by this book, is the information upon which such views were based and whether better information might have produced different behavior, involving less risk exposure.

1.3 The Maestro

Many commentators believe Alan Greenspan should get much of the blame for what has happened. He is a disciple of Ayn Rand. His setting of low interest rates and his libertarian views, favoring decreased regulation, are often criticized. While there is some truth to those criticisms, Greenspan's primary role in contributing to the crisis lies elsewhere: in being so good at what he does best.

During Volcker's chairmanship, Alan Greenspan was on the semi-annual Panel of Academic Advisors to the Federal Reserve Board,

---

7. Perhaps my views might be somewhat biased. I took Lucas's courses, while I was a graduate student at Carnegie Mellon University. Prescott had recently received his PhD from Carnegie Mellon and was on the faculty there, having returned from the University of Pennsylvania.

although paradoxically he had never been on the faculty of a university, so was not an "academic." I was on the staff of the Federal Reserve Board during most of those Volcker years and attended some of those Academic Advisors meetings. The meetings were held in the Board Room in the presence of the Board's Governors and some of their staff economists. Greenspan was very different from the rest of that panel. As is normal with serious academic researchers, the others tended to be cautious with their statements and rarely commented forcefully on topics and issues outside their own areas of research and expertise. Greenspan, in conspicuous contrast, was very flamboyant and presented himself as a person who could comment with great authority on anything of concern to the Board. Why the difference in approach, you ask?

Alan Greenspan ran the consulting firm, Townsend–Greenspan & Company, for nearly thirty years, since becoming the principal owner in 1958. The firm was organized in the 1930s by William Townsend and Dana Skinner. Greenspan joined the firm in 1953. The firm ceased operation, when Greenspan was appointed Chairman of the Federal Reserve Board in 1987. Writing an academic research paper for a peer-reviewed journal is very different from writing a consulting report. No customer, employing the services of a consulting firm, wants to be told that answering questions requires a couple of years of research and a government grant to fund graduate-student research assistants. The most important role of the principal owner of a consulting firm is—salesman. Townsend–Greenspan was a very successful consulting firm, largely due to the exceptional sales ability of Alan Greenspan. He did not just sell the firm and its services to clients. He sold himself and his personal authority and expertise. I saw his sales ability firsthand in some of the Academic Advisors meetings.

Others on the panel often included famous economists, such as Franco Modigliani, from whom I took a graduate course at MIT. In addition I interviewed Franco for the professional journal I edit and for the book, *Inside the Economist's Mind* (Barnett and Samuelson 2007). As I learned from personal experience as a student, an editor, and an interviewer, Modigliani was a very flamboyant and outgoing speaker. But Greenspan dominated much of the discussion at the Academic Advisors meetings, even when Modigliani was on the panel. If it had not been for his personality, Greenspan would have seemed out of place, because of his claims to know so much about everything, to be able to predict nearly everything, and to be able to determine the best policy under all possible circumstances. With such a formidable group in the room, such claims easily could have been dismissed. But that was never the case. He was such an interesting, outgoing, friendly person that everyone in the room treated him with respect.

The few research staff members invited to attend those semiannual meetings would leave the room together and take the elevator from the Board room level on the second floor down to the first floor, while sometimes shaking their heads in disbelief at Greenspan's "performance." I was no longer on the Board's staff, when President Reagan appointed Greenspan to be chairman. At that time I was at the University of Texas at Austin. But I would guess that many staff members at the Board were surprised by Greenspan's appointment.

During his chairmanship, the whole world witnessed Greenspan's skills as a salesman. He won over large numbers of persons, including influential members of Congress. Many began referring to him as "the Maestro," following the appearance of Woodward's (2001) book by the same name. But to my knowledge, he had never published a peer-reviewed research article in a major economics journal. His PhD dissertation at the New York University School of Business (no, not the Economics Department) was never published and is virtually unknown within the economics profession. In sharp contrast, Ben Bernanke, a professor at the Princeton University Economics Department, is a highly regarded scholar, who has published extensively in major journals.[8]

I have no doubt that Greenspan did the best he could as chairman of the Federal Reserve Board, and he certainly cannot be faulted for having an exceptionally commanding sales personality. If he didn't, Townsend–Greenspan would never have become as successful as it

---

8. Some people think a person with business experience, such as Greenspan's business consulting experience or G. William Miller's corporate background, is better qualified to be chairman of the Federal Reserve Board than an eminent academic such as Ben Bernanke. If that is your view, I recommend that you read part II of this book. You also might want to consider the consequences of Miller's and Greenspan's chairmanships. G. William Miller was the first, and so far only, Federal Reserve chairman to come from a corporate background, rather than from economics or finance. He had previously been chairman and CEO of Textron, Inc. He was appointed in January 1978 by President Carter and removed from that office by President Carter on August 1979, as one of history's most unsuccessful and least respected Federal Reserve chairmen. When presented with staff economists' research at Board meetings, Miller's response was usually to flatter them for their presentations, which he often admitted he did not understand. We thought he was a very nice guy, who didn't have a clue.

did.[9] What set Townsend–Greenspan apart from the others was—Alan Greenspan's persona. But that was the problem. During Greenspan's chairmanship, Wall Street began talking about the "Greenspan put," according to which no need existed to worry about declining asset prices, since the Maestro could be depended upon to intervene successfully. This unjustified belief fed into the misperceptions about the Great Moderation, further increasing the widespread confidence in permanently decreased systemic risk.[10]

The economics profession knew Greenspan had never published well-regarded research in major peer-reviewed journals. It would be comforting to believe that the economics profession did not fall into the trap of viewing him as the Maestro. But sad to say, that is not the case. A primary channel for academic dissent had been the Shadow Open Market Committee (SOMC), founded by Karl Brunner at the University of Rochester and Allan Meltzer at Carnegie Mellon University. The SOMC, comprising a group of eminent economists, met at the same time as the Fed's policy-making Federal Open Market Committee (FOMC). The SOMC issued a dissenting opinion, along with its policy recommendations, following each such meeting. The SOMC opinions and reports were widely influential in the financial press, especially *The Wall Street Journal*. During the Greenspan years, criticism of the Fed by the SOMC was greatly toned down, thereby muting the most visible channel for dissent from within the economics profession. In addition, during most of the years leading up to the recent financial crisis and recession, the SOMC did not meet at all.[11] Between 1997 and 2009, the SOMC met only once, and that was not until 2006.

When I was hired by the Federal Reserve Board, I was informed that I was to fill the position left by Bill Poole, who had moved to the Boston Federal Reserve Bank and then to Brown University. He left the Board

9. That firm had a mathematical (econometric) model used in its consulting. There were other major consulting organizations, some at universities and some at banks, having well known models. The Townsend–Greenspan model was largely unknown to the econometrics profession.

10. The term, "Greenspan put," was coined in 1998, after the Fed lowered interest rates following the collapse of the firm, Long-Term Capital Management.

11. At the time that Greenspan became chairman, Karl Brunner had died. Allan Meltzer, a founder of the SOMC, is a formidable authority on monetary policy and has been working for many years on a series of important books about the history of the Federal Reserve. He is a professor at Carnegie Mellon University, from which I received my PhD. I know him well and respect him greatly. During the Greenspan years, I asked him why the SOMC's policy critique had become so muted. His reply was "Greenspan is a different kind of a guy." Clearly, Allan liked Greenspan a lot. Ah, the Maestro's sales ability again at work!

under a cloud of trouble. I was told that his departure was not entirely voluntary. As was explained to me, he had sent to *The Washington Post* a letter-to-the-editor in opposition to the Burns/Nixon wage and price controls. Arthur Burns, chairman of the Fed's Board at the time, was angry about the letter-to-the-editor and had some role in Poole's move out of Washington, DC.[12] At academic conferences there often were sessions at which former Fed staff economists would speak. It seemed to me that Poole had become the angriest, most uncompromising critic of Federal Reserve policy. He then was brought into the SOMC and acquired a regular byline in a newspaper called the *American Banker*.

Some of the Board's senior staff members were worried about Poole's byline, since they knew he was angry at the Fed and was under pressure to write a regular article for the *American Banker*. Previously, staff research economists could submit their research to peer-reviewed journals without prior approval from the Board. When Poole began his byline, a new Fed policy was instituted. Before submitting to a peer-reviewed journal, we were required to send our paper to a high ranking Board staff officer, who would edit the wording. I was puzzled by the nature of the rewording. It was always harmless, never changing my intent, and the changes never were substantive in any way. I asked what the purpose of the censorship was. I was told it was to ensure that the paper would not include wording Poole might consider to be quotable in the *American Banker*.

When Greenspan became chairman, he understood, as a business consultant, that the best way to silence dissent and minimize competition is to bring in the dissenters and merge with the competition. The St. Louis Federal Reserve Bank's Board of Directors employed a firm to search for a new president, when the bank's prior president retired. Poole was selected. To my astonishment, Greenspan did not prevent Poole from becoming president of the St. Louis Fed. At the time, I mentioned to Allan Meltzer that I was amazed Poole had been brought back into the Fed in such a high position, despite the history of bad feelings. Meltzer told me he and the SOMC had a role in that decision. [13]

---

12. This is what I was told at the Federal Reserve Board, when I was on its staff in Washington, DC. I have recently heard that Poole could already have been planning to leave the Board at the time he sent the letter to *The Washington Post*.

13. During the years I was at the Board, Karl Brunner and Allan Meltzer were very visible critics of Board policy through the SOMC they had founded. But there was a difference in their degree of willingness to be cooperative with the Board. Allan, who got along well with the Board, was often included among the Academic Advisors to the Board. However, Brunner, who tended to be uncompromising in his policy advocacy, was banned from

Again, recall the critical importance of the information sets in guiding expectations relevant to the success of a decentralized economic system. There was the Great Moderation; there was the "Greenspan put"; and there was the near silence of the SOMC's primary channel of dissent. Is it a surprise that so many major financial players believed the Fed had succeeded in ending the business cycle through superior monetary policy? Is it a surprise that even the great Nobel laureate Robert Lucas had reached that conclusion? So, of course, increasing private risk appeared to be prudent.

But there was a problem. It was not true. It was all a myth. There were no great improvements in monetary policy design, which was based fundamentally on the same approach used for over a half century. The sources of those appearances of improvements were developments outside the Federal Reserve System. The one genuine, noteworthy change in Fed activities was the decline in data quality. When more and better data were needed by the private sector, as the complexity of financial products grew, the quantity and quality of Fed data declined.

1.4 Paradoxes

Going back to 1974, Federal Reserve monetary data have produced a series of paradoxes, continuing to the present time. These paradoxes were purported to demonstrate that behavior by consumers and firms was irrational and thereby raised questions about the relevancy of economic theory. The paradoxes were the subject of research in major economics journals and resulted in hundreds, perhaps thousands, of published articles and books. The central banks throughout the world, and most conspicuously the Federal Reserve, used those paradoxes to justify their advocacy of increased discretionary power and less oversight, based upon the need for judgmental policy free from accountability to Congress. The story was: *you can't understand this; just trust us; we*

---

the Board building. In fact the security guards at the entrances were instructed never to permit Brunner to enter the building. Brunner once confided to me that the ban had done wonders for his career.

There had been security guards at the entrance to the building, since Burns had become chairman. Anti-Semitic conspiracy theorists had threatened Burns's life, when he was appointed as the Board's first Jewish chairman. But those guards rarely interfered with the public's access until years later, while Greenspan was chairman, after the staff found a critic wandering the building with a shotgun. The ban on entry by Brunner was subsequent to the posting of guards to protect Burns and prior to Greenspan's stepped up security.

know best; even the economics profession can't understand this; only we can. In fact a high-ranking, staff officer of the Federal Reserve Board stated in a meeting that he did not trust academics, whom he considered to be "glory seekers." On the contrary, excessive confidence in the Fed, free from dissent, is inconsistent with proper functioning of a decentralized economy. But the Fed's growing influence within the profession tends to limit dissent, as has been documented by White (2005). The economy's private sector needs to have a clear understanding of the risks it is taking.

As this book establishes, the paradoxes resulted from Federal Reserve bad data, inconsistent with the economic-measurement methodology established by the profession. The paradoxes fed into the misperceptions that distorted expectations and thereby eventually damaged the economy. Internal inconsistencies exist between the way the data were produced and the way they were used. Those internal inconsistencies have become known as the "Barnett critique" (see Chrystal and Mac-Donald 1994; Belongia and Ireland 2010).

Recently it has become fashionable to criticize the scientific basis for modern economic theory. Such criticisms often argue that macroeconomics is founded upon distorting oversimplifications. I would not disagree. Indeed the problem is not the use of too much economic theory, but rather the use of too little theory for purposes of analytical simplification. I have published extensively on the need to bring into macroeconomics more of the recent advances from the physical sciences and mathematics in nonlinear dynamics.[14] I also believe that the economics profession should take more seriously the distribution effects of macroeconomic policy. But there is a deeper question. Why are distorting oversimplifications in macroeconomic modeling so widely acceptable to the profession? Why are we not better able to determine which simplifications provide justifiable approximations and which are distorting oversimplifications. The following simple Aristotelian syllogism could shed some light on that question:

Major premise: Good science is not possible without good data.

Minor premise: The Federal Reserve Board is not providing good data.

Conclusion: _____ (fill in the blank).

---

14. See, for example, Barnett and Duzhak (2008, 2010), Barnett, Serletis, and Serletis (2006), Barnett et al. (1997), and Barnett, Geweke, and Shell (1989). This literature is well established and respected in economics but is not at the center of the field. See Caballero (2010).

While this logic may appear to be harsh, I do not consider myself to be a general critic of the Federal Reserve, which I respect as being among the world's most distinguished central banks. I consider myself to be a scientist. My statements in this book are directed solely at the mathematically provable fact the Federal Reserve Board is not producing data based on best-practice principles of the economics profession. For that mathematical proof, see part II of this book.

In contrast, what the real critics of the Fed say is far harsher than what I am arguing in this book. Consider, for example, the devastating book by the great Princeton economist, Oskar Morgenstern (1965), *On the Accuracy of Economic Observations*, from which a brief quotation is provided at the start of this chapter.[15] Everything in Morgenstern's book is as relevant today as it was then.

1.5   Conclusion

Decisions are made conditionally on information. Yes, many bad decisions were made by many people and firms, as well as by central banks, economists, and governments. But insulting those who made bad decisions fails to get to the root of the problem: the information on which the decisions were made was defective. Fraud was not a new invention. Clearly, something was wrong with the information on which decisions were being made. What was it and why? How did it get transmitted throughout the economy?

This book does not seek to provide easy answers to difficult problems, but rather to deepen insight into the root causes of the economy's problems. Those causes have not been remedied by the Band-Aids applied so far.

---

15. I am indebted to Steve H. Hanke at Johns Hopkins University for recommending to me the Morgenstern (1965) book.

2 Monetary Aggregation Theory

Economic measurement is a formidable subfield within the field of economics and has been evolving with increasing sophistication over more than a century. Economic measurement includes "aggregation theory" and "index-number theory." Perhaps the most widely known applications of that subfield are the consumer price index (CPI) and the national income accounts. Economic measurement is not simply accounting. Flow of funds accounting is taken as given in economic measurement, which goes far beyond accounting and makes extensive use of economic theory. Aggregation theory can become very mathematical, but the basic ideas can be understood without the mathematics. This chapter makes the basic principles accessible.

2.1 Adding Apples and Oranges

Economic theory deals primarily with flows of services, including the demand and supply for those services. To apply economic theory, measurement of the quantity and price of the service flows is necessary. With perishable goods, the service flow is the same as the stock, and the price of the service flow is the same as the price of the stock. If you purchase an apple, all of its services must be consumed in the current time period before it spoils, so purchasing one apple provides the total services of one apple during the current period of time. The same is true for an orange. Durables providing services for multiple periods are a more complicated matter. When you buy a house, you are purchasing the service flow over the lifetime of the house, not just its services during the current period. As a result, renting the services for only one period is less expensive than buying the house.

This section considers initially only the case of perishable goods, so that the stock and the service flow are the same. Suppose that you want to measure the service flow from fruit, consisting of apples and oranges. Perhaps you have five apples and four oranges. Clearly, the service flow from the apples can be measured as five apples, while the service flow of the oranges can be measured as four oranges. But would you wish to measure the service flow of the basket of fruit to be nine units of aggregate fruit, regardless of the prices of oranges and apples and your preferences over them? Suppose that it was five grapes and four watermelons? Is that nine "fruit" units, the same as for nine grapes or nine watermelons? A sophisticated area of economic theory deals with that problem. The theory is called "aggregation theory," along with the closely related area of "index-number theory." The specialized professional literatures on aggregation theory and index-number theory comprise the foundations for "economic measurement." Major advances have been made in those areas of research over the past century, and the relevancy and validity of that literature are accepted by all economists. While the literature is highly mathematical and sophisticated, the basic insight is easily understood by everyone and is consistent with a common admonition: "you can add apples and apples but not apples and oranges." *That's it!*

That idiom is in fact widely known; it exists in similar forms in most languages throughout the world, as explained in the Wikipedia. In Quebec French, it takes the form *comparer des pommes avec des oranges*, while in European French the analogous saying is *comparer des pommes et des poires*. In Latin American Spanish, it takes the form *comparar papas y boniatos* or *comparar peras con manzanas*, while in Spain it becomes *sumar peras con manzanas*. In Romanian the popular idiom takes various forms: *a aduna merele cu perele; baba şi mitraliera; baba şi mitraliera, vaca şi izmenele;* or *ţiganul şi carioca*, while in Hungarian the expression *ízlések és pofonok* has similar meaning. In Serbian it becomes *Поредити бабе и жабе*, while in Welsh it takes the form *mor wahanol â mêl a menyn*. An equivalent Danish idiom is *Hvad er højest, Rundetårn eller et tordenskrald?* In Russian, the phrase *сравнивать тёплое с мягким* is used. In Argentina, a common question has that purpose: *En qué se parecen el amor y el ojo del hacha?* In Colombia, a similar version is well known: *confundir la mierda con la pomada*. In Polish, the expression *co ma piernik do wiatraka?* is used. In British English, the phrase *chalk and cheese* is used for that purpose instead of *apples and oranges* and perhaps makes the point more clearly.

It is not necessary to understand the mathematics in this book's appendixes to recognize the basic principle on which economic measurement is based. You need only speak any of the world's major languages to recognize the principle as a truism known to everyone. To make the point more clearly, let's change from apples and oranges (or chalk and cheese in the British English version) to subway trains and roller skates. Suppose that the city includes 10 subway trains and 10,000 pairs of roller skates. To measure the city's transportation services, would you be willing to say it is 10,010? Of course, not! A subway train provides far more transportation services than a pair of roller skates. The two are not perfect substitutes in the production of transportation services. Translating the common idiom into technical economics terminology, economists would say: you can aggregate over the quantities of goods by addition, only if all of them are indistinguishable perfect substitutes. If they are not perfect substitutes, quantity aggregation by addition is wrong.[1] It is tempting to think perhaps the solution is to multiply the quantities by prices and then to add up the cost of buying the 10 subway trains and 10,000 roller skates. But that can't be right either, since the result would be in units of dollars. Expenditures are in units of dollars, but not service flow quantities.[2] The services from consuming a good need not change, if its price changes. We are seeking to measure the quantity of services produced by the goods, not the dollar expenditure on them. The latter is a subject of accounting flow-of-funds measurement. The former is a subject of economic measurement.

Clearly, some sort of weighting is needed. We need to weight each subway train far more heavily than each pair of roller skates in aggregating over roller skates and subway trains to measure the city's flow of transportation services. How to produce that weighting is the subject

---

1. There is a vast literature on the appropriateness of aggregating over monetary asset components using simple summation. Linear aggregation can be based on Hicksian aggregation (Hicks 1946), but that theory only holds under the unreasonable assumption that the user-cost prices of the services of individual money assets do not change over time. This condition implies each asset is a perfect substitute for the others within the set of components. But simple-sum aggregation is an even more severe special case of that highly restrictive linear aggregation, since simple summation requires the coefficients of the linear aggregator function all to be the same. This in turn implies that the constant user-cost prices among monetary assets must be exactly equal to each other. Not only must the assets be perfect substitutes, but must be perfect one-for-one substitutes—that is, must be indistinguishable assets, with one unit of each asset being a perfect substitute for exactly one unit of each of the other assets. In reality, financial assets provide different services, and each such asset yields its own particular rate of return, so has its own unique user-cost price.
2. There also is the problem of durability, since subway trains and roller skates are not perishable goods providing services for only one time period. But in this section we are not yet introducing the solution to that problem.

of economic aggregation and index-number theory, and many economists are specialists in that field. The appendixes to this book provide the derivation of the theory needed to aggregate over financial services. Provided here is only the relevant intuition.

Simply applying weights to the quantities of subway trains and roller skates and computing the weighted average is not an adequate solution. Suppose, for example, that we apply a weight of a million to each subway train and a weight of one to each pair of roller skates and then compute the weighted average. The conclusion would be the city's transportation services can be measured as 10,000,000 + 10,000 = 10,010,000. That would certainly seem to be more reasonable than the previous conclusion of 10,010, and would recognize the fact that a subway train provides far more services than a pair of roller skates. But there remains a problem. We would implicitly be assuming the services of one subway train are always perfect substitutes for exactly one million pairs of roller skates, regardless of the number of subway trains and roller skates existing in the city. But the nature of the services of a subway train is different from the nature of the services of a pair of roller skates, and the services of another subway train or another pair of roller skates is not independent of the number that already exists in the city. If the city already has a large number of subway trains crowding the tracks, acquiring another one might be far from desirable. So a simple linear weighted average cannot reflect the imperfect substitutability of subway trains for roller skates. The magnitude of the error from such linear aggregation can be large, and the magnitude of the error from the more restrictive simple-sum aggregation is extremely large. For a formal derivation of that error range in appendix A, see equations (A.132) and (A.133) and the illustration in appendix A's figure A.3.

In the jargon of mathematics, the theoretically correct way to aggregate over imperfect substitutes is nonlinear. Linear aggregation, with or without weighting, implies perfect substitutability. The weights only change the units of measurement of the individual component goods. The correct formula, called the "aggregator function" in aggregation theory, must be nonlinear, often involving multiplication and division, not just addition. Readers familiar with elementary economics will recognize that "utility functions" and "production functions" are nonlinear functions, permitting imperfect substitutability. Such functions potentially can serve as valid aggregator functions.

The field of economic "aggregation theory" determines the valid aggregator functions. But there remains the need to measure the aggregate. Statistically estimating the theoretical, nonlinear aggregator function is a challenging application of "econometrics" and is the subject of many published articles in professional economics journals. But governmental agencies need a way to measure the growth rate of the aggregate, without using the economics professions' advanced statistical methodology. The field of "index-number theory" deals specifically with that need. Index-number theory determines formulas that can be used to measure the growth rate of the theoretical aggregate without the need for econometrics.

Elementary economics courses usually explain the "cost of living index," the "true cost of living index," the Paasche index, and the Laspeyres index. The "true cost of living index" is produced by aggregation theory, while the Paasche and Laspeyres indexes are produced from index-number theory to approximate the true cost-of-living index. For example, the Department of Labor's widely used CPI is a Laspeyres price index, and the Commerce Department's corresponding price index (the "implicit price deflator") has, until recently, been a Paasche index.

2.2   Dual Price Aggregation

The previous section emphasized quantity aggregation over imperfect substitutes. But that section did briefly mention the cost-of-living index, which is a price aggregate, and also mentioned the total expenditure in dollars, which is an accounting flow-of-funds concept. The three are rigorously interconnected through an area of mathematics called "duality theory," which can be found in the appendixes (e.g., equation A.46 of appendix A). But there is an easy way to see the connection without getting into that deep theory. Suppose that you have three numbers: a measure of the aggregate quantity of automobiles, Q, the aggregate price of automobiles, P, and total expenditure on automobiles, E. Clearly you would want Q multiplied by P to equal E. Satisfaction of that elementary accounting identity is a fundamental axiom in aggregation theory.[3] As a result the aggregate price of automobiles, P, must equal the total expenditure on automobiles, E, divided by the aggregate quantity of automobiles, Q.

---

3. That equation is called "Fisher's factor reversal test."

As explained in the previous section, a highly regarded literature exists on identifying the quantity aggregator function and measuring it, when the goods are imperfect substitutes. The corresponding "dual" price aggregate then can be computed by dividing the measured accounting expenditure on the goods by their quantity aggregate. In short, the correct quantity aggregate implies the correct price aggregate, and vice versa. The two are not independent concepts. They are linked together by the accounting identity requiring consistency with actual dollar expenditure.

Consider aggregating over automobile-tire prices and buggy-whip prices for use in the cost-of-living index. Would you compute the unweighted average of the two prices? That would give buggy-whip prices an equal role in determine the cost of living with automobile tire prices. Surely you would not do that. But in fact a century ago British newspapers did compute the inflation rate from unweighted averages of prices of goods. The need for nonlinear weighting from index-number theory has now been known and used by governmental agencies throughout the world for nearly a century.

But there is a complication. We have so far abstracted from the problem of durability. We now must take that into consideration. Consider a house or an automobile. You can buy either and then consume its services during its lifetime, or you can rent either and use its services for only one time period (perhaps a week, month, or year). The prices are not the same. To buy a house or car will cost a lot more than renting it for one period. The perfect-market price of the single-period services of a durable good is called the "user-cost price," and the mathematical procedure for determining that price is known to the economics profession. The rental rate is the valuation placed by the rental market on the theoretical user-cost price. If the rental market were a perfect market, the user-cost price and the rental price would be identical, and both would be much less than the price to buy and hold the stock of the good, in order to consume all of its services during the good's lifetime.

Recall that economic theory is primarily about the demand and supply for service flows per unit of time. For internal consistency with that objective, the correct price of a durable in a cost-of-living or other price index is the user-cost or rental price, not the purchase price of the stock. This fact is well understood in computation of the cost-of-living index and other price indexes in the national accounts.

2.3 Financial Aggregation

The discussion above is about consumer goods. But the same theory is relevant to financial assets, so long as they are treated as durables, providing financial services for more than one period. Clearly, financial assets are not perishables, immediately destroyed by consumption of their services. In particular, let us now consider monetary aggregation.

As is widely known, the Federal Reserve and most central banks compute and publish monetary aggregates. The Fed for many decades published four monetary aggregates: M1, M2, M3, and L. The aggregate M1 is the narrowest aggregate, defined to include only transactions balances used as a medium of exchange, such as currency and demand deposits (checking accounts).[4] The aggregate M2 is broader, including some close substitutes for money, such as bank saving accounts. The aggregates M3 and L are even broader, with L being the broadest aggregate, intended to measure total financial "liquidity" of the economy, hence the symbol L. The Fed has discontinued computation and publication of L. More recently, in 2006, the Fed discontinued supplying M3, leaving only M1 and M2.

Discontinuing M3 was particularly unfortunate, since assets in M3 but not in M2 include financial assets contributing a significant amount of liquidity to the economy. Studies have repeatedly shown that M3 or L, when properly constructed as an index number, is the most informative available monetary aggregate.[5] But the official simple-sum M3 and L were so badly distorted by improper component weighting as to be virtually useless. I fully agree with the Federal Reserve's discontinuing publication of the simple-sum M3 and L monetary aggregates. In fact the world's central banks should do what all other governmental agencies have done, since the publication of Fisher's (1922) book, and discontinue publishing all of their simple-sum and arithmetic-average aggregates. But when the Fed discontinued publishing simple-sum M3 and L, the Fed also discontinued supplying much of their consolidated, seasonally adjusted, monthly component data. As a result construction of reputable index numbers, using that component data, has

---

4. Technically speaking, demand deposits (checking accounts) are not "legal tender." Their acceptability as a means of payment is a contractual matter and is conditional upon clearing of the check at your bank and at the Fed. Many businesses will not accept personal checks at all. M0, the monetary base, is sometimes viewed as a monetary aggregate, but in a different sense, more relevant as a Federal Reserve policy instrument than as a measure of the monetary services available to the public.

5. See, for example, Barnett (1982).

become needlessly difficult. The cost of supplying the component data was negligible to the Fed. Then why did they discontinue it? I would not presume to answer that question for the Fed, but here might be an unpleasant "clue." M3 picked up repurchase agreements (repos), which were huge elements of the shadow banking system's creation of money.[6]

Perhaps even more puzzling is the fact that the Federal Reserve has terminated publication of all interest rates paid by banks on deposits, such as average interest rates on checking accounts, small certificates of deposit, and savings accounts. Nearly every other central bank in the world provides interest rates paid on the country's various categories of bank deposits, averaged across banks. Unlike most of the world's central banks, the Federal Reserve no longer acquires those interest rates directly from banks, but instead purchases that information for internal use from Bank Rate Monitor. Bank Rate Monitor will not provide the historical data to the public, since the contract between Bank Rate Monitor and the Federal Reserve permits publication of the back data only by the Fed, which is not doing so. If that data were not useful for policy research by Fed staffers, the Fed would not subscribe to the expensive Bank Rate Monitor Survey. By failing to make the data public, the Fed hampers research on monetary policy by academic economists and investors.

Yes, the Federal Reserve should retain, solely for internal use, the interest rate data on individual banks. But it is not in the public interest to withhold interest rate data averaged over the country's banks. Here are a few of the central banks that do provide that data to the public: the central banks of Turkey, Saudi Arabia, Iran, Pakistan, and China, each of which has more understandable reasons to be hesitant about making that data available than the Federal Reserve does. I can indeed think of another central bank that does not provide that data—the central bank of North Korea.

Now let us consider only M2, which is still being computed and supplied by the Fed. Among the assets included in M2 are currency, demand deposits, and savings deposits. Would you consider savings deposits to be perfect substitutes for cash? Cash pays no interest, and

---

6. Nonbanks used AAA-rated mortgage-backed securities (MBS) in overnight repo trades for cash on a daily basis, effectively creating money from a growing stock of AAA MBS. M3 contained only repos of maturity greater than one day at commercial banks, so would not have picked up all of that shadow banking activity. But surely it would have revealed growing repo usage generally. Further information about M3 can be found on Williams's "Shadow Statistics" site at www.shadowstats.com.

savings deposits are not legal means of payment. To pay a bill with noncheckable savings deposits, you must withdraw cash from those deposits or transfer funds from the savings account to your checking account. Savings deposits are a "joint product," providing both monetary services (liquidity) and investment yield (interest income). Currency is pure money providing only liquidity.

Monetary assets are durable goods, and hence the user-cost prices of their services need to be determined. That formula is derived in Barnett (1978, 1980a).[7] The proof is repeated in the part II of this book, and the resulting formula is provided as equation (A.5) of appendix A. Without going into the details of the proofs or of the formula, the basic intuition is the following: the user-cost price of consuming the services of a monetary asset is its opportunity cost, measured by the interest forgone by employing the services of the asset. If the asset is currency, which yields no interest at all, then the foregone interest is the interest rate that could have been earned on the best available pure investment, called the "benchmark interest rate." Alternatively, suppose that the asset is a savings deposit. Then the forgone interest is the benchmark interest rate minus the interest rate paid on the savings deposit. The user-cost price of a monetary asset is not its own rate of interest, which is not a price paid for using the liquidity services of the asset, but just the opposite. The return received on the asset's nonmonetary investment services needs to be subtracted out of the benchmark rate to compute the user-cost price of its liquidity services.

---

7. There is a long history regarding the "price of money." See, for example, Greidanus (1932). Keynes and the classics were divided about whether it was the inflation rate or the rate of interest. The latter would be correct for noninterest bearing money in continuous time. In that case, as can be seen from equation (A.5) in appendix A, the user cost becomes R_t, since the denominator disappears in continuous time and $r_{it} = 0$ for non–interest-bearing money. More recently Diewert (1974) acquired the formula relevant to discrete time for noninterest bearing money, $R_t / (1 + R_t)$. Perhaps the first to recognize the relevance of the opportunity cost, $R_t - r_t$, for interest bearing money was Hutt (1963, p. 92n), and he advocated what later become known as the CE index derived by Rotemberg, Driscoll, and Poterba (1995). The best-known initial attempt to use aggregation theory for monetary aggregation was Chetty (1969). But he used an incorrect user-cost formula, which unfortunately was adopted for a few years by many other economists in subsequent research in monetary aggregation. Through analogous economic reasoning, Donovan (1978) acquired the correct real user-cost formula. As a result of the confusion produced by the competing user-cost formulas generated from economic reasoning, application to monetary aggregation was hindered until Barnett (1978, 1980a) formally derived the formula by the normal method of proof using the sequence of flow-of-funds identities in the relevant dynamic programming problem. Regarding that formal method of proof, see Deaton and Muellbauer (1980). Barnett's proof and his derivation within an internally consistent aggregation-theoretic framework marked the beginning of the modern literature on monetary aggregation.

For future reference, we now provide a formal definition of the user cost of money.

Definition 1   *The "user cost price of a monetary asset" is the forgone interest from holding the asset, when the interest yielded by the asset is less than the interest rate that could have been earned on an alternative investment.*

In the most elementary case, the forgone interest is the difference between the two interest rates mentioned in the definition, although the formula in the appendixes incorporates some refinements.[8] The complete formula, provided in this book's appendix A as equation (A.5), is more formally derived in appendix B as equation (B.4). Even if you do not choose to read the proof, it is important to understand that the formula is not just a matter of opinion based on plausible reasoning. What is provided in the appendix is a mathematical proof, deriving the formula directly from the microeconomic theory of rational decision-making by consumers and firms.

In accordance with the principles explained in the prior sections of this chapter, currency and savings deposits should not be aggregated by addition, since they contribute differently to the economy's monetary service flow and have different user-cost prices. Index-number theory needs to be used to measure the service flow properly. In this regard a short quote from the Federal Reserve Act, Section 2a, may be instructive:

The Board of Governors of the Federal Reserve System and the Federal Open Market Committee *shall maintain long-run growth of the monetary and credit aggregates* commensurate with the economy's long-run potential to increase production, so as to promote effectively the goals of maximum employment, stable prices, and moderate long-term interest rates.

[12 USC 225a. As added by act of November 16, 1977 (91 Stat. 1387) and amended by acts of October 27, 1978 (92 Stat. 1897); Aug. 23, 1988 (102 Stat. 1375); and Dec. 27, 2000 (114 Stat. 3028).]

Central banks produce a product. It is the liquidity of the economy. Without money, there would be only barter and extreme illiquidity. In

---

8. These refinements include discounting to present value, distinguishing between the nominal and real user cost, incorporating risk adjustment, and adjusting for taxation. Subsequently Barnett (1987) derived the formula for the user cost of supplied monetary services, provided as equation (A.22) in appendix A to this book. A regulatory wedge can exist between the demand- and supply-side user costs, if nonpayment of interest on required reserves imposes an implicit tax on banks, as displayed in figure A.2 in appendix A and provided mathematically in that appendix's equation (A.25). Another excellent source on the supply side is Hancock (1991), who correctly produced the formula for the implicit tax on banks.

particular, Fed open market operations (purchases and sales of Treasury securities in New York) change the balance sheet of the Federal Reserve and thereby change what, in economics jargon, is called "high-powered money," the "monetary base," or "outside money" (currency plus bank reserves). Changes in high-powered money, the primary product, are transmitted through the banking system to produce the economy's monetary services and thereby the liquidity of the economy. That liquidity is heavily dependent on the "inside money" produced by private firms as intermediate products, conditionally upon the Federal Reserve's production of outside money.[9] Properly computed monetary aggregates are designed to measure that service flow in the economy. The Fed does not "produce" interest rates. The economy itself produces interest rates, although the Federal Reserve intervenes to influence some of them. Focusing solely on interest rates, while ignoring monetary aggregates, ignores the product produced by the central bank. The relevancy of that product to public understanding of monetary policy is independent of whether or not the central bank itself targets or otherwise uses measurements of that product in conducting its monetary policy.[10]

Yet in recent years the Fed has not produced and supplied monetary aggregates consistent with modern index-number theory. The Fed discontinued providing M3 and L and supplies simple-sum M1 and M2 aggregates inconsistent with index-number theory. As you will learn from this book, these data defects are far from trivial. They have done much damage to policy, to the profession's research, to the expectations of the private sector—and to the world's economies. Is it reasonable to expect Wall Street firms, commercial banks, mortgage lenders, mortgage borrowers, the press, and the economics profession to have assessed systemic risk correctly when the Fed was minimizing its own information-reporting responsibilities under the Federal Reserve Act? How much confidence should we have in the Fed's own monetary policy, formulated without access to highly relevant data?

This observation is not unknown within the Federal Reserve System. The president of the St. Louis Federal Reserve Bank, James Bullard (2009), has written recently:

---

9. An alternative, and more detailed, explanation of the transmission mechanism of monetary policy emphasizes the payments system and the use of high-powered money by banks for payments to other banks via check clearing and wire transfers. This equivalent explanation does not change any of the conclusions.

10. For example, is it reasonable to expect people transacting daily in the repo market, thereby creating money in the shadow banking system, to be able accurately to assess the riskiness and widespread use of their activities without the aggregate measure, M3, which contained repos?

I have described three funerals. . . . The ongoing financial market turmoil may have caused the death of many cherished ideals about how the macroeconomy operates. One funeral was for the idea of the Great Moderation. . . . A second funeral was for our financial system as we have known it. . . . A third funeral was for monetary policy defined as nominal interest rate targeting . . . . The focus of monetary policy may turn to quantity measures.

Indeed this assessment is long overdue. But again, availability of reputable monetary quantity measures to the public is important, regardless of what the Federal Reserve chooses to target in its policy.

More recently Greg Robb (2009) has reported:

The Federal Reserve should return to the practice of setting monetary policy by targeting the growth of monetary aggregates, St. Louis Fed president James Bullard said Tuesday. Bullard said the Fed should set a target for expanding the monetary base because it needs a credible weapon to fight the risk of deflation. Although the Fed has already expanded its balance sheet by about $1 trillion, much of the increase to date has come from temporary programs that could quickly be reversed and so do not count as an expansion of money, he said. The Fed needs to communicate that it is expanding the money supply, which has historically created inflation, he said. This will end market expectations that a general decline in prices might take hold in the US as it has in Japan.[11]

I wish to emphasize that I am not personally an advocate of any simplifying "ism," whether it be monetarism, new-monetarism, Keynesianism, New-Keynesianism, Post-Keynesianism, Austrianism, or Marxism. I am an advocate of professional scientific standards for economic measurement. The economy responds strongly to the information available to private economic agents, governmental policy makers, and academic researchers. Inadequate, distorted, and fraudulent information is damaging to the economy as a whole, not just to those who have used that information personally.

When I was an engineer at Rocketdyne, we would never have been able to develop the rocket engines for Apollo, if we had not heavily instrumented the rocket engines we tested nearly every day on test stands in the Santa Susana Mountains north of Los Angeles and at Edwards Air Force Base. When something went wrong during a rocket engine test, we poured over voluminous data to determine the cause. Theory alone or talk alone was never acceptable as an answer. The cost of those tests was enormous but necessary for success. Economic measurement

---

11. I do not know whether Robb's statement is an entirely accurate representative of President Bullard's views. In particular, I do not think that Jim Bullard's statement necessarily implies clear advocacy of targeting a monetary aggregate.

is even more challenging, since the measurement methodology needs to be related to aggregation theory. All economic data from the economy is aggregated over goods and over economic agents.

2.4 The Commerce Department and the Department of Labor

The first modern monetary aggregate, based on averages of daily data, was constructed by William Abbott and Marie Wahlig of the Federal Reserve Bank of St. Louis and published in Abbott (1960).[12] By their definition, "money," labeled M1, consisted only of currency plus noninterest-bearing demand deposits (bank checking accounts). Interest-bearing NOW checking accounts and interest-bearing, checkable, money-market deposit accounts (MMDAs) did not exist. Savings deposits were not viewed as producing any monetary services at all without the current ease of transfer among accounts by online banking. As a result saving accounts were not included in that monetary aggregate. In those days, over half a century ago, the components of the monetary aggregate, M1, could reasonably be viewed as perfect substitutes. Both currency and demand deposits were means of payment, and both produced no investment return.[13] Currency and demand deposits had the same user-cost price, with the entire benchmark rate being forgone to consume the services of either cash or demand deposits. Hence both were considered to be "pure" money. Adding them up made sense and was consistent with aggregation and index-number theory, since aggregation by summation is correct over perfect substitutes having identical prices. But that is "ancient history." Most assets in monetary aggregates now yield interest. Monetary aggregation by addition has been inconsistent with economic theory and best-practice measurement for over a half century.

In contrast, the other data-producing agencies in Washington, DC have been using index-number theory to compute and publish their data for many decades. The two primary data-producing agencies, the Commerce Department and the Department of Labor, have separate data-producing bureaus with authority to produce best-practice data, and those autonomous organizations employ experts in aggregation and

---

12. See Anderson and Kavajecz (1994).
13. There has been much research on imputation of implicit rates of return on demand deposits through services provided, especially for large business checking accounts. But in the early days of monetary aggregate publication, the legal restriction requiring nonpayment of interest on demand deposits was usually assumed to be binding.

index-number theory. The Department of Labor has the Bureau of Labor Statistics (BLS), which is respected in academe for its expertise in economic measurement. The BLS produces the well-known CPI along with many other valuable data series. The BLS has never used simple-sum aggregation or unweighted arithmetic-average aggregation. The BLS has always recognized that it is aggregating over imperfect substitutes and needs to use the procedures available from index-number theory. Similarly the Department of Commerce has the Bureau of Economic Analysis (BEA), which employs experts in economic index-number theory. The BEA produces the national accounts of the United States. The BEA has never used simple-sum or unweighted arithmetic-average aggregation and has always based its data on economic index-number theory.

The Federal Reserve has no autonomous data-production bureau, such as the BEA or BLS. The Fed certainly could produce a similar autonomous data bureau within the Federal Reserve System. Data published by the BEA and BLS are far from flawless. But the contrast between the BEA and the BLS, on the one hand, and the Fed, on the other hand, is clear—there is no "Bureau of Financial Statistics" anywhere within the Federal Reserve System. Expertise in index-number theory is marginalized and spread very thinly throughout the Federal Reserve. Setting up such a bureau might be viewed as inconsistent with the self-interests of the Federal Reserve. If so, perhaps the Treasury, which tracks some international financial statistics, could institute such an independent bureau for US financial statistics; or Congress could create a new independent bureau for that purpose. In effect such a potential office now exists within Washington, DC, the Office of Financial Research (OFR), set up under the recently passed Dodd–Frank Act. In section 2.7.6 below, I consider whether the OFR might be able to provide a satisfactory solution to this serious problem.

Exceptions within the Federal Reserve are few and far between, such as the Fed's industrial production index, which admirably does use reputable index-number theory with input from the BLS and industrial trade organizations. This fact raises another interesting question. Why does the Federal Reserve Board recognize the measurement issue and use the best available methodology in measurement of industrial production, over which Fed policy has limited influence, but is unwilling to devote comparable resources to state-of-the-art measurement of the most fundamental variable over which a central bank does have influence—money? Why is the Board's staff unique in Washington, DC, in selectively resisting the fundamental principles of aggregation and index-number theory, accepted by the profession for over a half a century? Perhaps by the time you have finished reading this book, you may have an opinion on this question.

We examine the question in a later section, but it is worthwhile at this point to observe that the Federal Reserve Board staff is unique in another way. Most bureaucracies in Washington, DC, have little influence, through their own policies, on the variables they measure. The policy decisions of the Department of Labor have little, if any, effect on the country's inflation rate, measured by the CPI. The policy decisions of the Commerce Department have little effect on the country's gross domestic product or other variables in the national accounts measured by the BEA. The industrial production index, which the Federal Reserve Board's staff supplies in a manner consistent with best-practice standards of the profession, does not contain financial or monetary data heavily influenced by Fed policy. In contrast, the financial and monetary data produced by the Federal Reserve measure economic variables heavily influenced by the Fed's own policy decisions. The Federal Reserve is accountable to Congress and to the public for its actions, but the Fed itself measures and produces the financial and monetary data relevant to monitoring the product that the Fed produces: the liquidity of the economy. Is there a conflict of interests? We will return to that question in a later section.

2.5   The Major Academic Players

The first wave of research, on which this book's research is based, appeared in Paris (François Divisia) and Princeton (Irving Fisher) early in the twentieth century. Controversies regarding the lives and work of Divisia and Fisher extended far outside the field of economics. The second wave appeared in the 1960s and early 1970s and came primarily from the University of California at Berkeley (Dale Jorgenson and W. Erwin Diewert) and the University of Chicago (Milton Friedman and Henri Theil). Intellectual activity at Berkeley and Chicago was far from dull and calm in those days. During the 1960s and early 1970s at Berkeley, there were two explosions. One was the student rebellion against the university's administration and the war in Vietnam. That rebellion became known internationally as the "Free Speech Movement." The other explosion at Berkeley took place inside the economics department's building, where many of the tools used in this book were evolving with remarkable speed through the research of the faculty and students. At the University of Chicago, research emphasized the application of the same approach, called "neoclassical," based on the use of calculus. But the Department of Economics at the University of Chicago was at the other end of the political spectrum from the student explosion at Berkeley, with conservatism being central to the Chicago department's philosophy. A Chicago professor, Arnold Zellner, once said to me: "As we say at Chicago, if you don't know which way to go, turn right." This section tells the stories of the major players and how their work is needed to understand the contributions of this book.

2.5.1   Irving Fisher

As in all areas of important research, there are "major players," whose contributions to the field were pathbreaking and whose names are forever attached to the subject. While index-number theory and associated areas of economic measurement have been evolving for over a century, the first enormous contribution was the classic book, Fisher (1922), by the famous American economist, Irving Fisher (1867–1947). To clarify the discussion that follows, I'll now provide a relevant definition. This definition applies equally to a price or quantity index number, so the definition is provided in a form that can be used for either.

Definition 2   *A quantity (or price) "statistical index number" measures the change in the aggregated quantity (or price) of a group of goods between two time periods. The index number must be a formula depending on both the quantities and prices of the goods in that group during the two time periods. The index number cannot depend on any other data or on any unknown parameters.*

As can be seen from that definition, there is an enormous number of such formulas that can be viewed as contenders, so long as they depend only on prices and quantities of the component goods in the two periods and contain no unknown parameters. Indeed by the time that Fisher's book appeared in 1922, a large number of such formulas had been proposed. What Fisher did, in a very thick book, was to define many good and bad properties of possible index numbers. He then classified all of the existing formulas in terms of how many good and how many bad properties each had. Among the indexes he concluded did best in those classifications, the one that later became known as the "Fisher ideal index" was the one he liked best. But there were others that remained serious contenders. In contrast, only two met his criteria for "worst": the simple-summation index and the arithmetic-average index.

On p. 29 of that book he wrote:

The simple arithmetic average is put first merely because it naturally comes first to the reader's mind, being the most common form of average. In fields other than index numbers, it is often the best form of average to use. But we shall see that the simple arithmetic average produces one of the very worst of index numbers, and if this book has no other effect than to lead to the total abandonment of the simple arithmetic type of index number, it will have served a useful purpose.

On p. 361 Fisher wrote:

The simple arithmetic should not be used under any circumstances, being always biased and usually freakish as well. Nor should the simple aggregative ever be used; in fact this is even less reliable.

At the time Fisher's book appeared, government agencies were not the source of British price-index data. British newspapers computed the inflation rate from unweighted averages of prices of goods. Following the appearance of Fisher's book, the British newspapers stopped their use of unweighted averages of price changes and instead adopted index numbers that performed well in Fisher's book.

Fisher was a giant in the field of economics, and within the economics profession his name is equated with his famous research in economic science. In the minds of most American economists, Fisher ranks among the top five economists in American history. Milton Friedman (1994, p. 37) called Fisher "the greatest economist the United States ever produced." But while he was alive, Fisher's visibility to the public spanned many other areas. He did not shy away from controversy. Among his most controversial views were his advocacy of prohibition, his views on health, and his advocacy of eugenics. Even his views in applied economics created controversy in his time, since he published favorable views of the stock market shortly before the 1929 crash. After the crash he continued to publish reassurances that recovery was just around the corner. As a public spokesman on economics and the stock market, his reputation was destroyed for the rest of his life.

On the subject of prohibition, he published three books favoring total abolition of alcoholic beverages. His views on health were even stranger. He argued that avoidance of exercise is a health benefit. He was an outspoken advocate of the "focal sepsis" theory of physician Henry Cotton, who believed mental illness was caused by infections in various locations in the body and advocated surgical removal of the infected materials. When Fisher's daughter was diagnosed with schizophrenia, he had surgical removals done at Dr. Cotton's hospital, resulting in his daughter's death. In eugenics, his publications, along with that entire field, were discredited during and after the Second World War, because of the association of eugenics with the racist views of the Nazis.

Greatness in science is not always associated with greatness in other areas. This book is associated with Fisher's research only in index-number theory. His book on that subject is acknowledged by all economists to be historic. In many other areas of economic science, he was similarly among history's greatest researchers. In other fields—well—you can judge for yourself.

2.5.2 François Divisia

The next major contribution, which changed the field forever, was produced by a brilliant French engineer and mathematician, François Divisia. He was born in Tizi-Ouzou, Algeria, in 1889 and died in Paris in 1964. Divisia contributed extensively to the field of economics, as evidenced by his books, Divisia (1926b, 1928, 1950, 1962). Some economists believe Divisia's macroeconomic theory was more advanced than the well-known theory of John Maynard Keynes, and perhaps Divisia's views may have been closer to a more modern theory, now called New Keynesian economics.[14] Divisia (1963) rejected the research published by Keynes as not based on microeconomics, but of course the microfoundations of New Keynesian economics did not exist at the time. Divisia's macroeconomic theory is less widely known than that of Keynes, but Divisia published in French, which might have constrained his visibility. Also, by not accepting Keynesian economics, his influence within the growing Keynesian movement was marginalized. In France, Divisia's most celebrated book is his book on mathematical economics, Divisia (1928), rather than his criticisms of Keynesian economics.

Although less well known than Keynes in macroeconomics, Divisia was among the French intellectual elite and a leader of the French school of mathematical economics. After studying at the École Polytechnique and the École Nationale des Ponts et Chaussées, two of the greatest French Grandes Écoles, he worked as an engineer for ten years. As an engineering graduate student, he had previously been mobilized as an engineer at the beginning of World War 1 in 1913 as "an officer of genius." Rapidly promoted to captain and wounded, he was named chevalier of the Légion d'Honneur. Following his ten years as an

---

14. See, for example, Lemesle (1998) and Gay (2008).

engineer after the war, he worked for the rest of his career as an economist, although his education was as an engineer and mathematician.
He was a professor at the École Polytechnique and the Conservatoire
Nationale des Arts et Métiers from 1929 to 1959. He also was a professor at the École Nationale des Ponts et Chaussées from 1932 to 1950 and
was one of the founding members of the Econometric Society and its
president in 1935. During the latter years of his life, he was out of touch
with his family and friends. It is not clear why.[15]

Divisia's famous articles and book on index-number theory, Divisia
(1925, 1926a, b), are historic and justly famous. Even by current standards, that book is astonishingly brilliant. Prior to the publication of
that book, all economists publishing in index-number theory proposed
approximate formulas. At best, those index numbers were shown to
have some good statistical properties, as systematically classified by
Fisher (1922). But such classifications by properties could not conclude
that an index was the exactly right one to measure aggregate quantity
or aggregate price. In an astonishing *tour de force*, Divisia proved that
one formula would exactly track the unknown aggregator functions of
economic theory, so long as the aggregator functions were consistent
with rational economic behavior.[16]

Recall that the aggregator functions are derived directly from economic theory and are uniquely correct for aggregation over quantities
and prices. This book's appendixes derive those functions for consumers, firms, and financial intermediaries. The aggregator functions of
economic theory depend on unknown functional forms and unknown
parameters, which, at best, can be estimated by statistical inference
methods. But index numbers, which do not depend on unknown functional forms or unknown parameters, are easily computed formulas.
As a result, index numbers are much preferred by data-producing
governmental agencies to aggregator functions. François Divisia's
proof of the existence of such an index number, which can track any
theoretical aggregator function perfectly, stunned the profession. His
index-number formula measures without error, regardless of the degree

---

15. See Roy (1964), which was translated for me by Marcelle Chauvet. I have heard rumors about the reason for Divisia's isolation from family and friends in the latter years of
his life, but the rumors do not seem to be consistent with the available information. I am
indebted to Steve Hanke for pointing out to me this time inconsistency.

16. Divisia's proof applied to data from the rational decisions of one consumer or firm.
Aggregation over consumers and firms is a very complicated subject, which is hard to explain without the use of much mathematics, but discussion of that literature can be found
in the appendixes to this book. See, for example, section A.9 of appendix A.

of substitutability among the goods over which the index aggregates. There was a reason that he was able to derive that proof, while no economist had previously been able to do so. He used an area of advanced mathematics, the "line integral," known to engineers and mathematicians, but not known by many, if any, economists at that time.

The precise mathematical formula for the Divisia index is provided in appendix A as equation (A.79), or in its approximate discrete time form as equation (A.80). Less formally, here is his remarkably simple formula, which is exactly correct in aggregating over quantities or over prices:

Definition 3   *The growth rate of the "Divisia quantity (or price) index" is the weighted average of the quantities (or prices) of the component goods over which the index aggregates, where the weight of each good is that good's expenditure share in the total expenditure on all of the goods over which the index aggregates.*[17]

While this formula is deceptively simple in its appearance, computation, and use, the mathematics in Divisia's paper, proving its exact tracking ability, are not at all simple.[18] Divisia was so far ahead of his time that economists continued suspecting his index was flawed ("path dependent"), until the Divisia index was proved to be free from that mathematical flaw, a half century later by the American economist Hulten (1973) in the journal, *Econometrica*.[19]

---

17. Formally speaking, the Divisia index is derived in continuous time, requiring growth rate data at every instant of time; and the formula uses calculus. But the Finnish economist, Törnqvist (1936), subsequently produced the accepted discrete-time version of the formula, requiring only one measurement during each time period. The formal distinction between the Divisia index and the Törnqvist index is usually made only by professionals working in the index-number theory. Other economists call both indexes the Divisia index. While the Divisia index is exact in continuous time, the Törnqvist discrete time approximation has a small, third-order error in the changes.

18. The direction in which an asset's growth rate weight will change with an interest rate change is not predictable in advance. Consider Cobb–Douglas utility. Its shares are independent of relative prices, and hence of the interest rates within the component user-cost prices. For other utility functions, the direction of the change in shares with a price change, or equivalently with an interest rate change, depends upon whether the own price elasticity of demand exceeds or is less than minus 1. In elementary microeconomic theory, this often overlooked phenomenon produces the famous "diamonds versus water paradox" and is the source of most of the misunderstandings of the Divisia monetary aggregate's weighting, as explained by Barnett (1983b) and in appendix E to this book.

19. Hulten proved that the appearance of a mathematical flaw in the Divisia index was not relevant, unless no aggregate exists to be measured. Of course, the index cannot measure something, if nothing exists to be measured. The mathematical condition for existence of something to be measured is "weak separability" of the mathematical structure. The appendixes in this book's part II provide the relevant mathematics.

2.5.3 Henri Theil

Although controversy remained about Divisia's proof until Hulten's paper appeared in 1973, a Dutch econometrician, Henri Theil (1924–2000), in a citation classic book, Theil (1967), made extensive use of the Divisia index. Theil demonstrated its value in applications and its connection with well-known economic models. The book appeared one year after he moved from the Netherlands to accept an endowed chair at the University of Chicago. In addition, Theil demonstrated that the Divisia index can be derived from the field of "information theory," associated with an engineer, Shannon (1951), working at Bell Laboratories on measuring information transmitted over telephone lines.

I have mentioned the role of the First World War in the life of François Divisia. Theil's life was heavily influenced by the Second World War. Theil was an exceptionally determined man, who did not easily compromise and was dedicated to his work. He published 15 important books, of which three are citation classics, and over 250 articles. Much of his research established the central role of the Divisia index in applied economic modeling and in economic measurement. His decisiveness was more than evident to me, during a two-day stay in his Michigan weekend home. The source of his single-minded determination and dedication has been the subject of speculation by many economists, including his own colleagues at the University of Chicago.

Here is a possibly relevant source, as explained to me by Theil after he had retired from the University of Chicago. During the Second World War, he was a student at a university in Amsterdam. The Wehrmacht (German Army) required all students to sign a loyalty oath to Germany. Theil was a patriotic Dutchman who refused to sign the oath. The penalty was deportation to Germany into forced labor in a factory. He hid in the crawl space below his parents' home with nothing but a radio to use to listen to the BBC. Eventually he was caught and deported to a factory in Germany. His parents were well off and well regarded in the Netherlands, so were able to bribe the German officials to get him released. When he was back in Amsterdam, the Wehrmacht soldiers came looking for him again with the loyalty oath in hand. He refused to sign, and went back into hiding. This happened three times. The last time he was in forced labor in Germany, he was near death, when the war ended. How many people are so patriotic and determined as to be willing to die to avoid signing a meaningless piece of paper? Yes, he was a person whose dedication was beyond admirable, and his contributions to index-number theory, aggregation theory, and econometrics are of historic proportions.

His influence on a generation of econometricians is, to this day, not fully recognized. Divisia and Theil were extraordinary people, whose roles in this literature are historic. To my knowledge, they never met, although Theil recognized the practical applications of Divisia's contribution long before most of the rest of the economics profession did and developed it in ways that still are not fully absorbed into mainstream economics.

2.5.4   Dale Jorgenson

In this professional drama, five more major players need to be introduced, before our discussion can be considered up to date. In economic theory, prices are opportunity costs: the costs in forgone resources to buy one more unit of the services of the good being priced. As we have seen, no ambiguity arises, when the goods are perishable. But with a durable good, the price of services per unit of time is not the same as the price to purchase the services of the good for its lifetime. The mathematical implications of that distinction did not become clear until Dale Jorgenson (1963) derived the user-cost price of consuming the services of a durable capital good.[20] He published that famous paper, while a professor at the University of California at Berkeley. He moved to Harvard six years later, where he is an endowed full professor to this day.

Prior to Jorgenson's paper, capital theory had been troubled by paradoxes created by using the purchase price of the capital stock, when the rental price should have been used. Such misunderstandings were central to much of the confusion in Marxist theory, which purported to dispute mainstream capital theory. Financial assets are durable goods, subject to the same potential problems. In fact similar confusion evolved over many decades on the "price of money." Is it the inflation rate, an interest rate, or what? As we have seen in definition 1, the correct answer is the user-cost price of the monetary asset, as first derived mathematically by Barnett (1978) and provided as equation (A.5) of this book's appendix A.

In the 1960s, while Jorgenson was a professor at the University of California, three Berkeley PhD students had become well known: W. Erwin Diewert, Lawrence Lau, and Laurits Christensen. In a subsection below, Diewert's important role in this literature will be discussed. Regarding Christensen and Lau, they coauthored important work with their former professor in their papers, Christensen, Jorgenson, and Lau

---

20. Also see Jorgenson (1967) and Hall and Jorgenson (1967).

(1971, 1973, 1975), originating a modeling approach called "translog."[21] The translog also was important in the work of Erwin Diewert, since the translog "aggregator function" connected the Divisia index to aggregation theory.

At the height of the political and intellectual turmoil at Berkeley, there was another graduate student there. But he was not an economist, yet. He was on leave from his work as an aerospace engineer in Los Angeles. He did not know Jorgenson, Christensen, Lau, or Diewert at that time. His name was William A. Barnett. We'll get to that guy later.

2.5.5 Milton Friedman

The scene is now set for the arrival of the great monetary economist and Nobel laureate, Milton Friedman (1912–2006), at the University of Chicago. *The Economist* magazine described him as "the most influential economist of the second half of the 20th century (Keynes died in 1946), possibly of all of it [the century]."[22] He became such a well-known economist to the public that nearly everyone has heard of him. But what is less well known is there were two Milton Friedmans. (1) There was the mathematical statistician, who produced the important Friedman rank test before the Second World War and worked as a statistician for the federal government during the war. The Friedman rank test is a classical statistical test in the highly technical field of nonparametric statistical inference. That test is known to all serious mathematical statisticians. (2) There also was the economist Milton Friedman, known to all economists as well as to almost everyone else. What is not so widely known is that the two Milton Friedmans were—the same person.[23]

As an economist, Friedman was the world's best-known "monetarist." He was a strong advocate of controlling the rate of growth of the money supply, which he viewed as causal for inflation in the long run and for the business cycle in the short run. Although he based most

---

21. Translog is quadratic in the logarithms.
22. "Milton Friedman, a Heavyweight Champ, at Five Two," *The Economist*, November 23, 2006. Yes, he was five foot two inches tall. While teaching his graduate course in macroeconomics, he stood on a platform at the front of a large room. Since he was an intellectual giant and stood on a platform, he seemed larger than life to the students in his class. I was astonished by his height, when I first walked up to ask him a question after a class.
23. He initially planned to be an actuary and began his employment as a statistician in Washington, DC. His first academic position was as an economist at the University of Wisconsin-Madison, but he left that position to return to statistics in Washington, DC, as a result of anti-Semitism encountered in his first academic position. At the end of the Second World War, he moved back into economics at the University of Chicago and remained an economist for the rest of his career.

of his advocacy on the official simple-sum M2 monetary aggregate, he was well aware of the serious and growing problems with the official monetary aggregates. Distant substitutes for money were evolving and growing, while providing less monetary services per dollar of asset than the more liquid means-of-payment monetary assets, currency, and demand deposits. Friedman with his coauthor Anna Schwartz (1970, pp. 151–52) published, in their landmark book on United States monetary history, the following statement:

This [simple summation] procedure is a very special case of the more general approach. In brief, the general approach consists of regarding each asset as a joint product having different degrees of "moneyness," and defining the quantity of money as the weighted sum of the aggregated value of all assets, the weights for individual assets varying from zero to unity with a weight of unity assigned to that asset or assets regarded as having the largest quantity of "moneyness" per dollar of aggregate value. The procedure we have followed implies that all weights are either zero or unity.

The more general approach has been suggested frequently but experimented with only occasionally. We conjecture that this approach deserves and will get much more attention than it has so far received.

In a long footnote to that statement, Friedman and Schwartz listed the PhD dissertations of many of Friedman's students at the University of Chicago. Those dissertations attempted to produce weighted sums of monetary assets, but without use of index-number theory or aggregation theory. Such *ad hoc* weighted averages were "experimented with" by Friedman's students in his famous monetary economics workshop at the University of Chicago, but were never accepted by the profession. Those students did not yet have available the derivation of the user-cost price of monetary assets in Barnett (1978) or the unification of index-number theory with aggregation theory in Diewert (1976). The literature on rigorous monetary-aggregation theory and the resulting monetary index numbers began with Barnett (1980a), who at that time had available the necessary tools for the derivation.[24]

When Barnett (1980a) first appeared, Friedman had retired from the University of Chicago and was at the Hoover Institution at Stanford University. Arnold Zellner, who was on the faculty at the University of Chicago, was a friend of Milton Friedman. Zellner had lunch with Friedman at the Hoover Institution, and Friedman raised the subject of my 1980 paper. He requested Zellner to ask me to cite his above

---

24. In practice, there is little difference between the Fisher ideal and the Divisia monetary index. This book emphasizes Divisia, since the Fisher-ideal index is more difficult to explain without the use of mathematics.

statement in the Friedman and Schwartz book, as evidence that he had recognized the problem ten years before I solved it, although he and his students did not yet have the tools needed to solve the problem themselves. I was happy to cite Friedman and Schwartz's valid statement and have done so in many publications since then.

Friedman was well aware of the seriousness of the problems produced by the Fed's simple-sum monetary aggregation. By equally weighting components, simple-sum aggregation can badly distort an aggregate and obscure the effects of policy. As an example, suppose that the money supply is measured by the Fed's former, broadest simple-sum monetary aggregate, L, which included much of the national debt of short and intermediate maturity. That debt could be monetized (bought and paid for with freshly printed currency) without increasing either taxes or L, since the public would simply have exchanged component securities in L for currency, which also is in L. The inflationary printing of money to pay the government's debt would be successfully hidden from public view.[25]

However, if the Divisia aggregate over the components of L were reported by the Fed, that valid aggregate would not treat this transfer as an exchange of "pure money" for "pure money." Divisia L would instead rise at about the same rate as the resulting inflation in prices, since Divisia L would weight the growth of currency more heavily than the decline in government debt. The inflationary consequence of the policy would be revealed to the public and to the Congress.

The traditionally constructed high-level aggregates (e.g., M2 or the now discontinued M3 and L) implicitly view distant substitutes for money as perfect substitutes for currency. Rather than capturing only part of the economy's monetary services, as M1 does, the broad simple-sum aggregates swamp the included monetary services with excessively weighted, nonmonetary services. The need remains for an official aggregate capturing the monetary-services contributions of all monetary assets in accordance with best-practice economic measurement, as by Divisia or Fisher-ideal aggregation.

Milton Friedman's successor at the University of Chicago is Robert E. Lucas. In an article in the journal, *Econometrica*, Lucas (2000, p. 270) wrote:

---

25. This interesting anecdote should not be taken too literally, but rather as an illustration of how serious the defects of broad simple-sum monetary aggregation can be. Formally speaking, the aggregate, L, which the Fed no longer supplies, contained only those asset quantities held by domestic non–money-stock issuers. Treasury securities held by banks or held abroad were not included.

I share the widely held opinion that M1 is too narrow an aggregate for this period [the 1990s], and I think that the Divisia approach offers much the best prospects for resolving this difficulty.

Amen.

2.5.6 W. Erwin Diewert

Index numbers, as defined above, depend on both prices and quantities. As a result, a valid index-number-theoretic money aggregate must contain both prices and quantities. Dale Jorgenson's concept of the user cost of a durable good was needed to be able to derive the user-cost price of the services of a monetary asset. My derivation of that formula for "the price of money" removed one source of arbitrariness from construction of a monetary quantity index number.

But there remained another source of non-uniqueness. While François Divisia's famous formula provided an immediate good choice, Fisher had shown that many index-number formulas move very closely together and have excellent properties, including his own preferred Fisher-ideal index. This fact had produced a wedge between economic theorists, who advocated estimating the exact aggregator functions of economic theory, and index-number theorists, who advocated easily computed statistical index numbers. In particular, how should we choose among the index-number formulas shown to have good properties by Fisher? While Theil clearly advocated and used the Divisia index, other index-number theorists advocated other formulas having good properties. What was needed was a link between the best index numbers and the underlying theoretical aggregator functions of pure economic theory.

Precisely that result was provided in a transformative paper by W. Erwin Diewert (1976) at the University of British Columbia in Canada. He proved that all of the index numbers in a particular class of index-number formulas track the exact aggregator function equally well in discrete time. He called those index numbers "superlative" index numbers.[26] He had thereby unified aggregation theory with index-number theory, since all index numbers in the superlative class have equally good ability to track the exact, aggregator function. His superlative index-number class included both the Fisher-ideal index and the (discrete time) Divisia index. Barnett (1980a) advocated either the Divisia index or Fisher ideal index with user-cost prices to measure the economy's monetary-service

---

26. In the language of mathematics, all index numbers in that class have third-order remainder terms in tracking the exact aggregator function's growth rates.

flow. The two formulas move so closely together that there usually is little reason to prefer one over the other. The differences in growth rates among index numbers in the superlative class are usually less than the round off error in the component data used in the index.

It is interesting to observe that Diewert got his PhD from the University of California at Berkeley at the time that Jorgenson was a Berkeley professor, producing his famous user cost of capital paper. In addition Diewert's first faculty position was as an assistant professor at the University of Chicago, at the time that Theil was producing his famous research on the Divisia index. I got my MBA degree from the University of California at Berkeley at the time that Jorgenson and Diewert were there. No, I never met Divisia, but few, if any, American economists ever did. The famous engineer and economist, François Divisia, died in 1964, long before I had become an economist, but while I myself was working as an engineer at Rocketdyne.

With definitions 1 and 3 providing the Divisia index and user-cost price of money, and with Erwin Diewert's definition of "superlative index numbers," the scene is now set to provide a formal definition of the Divisia monetary aggregates, in accordance with Barnett (1980a).

Definition 4   *The "Divisia monetary aggregates" are produced by substituting into the Divisia quantity index formula, definition 3, the quantities of individual monetary assets and their corresponding user-cost prices, in accordance with definition 1.*

The resulting index is a "statistical index number," in accordance with definition 2, and hence the entire literature on index number and aggregation theory is relevant, including Diewert's and Theil's work, as well as Divisia's famous proof.[27] Several authors have studied the empirical properties of the Divisia monetary-quantity index compared with the simple-sum index.[28] The theory developed at this stage of the

---

27. In practice, the Fisher ideal formula has advantages over Divisia during time periods when new assets are being introduced. A "reservation price" needs to be imputed for the period prior to the introduction of the new asset.

28. The earliest comparisons are in Barnett (1982) and Barnett, Offenbacher, and Spindt (1984). Barnett and Serletis (2000) and Barnett and Chauvet (2011b) collect together and reprint seminal journal articles from this literature. More recent examples include Belongia (1996), Belongia and Ireland (2006), and Schunk (2001), and the comprehensive survey found in Barnett and Serletis (2000). Other overviews of published theoretical and empirical results in this literature are available in Barnett, Fisher, and Serletis (1992) and Serletis (2006). For textbook treatments, see Serletis (2006,2007). Barnett (1997) has documented the connection between the well-deserved decline in the policy credibility of monetary aggregates and the defects peculiar to simple-sum aggregation.

literature's evolution is summarized in this book's appendix A and is fundamental to modern monetary aggregation.

I mentioned previously that I was at Berkeley as a graduate student at the peak of the Berkeley intellectual and political explosion in the 1960s, while on leave from my Rocketdyne employment. What about the subsequent intellectual explosion at the University of Chicago in the early 1970s? I knew about that too, and yes, I was there on another leave from Rocketdyne. Friedman, Diewert, and Theil were on the faculty. I took their courses. In those days of cost-plus-fixed-fee contracts and the race to the moon, Rocketdyne provided one year of educational leave for each year of engineering work completed. I took full advantage of those opportunities.[29]

2.5.7   James Poterba and Julio Rotemberg

When I derived the theory summarized in appendix A and began to apply it empirically, I thought that was the end of the story. The theory unified aggregation theory, index-number theory, and monetary economics in a manner uniquely internally consistent. In addition the theory was proving to be very successfully applied in empirical research, including research at many central banks throughout the world. But I was stunned when Julio Rotemberg, then a professor at the Massachusetts Institute of Technology's (MIT) Department of Economics, presented a startling paper at a conference I organized at the University of Texas at Austin.[30] Rotemberg's paper was coauthored with James Poterba, also at MIT. Their paper challenged the state of the art of index-number theory and thereby brought into question whether using that theory in monetary aggregation was really the "end of the story." Poterba now is not only the Mitsui Professor of Economics at MIT, but also is the president of the National Bureau of Economic Research. Rotemberg now is the William Ziegler Professor of Business at the Harvard University Business School.

Poterba and Rotemberg (1987) emphasized the fact that user-cost prices of monetary services for monetary-assets are not known with

---

29. The intent was for me to return to Rocketdyne as a statistician to work in its new advanced research facility on possible future space exploration projects. But by the time I completed my last educational leave, at Carnegie Mellon University, the space program priority had given way to military funding for the Vietnam War, and the new Rocketdyne advanced research facility was closed down. Instead of returning to Rocketdyne, I accepted my first position as an economist, at the Federal Reserve Board in Washington, DC.
30. The proceedings of the conference were for publication in a monograph series I was editing for Cambridge University Press. I was editing that volume jointly with Kenneth Singleton, who now is on the faculty at Stanford University.

perfect certainty, since interest rates are not paid in advance. So, for example, if you deposit money into a passbook savings account at a bank, you cannot be certain how much interest you will be paid that month. In contrast, prices of most consumer goods are known at the instant of purchase of those goods.[31] For that reason, the classical literature on index-number theory, including the work of Fisher, Theil, and Diewert, assumed prices are known at the instant of purchase. The issue is not knowledge of future prices or interest rates. Risk and uncertainty about future prices and interest rates have been shown not to be a problem for index-number theory.[32] But risk about current-period purchase prices is ignored in classical index-number theory, although is potentially relevant to monetary aggregation, if current-period interest rate risk is not negligible. This distinction had not previously occurred to me.

Julio Rotemberg's presentation at the conference at the University of Texas excited the audience with the challenge it presented to us. Leonard Rapping, who was one of my former professors, when I was a student at Carnegie Mellon University, was in the audience. He walked over to me after Rotemberg's presentation and said to me with great enthusiasm that I should take the challenge seriously and seek to advance the field in a manner dealing with the fundamental issues raised by Poterba and Rotemberg. Sadly Rapping did not live to see that happen. He had serious problems with his heart. But I have fond memories of his excitement at what he saw and recognized at that conference.

In their paper, Poterba and Rotemberg proved that some of the fundamental tools of classical index-number theory are undermined, if current prices are not known with certainty. In the case of monetary aggregation, Poterba and Rotemberg advocated instead the direct econometric estimation of monetary aggregator functions by advanced statistical methodology permitting risk. I accepted that idea and used it with two coauthors in Barnett, Hinich, and Yue (1991, 2000). While that approach is elegant and suitable for publication in professional journals, it would not be appropriate as a data production procedure for a governmental agency. Such organizations produce their data using index-number theory, specifically designed for that purpose. Index-number theory does not require econometric modeling or estimation.

---

31. The problem does not exist for perishable goods, since the purchase price then is for all of the services of the good. But the Poterba and Rotemberg critique is relevant to durable consumer goods, since the cost of consuming the services of a durable good during one period, the "user cost," depends on the price at which it can be sold at the end of the period, unless the good is rented, rather than bought and sold. The sale price is not known with certainty at the end of the period.

32. See Barnett (1995). The proof assumes intertemporal separability of preferences.

In thinking about this problem, it occurred to me that there should be a way to extend index-number theory to incorporate risk by using techniques developed in the field of finance. After leaving the University of Texas for Washington University in St. Louis, I suggested the approach I had in mind to two of my PhD students at Washington University. We succeeded in producing that extension and published it in Barnett, Liu, and Jensen (1997). The resulting extension of the literature on index-number theory to include risky prices is presented in sections D.1 through D.6 of this book's appendix D.[33]

But a further challenge remained in this direction of research. The common finance approach to adjustment for risk is known to produce an inadequately small adjustment for risk. This under-adjustment has become known as the "equity premium puzzle." I delayed addressing this problem for a few years, while the controversy played itself out in the finance literature. After leaving Washington University for my current position at the University of Kansas, I worked with my colleague, Shu Wu, on application of the newest approach from the finance literature.[34] The result was Barnett and Wu (2005), summarized in sections D.8 through D.10 of this book's appendix D. That research, in many ways, represents the state of the art of monetary aggregation and currently is motivating research by many economists throughout the world. The risk-adjusted Divisia monetary aggregates are especially relevant to countries in which substantial foreign-denominated money-market assets and accounts are held. In such cases interest rates can be subject to substantial exchange rate risk.

Well, that was not all from Poterba and Rotemberg. With one of their students at MIT, they subsequently published Rotemberg, Driscoll, and Poterba (1995), applying a new monetary-aggregation formula, called the currency equivalent (CE) index. That index was first proposed by Rotemberg (1991). I was able to prove that the CE index, as the flow index they advocated, was a special case of my Divisia monetary index, and hence seemed to provide no gain over the monetary aggregates I was advocating. But I had learned never to take Poterba and Rotemberg lightly. Looking at their index more carefully, I found that I could derive it in a different manner as a measure of the economic capital stock of

---

33. That extension of the field of index number to include risk can be adapted to consumer durables. As explained in the prior footnote, the price at which a durable can be sold at the end of a period is not known with certainty, so extension of index-number theory for risk is relevant to consumer durables as well as to financial assets.

34. The approach permits intertemporal nonseparability and is a response to the "equity premium puzzle."

money. The capital stock evaluates the discounted present value of the future flow, rather than only the current flow of monetary services. I published that alternative derivation in Barnett (1991). Here was now a new challenge. Measuring the economic capital stock, depending on future service flows, requires the ability to forecast future flows. Improvements to the CE index's measure of future flows have motivated much of my current research with students and colleagues.[35] You can find an introduction to that research in this book's appendix B. Poterba and Rotemberg have certainly been keeping me busy with their deep and challenging insights.

From the early path-breaking work of Fisher and Divisia through the recent developments motivated by the prodding of Poterba and Rotemberg, there has been a long progression of insights and developments. That progression and those developments have led to the most recent, state-of-the-art Divisia monetary aggregates. Are there any shortcomings in measurement to prevent a central bank from using Divisia monetary aggregates? Is there any reason at all to prefer the disreputable simple-sum monetary aggregates to the state-of-the-art Divisia monetary aggregates? The answer to both questions is one simple unequivocal word—*no*! In measurement, central banks should do the best they can, not the worst they can. It doesn't get any worse than simple-sum aggregation.

2.6 Banks throughout the World

Divisia monetary aggregates exist for over 37 countries throughout the world and are available within many central banks.[36] But let's look at

---

35. My initial proof assumed martingale forecasting.

36. For example, Divisia monetary aggregates have been produced for the following countries:

North America: United States (Barnett 1980a; Anderson, Jones, and Nesmith 1997), Mexico (Alfredo Sandoval, unpublished), and Canada (Cockerline and Murray 1981; Hueng 1998; Serletis and Molik 2000; Longworth and Atta-Mensah 1994).

South America: Brazil (Divino 1997, 2000; Neto and Albuquerque 2002), Chile (Katerina Taiganides, unpublished), and Peru (Veronica Ruiz de Castilla, unpublished).

Europe: Britain (Batchelor 1988; Drake 1992; Hancock 2005; Belongia and Chrystal 1991), Denmark (la Cour 2006), Switzerland (Yue and Fluri 1991; Mullineux 1996, chapter by H. Genberg and S. Neftci), Poland (Cieśla 1999; Kluza 2001), Bulgaria (Ganev 1997), Italy pre-euro (Binner and Gazely 1999; Mullineux 1996, chapter by E. Gaiotti), France pre-euro (Mullineux 1996, chapter by S. Lecarpentier), the Netherlands pre-euro (Fase 1985), Austria pre-euro (Driscoll, Ford, Mullineux, and Kohler 1985), Germany pre-euro (Herrmann, Reimers, and Toedter 2000; Gaab 1996; Belongia 2000), and the European Monetary Union the differences among some of the most relevant central banks in this regard.

2.6.1   The Federal Reserve Board

As the originator of the Divisia monetary aggregates and, nearly equivalently, the Fisher-ideal monetary aggregates, I was the first to compute them, while on the staff of the Special Studies Section of the Federal Reserve Board (FRB) in Washington, DC. Later sections of this book provide information about what transpired in those and subsequent years at the Fed. But this section will mention only the start. When I first produced the Divisia monetary aggregates for the United States, I was asked to produce a monthly memorandum reporting on those aggregates and their implications for the economy. The monthly memorandum was to be delivered to Stephen Axilrod, the staff director of monetary policy, which was the highest policy position on the FRB's staff.[37] He was the most powerful person on the Board's staff and was occasionally more influential on policy than some of the governors. In fact, while the weakest of the chairmen, William Miller, was there, Axilrod was widely believed to be running the show.

I do not know whether Axilrod ever passed my memoranda on to the governors, who were being provided with the severely defective, official simple-sum monetary aggregates. But during a Board meeting, I was asked to provide information about the Divisia monetary aggregates directly to the governors. To my surprise, three of the governors turned to me and asked me to send them a memorandum answering

---

(Fase and Winder 1994; Spencer 1997; Wesche 1997; Fase 2000; Beyer, Doornik, and Hendry 2001; Stracca 2001; Reimers 2002).

Asia: Japan (Ishida 1984; Mullineux 1996, chapter by K. Hirayama and M. Kasuya; Belongia 2000), South Korea (Hahm and Kim 2000; Habibullah 1999), China (Yu and Tsui 2000), Malaysia (Dahalan, Sharma, and Sylwester 2005; Habibullah 1999; Sriram 2002), India (Acharya and Kamaiah 2001; Jha and Longjam 1999), Taiwan (Shih 2000; Wu, Lin, Tiao, and Cho 2005; Habibullah 1999; Binner, Gazely, Chen, and Chie 2004), and Indonesia, Myanmar, Nepal, Philippines, Singapore, Sri Lanka, and Thailand (all in Habibullah 1999).

Australasia: Australia (Hoa 1985).

Middle East: Turkey (Celik and Uzun 2009; Kunter 1993), Iran (Davoudi and Zarepour 2007), Israel (email Offenbacher at akoffen@bankisrael.gov.il or Bank of Israel Information and Statistics Department at statistics@boi.org.il), Pakistan (Tariq and Matthews 1997), and Saudi Arabia (Mamdooh Saad Alsahafi, unpublished).

Caribbean: Barbados (Kurt Lambert, unpublished).

For collections of cross-country results, see Belongia and Binner (2000), Mullineux (1996), and Habibullah (1999). More international data and results can be found online at the website of the Center for Financial Stability in New York City.

37.   He mentioned nothing about any of this in his recent MIT Press book, Axilrod (2009).

questions they asked. Of course, I immediately agreed and was pleased by the display of interest. But when I returned to my office, two high-level staff members came to my office looking alarmed. One was the director of research, whom I had never before met, since our offices were in different buildings. The two of them instructed me to write the memorandum and send it to them. They told me they might let me reply to the governors' request at a later date, once they approved of my reply. So I wrote the memorandum and sent it to them. One of them sent me comments for revision. The primary comment was about what to call the Commerce Department's inflation index. I changed the terminology to the one he requested and sent the revised memorandum back to both of them. The other officer then sent me comments. His primary comment was to change the terminology back to the one I originally had used. The memorandum bounced back and forth between the two staff officers in that circular manner for many months. Eventually they both said the memorandum was OK and would be delivered to the three governors. I was not permitted to deliver it myself, so I have no way of knowing whether the governors ever received it. But if they did, they probably had forgotten about the questions they had asked.

As mentioned earlier, I left the Fed in 1981 for the University of Texas. My first PhD student at Texas was a very dedicated man, with a prior background in engineering. He had the technical background to work with me on research using my Divisia monetary aggregates. To be able to explore policy problems in the past, I needed back data. The student produced those data extending back to 1959. For long-run research in this area, his PhD dissertation data remain the authoritative source of the early data to this day. He was a determined and unusual person. But I could not have anticipated he would one day end up in the position he now holds. His dissertation is Fayyad (1986). Yes, he is Salam Fayyad, the current prime minister of the Palestinian Authority.

The contrast in economic measurement expertise between the Fed and the BEA or BLS is evident from the following example. When I first originated the Divisia monetary aggregates, while on the staff of the FRB, a number of reporters wanted to interview me about it. Articles appeared in *Business Week*, *The Boston Globe*, and *The Wall Street Journal*. The *Business Week* article appeared in the September 22, 1980 issue (p. 25) shortly after my paper, Barnett (1980a), had appeared in the *Journal of Econometrics*. The *Business Week* reporter had attended my presentation at the annual meetings of the American Economic Association and interviewed me in the lobby of the Hilton Hotel later that day. He asked me many good questions, seemed genuinely interested, and appeared to understand what I was saying, including my explanation of the role of user-cost prices in computing the weights in quantity index numbers. When his article appeared, he devoted a half page to reporting in a very positive manner on my presentation at the conference. I was pleased to see such a supportive article in that magazine, but he made a mistake in describing the weighting formula. He wrote that I was using "turnover rates" as the prices in the quantity index. Of course, this was wrong. The user-cost price measures opportunity cost, which for a monetary asset is forgone interest. I cut out the article and posted it on a bulletin board at the Board in Washington, DC. I underlined the statement about turnover rates, assuming the economists would realize that I had done so as a joke. Turnover rates make no sense as user-cost prices in quantity indexes.

A few months after I left the Board for the University of Texas, I learned, to my astonishment, that one of my former colleagues had actually begun producing monetary aggregate "index numbers" using turnover rates as prices. Perhaps my joke had been taken seriously. The resulting new index was called MQ and was supplied to the profession for a couple of years.[38] No one at the BLS or BEA would have taken my joke seriously. They are sophisticated people in economic measurement and understand the connection with economic aggregation theory.

2.6.2   The Bank of Japan

Four years after I had originated the Divisia monetary aggregates, I was invited to speak on my research at a conference in Tokyo on the topic of "Information and Data Management." At that time, I was on the faculty of the University of Texas at Austin. The invitation was very appealing. It included air fare for both my wife and me, a room at one of Tokyo's best hotels, all meals and transportation, along with other special arrangements. This was in 1984, when Tokyo was in a dramatic boom, and the cost of living in Tokyo was very high. When invited to conferences, I am accustomed to being told the amount of time I have

---

38. At conferences, I then found I was often being viewed as having advocated MQ and was asked to defend it. Even the great economist Franco Modigliani, confronted me with MQ at a conference and criticized me for having had anything to do with it. But, of course, I never did. It was just a joke, based on a misunderstanding by a *Business Week* reporter and then evidently by one of my former colleagues at the Fed. As a result I had to publish a proof that MQ made no sense in economic theory. See Barnett and Serletis (2000, pp. 97–98) and this book's appendix A, section A.12.2, equations (A.129) and (A.130).

for my presentation, the topic of the session, and the time available for open discussion. Although I was a friend of the conference's primary organizer, Ryuzo Sato, I could not get an answer to such questions from any of the organizers. All I was told was that the financial arrangements and accommodations would be first rate, and indeed they were. The organizers did not ask me to prepare a paper or to provide the subject or title of a talk.

I began to recognize the nature of the situation, while on my JAL flight to Tokyo. The airline's magazine, at every seat in the airplane, contained an article about the experiences of scientists invited to speak at conferences in Tokyo. What I was experiencing and what happened subsequently in Tokyo fit what I read. The article explained that the procedure was designed to acquire information by putting scientists in a high-pressure situation. The article also said that Carnegie Mellon University, from which I had received my PhD, prohibited its faculty from participating in any of those conferences. The University of Texas was subject to no such prohibitions. I did want my work to be used, so if the Bank of Japan might act faster than the Fed, that was fine with me.

The conference was held in a very large auditorium with hundreds of people in the audience. I was on the stage as a panel member for an entire day, with only two coffee breaks and a break for lunch. I was not permitted to present a prepared paper. The other people on the stage were speaking many languages, including Japanese, German, French, and English, among other languages. We all were wearing headphones providing simultaneous translation of what was being said, and the simultaneous translation was into many languages. I had my headphones set for translation into English. Simultaneous translation of technical discussion is far from flawless, so it was hard to know precisely what was being said. One of the speakers on that panel was Marvin Minsky at MIT. He was America's leading authority on artificial intelligence and cofounder of MIT's Artificial Intelligence Laboratory. Isaac Asimov (1980, p. 217 and 301) described Minsky as one of only two people he would admit were more intelligent than he was, the other being Carl Sagan.

Being on the stage so long with confusing simultaneous translation from other languages was stressful, especially with no ability to present a prepared paper. The moderator sat at the head of the table. He was my old friend, Ryuzo Sato, who spoke fluent English and Japanese. If you were not regularly participating in the conversation, he would turn to you and ask you a question. No one wanted that, since he asked unexpected, difficult questions. In short, we all were under pressure to continue participating in the discussion all day long. About the only way to do that was to reveal whatever you knew about the subject of the conference. Indeed Minsky revealed much about his research on artificial intelligence, and I revealed much about my research on monetary aggregation theory. It was becoming clear how Japanese industry was acquiring so much information about American research, and then adopting it faster than American industry was.

At lunch, I sat at a table in a group including a Japanese economist, who had been educated in the United States. I mentioned to him that Carnegie Mellon University, which is a leader in artificial intelligence research, did not permit its faculty to participate in conferences in Japan. His reply was, "they are smart." I also asked him about the unusual conference procedure, which I had never experienced anywhere else in the world. He explained the intent was to induce speakers to reveal what they knew. But he also said that it was designed to attract a large Japanese audience. In Japan, arguing in public is frowned upon as a "loss of face," so such public arguments are not often seen. By setting up a procedure inducing foreign speakers to be argumentative, the conference provided a form of unusual entertainment for the audience.

My Divisia monetary aggregates were unavailable to the American public at the time. In section 2.7.3 below, I explain the secretive way in which they were being used at the FRB by the model manager, after I moved to Texas. But to my astonishment, a few months after I returned to Texas from Tokyo, I saw an article by Ishida (1984) in the Bank of Japan's official publication. He published a collection of empirical comparisons demonstrating that Divisia monetary aggregates for Japan work better than the official monetary aggregates. I had no doubt that Ishida's research had been motivated by what I had said in the Tokyo conference. Because I was pleased by the results in Ishida's paper, I wrote to him. He did not reply. I wrote again. He did not reply. Serious scientists throughout the world correspond freely. I had never before encountered an author who used and properly cited my work, but failed to reply to my correspondences. I then asked my friend, Ryuzo Sato, whether he could explain that odd behavior. Sato told me this is a common problem among Japanese government employees, since their written English is often not very good, and they do not want to make that evident by replying to a letter. I found that odd, but I assumed it was true. Two years later I met Ishida at a conference in the United

States. He got his PhD from the London School of Economics, and his English is perfect.

2.6.3   The St. Louis Federal Reserve Bank

I remained on the faculty of the University of Texas for eight years, until I was offered a professorship at Washington University in St. Louis with a reduced teaching load. I welcomed the proximity to the St. Louis Federal Reserve Bank, at which I have friends and colleagues. In fact two of my PhD students at the University of Texas got their first positions at that Reserve Bank, including Salam Fayyad. At the time, a senior officer of that bank, Michael Belongia, had a full understanding of the Board's defective measurement procedures and was publishing valid criticisms of them himself (e.g., see Belongia and Chalfant 1989 and Belongia 1995, 1996).

The St. Louis Fed decided to take over production and distribution of my Divisia monetary aggregates and to make the data available to the public. The database was constructed and announced to the public in the publication, Thornton and Yue (1991). Dan Thornton is a well-known, highly published, vice president at the bank and Piyu Yue was a former PhD student of mine at the University of Texas. Although the new Divisia data were produced and used in research there, no mechanism was set up for regular monthly updates to be made available to the public. Subsequently Mike Belongia left for a university position, when the director of research at that bank retired. The two were close friends.

Subsequently the St. Louis Fed hired a new director of research, William Dewald. He was a well-known academic economist, who had been a professor at Ohio State University for many years, and had been the long-time editor of a respected journal, *The Journal of Money, Credit and Banking*. Fortunately, Dewald's commitment to continuation and improvement of the Divisia data was clear. I've heard he regularly said to his staff that "data live forever and data collection and dissemination are a fundamental purpose of a central bank." Dewald's professionalism played a key role in continuing the availability of those data.

Dewald's commitment resulted not only in a substantial upgrade in the quality of the data, but also in the creation of an internal procedure for regular monthly distribution of the data on the bank's website. The importance of this commitment cannot be overestimated. Setting up that database for regular public release was not a trivial matter. The economist Dewald put in charge was Richard Anderson, a vice president at the St. Louis Fed. He was previously on the staff of the Money and Reserves Projection Section at the Federal Reserve Board in Washington, DC, where he had been in charge of producing the Fed's monetary aggregates for its official release (called the H.6). His PhD in economics is from MIT. He is a senior Fed insider with expertise in monetary data construction and policy. He employed two of my PhD students at Washington University to help with improving the database. One was Barry Jones, now a professor at the State University of New York at Binghamton. The other was Travis Nesmith, now a senior economist on the Federal Reserve Board's staff in Washington, DC. In addition I was myself included on the Advisory Board for the St. Louis Fed's Divisia database.

There was good reason to set up the database at the St. Louis Fed, which has long been a major source of Federal Reserve data. As I've mentioned above, the only person who had regular access to the Divisia monetary aggregates, while I was on the Board's staff, was the staff director of monetary policy, a position that no longer exists at the FRB. There was no official channel allocated to making the data available to the public. As discussed in section 2.7.3 below, the internal use of the Divisia monetary aggregates after I left became more secretive, unknown even to the Board's governors. They were making policy decisions based on model simulations, without knowing that their own model contained Divisia M2, not the Board's official simple-sum M2.

Anderson, Jones, and Nesmith (1997) set up the revised database, making it available to the public online on the Bank's website, and provided the details of the construction process in an issue of the St. Louis Fed's *Monthly Review* publication. Instead of calling the aggregates the Divisia monetary aggregates, as I do, they called them the monetary services index (MSI). Two reasons exist to use the MSI terminology. One is the emphasis on the index's measure of service flow. The other is to emphasize that any index number formulas can be used from Diewert's superlative index-number class, such as the Fisher ideal or Divisia, so long as the prices in the formulas are measured using the user-cost price formula. I nevertheless continue using the terminology, Divisia monetary aggregates, to emphasize the roots of modern index-number theory in the brilliant work of François Divisia in Paris. In addition the Divisia index formula is more easily explained without mathematics (see definitions 3 and 4 above) than the Fisher-ideal index and provides access to the dispersion measures defined in appendix C, section C.7.

However, there was a rather disturbing note to the St. Louis Fed's admirable work in making its Divisia index available to the public. The database was "temporarily" frozen in February 2006 for "revisions." Those minor revisions, requiring no extensions to the theory, should not have taken five years to complete. At the time of the freeze, the economists responsible for the revisions posted online that the freeze would last for a few months, not years. Throughout the five years of the data freeze, the target date for revisions' completion changed repeatedly from months to years. I am aware of no credible reason for denial of public access to the Divisia data for so many years. But it is worthwhile to consider the time period, during which we all were denied access to those data. Keep in mind that the housing downturn, which started in 2006, is a primary cause of the recession that followed. Is it a coincidence that the MSI (Divisia) data were frozen at precisely the time that the economic malaise began and remained frozen during the financial crisis and the recession? Is it a coincidence that a month later, in March 2006, the M3 data were closed down permanently?[39] The most charitable explanation would be that there is something wrong with the Fed's priorities. But if I were a comedian, I'd conclude that the devil made them do it. That is about as good an explanation as any I heard during the five-year freeze.

Sometimes a system is more than the sum of its individuals and has a life of its own. The economics profession has been hearing that for nearly a century from economists who call themselves "institutionalists" specializing in "institutionalism."[40] During the five years of the MSI data freeze, there were substantial changes in the high-level officer staff at the St. Louis Fed, including the director of research and the president of the bank. When the freeze began, most of those having authority over funding decisions for the Divisia project were no longer at the bank. In addition the St. Louis Fed, along with the other regional reserve banks, is not fully autonomous of the Federal Reserve Board in Washington, DC. Hence the multidimensional, institutional complexities of decisions at the St. Louis Fed cannot be understood independently of pressures from the Board in Washington, DC. See Toma and Toma (1985), regarding penalties that the Board has imposed on "maverick" regional reserve banks.

Here is the good news. The revisions of the Divisia MSI database are now complete, and MSI went back online in April 2011, with monthly

---

39. It is sometimes argued that the loss of availability of M3 component data explains the freeze of MSI. But the loss of M3 data could not have prevented continued availability of MSI M1 and M2.

40. The authoritative source on the evolution of the Federal Reserve System from its origins to the present day is the massive Meltzer (vols. 1 [2002] and 2 [2010]).

updates expected, at http://research.stlouisfed.org/msi/index.html. But the interest rate (user cost) aggregates and component data are still being withheld from the public. The documentation on the revisions is in Anderson and Jones (2011). Particularly positive is the fact that the new vintage of the MSI Divisia data is expected eventually to be included within the St. Louis Fed's excellent, interactive, relational database, called FRED (Federal Reserve Economic Data).

The long-delayed, updated data were available within the St. Louis Fed from mid-2010. The St. Louis Fed withheld the data from the public until April 2011, shortly after the manuscript for this book was completed and delivered to MIT Press. I am nevertheless displaying two figures supplied by one of my coauthors, Marcelle Chauvet, using the new vintage Divisia data. She had authorized access to those data, prior to their going online. Those results are in this book as figures 4.11 and 4.12 in section 4.3.3 of chapter 4. The St. Louis Fed graciously provided me with the new vintage Divisia data, when the data first became available for internal use. But I was not willing to use the data in my own research prior to the data's availability to the public. Since February 2006, there has been a dark cloud over the entire world from the financial crisis and the subsequent Great Recession. During that same time period, there has been a gray cloud over the highly relevant Divisia database. The gray cloud seems to be lifting, and what now is appearing may be better than what was previously there. Let's hope the same for the economy.

Regarding transparency of policy, the reappearance of the Divisia database is some of the best news that has come out of the Federal Reserve System in years, but is only a first step in the right direction. In fact even the encouraging reappearance of the Divisia database should give us pause. I have been confronted frequently with the following questions at conferences: (1) What should we do the next time the Fed decides to deny public access to Divisia monetary aggregates data, as it did throughout the entire financial crisis and Great Recession? (2) The economist who maintains the Divisia database is admirably motivated by his own research and publications using those data. What will happen if he retires or leaves the St. Louis Fed?[41] You think someone else at the St. Louis Fed would pick up the ball? Without FRB advocacy in Washington, don't bet on it. (3) Since no autonomous Bureau of Financial

---

41. In fact he told me to expect the Divisia database to be discontinued by the St. Louis Fed under those circumstances, in much the same way that the Board incomprehensibly dropped its simple sum M3 and L.

Statistics exists within the Federal Reserve, what would happen if the person who maintains MSI is subjected to Fed policy-advocacy pressures from the Board or is confronted with data problems about which inadequate expertise exists within the Federal Reserve? As can be seen from part II of this book, economic measurement is a formidable area of expertise. (4) Since the Fed stopped publishing its broad aggregates, M3 and L, the Federal Reserve no longer supplies consolidated, seasonally adjusted, monthly data on much of the highly liquid money market. Why not acquire whatever data exist from available sources, regarding those highly relevant assets, and produce a properly weighted, broad Divisia monetary aggregate?

Since I originated the Divisia monetary aggregates in 1980, I have never wanted to spend time personally maintaining that database, despite growing "popular demand" for me to do precisely that. But because of the questions I have just enumerated and the frustration of many experts with the five-year MSI freeze, I have reluctantly agreed personally to supervise an independent Divisia monetary aggregates data site, hosted by a major international research center, the Center for Financial Stability (CFS). The CFS is a nonpartisan, nonprofit, independent, global think tank, focused on financial markets. I am indebted to Steve Hanke at Johns Hopkins University for suggesting this option. The CFS Divisia database should be online by the time this book is in print and can be found at www.CenterforFinancialStability.org . The Divisia data are planned to be in a CFS section called Advances in Monetary and Financial Measurement (AMFM), under my direction. Additional information can be found at the "Data" tab of my personal website, hosted by Carnegie Mellon University and linked to the following URL at the Massachusetts Institute of Technology: http://alum .mit.edu/www/barnett.

Initially the information in AMFM will be similar to the Divisia database maintained by the St. Louis Fed, but with minor refinements, full disclosure, broader aggregation, and my analysis. Among the objectives will be to serve as a hedge against the possible MSI problems enumerated above. In addition the initial data are expected to include broader monetary aggregates, incorporating data from non-Fed sources, and more adequate accounting for shadow banking system activities. The primary new monetary aggregate will be called Divisia M4. But in the future the AMFM data will introduce more advanced extensions, such as the adjustment for risk in appendix D's section D.7, the discounted monetary capital-stock measurement in appendix B's section B.5, and the closely related Fisher-ideal and distribution-effect measures of appendix C's section C.7.

AMFM should be particularly useful to researchers interested in recent advances in economic measurement; properly weighted, broad measures of the economy's financial liquidity; and rapid adjustment to structural changes in financial markets. The scope of AMFM will be wider than Divisia monetary aggregation and will encompass state-of-the-art advances in monetary and financial measurement. I also expect to provide relevant international data, such as the admirable, official, Divisia monetary aggregates supplied by the Bank of England and the National Bank of Poland, along with the newly available Divisia monetary aggregates provided by the Bank of Israel. If the European Central Bank and the Bank of Japan should decide to make their Divisia monetary aggregates public, AMFM will provide them. International multilateral aggregation, in accordance with this book's appendix C, will likely also be incorporated eventually within AMFM, as economic globalization progresses. Periodic commentaries also are contemplated within AMFM. But as director of AMFM, my initial priorities are focused on the measurement science.

The Fed should put much higher priority on the competent use of economic index-number theory and reputable economic measurement and should create an autonomous Bureau of Financial Statistics. The Divisia monetary aggregates are only the tip of the iceberg. The public has the right to know. The public has the need to know.

2.6.4 The Bank of England

It is interesting to compare the way the Federal Reserve Board (FRB) has dealt with the Divisia monetary aggregates with the way the Bank of England (BOE) has. Although the origins of the Divisia monetary aggregates were at the FRB, when I was on the Board's staff, the FRB has never made those data available in its official data releases to the Congress and the public. The Board's official data releases do not include data produced and supplied by the St. Louis Fed. However, the Board's staff has continued to supply to the public its official monetary aggregates, based on the simple-sum index, disreputable among professionals in economic measurement for nearly a century. Many other examples exist of FRB poor-practice economic measurement, such as reporting of negative values of nonborrowed reserves (an oxymoron) and distortion of demand-deposit data by about 50 percent through failure to report "pre-sweep" data, as explained in detail in section 4.2 of this book's chapter 4.

In contrast, the BOE has gone about this in precisely the right way. That central bank provides to the public a Divisia money data series— *officially*. When that central bank decided to start producing Divisia data many years ago, the bank's economists corresponded extensively by fax with experts in the field, including me. Once the data were constructed, the BOE continued providing them monthly to the present day. The data never were frozen for any reason. What the BOE did was professional and admirable, and is what every central bank in the world should have done long ago. In getting it right officially and publicly, the BOE is not alone. The National Bank of Poland also produces Divisia monetary aggregates officially and provides them to the public on its web site. The Bank of Israel similarly plans to be providing Divisia monetary aggregates to the public by the time this book is in print.

2.6.5 The European Central Bank

When the European Central Bank (ECB) in Frankfurt took over producing the euro currency for countries in the European Monetary Union (EMU), a challenging problem arose in application of index-number theory to monetary aggregation. The ECB needed the ability to aggregate over monetary assets within countries and then over countries. This two-stage nested procedure is called "multilateral" aggregation. No one had ever previously worked out the theory of multilateral Divisia monetary aggregation, since separate monetary aggregation within the individual states of the United States has never been of interest. But within the EMU, good reason exists to monitor the distribution effects of ECB monetary policy across countries.[42] Changing the total supply of euro-denominated monetary assets does not necessarily affect all countries within the monetary unions in the same way or to the same degree.

The ECB employed me as a consultant to derive the relevant theory for multilateral Divisia monetary aggregation. I met with the relevant economists at the ECB in Frankfurt a few times and derived the theory they sought. I wrote a working paper available from the ECB in its

---

42. Regarding the relevancy of Divisia second moments to measuring and monitoring distribution effects of policy, see Barnett and Serletis (1990). An extension to this modeling could incorporate both political and economic aggregation, as in Azzimonti, Francisco, and Krusell (2008), but political aggregation is beyond the scope of this book.

working paper series. Since the result was a contribution to economic theory, a version of the paper was published in the *Journal of Econometrics* (Barnett 2007). My theoretical results, which are applicable to any multicountry economic union, are provided in appendix C to this book. The theory provides the internally consistent aggregation procedure applicable to three stages of economic progress toward convergence of an economic union, along with the formulas needed to monitor that progress. Those formulas, based on Divisia variances across countries, are provided in section C.7 of appendix C.

While I was in Frankfurt, one of the ECB economists provided me with graphs of the behavior of some of their Divisia monetary aggregates, produced using my theory. I have displayed what they provided in section 4.1 of this book's chapter 4. But oddly they have not made those data available to the public. I do not know why. Until very recently I did not even know whether the ECB was using the data internally. In May 2010, when I visited the Bank of Greece in Athens, a high-level official informed me that the ECB is providing Divisia monetary aggregates to the ECB Governing Council, along with policy analyses of the implications of those data. If the data are useful to the highest level officials of the EMU, why would the data not be useful to the public? Is this "transparency" of central bank policy?

Based on what is being made available to the ECB Governing Council, I'd say that the ECB is dealing with these matters in a better way than the FRB and its staff in Washington. But in this area, neither the ECB nor the Fed meet the standards of openness and genuine transparency of the Bank of England, which is the model of a central bank that fully recognizes and respects its obligations to the public. The National Bank of Poland also provides its Divisia monetary aggregates to the public. The Bank of Israel and the Bank of Japan are similar to the ECB in keeping its Divisia monetary aggregates internal to the central bank, although the Bank of Israel has plans to begin making its data available to the public, perhaps through the Center for Financial Stability in New York City.

2.6.6   The International Monetary Fund

The International Monetary Fund (IMF) is an unusual organization, having the luxury of being above the fray of local politics within individual countries. The IMF is an institution within the United Nations system. The Bank's formal relationship with the United Nations is defined by a 1947 agreement, which recognizes the Bank as an independent, specialized UN agency. Although the IMF is located in Washington, DC, its staff is international and very highly qualified, including many very sophisticated economists. In addition, employees of the IMF are not subject to US income tax. The IMF's high after-tax salaries make it possible for them to employ and retain exceptional economists. When I first moved to Washington, DC, my real estate agent told me about the neighborhoods to avoid, since only IMF and World Bank economists could afford the housing in those neighborhoods.

With its exceptional expertise and independence of national political pressures, the IMF's views on this subject are interesting. The IMF produces an official document, called *Monetary and Financial Statistics: Compilation Guide*.[43] The most recent edition is dated 2008. Its sections 6.60 through 6.63 are on the subject of "Divisia Money." Without comment, I provide the following direct quotations from pages 183 and 184 of those sections.[44] The quotations speak for themselves:

In constructing broad-money aggregates, it is necessary to evaluate the degree of *moneyness* of a wide array of financial assets, focusing on the extent to which each type of financial asset provides *liquidity and a store of value*.

Divisia money is a measure of the money supply that weights the money components—currency, transferable deposits, time deposits, etc.—according to the usefulness of each component for transactions purposes.

A monetary aggregate that is an unweighted sum of components has the advantage of simplicity, but a monetary aggregate with weighted components may be expected to exhibit a stronger link to aggregate spending in an economy.

In a Divisia money formulation, the money components are weighted unequally in accordance with their relative usefulness for making transactions.

By weighting the monetary components, a Divisia money formulation takes account of the trade-off between the medium-of-exchange and store-of-value functions of holding of money components.

It is assumed that relatively illiquid deposits are less likely to be used for transactions purposes than highly liquid financial assets in the money supply and that higher interest rates are paid on the less liquid money components.

The largest weights tend to be attached to components that are directly usable as media of exchange (national currency and noninterest-bearing transferable deposits), but that are least useful as stores of value.

---

43. I am indebted to Steve Hanke for informing me about that IMF source.
44. Well, not entirely without comment. While the intent and spirit of these IMF statements are admirable, they are not quite accurate. The Divisia index does not "weight" quantities. The index weights growth rates of quantities. See appendix E for clarification.

Divisia money formulations originated in the United States, but have become most prominent at the Bank of England (BOE), which has published Divisia money series since 1993.

The BOE publishes a Divisia money series for a broad money aggregate, as well as Divisia series for the money-holdings of separate money-holding series—that is, for the household sector, private nonfinancial corporations sector, and OFCs sector.

On the development of the Divisia index for monetary aggregates, see Barnett (1980a); Barnett, Offenbacher, and Spindt (1984); and Barnett, Fisher, and Serletis (1992).

2.7   Mechanism Design: Why Is the Fed Getting It Wrong?

2.7.1   The Theory

I frequently present research on this subject at conferences, often as keynote speaker. At the end of my presentation, there is one question someone almost invariably asks me. It goes something like this: "We know that the Federal Reserve Board's official monetary aggregates are nearly useless. You make a very good case for adoption of your Divisia monetary aggregates, which in fact are computed and made available by the St. Louis Federal Reserve Bank and are official data at the Bank of England and the National Bank of Poland. Why does the Federal Reserve Board's staff in Washington, DC, not adopt them as official data for the United States and provide them to the public, the profession, and the Congress through Board release channels?"

I hate being asked that question. My usual initial reply is: "I am not responsible for the FRB's bad data. Ask them. It's their problem, not mine." Recently I also have added that I am very happy the FRB is "getting it wrong," since that is in my own personal best interests. I doubt I would have received such an attractive contract from MIT Press for this book, if it had been titled, *Getting It Right*. This usually gets a laugh and some knowing smiles, but rarely stops the questioning. As is often then observed, I was on the Board's staff in Washington, DC, for eight years, so I should know why the Divisia monetary data have still not been made official in Washington, DC.

This is a serious question, but the answer is much more complicated than might seem to be the case. Accusing the Board's staff of incompetence in this area is a shallow oversimplification. The FRB's staff is highly sophisticated in many areas and far from "stupid." But there is a highly mathematical area of economic research, called "mechanism design," originated by and developed by Nobel laureates Leonid Hurwicz and Eric Maskin. The field seeks mathematically to design economic systems and organizations in such a manner as to meet certain desirable objectives. The literature makes extensive use of mathematical game theory.[45] A key property of a successful mechanism design is "incentive compatibility," as defined by the brilliant mathematician Leonid Hurwicz. Formally, a process is defined to be incentive compatible if all of the participants fare best when they truthfully reveal any private information asked for by the mechanism. Incentive compatibility assures that satisfaction of the optimal outcome of the mechanism is consistent with decentralized pursuit of personal best interests by all participants. In that deeply mathematical literature, nothing is more important than the mechanism's design for acquisition, allocation, and distribution of information in an incentive compatible manner. *There is the key!*

With this in mind, consider the different ways in which the Bank of Japan, the BOE, the National Bank of Poland, the ECB, the FRB, the St. Louis Fed, the Bank of Israel, and the IMF have dealt with these data and information matters. How would you explain, for example, the difference in behavior between the Bank of England and the Federal Reserve Board staff in Washington, DC? Clearly all of the central banks I've listed above are structurally designed differently—very differently. So there is the answer. It is a "mechanism design" problem.

Consider an analogy between the chairman of the Federal Reserve Board and the chairman of the board of directors of a corporation, such as Enron. It is widely believed that the CEO of Enron was fully informed and involved in the major decisions of the corporation, while the stockholders were not. Clearly, there was an incentive compatibility problem. In the literature on mechanism design, such problems are called "principal-agent" problems. In political science and economics, the principal-agent problem arises under conditions of incomplete or asymmetric information, when a "principal" hires an "agent" and needs to find an incentive system that will align the interests of the agent in solidarity with those of the principal. The problem arises in most employer–employee relationships and in the delegation of legislative authority to bureaucratic agencies. Because of the design of the Federal Reserve System, there is reason to be concerned about such matters. But mechanism design is an extremely complicated area of economic theory. Attempts at reform can have very negative consequences,

---

45. Since much of that literature is produced by mathematicians for mathematicians, the results are usually not easily accessible to the general public or even to undergraduate students in economics. But for an example of its nonmathematical use to analyze the recent "bailouts," see Anderson and Gascon (2011).

if motivated more by politics than by a full understanding of the problem's complexities. In fact misguided "Fed bashing" is dangerous.

I am not an authority on economic mechanism design. Also I am not a political scientist. It would be unprofessional of me to presume to know how best to modify the design of the Federal Reserve System or how to isolate and identify the system's design defects. An extensive comparison of the BOE with the Fed could be productive in that regard, but such research is far outside my areas of expertise.

2.7.2   NASA's Space Program

While I do not presume to explore the design of the Federal Reserve System, I can provide an observation that may be analogous. This possible analogy is based on my early experience as a rocket-engine systems engineer on the space program long ago. While the work of engineers on the Apollo project was very different from the work of economists at central banks, there is something in common: existence of governmental oversight. The contractors that produced Apollo were subject to oversight by NASA (National Aeronautic and Space Administration), while the Federal Reserve is accountable to the Congress, which created the Fed.

I worked for Rocketdyne Division of North American Aviation (now part of the Boeing Corp). Rocketdyne produced the rocket engines for all three stages of the *Saturn* vehicle for the Apollo Project. Many years earlier another aerospace contractor, Lockheed Corporation, was exceptionally successful with a military contract to produce the *Polaris* submarine for the Navy. Lockheed completed the design, development, and delivery of *Polaris* ahead of schedule and at below the estimated cost. With the "cost-plus" military contracts of the time, such ahead-of-schedule under-contract-cost completion was virtually unheard of. Lockheed credited its dramatic success with a project-planning tool the corporation used for the first time on that project. The innovation was called a PERT chart, standing for Program Evaluation and Review Technique.

The fact that the PERT chart's success became widely known was itself rather surprising at the time. Of the large aerospace contractors, the most secretive was Lockheed. For example, Lockheed had a super-secret division in Burbank, California, known to the locals as "the Skunk Works," which had developing the U-2 spy plane. When I was at Rocketdyne, also in the San Fernando Valley of Los Angeles, most of the engineers had Confidential Security Clearances. For a couple of years I needed and had a higher level, Secret Security Clearance. But I never heard of any Rocketdyne engineers having the even higher level, Top Secret Security Clearance, despite the fact that some of the Rocketdyne engineers worked on military rocket engines for ICBM missiles. In contrast, everyone at the Skunk Works was reputed to have a Top Secret Security Clearance. The security level was so high that employees were not even permitted to reveal their employer to their families. As a result, if PERT had been originated by Lockheed, we might never have learned about it. But PERT was developed for Lockheed by Bill Pocock, Booz Allen Hamilton, and Gordon Pehrson of the US Navy Special Projects Office, as an innovative application of the "scientific management" literature of the time.

The PERT chart is a tree-diagram flowchart with each node representing tasks during the development process. At the far right of the chart is only one node: project completion. At the far left of the flowchart are many nodes, identifying many development tasks needed to start up the engineering design and development. The tree eventually converges from its many branches at the start of the project to the final completion node. At each node, various numerical values had to be entered, identifying progress completed and remaining to be completed at that node. All of the node information was entered into a computer periodically to determine the critical path delaying completion. Resources then were reallocated to the critical path.

NASA found out from the Navy about the success of PERT. Rocketdyne had a PERT chart for the F-1 rocket engine program, on which I worked. NASA, knowing about the technique and its success at Lockheed, insisted that Rocketdyne supply the PERT chart to NASA on a regular basis. I observed that two groups of planners worked on the PERT chart. One group regularly came around asking for information on each group's progress and plans. The other group never did. I asked an engineering executive in the project office why we never seemed to see anyone from the other PERT group. What was the reply? That group produced a different chart supplied to NASA. I assume you "get the picture."[46]

---

46. Many years after I left Rocketdyne and was a professor at the University of Texas, I read that there was a federal investigation into such practices by aerospace contractors. But considering the nature of the incentives, preventing such practices completely is next to impossible.

I have been out of that industry for decades, but at that time the attitude of Rocketdyne engineers regarding NASA was that oversight by NASA was often an obstacle and a nuisance. The unspoken "message" in the minds of many Rocketdyne engineers toward NASA administrators was: "Leave us alone. We know what we need to do better than you do. You are just in our way."[47] Rightly or wrongly, the attitude of the FRB's staff toward the Congress is similar, as is well known to any congressional economics staffer or to any employee of the FRB's Congressional Liaison Office, which serves as an information filter.

As mentioned, when I was on the staff of the Federal Reserve Board, I was told to send my Divisia monetary aggregates only to the staff director of monetary policy, to delay replying to requests from the governors, and to stay far away from the Congressional Liaison Office. These requirements all had a very familiar ring to me, going back to the years I was an engineer at Rocketdyne. Unlike the other economists on the staff of the FRB, I also was not surprised when Chairman Arthur Burns brought in the FBI to investigate his entire staff, including hundreds of economists, to track down the economist who had provided bank interest rate data to *Consumer Reports*. That magazine published a series of articles revealing which banks in the United States were paying the highest interest rates on various categories of saving accounts and certificates of deposit. Of course, anyone can call any bank and ask for the interest rates offered on its accounts. But Burns immediately recognized that the only computer file having information on interest rates paid by every bank in the country was at the Federal Reserve Board, so the source must have been an FRB staff member. The FBI found the person who did it, and Burns fired him.[48]

I have no doubt that the fired employee never dreamed he would be hunted down by the FBI, since no bank hides the information on its interest rates offered. But he would not have been surprised, and would not have provided the requested information, if he had previously worked for an aerospace contractor or had been an expert in economic

---

47. The attitude toward the Air Force on Air Force contracts was much more friendly.
48. The announcement to the staff of the firing did not reveal the identity of the person fired. I do not know who it was, although I have heard an unsubstantiated rumor. The reason for Burns's shocking reaction was that the data in that file (the FR2042 report) were provided voluntarily by banks under a promise of anonymity. It was probably a violation of federal law for a staff member to furnish data to the public in violation of the contractual terms under which the data had been collected, even though what he provided was not the sensitive information motivating the anonymity agreement.

mechanism design. He would have understood the rational constraints on information availability by organizations subject to oversight.

Are you still wondering why the FRB does not provide Divisia monetary aggregates through its official releases? If so, perhaps it will be clearer by the time you finish reading this book.

2.7.3   The Locked Office

The Board has an econometric model used in policy decisions. Years of problems have existed with such models. In section 3.1 of this book's chapter 3, I provide graphs demonstrating those problems resulted from the use of the Board's simple-sum monetary aggregates and could have been avoided by adoption of index-number-theoretic data. The model manager at the time was a very fine economist by the name of Jerry Enzler. He had seen my research, which had independently been confirmed by two other economists at the FRB, but Jerry never discussed the subject with me.

After I had left the Board for the University of Texas, I received a surprising telephone call from a senior economist at the Federal Reserve. He told me that Jerry sadly had been in a serious automobile accident, suffered brain injury, and had to go on permanent disability. Unlike the other economists in the Special Studies Section and its sister section, Econometrics and Computer Applications, Jerry had a lock on his door. No one had access to the work in his office, unless he provided it. The primary reason he had a lock on his office was his access to some classified CIA data.[49] When he went on disability, one of his colleagues was given the key to Jerry's office. His colleague, an economist in the same section, discovered Jerry had changed the M2 monetary aggregate used in the model from the Board's official, simple-sum aggregate, to my Divisia M2 aggregate. As a result, for a few years, the model simulations, sent to the governors for use in policy decisions, were based on my Divisia M2 data, not the official M2 data.

The model manager is fully authorized to use whatever data and whatever equations he finds to be useful in producing policy simulations for the Board and the FOMC. In addition, the monetary aggregates were neither a final target of policy nor a policy instrument at that time. As a result his policy simulations transmitted to the Board did not likely mention the role of the monetary aggregates, which were internal

---

49. In operating sections, there were economists with locks on their offices for other reasons without access to CIA data.

to the model's transmission mechanism of policy, along with hundreds of other variables. No breach of fiduciary responsibility was involved in his use of Divisia M2 within the equations of the model.

Unfortunately, Jerry's colleague revealed what Jerry had done and switched back to the official simple-sum M2 data. Jerry, as the model manager, had never revealed his use of Divisia M2 to anyone, including me. Even the governors did not know. Unfortunately, not many economists like Jerry Enzler have positions in governments anywhere in the world. I wish there were more.

2.7.4 The Relationship between the Board's Staff, the Governors, the FOMC, and the Regional Banks

The relationships among the Board's staff in Washington, DC, the governors, the FOMC, and the regional banks are often misunderstood. The chairman of the Board of Governors is sometimes viewed as analogous to the CEO of a large corporation. A closer, but not entirely accurate, analogy might be with the chairman of the board of directors of a corporation.

The Board's staff, although not formally part of the civil service, consists of career bureaucrats; and the Board's staff operates in a manner similar to the civil service. For example, Board staff salaries are on a table of levels and steps, similar to that for the civil service. The governors are not career civil servants. A field of economics, called "public choice," studies and models the ways in which bureaucracies function. Public choice is closely connected with political science formal theory, as well as with mechanism design. Serious consideration is given to problems of incentive compatibility. In contrast, the governors, not being part of the staff's bureaucracy, tend to be dedicated solely to the pursuit of the public interest. Many studies have sought to find conflicts of interests among the governors. None of those studies has ever found convincing evidence of conflicts of interests. In fact many of the governors are paid significantly less as governors than they were paid in their prior employment. About the only significant material benefit that they receive from their positions as Federal Reserve Governors is an exceptionally dramatic office in the Board Building.

Conspiracy theorists are fond of viewing the Fed as being nongovernmental and under the control of mysterious private interests. In fact the FRB staff and the Board of Governors are 100 percent federal government employees, but with some differences in motivation and self-interests. The regional banks are semi-governmental and semi-private.

The decentralization designed into the system by creation of the regional banks is noteworthy in many ways, providing closer contact with the commercial banks and the university professors in their regions and a channel for policy dissent.

Much of the role of the Fed in monetary policy is executed through the actions of the FOMC, which meets in Washington, DC, but provides its instructions to the Open Market Desk located at the New York Federal Reserve Bank in New York City. The Open Market Desk buys and sells securities as a means of influencing interest rates and the money supply. The FOMC includes representation from the regional banks, as well as heavy influence from the FRB in Washington, DC. Dissent by presidents of the regional banks takes place at FOMC meetings and often in a more visible manner in public speeches and interviews. The complexity and sophistication of the system is evident at the FOMC, along with the balance between centralization in Washington, DC, and decentralization to regions throughout the country.

But the independence of the regional banks from the Board should not be overestimated. Prior to the three years of the "monetarist experiment" in the United States (1979–1982), the research staff of the Philadelphia Federal Reserve Bank produced a large document containing research supporting a change in policy direction—the same change in direction that subsequently was adopted by Paul Volcker during the years of the "monetarist experiment." The purpose was to deal with the accelerating inflation of the 1970s. But that research at the Philadelphia Fed was prior to the arrival of Paul Volcker as chairman of the FRB. Since the Board was not yet favoring Volcker's subsequent change in direction, the Board staff at the time was instructed to crush the research at the Philadelphia Fed and discredit its staff.[50] The Board staff succeeded to the degree that almost the entire research staff of the Philadelphia Fed resigned. Prior to their resignation, I was invited to the Philadelphia Fed as a possible new hire, who might be able to help hold the staff together. I had said nothing about this invitation at the Board. But on the morning I returned from Philadelphia to the Board staff in Washington, DC, I was called into the office of the director of personnel and given an immediate raise along with instructions not to help "those bad people" in Philadelphia.

The Philadelphia Fed at that time had an eminent group of vice presidents, who supported their research economists' critique of Board policy.

---

50. The resulting controversy made its way into the press. See "The politicization of research at the Fed," *Business Week*, July 16, 1979, pp. 106–15.

But there was an exception. One vice president backed the Board against his bank's own staff. Yes, you guessed it. He was promoted to president of the bank. Most of the research staff left. While I witnessed this evolve firsthand, what happened was far from unique. Toma and Toma (1985) provided evidence that some regional reserve banks received systematic and significantly lowered budget increases than the other regional reserve banks for their "maverick" views on monetary policy.

Not long after the purge of the research staff in Philadelphia, as inflation was becoming intolerable to the Carter administration, Paul Volcker was moved from the New York Fed to become Board chairman in Washington, DC. He then instituted the policies previously advocated by the former staff at the Philadelphia Fed. Chairman Volcker, knowing that his staff in Washington had been geared up to oppose precisely that approach, did not confer with or inform his large staff before his announced policy change. Reputedly only three staff members at the top were informed of the impending change. The rest of us learned from the newspaper the next morning. That morning, I had breakfast at the Board's cafeteria and observed the stunned looks on the faces of the staff and the bewildered conversations among us over our eggs and coffee. In contrast, Professor Carl Christ was visiting from Johns Hopkins University that day and joined us at that breakfast. He was clearly amused and pleased by what had just happened.

2.7.5   The Right and the Wrong Kinds of Reform

Not being an expert in mechanism design, political science, or public choice economics, I would not presume to recommend fundamental change to the structure of the system. But my experience does tell me that some congressional proposals for reform of the Fed reflect lack of appreciation of the merits of the system. In the following section, I discuss some of those proposals and their history, and offer a suggestion for an overlooked minor reform, which would have only positive effects, as opposed to the more sweeping, and potentially damaging, reforms periodically proposed in the Congress. First, let us look at the context relevant to the recently passed reforms and others still circulating among congressional staffers.

Fed Chairman Ben Bernanke spoke out against congressional bills to audit the Federal Reserve. Why? Proponents argue that the purpose of the audits would be to increase the transparency of policy and improve the quality of Fed data. Aren't these purposes both in the public interest? Growing evidence exists that defective Fed data played a role in producing the misperceptions of decreased systemic risk, leading up to the current recession.

Discussion of the debates about auditing the Fed can be found in my *New York Times* article, Barnett (2009), and my journal article, Barnett (2010). A Rasmussen reports survey found that 75 percent of Americans favored auditing the Fed and making the results available to the public, while only 9 percent opposed it, with 15 percent being unsure. After all, as a previous New York Fed president remarked, the Fed is independent within the federal government, but not of the federal government.[51] Since the Federal Reserve was created by the Congress, the Fed is inherently accountable to the Congress. Isn't therefore an audit in the interests of good governance? Despite the public support, the bills failed to pass.[52] Let's consider the ramifications of this outcome.

The debate needs to be set against the background of long-running tensions among the central bank and the legislative and executive branches of government. When in 1978 the Congress passed a bill mandating audits by the Government Accountability Office (GAO) for most government agencies, the bill excluded from audit a vast sweep of the Federal Reserve System's activities. Operations of some Fed activities, including monetary policy, were also addressed in the same year in the Humphrey–Hawkins Act. The following year Chairman Paul Volcker made major policy changes to lower the inflation rate. Bernanke has stated that the 1978 audit exclusions were necessary to allow Chairman Volcker's ability to act decisively. Personally, I doubt this. I was on the staff of the Board in Washington at that time. Paul Volcker was a determined chairman, whose actions were based on his own strong convictions. Since the GAO has no policy-making authority, the GAO could not have prevented him from implementing his chosen policy.

Certainly the Fed has reasons to oppose an increased role in monetary economics by the GAO. From the standpoint of the Federal Reserve, the biggest danger would be that increased audit authority by the Congress would allow politicians to second-guess unpopular policy actions, which might have been chosen for good reasons by the Federal Reserve. Indeed the Fed should avoid short-term politics and focus on policies that are good for markets and the economy over the long run. The recent Dodd–Frank Act provided for an audit of the Fed—once.

---

51. The statement was by Federal Reserve Bank President Allan Sproul in an April 1952 hearing before the Joint Economic Committee of Congress.
52. During 11th hour debates on the Senate floor over the Dodd–Frank Act, Bernie Sanders watered down his audit bill to the dismay of Ron Paul.

However, audit authority is hardly necessary for the Congress to take an interest in the Fed's business, as has been demonstrated time and again by the actions of past congress members, senators, and presidents. From its point of view, the Congress created the Fed and thereby has responsibility for its oversight.

There are well-known examples of such pressures. When I had lunch with Arthur Burns, following his term as Federal Reserve chairman (1970–1978), I asked him whether any of his decisions had ever been influenced by congressional pressure. He emphatically said no—not ever. On the other hand, Milton Friedman reported Nixon himself believed he had influenced Burns.[53] Similarly Fed Chairman William M. Martin (1951–1970) discussed pressures from President Lyndon Johnson.[54] Chairman Martin emphasized that, in his views, the Congress and the president set the nation's economic priorities, including spending, taxes, and borrowing. The role of the Federal Reserve, in Martin's view, was to assist in fulfilling those policies, including facilitating Treasury borrowing at reasonable interest rates. In 1966, when he led a sharp contraction of monetary policy to offset aggregate demand pressures from President Johnson's policies, Martin was sharply reprimanded by President Johnson. In 1969 the FOMC did respond unwisely to administration pressures to ease policy. Occasionally presidents have been supportive. President Reagan's support was important to the success of Chairman Volcker's anti-inflation policy.

Perhaps the closest antecedent to recent congressional audit proposals was the upswell of monetarist sentiment in the Congress in 1975 to 1978, following puzzling phenomena in 1974 money markets. Later analysis revealed flaws in the published monetary aggregates during that period. Those flaws contaminated economic research for years afterward and remain a source of misunderstanding to the present day.[55] Two congressional measures—House Concurrent Resolution 133 in 1975 and the Humphrey–Hawkins Act of 1978—subsequently required the Fed chairman to appear twice each year before the Congress

---

53. Barnett and Samuelson (2007, p. 116). Also see Abrams (2006).
54. See, for example, Bremmer (2004).
55. These results are presented in chapter 3 of this book. The bad data produced extensive confusion in academic research and led to the erroneous belief the demand for, and supply of, money had, without reason, mysteriously shifted in 1974 and were unstable. But the seemingly unexplainable economic structural shifts were shown to disappear, when the data flaws were corrected. For the original research on this subject, see Barnett, Offenbacher, and Spindt (1984).

to report the FOMC's target ranges for money growth.[56] The Federal Reserve bristled under such supervision. Never before in the Fed's history had the Congress imposed a reporting requirement on Fed policy makers—and a requirement far less invasive than a GAO audit. The Humphrey–Hawkins Act reporting requirement came up for renewal in 2003 but quietly was allowed to expire. Semiannual reports to the Congress continue but without the force of law.

There are several instances when faulty monetary data led policy makers astray. My research, summarized in section 3.3 of this book's chapter 3, shows that Volcker's disinflationary policy was overdone and contributed to an unnecessarily severe recession. Poor monetary aggregates data led Volcker inadvertently to decrease monetary growth to a rate that, appropriately measured, was *half* what he thought it was.[57] Volcker wrote to me years later that he "still is suffering from an allergic reaction" to my findings about the actual monetary growth rate during that period. Suppose that a GAO audit had investigated whether data being published were best practice among experts in economic measurement, and concluded that they were not. With better data, would Volcker have selected a more gradual disinflationary policy?

Focus, for a moment, on the Federal Reserve's published monetary data. Is its quality the best possible? Are the reported items constructed appropriately to the task of operating and understanding the path of monetary policy? Unfortunately, no. Consider, for example, the important and widely monitored data on banks' "nonborrowed reserves." Every analyst understands that banks hold reserves at the Fed to satisfy legal requirements and to settle interbank payments, such as wire transfers and check clearing. The total of such reserves may be partitioned into two parts: the portion borrowed from the Federal Reserve and the portion that is not. Clearly, the borrowed portion of reserves cannot exceed total reserves, so nonborrowed reserves cannot be negative. Yet recently Fed reported values of nonborrowed reserves were minus 50 billion dollars, as shown in section 4.2 of this book's chapter 4. How can

---

56. One widely held theory is that the congressional actions were precipitated by over-tightening by the Fed in 1974 in response to faulty monetary data. There is controversy about precisely what precipitated these congressional actions. See, for example, Poole (1979). But what is well established is that the structural shifts the Fed and the profession believed occurred in 1974 did not occur and were inferred from defective data, as shown by Barnett, Offenbacher, and Spindt (1984) and reproduced in chapter 3 of this book.

57. These results are presented in a later chapter of this book. For the original research see Barnett (1984).

this happen?[58] Such confusing accounting practices would not likely survive scrutiny by an outside audit, assuming it was competently performed. Ah, but that is the problem. Is GAO audit the best solution? I have my doubts.

Other serious defects exist in the data currently published. According to Section 2a of the Federal Reserve Act, the Fed is mandated to "maintain long run growth of the monetary and credit aggregates commensurate with the economy's long run potential. . . ." Neglecting these instructions, Fed policy makers have stated that monetary aggregates currently are unimportant to their decisions. Whatever the merits of this attitude might be, external analysts and researchers continue to depend on monetary aggregates to obtain an accurate picture of the stance of policy, and many other central banks throughout the world continue to report data on multiple monetary aggregates. During the 30 years since the Congress excluded monetary policy from GAO audits and mandated reporting of money growth in the Humphrey–Hawkins Act, two of the then four published monetary aggregates have been discontinued: M1 and M2 remain, but M3 and L do not. In quiet times, perhaps this is of little importance, but these broad monetary aggregates and the underlying data detail were greatly missed during the 2008 financial crisis.

Furthermore the M1 aggregate is severely biased downward. Since 1994, banks have been permitted by the Fed to reclassify, for purposes of calculating legal reserve requirements, certain checking account balances as if they were MMDA saving deposits. The reclassified deposits are euphemistically called "sweeps." Banks supply to the Federal Reserve only the post-sweeps checking account data. The resulting published data on checking deposits understate, *by approximately half*, the amount of such deposits held by the public at banks. Why doesn't the Federal Reserve require banks to report the pre-sweeps data? Does such published monetary data satisfy the requirement of the Federal Reserve Act? Again, it seems unlikely that such an omission would survive an unconstrained examination by persons qualified in economic index-number theory. But who should those persons be?

Now we come to the bills recently debated in the Senate and the House to expand upon GAO audit authority. The House bill was

---

58. In its definitions, the Federal Reserve chose to omit from "total reserves" large amounts of funds borrowed from the Fed, but included in published figures for borrowed reserves. Those term auction borrowings should be included in both borrowed and total reserves or in neither, depending on whether they are or are not held as reserves.

introduced by Texas Republican Congressman Ron Paul and had 317 cosponsors, including over 100 Democrats. The Senate bill was introduced by Vermont Independent Senator Bernie Sanders; bipartisan cosponsors included Kansas Republican Senator Sam Brownback and Wisconsin Democratic Senator Russell Feingold. In Washington, DC, I met with a senator and his staff, who supported the Senate bill, and with a Federal Reserve Board division director, who opposed part of it. Since my conversations in Washington were about the Senate bill, I comment on only that failed bill.

Current law contains four audit exclusions for the Fed. That Senate bill would have removed all four of the current audit exclusions. The four exclusions are:

1. transactions for or with a foreign central bank, government of a foreign country, or nonprivate international financing organization;
2. deliberations, decisions, or actions on monetary policy matters, including discount window operations, reserves of member banks, securities credit, interest on deposits, and open market operations;
3. transactions made under the direction of the Federal Open Market Committee; or
4. a part of a discussion or communication among or between members of the Board of Governors and officers and employees of the Federal Reserve System related to clauses 1, 2, and 3 of this subsection.

Exclusions 1 and 3 are arguably not in the public interest and could have been removed. I would not support unconditional removal of the other two exclusions, because they appear to overlap roles outside the GAO's primary areas of expertise.

Many economists signed a "Petition for Fed Independence," often interpreted as opposing audit of the Federal Reserve. However, the petition makes no mention of auditing the Federal Reserve. The petition opposes possible infringements on Fed policy independence, and I support that view. Audits ask whether a firm or organization is following best practice and existing regulations in its business dealings. Audits do not tell management how to run a business or conduct policy. But again, the question remains: Who has the relevant expertise to provide such oversight for the Federal Reserve?

With respect to the collection and publication of accurate data, creation of an independent data institute for monetary and financial data would be preferable to expanded audit, since such institutes possess specialized expertise in economic measurement, including the latest advances in index-number and aggregation theory. An obvious potential for a conflict of interests exists in having data reported by the same agency that influences data through its own policy actions. Perhaps an economy of scale exists in such collection, but the risks outweigh any benefits, unless those responsible for producing the data have a relevant degree of autonomy and authority, as through the creation of a data bureau within the Federal Reserve. I return to this subject in section 2.7.6 below.

Such autonomous bureaus exist elsewhere in the government. The Bureau of the Census, the BEA, and the BLS, collect data later used for policy purposes by the administration and the Congress. An "independent" federal data institute need not be outside the Federal Reserve System. Varying degrees of independence exist within the admirably decentralized Federal Reserve System, with, for example, regional bank presidents free to vote against the Federal Reserve Board's positions at FOMC meetings. The deeply respected BLS is within the Department of Labor, but has sole responsibility for production of Department of Labor data and employs a staff of formidable experts in economic aggregation and index-number theory. Expertise in those areas within the Federal Reserve System is minimal and is not centralized into any autonomous single group anywhere within the system.

Regarding Federal Reserve independence, concern should be focused on the recently renewed "coordination" of Fed monetary policy with Treasury fiscal policy. That coordination is in conflict with the 1951 Treasury–Fed Accord that established independence of the Fed from the Treasury. Unwise Federal Reserve actions in support of Treasury bond prices during periods of heavy Treasury borrowing have ignited inflation twice before: once following World War II (a trend that ended with the 1951 Accord) and once following Chairman Martin's capitulation to President Johnson's Great Society pressures, as already mentioned. During World War II, good reason existed for the Fed to be expected to assist the Treasury in its financing of the war through bond issues. After the war, the Treasury tried to retain that obligation of the Federal Reserve to assist the Treasury; but the Fed, recognizing the inflationary implications of printing money to finance federal debt, resisted. Following a long struggle, the Accord was reached, by which the Federal Reserve was freed from further obligations to assist in Treasury financing. The violations of the Accord that took place during the recent financial crisis and Great Recession could have long-run consequences.

Federal Reserve spokesmen are right to warn of the risks and dangers that expanded audit would entail. The best solution would be to set up an independent institute for monetary and financial data. The

Fed could create such an institute on its own within the Federal Reserve System, without the need for congressional intervention. I admire and respect the role that the St. Louis Fed plays in producing high-quality data. But the only Fed data having widespread visibility to the public and the press are the official data produced and distributed by the FRB staff in Washington, DC. The cause of the existing inadequacies is the failure of the original design of the system to recognize the conflict of interests inherent in having a system, with policy authority, report the data that the Fed itself influences. However, expanded audit would be an inferior solution to the creation of an independent data institute. While it has expertise in accounting, the GAO is not known for its expertise in economic aggregation and index-number theory. Those areas of expertise are of greatest importance to any federal economic data institute, such as the BLS.

But sad to say, within the Federal Reserve System, which employs thousands of highly educated professionals, I currently can think of only three economists who have demonstrated published knowledge in the field of economic measurement (i.e., economic index-number and aggregation theory): Richard Anderson, vice president at the St. Louis Fed; my former student, Travis Nesmith, senior economist at the FRB; and my former student, Mark Jensen, financial economist and associate policy adviser at the Atlanta Fed. No two of them are in the same group, or even the same city. This is in stark contrast with other major data and information generating federal agencies in Washington, DC.

While the subject of audit of the Fed has been an issue in Washington recently, and may return in the future, more troubling proposals exist for fundamental structural change to the Federal Reserve. While the most worrisome of them have not passed in the Congress, the fact that they appeared in a major bill is disturbing. These proposals for major structural change have made the mistake of blaming the regional banks for the financial crisis and recession. Shooting from the hip, when you're target is bank regulation reform, overlooks the complexity of mechanism design, public choice, and political science. Some examples, which could have done more harm than good, appeared in Senator Christopher Dodd's original bill and Representative Gary Peters' original proposal.

The Federal Reserve is built on a decentralized structure encouraging businesses, banks, and the public to participate and cooperate in getting things done. For any single group—including the Congress—to dominate decision making, is nearly impossible. Parts of Dodd's original bill threatened that structure under the guise of removing conflicts of interest. Those parts would only have reduced the professionalism of the Federal Reserve and increased the political role of the Congress in monetary policy.

The choice of Federal Reserve Bank presidents is at the core of the Fed's populism—and success. The selection process balances the interests of business, the public, and banks, while also giving voice to the small, medium, and large entities within each group. No Federal Reserve Bank ever "appoints" a president—a candidate becomes a president only after having been nominated by the regional Federal Reserve Bank's directors and approved by the Fed's Board of Governors. This veto power in Washington assures only well-qualified persons are nominated and, eventually, accepted.

Dodd's original bill proposed Senate confirmation power over appointment of Federal Reserve regional bank presidents. This reform would have been misdirected and fortunately did not pass. Even worse would have been Representative Gary Peters's proposal to take away the vote of Federal Reserve regional bank presidents on the FOMC.

Dodd's original bill would have changed the current approach into a Washington-centric one laced with opportunities for political meddling. His bill would have increased the power of the Federal Reserve Board at the expense of the system's regional banks. The bill also would have created a new centralized regulatory agency, vulnerable to regulatory capture by the powerful, as happened to the now defunct Interstate Commerce Commission.

Poorly conceived attempts to fix the Fed's problems risk losing its best features. One great asset is the Fed's intellectual capital. Many of the Fed's economists are thought-leaders in their fields, both publishing in, and serving as associate editors of, professional journals. For example, Jim Bullard, president of the St. Louis Fed, is a well regarded economic researcher, who has published in some of the profession's best journals, including the one I edit.

Since I left the Federal Reserve Board staff 28 years ago, the economics profession's respect for the research staffs and presidents at those regional banks has steadily grown. The vast majority of the 12 presidents are PhD economists. The only other central bank in the world having comparable research competence is the ECB in Frankfurt.

Yet there are some regulatory changes that need to be made. The 1980 Monetary Control Act granted all banks, along with other depository financial institutions, the right to offer checkable deposits, settle payments at the Federal Reserve, and borrow from the Fed's discount window—but it did not require them to become members of the Federal Reserve System. It is time that all banks were required to be Fed members. That would eliminate "regulatory shopping," by which banks seek the most permissive regulator among state regulators, the FDIC, the comptroller's office, and the Fed. Such behavior produces an incentive for regulators to adopt lax regulatory policies.

I am also concerned about the 1956 Bank Holding Company Act and its Gramm–Leach–Bliley revision. Under this act the Federal Reserve regulates all large financial holding companies, including most large commercial banks and the surviving investment banks. The problems of troubled Citicorp do not speak well of the existing approach. But that regulatory authority is centralized to the FRB staff's Supervision and Regulation Division in Washington, so Citicorp's problems cannot be blamed on the regional banks. In fact, involving the decentralized Federal Reserve Banks in that supervision might be a positive change, by reducing opportunities for political meddling.

Many Fed reform proposals reflect inside-the-beltway politics, seeking increased centralization of Fed policy. GAO audit, instead of bringing in autonomous expertise in economic measurement, as exists in the BLS and the BEA, would introduce oversight from another Washington bureaucracy, having no established expertise in index-number theory or aggregation theory. In the published professional literature on economic measurement, I have seen many important articles published by economists at the BEA and BLS over the years. I have known many of those economists, and those agencies frequently hire PhD economists with expertise in those areas. While I can think of only three such economists within the Federal Reserve System, which has no such autonomous data production bureau, I can think of none at all at the GAO; and I do not recall having ever read any serious contributions to the relevant professional literature from employees of the GAO.

While there may be some merit to increased accounting audit of the Federal Reserve data in some areas, the net effect of a significantly increased role for the GAO in central bank policy would be increased centralization to a federal agency having little claim on relevant expertise in the area. Similarly the congressional bills designed to decrease the policy role of the regional banks would have increased the role of the Federal Reserve Board and its staff at the expense of the decentralized regional banks—again, increasing centralization to inside-the-beltway Washington, DC. While the media have made much of the questionable actions of the regional banks in bank regulation prior to the financial crisis, the media seem to have overlooked the fact that the FRB in Washington contains three divisions, one of which is the Division of Supervision and Regulation. Why have the media failed to take into consideration the failures of that large Division inside the beltway?

Transparency and information-availability from the Fed are critical to the successful role of decentralized free enterprise. As this book documents, the quality of data coming from the Federal Reserve Board staff has been declining for years, as the need for data has grown in the face of increasing complexity of financial markets and instruments. In contrast, data coming from the St. Louis Fed have been improving, but are less visible than the official data provided by the FRB. With decreasing data quality coming from the Board in Washington, DC, and growing need for those data by the public, an increasing need for regulation is unavoidable to constrain poorly informed decisions by the private sector. The preference in Washington appears to be for increased regulation to be centralized there, as a means of dealing with the effects of the problem, rather than the cause.

Finally, little in Dodd's original bill would have addressed the problems of inadequate policy transparency, the sometimes shockingly low Federal Reserve data quality, and the anticompetitive concept of "too big to fail." But there is a very positive exception, which is the subject of the next section. Regarding Federal Reserve policy, the Congress has been asleep for 25 years. Now that it is waking up, I am worried that sooner or later the sleeping giant may stomp in the wrong places.

2.7.6 The Office of Financial Research

The existence of a system design problem at the Federal Reserve was recognized within Title 1 of the Dodd–Frank Act, by creation of the new Office of Financial Research (OFR), currently housed within the Treasury building. The broad charge of the office is in Section 151 of Subtitle B of Title 1 of the Dodd–Frank Act. That charge is to acquire and report to the Congress data relevant to monitoring and regulating systemic risk. The director of OFR does not report to the Secretary of the Treasury, and the OFR's budget does not come from the Congress. The director of OFR is appointed by the president and confirmed by the Congress. The Secretary of Treasury has no authority to require the OFR's director to submit in advance any documents, speeches, or testimony. The OFR's budget comes from the Federal Reserve initially, but that arrangement is only temporary. Once fully established within two years, the OFR will acquire its budget from banks via levy. As a result Dodd–Frank has made the OFR an independent federal agency.

The creation of the OFR by the Congress is a rebuke to the Fed's stewardship of the financial system. The prior view of political scientists was that the Congress does not and cannot know all future regulatory and monetary policy risks. That view resulted in the theory of "delegated monitoring," by which the Federal Reserve is charged with bringing to the attention of the Congress any and all innovations presenting risks to the financial system. The creation of the OFR reflected the congressional view that the Fed did not adequately monitor the economy for systemic risk and failed to bring to the Congress needed reforms. According to that point of view, the Fed assumed markets would self-regulate, investors would not buy instruments they did not understand, and owners of financial firms would not allow managers to undertake undue risk, which would harm the brand name of the firms.

Aren't aggregated financial data relevant to systemic risk? Of course, they are. The systemic risk at the root of the financial crisis and the Great Recession was the risk of recession. That risk was underestimated by those who imprudently increased their personal risk exposure. The financial data relevant to inflation and the business cycle are aggregated financial data, such as the monetary aggregates, dealt with by the FRB in an irresponsible manner. But at present the OFR is concentrating on disaggregated micro data about individual firms.

The OFR's current focus on micro data is down to the individual loan and security level, with particular emphasis on derivatives and securitization and on whether the outstanding set of securities is consistent with market stability. The emphasis is on assessing, as a regulator, whether entities/markets are pricing risk correctly. Ongoing debate within the OFR is focused on the extent of analysis and information to be returned to the market. In particular, concern exists about whether the results of analysis should be held confidential and used for regulation, or whether aggregated results should be made public to assist the public in making correct decisions. Anyone reading this book should have no difficulty in guessing my views on that debate.

The charge of the OFR under the Dodd–Frank Act easily could encompass aggregated financial macro data. How could it not? The micro sources of risk that evolved, and now rightfully will be monitored by the OFR, were consequences of the misperceptions of macro systemic risk. This book distinguishes between cause and effect. No mistake is involved in governmental policy makers concentrating on availability and quality of aggregated macro data.

Need exists for the creation of a new Bureau of Financial Statistics (BFS) to provide competently aggregated macro financial data to the

Congress and to the public. As this book documents, the Federal Reserve Board has been failing in that area, and therein lies much of the misperception of systemic risk, which led to the financial crisis and the Great Recession. To be consistent with the basic principles of mechanism design and incentive compatibility, data production must be logically prior to data use. Those who produce economic data should be experts in index-number and aggregation theory and should have no role in the use of those data in policy. The BFS could be created as an autonomous group within the Federal Reserve, in a manner analogous to the role of the BLS within the Department of Labor.

But considering the poor record of the Fed in production and distribution of aggregated financial data, I would not be at all surprised, if the Fed were to believe that providing adequate, professionally produced financial data would be inconsistent with the Fed's best interests. Such data are relevant to Fed policy oversight by the Congress, the profession, and the public. No rational bureaucracy voluntarily seeks to facilitate or increase oversight. As a result the OFR may very well recognize the need for a BFS and decide to create the BFS within the OFR. Since the OFR has the authority to recommend policy to the Congress, the employees of the BFS, if within the OFR, should be separated from that policy authority. The sole responsibility of the employees of the BFS should be best-practice economic measurement of financial aggregates, which this book documents are being poorly produced and inadequately supplied by the Fed.

It should be emphasized that nothing I have written in this section or anywhere else in this book recommends decreasing the Federal Reserve's autonomy, independence, or authority in making monetary policy. In fact separation of the reporting role from the policy-making role would increase the independence of the Fed's policy makers, by removing an overlap creating a conflict of interests within the system—a fundamental violation of elementary principles of mechanism design.

2.7.7 A Quiz: Answer True or False

In a sense, a large gap exists between part I of this book and the first four appendices in part II. Part I assumes little, if any, prior knowledge of economic theory. In contrast, part II assumes extensive prior knowledge of the relevant literature on index-number theory and aggregation theory and is provided for the benefit of professionals in those areas of specialization. Appendix E addresses the middle ground:

people having some knowledge of microeconomic theory, but without prior expertise in aggregation and index-number theory. That group includes a large percentage of potential users of the Divisia monetary aggregates. If you read this section, you will find out whether you are in the middle-ground group, who would benefit from reading appendix 5. *If you already know the answer to that question, just skip this section and move on to chapter 3.*

In teaching the relevant economic theory to my students, I sometimes give examinations containing true or false questions, to see if my students have misunderstood the economic implications of definitions 1, 2, and 3. If I give such an exam soon after the students have seen that material for the first time, some students often will answer "true" to the following intentionally misleading questions.

Question 1:   If the interest rate on a monetary asset increases, its user cost price will decline. Hence the weight given to that asset in the Divisia monetary aggregate will necessarily decline. True or false?

Question 2:   If the interest rate on a monetary asset is high, its user cost will be low. Hence monetary assets with high interest rates necessarily contribute less to the Divisia monetary service flow than monetary assets with low interest rates. True or false?

Question 3:   Quantity aggregator functions contain only quantities, but quantity index numbers contain both prices and quantities. As a result something must be wrong with the entire field of index-number theory. Index numbers cannot accurately measure the correct quantity aggregate, which does not include prices (or interest rates, in the case of monetary aggregation). True or false.

The correct answer in all these cases is "false." Once the students have completed reading appendixes A through D, no students get those questions wrong. But since some readers of this book may not read those appendixes, written for professional economists, I have provided another appendix (appendix E), which explains why the correct answer to all of those questions is "false." Appendix E, while not assuming knowledge of appendixes A through D, does assume knowledge of technical jargon not explained in part I.

Anyone who teaches economics would recognize question 2 immediately, since it is a variation on a famous trick question, appearing in almost every elementary economics textbook as the "diamonds versus water paradox." The lower price of water does not imply that the total stock of the world's water, which is needed for survival, has less value than the total stock of the world's diamonds. If you have taken an elementary course in economics, you will surely have seen this before and will recognize the following technical statement: low "marginal utility" does not imply low "total utility."

Questions 1 and 2 both reflect an inaccurate reading of definition 3. Recall that the "weights" in the Divisia index are not prices. The weights are expenditure shares. But even students who recognize that fact often are tricked into answering "true" to question 2. It is tempting to think that increasing the price of a good will increase the share of income spent on that good and thereby its weight in the Divisia quantity index. But increasing the price of a good will change the quantity of that good purchased, as well as the quantities of other goods purchased. Whether the share of expenditure spent on that good will increase, decrease, or stay the same is not predictable.[59]

Question 3 contains an implicit misrepresentation of the objectives of index-number theory. Index-number theory does not seek to reveal the complete aggregator function along with all of its properties and everything it can do. Index-number theory seeks only to track the value of the aggregate actually attained by the economy. In continuous time, the Divisia index tracks that value exactly correctly without any error at all. The Divisia index cannot reveal values of the aggregate that may be possible but are not attained by the economy. You may recognize the analogy with Paul Samuelson's famous theory of "revealed preference," and you may have seen an explanation of how the CPI, provided by the BLS, tracks the "true cost-of-living index." The true cost-of-living index contains only prices and no quantities, but the CPI contains both prices and quantities.[60] The CPI accurately measures that actual cost-of-living in the economy but cannot answer "what if" questions about what the cost-of-living might be under different circumstances. Only the "true cost of living index" can do that. The reason is the same.

Hopefully you have not gotten questions 1, 2, or 3 wrong and have no need for further explanation of those "trick" questions. If you got

---

59. Readers who have taken an elementary economics course will likely recognize that the direction in which the expenditure share will change depends on whether the own "price elasticity" of demand for that good is greater than or less than 1.0.

60. When quantities and prices are of consumer goods, the formula for the theoretical true cost-of-living index is in appendix A as equation (A.96). The formula can depend on the base-period welfare level as well as prices. In the more commonly used special case, not depending on a fixed welfare level, the formula is provided in that appendix as equation (A.46). See section A.7 of appendix A for Samuelson and Swamy's (1974, p. 592) "Santa Claus" hypothesis, causing equation (A.96) to reduce to (A.46).

any of those questions wrong and feel the need for further explanation, you can find the full explanations in appendix E, but with some prior knowledge of microeconomic theory assumed.

2.8 Conclusion

In this chapter you have met some of the star players on the team: Fisher, Divisia, Theil, Jorgenson, Diewert, Poterba, and Rotemberg. They are among the best of the best. Are you still wondering why the FRB is "getting it wrong"? I have a better question for you to consider. Why are the BOE, the National Bank of Poland, the Bank of Israel, the ECB, the IMF, the St. Louis Fed, and every other federal data-producing agency in Washington—"getting it right"?

By creating the new OFR within the Treasury, the United States Congress has clearly recognized the existence of a Federal Reserve system-design problem. Through the OFR, the Dodd–Frank Act has taken away from the Fed part of its role in monitoring systemic risk. As this book documents, good reason does exist to be concerned about the role of the Federal Reserve in providing the needed information relevant to assessment of systemic risk. But the OFR has been concentrating primarily on disaggregated financial micro data about individual firms, rather than aggregated financial macro data about the economy as a whole. The financial crisis and the Great Recession were produced by excess risk-taking in response to underestimation of the systemic risk of the macroeconomy. The data relevant to inflation, unemployment, and recession are aggregated financial macro data.

By creating the OFR, the Dodd–Frank Act was critical of the Fed's performance in reporting systemic-risk information to the Congress. But that reporting problem is not limited to financial micro data. The problem is even greater regarding financial macro data. A new BFS needs to exist to provide competently aggregated financial statistics. The BFS could be either within the Federal Reserve or within the OFR, but would need to be dedicated to economic measurement and should employ experts in index-number and aggregation theory. The BFS should have no authority over policy, since economic measurement is logically prior to use. The role of the BFS would be analogous to that of the BLS within the Department of Labor. Overlap between measurement and policy-use authority produces conflict of interest—a fundamental mechanism design defect violating incentive compatibility.

3 The History

The systemic-risk misperceptions leading up to the current economic malaise evolved over more than three decades and accelerated during the last decade. This chapter presents the history of economic "paradoxes" associated with recent misperceptions. That history is presented in chronological order. Explaining what happened after the fact, and then saying you knew it all along, is always easier than at the time. This chapter avoids the appearance of such retrospective claims by using only the data available at the time and the results published in peer reviewed journals during each of the time periods considered, with new results left for the end of the chapter.

3.1 The 1960s and 1970s

The origins of the economy's current problems began to evolve in the 1960s and 1970s. That was a time period of unusual diversity, controversy, and dissent within the economics profession. Previously the profession was divided between those economists who advocated use of mathematics in economic theory, and those who opposed it. The economists who opposed it were divided between two groups: (1) those who advocated use of scientific methodology, but applying graphical techniques with minimal use of mathematics, and (2) those "institutionalists," who advocated a literary, liberal-arts approach to economics, resembling what now is sometimes called "postmodernism" or "deconstructionism." A leading figure among the institutionalists was Clarence Ayers at the University of Texas. Although he was a professor in the Economics Department, his PhD was in philosophy and his books read more like philosophy books than like modern economics books. By the time that the 1970s arrived, the value of mathematics in economics had become well established, and institutionalism was in a decline. But a new source of debate had arisen: the division between Keynesianism and monetarism, the latter of which was increasing in influence.

This section describes the earliest sources of the misperceptions about systemic risk, with emphasis on the year 1974, during which mysterious structural shifts were purported to have occurred within the American economy. Those shifts were often imputed to "missing money" and to other such phenomena outside the normal domain of the field of economics. Using a reputable measure of money based on state-of-the-art aggregation theory, I found no evidence of structural shifts and showed, with my coauthors, that the misperceptions at that time were caused by defective Fed data. The source of the results in this section, along with further details, can be found in Barnett, Offenbacher, and Spindt (1984) and Barnett (1982). As seen in subsequent sections below, these matters have been growing in importance, as asset substitution and financial innovation have progressed over time.

Demand and supply of money were fundamental to macroeconomics and to central bank policy until the 1970s, when questions began to arise about the stability of monetary demand and supply. In economic theory, microeconomics commonly determines relative prices, while the demand and supply for money determines the price level. But something was believed to have gone wrong in the 1970s. Central to the demand for money was the concept of monetary circulation "velocity," defined to be national income divided by the supply of money. According to the relevant theory, people are willing to hold a lot of cash and keep a lot of money in checking accounts, when the interest rates paid on alternative uses of money are low. But when interest rates increase, holding a lot of cash or checking account deposits foregoes the high interest rate that could have been received on alternative investments. As a result, cash and demand deposits are managed more aggressively to keep their balances low. Money passes from person to person more rapidly, increasing the turnover rate of money, and thereby monetary velocity. Interest is paid on assets as compensation for giving up monetary services. In short, with any valid definition of money, velocity of circulation should rise and fall with interest rates.

During the 1970s the relevant theory about the properties of the demand for money were widely viewed to have failed. The relationship between the demand for money and interest rates was presumed to have been reversed throughout that decade. In 1974 the demand and supply for money were viewed as having shifted without economic explanation, and a large amount of money was viewed as having

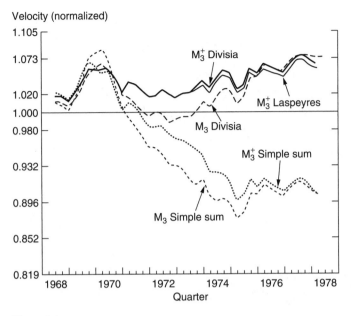

Figure 3.1
Seasonally adjusted normalized velocity during the 1970s

disappeared in the "missing money" paradox. At the time I called all of those puzzles the "space alien theories," since they argued that what happened had no explanation on this planet.

Now look at figure 3.1 and observe the behavior of the velocity of the FRB staff's aggregates, M3 and M3+ (later called L).[1] Based on the findings of Barnett (1982), those two broad aggregates were chosen to explore the demand for money puzzles in the 1970s. Also look at figure 3.2, which displays an interest rate during the same time period. Note that while nominal interest rates were increasing during the expanding inflation of that decade, the velocities of the simple-sum monetary aggregates in figure 3.1 were decreasing. While the source of concern is evident, note that the problem did not exist, when the data were produced from index number theory. Velocity behaved as expected from the theory in the three plots in figure 3.1, produced from reputable

---

1. To facilitate comparison of the plots in figure 3.1, all velocity series were normalized to equal 1.0 in the first quarter of 1968. It should be observed that all index numbers produced from index number theory must be normalized, since only growth rates of statistical index numbers are identified. Levels are determined by cumulating growth rates from the base period, during which the level of the index is set.

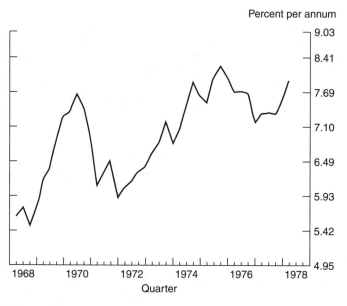

Percent per annum

Figure 3.2
Interest rates during the 1970s: Ten-year government bond rate

index numbers, the Divisia index and the Laspeyres index. Velocity goes up, when interest rates go up, and velocity goes down, when interest rates go down, in accordance with the theory about rational behavior of monetary-asset holders. While the Laspeyres index is not in Diewert's class of superlative index numbers, we decided to include it in that study, since the Laspeyres index is used in computing the Labor Department's CPI, which is familiar to almost everyone.

Most of the concern about economic "paradoxes" in the 1970s was focused on 1974, when a sharp, structural, money-markets shift was believed to have appeared, but could not be explained by interest rate movements. Figure 3.3 displays a source of that concern. Figure 3.3 plots velocity against a bond rate, rather than against time. In figure 3.3 a dramatic shift downward in velocity appears to have occurred in 1974, and clearly that shift cannot be explained by interest rates, since the shift happened suddenly, at a time when little change in interest rates was evident. But observe that this result was acquired using simple sum M3. Figure 3.4 displays the same cross plot of velocity against an interest rate, but with M3 computed as its Divisia index.[2]

---

2. In figure 3.4 velocity is normalized to equal 1.0 in the first period. As in figure 3.1, normalization is necessary, since only growth rates of statistical index numbers are identified.

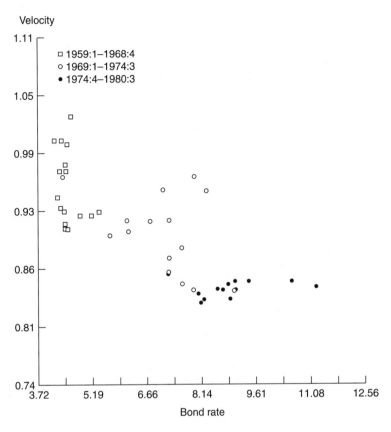

Figure 3.3
Simple sum M3 velocity versus interest rate: Moody's AAA corporate bond rate, quarterly, 1959:1 to 1980:3

Observe that velocity no longer is constant, either before or after 1974. But no structural shift appears, since the variations in velocity correlate with interest rates. The plot not only has no discontinuous jump at a particular interest rate, but is nearly along a straight (linear) line. Also note that the line slopes in the correct direction: velocity goes up, when interest rates go up.

Analogous concerns arose about the supply side of money markets. The reason is evident from figure 3.5, which plots the base multiplier against a bond rate's deviation from trend.[3] The base multiplier is the

---

3. On the demand side, the plots are against the AAA bond rate. On the supply side, the plots are against the BAA bond rate. These choices were based on the views and experience of my colleagues at the Federal Reserve Board at that time. It was a long time ago, and I do not recall the background that produced that preference. I did it the way that the

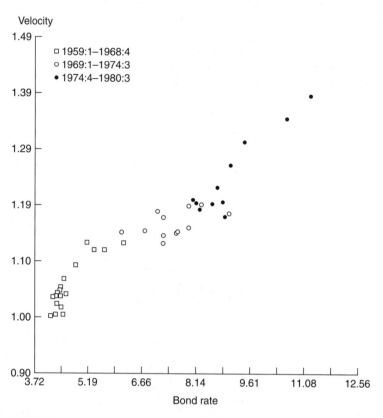

Figure 3.4
Divisia M3 velocity versus interest rate: Moody's AAA corporate bond rate, quarterly,
1959:1 to 1980:3

ratio of a monetary aggregate to the monetary base. Good reason exists
for looking at that ratio. The Federal Reserve's open market operations
(purchases and sales of Treasury Bills at the New York Federal Reserve
Bank) change the Fed's balance sheet. Those changes, in turn, change
the "monetary base," which also is called "high powered money," or
outside money. The monetary base is the sum of currency plus bank
reserves. Changes in the base work themselves through the banking
system and result in a change in the money supply. That is the normal
"transmission mechanism" for monetary policy to the money supply,

---

Fed wanted. I was told to suggest changing one thing at a time, or they would not listen.
My preference would have been to plot against the user-cost price, but changing both the
quantity aggregation method and the opportunity cost price would have been two things
at once.

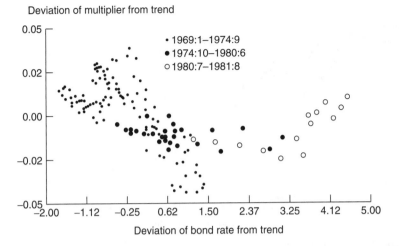

Deviation of multiplier from trend

• 1969:1–1974:9
• 1974:10–1980:6
○ 1980:7–1981:8

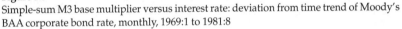

Deviation of bond rate from trend

Figure 3.5
Simple-sum M3 base multiplier versus interest rate: deviation from time trend of Moody's BAA corporate bond rate, monthly, 1969:1 to 1981:8

and thereby to inflation and the economy. The ratio of the money supply to the monetary base should exceed 1.0, since bank reserves back a larger amount of bank deposits, with only a fraction of the total deposits being held as reserves. The controllability of the money supply depends heavily on the ability to anticipate the ratio of the money supply to the monetary base. That ratio, also called the base "multiplier," need not be constant to ensure controllability of the money supply but should be stably related to interest rates, so that the multiplier can be anticipated from current interest rates. Then open market operations can be used to influence the money supply through changes in the monetary base, which is directly under the control of the Federal Reserve through its open market operations.

In figure 3.5 the monetary aggregate is again the simple-sum M3, as computed and officially provided by the Federal Reserve at that time. The base multiplier (adjusted for trend) is plotted against an interest rate. Observe the dramatic structural shift, which is not explained by interest rates. After 1974, the data are along a curved line, in fact a parabola. Prior to 1974, the data are along an intersecting, negatively sloped straight line. This figure displays what appears to be a shocking structural shift. To use the monetary base to control a monetary aggregate before 1974, it would appear to have been necessary to use the straight line to find the multiplier at the observed level of interest

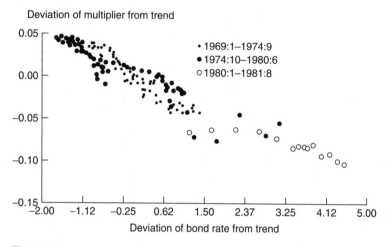

Figure 3.6
Divisia M3 monetary aggregate base multiplier versus deviation from time trend of Moody's BAA corporate bond interest rate, monthly, 1969:1 to 1981:8

rates. After 1974, it would have been necessary to use a completely different intersecting parabola to determine the multiplier at the observed level of interest rates. How could such a thing happen? Perhaps something supernatural happened? But again this puzzle was produced by the simple-sum monetary aggregate. In figure 3.6 the same plot is provided, but with the monetary aggregate changed to Divisia M2. The structural shift is gone.

During the late 1970s much was made of the presumed instability of the demand and supply for money. Hundreds of papers were published on the subject, and more significantly these paradoxes were used as a means of trying to discredit the monetarists, who were arguing that the Fed should be held accountable by the Congress for the rate of money creation. The presumed instability of the demand and supply for money was used by the Federal Reserve and some other central banks throughout the world to argue that central banks cannot be held accountable for something that cannot be understood, controlled, or predicted, because of structural shifts and inconsistencies with theory.

A more formal way existed to model the demand for money. The formal method at the time was based on the use of the Goldfeld demand for money equation, which was the standard specification used throughout the Federal Reserve System. The equation was originated by Stephen Goldfeld (1973) at Princeton University. That linear equation sought to explain a monetary aggregate as a function of national income, a regulated interest rate, and an unregulated interest rate.[4] As a result three coefficients were on the right-hand side of the equation: the coefficients of each of the three variables. The three coefficients had to be estimated by statistical regression. The equation was widely believed to have become unstable in the 1970s, since the three coefficients seemed to be varying over time. The coefficients were supposed to be constants, with only the variables varying.

P. A. V. B. Swamy and Peter Tinsley (1980), at the FRB in Washington, DC, had produced an approach to estimating a linear equation with the coefficients permitted to vary stochastically over time. The approach permitted testing the hypothesis that the three coefficients were constant with only random noise producing variation around the constants. In that case the appearance of nonconstancy would be statistically insignificant. At the time, Tinsley was my boss at the Federal Reserve Board, and Swamy was a very eminent independent-minded FRB econometrician, who had previously been a full professor at Ohio State University. I asked my boss to arrange for testing of constancy of the Goldfeld equation coefficients, using the Swamy and Tinsley methodology. I requested the test be done twice: once with simple sum M2 on the left-hand side of the equation, as was being done in the Board's quarterly econometric model, and once with Divisia M2 on the left-hand side. Tinsley passed the job on to Swamy, who had produced the computer program to run the test. He was viewed as being a person of exceptional professional integrity and was not subject to political influence within the system.

Swamy estimated the model's three coefficients at the Board with quarterly data from 1959:2 to 1980:4, and the results appeared in Barnett, Offenbacher, and Spindt (1984), which was published in the *Journal of Political Economy*. The estimated paths of the three coefficients are

---

4. Briefly, that demand for money equation is

$$\log\left(\frac{M_t}{p_t^*}\right) = a_0 + a_1 \log\left(\frac{M_{t-1}}{p_t^*}\right) + a_2 \log\left(\frac{Y_t}{p_t^*}\right) + a_3 \log(r_{1t}) + a_4 \log(r_{2t}),$$

where M_t is the monetary aggregate, p_t^* is the cost of living, measured by the Commerce Department's index, Y_t is GNP (gross national product), r_{1t} is a market interest rate, and r_{2t} is a regulated interest rate. The estimated coefficients are a_0, a_1, a_2, a_3, and a_4, which normally are treated as constants, but which we permit to vary stochastically over time. Figure 3.7 plots the realization of the stochastic process for a_2, figure 3.8 plots the realization of the stochastic process for a_3, and figure 3.9 plots the realization of the stochastic process for a_4. See equation 6 in Barnett, Offenbacher, and Spindt (1984) for the formal specification of the Goldfeld model's demand equation.

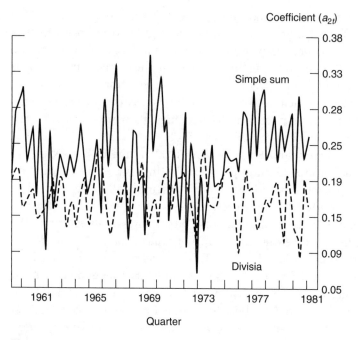

Coefficient (a_{2t})

Quarter

Figure 3.7
Time path of coefficient of income

displayed in figures 3.7, 3.8, and 3.9.[5] The solid line is the coefficient path, when money is measured by simple sum M2. The dotted line is the coefficient path, when the monetary aggregate is measured by the Divisia index. The instability of the coefficient is very clear, when the monetary aggregate is simple sum, but the paths look like noise around a constant when the monetary aggregate is Divisia. This conclusion is particularly clear from figures 3.8 and 3.9. Figure 3.8 shows that the coefficient of the unregulated interest rate exhibits clear cycles, when the left-hand side of the equation is simple-sum M2, but little more than noise around a constant, when Divisia M2. In the simple-sum case, the influence of the unregulated interest rate on money is not stable, and the variations in its multiplier are unpredictable.

Figure 3.9 is even clearer. Note that when the left-hand side of the equation is simple-sum M2, the coefficient of the regulated interest rate trends upward for almost half of the two decades, and then trends downward for the rest of the two decades. The influence of the

5. Formally speaking, they are the realizations of the coefficient stochastic processes. Other research in this area includes Serletis (1991).

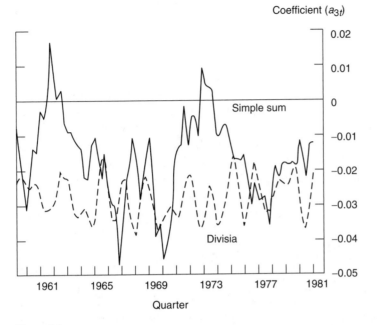

Figure 3.8
Time path of coefficient of market interest rate (commercial paper rate)

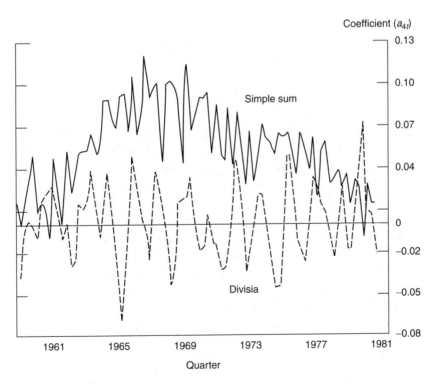

Figure 3.9
Time path of coefficient of regulated interest rate (passbook rate)

regulated interest rate on money grew for the first part of the period and then declined for the rest of the period, with no measured variable explaining the mysterious trends in that multiplier. In contrast, when the left-hand side of the equation is Divisia money, the coefficient of the regulated interest rate appears to be nothing more than statistically insignificant noise around a constant. In the formal Swamy and Tinsley hypothesis test, stability was rejected jointly for all three coefficients, when the monetary aggregate was simple sum, but not when computed as a Divisia index. In short, when simple-sum M2 was replaced by Divisia M2 on the left side of the Goldfeld equation, the equation worked just fine. No significant evidence existed of instability of the model. No space aliens had landed.

Since the Goldfeld equation was the demand for money equation in the Fed's model at the time, this result was of particular importance to the Board's model manager, Jerry Enzler. As discussed in section 2.7.3 of chapter 2, Jerry Enzler changed from simple-sum M2 to Divisia M2 in the Board's quarterly model, used to produce policy simulations. Those simulations provide a menu of "what if" scenarios. In particular, for each proposed policy path for the instruments under the control of the Federal Reserve, the simulation shows what the quarterly model predicts would happen to the economy. These simulations are supplied to the Governors for their use in making policy decisions.

3.2   The Monetarist Experiment: October 1979 to September 1982

Following the inflationary 1970s, Paul Volcker, as chairman of the Federal Reserve Board, decided to bring inflation under control by decreasing the rate of growth of the money supply, with the instrument of policy being changed from the federal-funds interest rate to nonborrowed reserves.[6] The choice of "instrument" of policy is particularly important, since the instrument is the tool the Fed seeks to bring directly under its control, as the means of influencing the inflation rate and general economy. Monetary policy operates through the Fed's chosen instrument. The period, October 1979 to September 1982, during which the nonborrowed reserves policy applied, was called the "Monetarist Experiment." The policy succeeded in ending the escalating inflation of the 1970s, but was followed by a recession. That recession, widely

---

6. The federal-funds rate is the interest rate that banks charge to each other, when banks borrow from other banks. Nonborrowed reserves are those bank reserves held by banks but not borrowed from the Federal Reserve. A more formal definition and discussion of nonborrowed reserves is provided in section 4.2 of chapter 4.

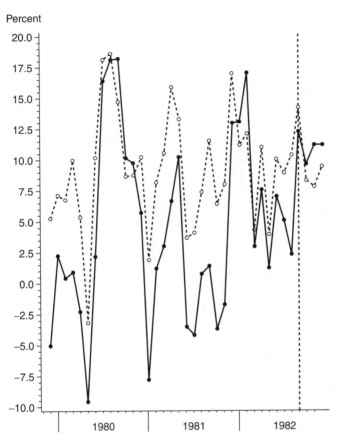

Percent

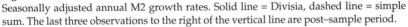

Figure 3.10
Seasonally adjusted annual M2 growth rates. Solid line = Divisia, dashed line = simple
sum. The last three observations to the right of the vertical line are post–sample period.

viewed as having been particularly deep, was not intended. The existence of widespread three-year negotiated wage contracts was viewed
as precluding a sudden decrease in the money growth rate to the intended long-run growth rate. The conclusion, based on a study published by the American Enterprise Institute in Washington, DC, was
that such a sudden contraction of monetary growth rate would produce
a recession. As a result, the Fed's decision was to decrease from the high
double-digit growth rates to about 10 percent per year and then gradually decrease toward the intended long-run growth rate of about 4 or 5
percent growth rate.

Figures 3.10 and 3.11 and table 3.1 reveal the cause of the unintended
recession. As is displayed in figures 3.10 and 3.11, for the M2 and M3

Percent

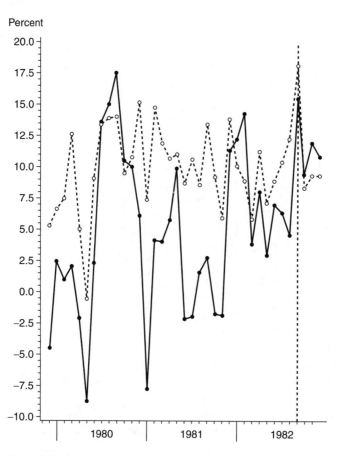

Figure 3.11
Seasonally adjusted annual M3 growth rates. Solid line = Divisia, dashed line = simple sum. The last three observations to the right of the vertical line are post–sample period.

levels of monetary aggregation, the rates of growth of the Divisia monetary aggregates were less than the rates of growth of the official simple-sum aggregates, which were the official targets of policy. As table 3.1 summarizes, *the simple-sum aggregates' growth rates were at the intended levels, but the Divisia growth rates were half as large, producing an unintended negative shock of substantially greater magnitude than intended. A deep recession resulted.* That table demonstrates that targeting the official simple-sum monetary aggregates resulted in precisely what was not intended: a rapid drop in the monetary growth rate to 4 or 5 percent per year. When a recession occurred, the unintended consequence was an embarrassment to monetarists, who subsequently denied that a monetarist policy

Table 3.1
Mean growth rates during the period

Monetary aggregate	Annual mean growth rate of the monetary aggregate during the Monetarist Experiment
Divisia M2	4.5
Simple sum M2	9.3
Divisia M3	4.8
Simple sum M3	10.0

had been in effect. But, as is well known to those who were on the FRB staff at the time, the Fed was doing precisely what it said it was doing, but relative to the simple-sum monetary aggregates.

I first published those two figures in the *American Statistician*, which is a publication of the American Statistical Association. The journal article is Barnett (1984). I am myself a journal editor, of the Cambridge University Press journal, *Macroeconomic Dynamics*, and have published extensively in professional journals; but submitting this paper was a unique experience. The normal procedure is for the editor to send a submission out to between one and three referees for peer review, before making the decision on whether to publish the article. In this case the editor sent me an astonishingly large number of referee reports, about ten, as I recall. This is virtually unheard of. All of the reports were very favorable, mostly emphasizing the paper's demonstration of the usefulness of statistics in government policy. In his letter, transmitting to me the unusually large number of very positive reports, the editor said he wanted to talk with me on the telephone. Suffice it to say that no other journal editor has ever asked to talk with me on the phone, and I've never asked any author to talk with me on the phone, when I am serving in my role as editor of *Macroeconomic Dynamics*. Such telephone conversations happen with newspaper article editors, but professional scientific journals simply do not operate that way.

Although surprised by the strange request, I called the editor. He told me the *American Statistician* has a letters-to-the-editor section, and he was afraid he would be swamped by angry letters to the editor, if he published my article. I responded I was sure my article could alarm some people, but none of them are readers of the *American Statistician*. He then published the article. No angry letters were sent to the editor.

As I have stated in section 2.7.5 of chapter 2, "Volcker wrote to me years later that he 'still is suffering from an allergic reaction' to my findings about the actual monetary growth rate during that period." The reason for that communication is interesting. With the great Paul Samuelson, I am coauthor of the book, *Inside the Economist's Mind* (Barnett and Samuelson 2007). The book contains a collection of the most important interviews I had previously published in the journal, *Macroeconomic Dynamics*. All the interviews published in that series of interviews are of very eminent economists. The book contains interviews of eight Nobel laureates, two central bank chairmen, and a chairman of the Council of Economic Advisors. One of the economists interviewed is Paul Volcker. With such a distinguished peer group, almost no one I have ever invited to be interviewed has declined, or even hesitated. But Paul Volcker hesitated. For many weeks, he did not respond to my letter of invitation. I wrote again. He then replied he was hesitant because of his "allergic reaction." He did not go into further detail to explain the reason for his Divisia-monetary-aggregates allergy "problem." But figures 3.10 and 3.11 and table 3.1 likely go a long way toward explaining his reply. I then assured him I would not personally conduct the interview; he would not be asked anything about my Divisia monetary aggregates; and he could choose the person to conduct the interview. He then accepted, and the interview was completed and published.

That interview is very informative and exceptionally interesting. For example, he makes clear he really did do what he said he was doing during the monetarist experiment, as I knew was true, since I was there. He was using "nonborrowed reserves" as an instrument of policy to bring monetary-aggregate growth rates, and thereby inflation, back down to more reasonable levels.[7] The frequently published statement by monetarists, that the Fed was not using nonborrowed reserves to bring down money-supply growth, seemed very strange to the Board's staff. The staff was being told to do research and provide support for what Volcker said he was doing—and indeed was doing.

The source of that controversy, which continues to the present day, is the fact that targets for the federal-funds interest rate continued to exist during the monetarist experiment period. Some economists were therefore under the impression that no attempt had been made to target nonborrowed reserves, and the policy had remained one of targeting interest rates.[8] But arguing it all was a fake amounts to a conspiracy theory, requiring the Federal Reserve Board to have been paying its

---

7. The concept of "nonborrowed reserves" is defined and discussed in section 4.2 of chapter 4.

8. For a serious presentation of that case, see Gilbert (1994).

hundreds of staff economists to work on something not being used at all, while systematically misleading the entire staff to believe otherwise. I do not find that view to be consistent with my experience on the Board staff at that time.[9]

As Volcker explained, undoubtedly correctly, in Barnett and Samuelson (2007, p. 178):

I used to rankle when some of the members of the Board, who were all enthusiastic about this turn of policy, would say, "Isn't this just a kind of public relations ploy to avoid being blamed for the rise in interest rates?" I never thought it was that, but a lot of people did think it was largely that. It was a very common thing to say that we just did it to obfuscate. We had no other good benchmark for how much to raise interest rates in the midst of a volatile inflationary situation.

Volcker was one of the Board's most highly qualified, effective, and brilliant chairmen. Too bad the Board was not using the Divisia monetary aggregates, so the outcome could have been as he had intended.

3.3   The End of the Monetarist Experiment: 1983 to 1984

Following the end of the Monetarist Experiment and the subsequent unintended recession, Milton Friedman became very vocal with his prediction that a huge surge had just appeared in the growth rate of the money supply, and the surge would surely work its way through the economy and produce a new inflation. Since the monetarists, led by Milton Friedman, had been embarrassed in the press by the unexpected recession, resulting from their advocated policy, good reason existed for Friedman to go out on a limb with this prediction, in the hope of recovering the reputation and influence of the monetarist point of view. He went even further by predicting there would be a Federal Reserve overreaction to the inflation, plunging the economy back down into a recession. He published this view repeatedly in the media in various magazines and newspapers, with the most visible being his *Newsweek* article, which appeared on September 26, 1983. The scanned article is provided in figure 3.12. Some excerpted sentences from that *Newsweek* article are below:

---

9. Formally speaking, a possible interpretation of the ambivalent-appearing policy would be that the Federal Reserve was using the federal-funds rate as its instrument and nonborrowed reserves as its intermediate target, where "instruments" of policy are defined to be more closely controllable than "intermediate targets." Examples of "final targets," which are the most difficult to control and the most distant in the transmission mechanism of policy, are inflation, unemployment, and economic growth.

MILTON FRIEDMAN

A Case of Bad Good News

President Reagan, politicians of all political persuasions, journalists specializing in economics, Wall Street, the business community—all these and many more are hailing the recent economic statistics showing rapid growth in output and employment as very good news indeed.

One group of economists—the monetarists—are a conspicuous exception. We were also an exception to what I labeled in February as "misleading unanimity" among economic forecasters (NEWSWEEK, Feb. 7, 1983). Almost to a person economic forecasters were predicting a slow and sluggish recovery. We predicted that "1983 will be a year of rapid and vigorous economic growth."

Monetary Explosion: That judgment was based on two considerations: the length and severity of the recession that ended in December 1982, and the monetary explosion that was then in process—a rise in M_1 at the annual rate of 15 percent from July 1982 to January 1983. It seemed to us that "this monetary explosion assures vigorous economic growth in the coming months"—but also that "unfortunately, if it continues much longer, it will also produce a renewed acceleration of inflation and a sharp rise in interest rates." The monetary explosion did produce vigorous growth. Unfortunately, it also did continue—at the annual rate of more than 14 percent from January to July. Interest rates have already risen sharply.

Inflation has not yet accelerated. That will come next year, since it generally takes about two years for monetary acceleration to work its way through to inflation.

The "good news," that output grew at the annual rate of nearly 9 percent in the second quarter of this year and may equal that record in the third quarter, is really bad news—the sign of an overheated economy headed for trouble. We do not need another sharp but brief expansion—like 1980 to 1981—followed by a relapse into recession. We need moderate growth at a rate that can be maintained for a long time along with continued reduction in inflation.

The only way to maintain anything like the recent hectic pace of real growth would

> The monetary explosion leaves no satisfactory way out of our present situation.

be to keep the monetary explosion going. But even if the Fed has learned nothing from experience, the market has—as its recent reactions to money-growth figures demonstrate. If the monetary explosion continued, both interest rates and inflation would react much more promptly than in the past. Both would head toward the sky. That reaction would make it nearly impossible for the Fed to continue the monetary explosion. However reluctantly, it will have to step on the brakes—as it already has apparently started to do.

The monetary explosion from July 1982 to July 1983 leaves no satisfactory way out of our present situation. The Fed's stepping on the brakes will appear to have no immediate effect. Rapid recovery will continue under the impetus of earlier monetary growth. With its historical shortsightedness, the Fed will be tempted to step still harder on the brake—just as the failure of rapid monetary growth in late 1982 to generate immediate recovery led it to keep its collective foot on the accelerator much too long. The result is bound to be renewed stagflation—recession accompanied by rising inflation and high interest rates.

Recession and the Election: The only real uncertainty is when the recession will begin. That will depend partly on the pattern of monetary growth over coming months, partly on other developments that cannot now be foreseen. Monetarists have always emphasized that the time delay between monetary change and economic change is not only long but also highly variable. Indeed, that is why we are so skeptical about the kind of monetary "fine-tuning" that the Fed has engaged in and why we favor steady monetary growth.

The precise timing of the recession will largely determine the political climate of election year 1984. Both President Reagan's supporters and his opponents are acting as if they expect recent favorable economic developments to continue through 1984—as evidenced by the search on the part of both for other issues to stress. They will be right if the recession does not begin before the third quarter of 1984. But if the recession should begin in the first or second quarter of 1984—as is entirely possible—the situation will be very different. In that case the election campaign would be conducted in an environment of declining output, rising unemployment, rising inflation and high interest rates—hardly an environment favorable to an incumbent.

Figure 3.12
Milton Friedman, *Newsweek*, September 26, 1983, p. 84

The monetary explosion from July 1982 to July 1983 leaves no satisfactory way out of our present situation. The Fed's stepping on the brakes will appear to have no immediate effect. Rapid recovery will continue under the impetus of earlier monetary growth. With its historical shortsightedness, the Fed will be tempted to step still harder on the brake—just as the failure of rapid monetary growth in late 1982 to generate immediate recovery led it to keep its collective foot on the accelerator much too long. The result is bound to be renewed stagflation—recession accompanied by rising inflation and high interest rates. . . . The only real uncertainty is when the recession will begin.

But on *exactly the same day*, September 26, 1983, I provided a very different view in *Forbes* magazine. That scanned article is provided in figure 3.13. As with many serious scientists, I rarely talk with the press, but in this case I knew Friedman's strong views and felt I should go on

Faces
Behind The Figures

Edited by John R. Dorfman

What explosion?

If you were measuring the nation's vehicle supply, you wouldn't give equal weight to roller skates and locomotives. But that, in effect, is what the Federal Reserve Board does in measuring the money supply, says William Barnett, an economist at the University of Texas (Austin).

The Fed has realized, Barnett says, that M1 excludes too many forms of money, such as the new money market accounts at banks. But the higher aggregates like M2 and M3, he says, suffer greatly from the "skates and locomotives" problem. Some of their components are much more liquid than others.

How can the Fed control money if it can't adequately define it? You have heard the question before. Barnett thinks he has the answer: Divisia aggregates, named after the late French statistician François Divisia, who published a famous paper on the subject in 1925. In Barnett's Divisia formula, the changes in the supply of various forms of money are weighted according to how liquid each form is. Checking accounts, for example, get more weight than certificates of deposit. To get his weighting factors, Barnett looks at the opportunity cost of holding such low-yield assets as checking accounts and passbook savings accounts. When you give up yield, his model figures, you are probably getting liquidity in exchange.

Economist William Barnett
A new set of "M" numbers?

Crunching Divisia numbers leads Barnett to two conclusions. One is that the Fed was much tighter than it intended to be during the period from late 1979 through mid-1982. For example, in 1982, M2, measured the usual way, was up 9.4%. But Divisia M2 was up only 7.8%.

The other conclusion is that people have been panicking unnecessarily about money supply growth this year. The new bank money funds and the super NOW accounts have been sucking in money that was formerly held in other forms, and other types of asset shuffling also have occurred. But the Divisia aggregates are rising at a rate not much different from last year's, Barnett says. Thus, the "apparent explosion" can be viewed as a statistical blip.

Is anybody listening? Yes, says Barnett, who was a research economist for the Fed for eight years until 1981. Some Fed members, including Governor Henry Wallich, regularly peruse his numbers. Such economists as Paul Samuelson, James Tobin and Milton Friedman also receive the Divisia numbers monthly. It's only a matter of time, he figures, before the Fed will go to Divisia aggregates as its official guide. "They've run out of other alternatives," says Barnett, "and are looking at this very seriously."—J.R.D.

Figure 3.13
William Barnett, *Forbes*, September 26, 1983, p. 196

the record. The following is an excerpt of some of the sentences from that article:

People have been panicking unnecessarily about money supply growth this year. The new bank money funds and the super NOW accounts have been sucking in money that was formerly held in other forms, and other types of asset shuffling also have occurred. But the Divisia aggregates are rising at a rate not much different from last year's . . . the "apparent explosion" can be viewed as a statistical blip.

Of course, Milton Friedman would not have taken such a strong position without reason. You can see the reason from figure 3.14. The percentage growth rates in that figure are monthly, not annualized. When annualized, the large spike in growth rate rises to over 30 percent per year, an enormous inflationary surge—if true. But that solid line is produced from simple sum M2, which was greatly overweighting the newly available, interest-bearing super-NOW accounts and money-market deposit accounts. No spike appeared in the Divisia monetary aggregate, represented by the dashed line, since Divisia removes the nonmonetary, investment motive, which at that time was receiving very high yield.

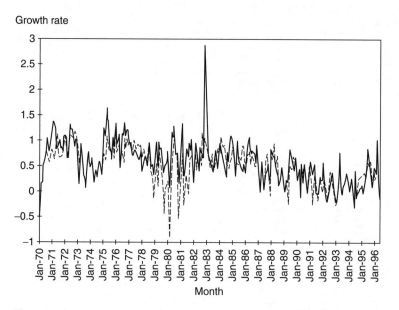

Figure 3.14
Monetary growth rates, 1970 to 1996, from St. Louis Federal Reserve's database. Solid line is simple-sum money; dashed line is Divisia. As originally published by Barnett (1997), the growth rates are not annualized.

If indeed the huge surge in the money supply growth had really happened, then inflation would surely have followed, unless money is extremely nonneutral (i.e., has no long-run effect on inflation), a view held by very few economists. Friedman undoubtedly was confident that he was right. But no inflationary surge occurred, and no subsequent recession resulted. This comparison of forecasts, published on the exact same day, is one of the few examples in the field of economics of such a documented, controlled-experiment in real time. Friedman's error resulted from his use of the Fed's official simple-sum monetary aggregates, which greatly distorted what had happened to the economy's monetary service flow.

3.4 The Rise of Risk-Adjustment Concerns: 1984 to 1993

As explained earlier, this chapter in chronological order presents and discusses the history of the "puzzles," along with the misperceptions those puzzles produced. The current problems in the economy are a consequence. We have now reached the period of 1984 to 1993. But the concerns that arose during that period deal with very technical problems. This section unavoidably surveys a literature that is difficult to explain without a lot of mathematics. If you are not comfortable about the technical jargon in this section, you might want to skim over some of this discussion. You can get the general flavor without biting too deeply into it. The relevant mathematics is presented in appendix D for the benefit of those who would like to acquire a complete understanding of what happened during those years. Some of the more technical details in this subsection are relegated to footnotes. While the rest of the book focuses on the field of economics and its available theory and practice, this section deals with the overlap between economics and finance. As a result much of the technical terminology is from the field of finance.

As described in previous sections, the exact monetary-quantity aggregate can be tracked accurately by the Divisia monetary aggregate, since that tracking ability is known under perfect certainty. But when nominal interest rates are uncertain, the Divisia monetary aggregate's tracking ability is somewhat compromised. That problem is eliminated by using the extended Divisia monetary aggregate derived by Barnett, Liu, and Jensen (1997) under risk. The extended Divisia monetary-aggregate formula requires risk adjustment, in a manner analogous to the use of "beta" risk adjustments in capital asset pricing in finance. The resulting very complicated formula is derived in appendix D and provided in theorem 1 of that appendix.

Interest rates are not paid in advance. If you were paid interest in advance, you'd take the interest payment up front and immediately withdraw your money from the account or sell the security. The same is true for wages. Workers are paid for their work at the end of the time period during which the work was done. Even with a savings account, you may be quoted an interest rate, when you deposit the funds, but the interest rate may change during the period of your planned holdings. As a rule, short-term interest rates on money-market accounts and securities are subject to low risk. While you cannot be sure of the interest you will receive at the end of the month, the interest payment is not likely to be greatly different from what you expected. So the interest rates in the user-cost price formula, needed to compute the Divisia monetary aggregates, usually can be viewed as low risk. The need for the risk-extended formula is most evident when substantial amounts of foreign denominated money-market and bank-account assets are held. Exchange rate risk can induce high risk into short-term interest rates.

Since Americans do not hold large amounts of such foreign denominated bank accounts, the risk adjustment in the formula is usually not significant.[10] But this is not always the case. During the period 1984 to 1993, use grew of money-market funds, stock market funds, and bond funds, all often within packages permitting easy transfer among the account types. The Board's staff found that once again their official monetary aggregates did not seem to be working properly, and this time the Fed thought the problem had to do with active transfer of funds among money-market funds, stock funds, and bond funds. The Board's official monetary aggregates included money-market funds but not stock or bond funds. Internalizing that substitution within the monetary aggregates would have required bringing stock and bond funds into the monetary aggregates, although the rates of return on investment in stock and bond funds are subject to substantial risk.

---

10. This conclusion of small risk adjustment with US data is based on the use of the CCAPM (consumption capital asset-pricing model) adjustment in appendix D's theorem 1. But it is well known in finance that CCAPM, assuming intertemporal separability, underestimates the risk adjustment. Barnett and Wu's (2005) extension to intertemporal nonseparability, provided in section D.7 of appendix D, has not yet been used to adjust the Divisia monetary aggregates. If the Federal Reserve begins again to provide the consolidated, seasonally adjusted component data on broad monetary aggregates, such as M3—*as the Fed should do*—then the magnitude of the risk adjustment should be reconsidered with the extended formula in section D.7 of appendix D.

During this time I moved from the University of Texas to Washington University in St. Louis. I produced the extended Divisia aggregate formula with two of my students there, Yi Liu and Mark Jensen, who based much of their doctoral dissertation research on that subject. The result was the extension of the field of index-number theory to the case of risk. François Divisia, along with others who had worked in the field of index-number theory, had based their research on the assumption of perfect certainty about current prices. Our research resulted in a fundamental extension of the literature on index-number theory to the case of uncertain prices and user costs.

With the risk-adjustment extension, Barnett and Xu (1998) demonstrated velocity will change, if the degree of risk of an interest rate changes.[11] Hence the variation in the riskiness of an interest rate cannot be ignored in modeling monetary velocity. Applying a small model of the economy, Barnett and Xu (1998) showed the usual computation of velocity will appear to produce instability, when interest rates exhibit varying degrees of risk over time.[12] But when the risk-adjusted user-cost variables are used, so that the variation in volatility is not ignored, velocity is stabilized.

Figure 3.15 displays a key role of velocity in the model of the economy, but without risk adjustment. The model was constructed to be stable. Consequently any evidence of instability is misleading. The figure displays a key property of the velocity function: its interest rate slope. We were investigating whether overlooking the risk adjustment could produce erroneous evidence of velocity instability.[13] Series 1 was produced with the least variation in interest rate volatility, series 2 with greater variation, and series 3 with even more variable volatility. Note that the plotted velocity property appears to be increasingly unstable, as volatility variation increases. By the model's construction, the plotted velocity property is constant, if the risk adjustment is used. In addition, with real economic data, Barnett and Xu (1998) showed the evidence of velocity instability in the literature is partially caused by overlooking the variation in the variance of interest rates over time.[14]

---

11. We measure risk by the conditional variance of the interest rate stochastic process and permit stochastic volatility.

12. The model was a dynamic stochastic general equilibrium model, which we calibrated.

13. The plotted property is the simulated slope coefficient for the velocity function, treated as a function of the exact interest rate aggregate, but without risk adjustment. All functions in the model are stable, by construction.

14. Subsequently, Barnett and Wu (2005) found that the explanatory power of the risk adjustment increases, if the assumption of intertemporal separability of the utility

Slope coefficient

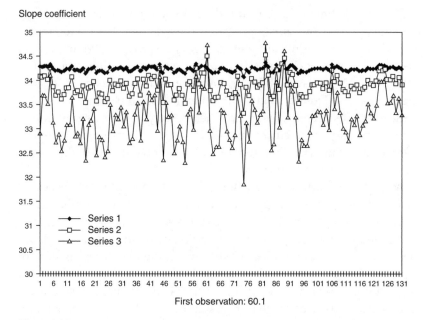

First observation: 60.1

Figure 3.15
Velocity's simulated interest rate coefficient when there is stochastic volatility of interest rates

Okay, if you have gotten this far, but are confused by the finance terminology, here is the bottom line. During this period of time there was much controversy about the appearance of monetary velocity instability and unpredictability. Here we have the "space alien theory" again, since this instability presumably had no natural economic causes. What my students and I demonstrated was that we could match the patterns of puzzling instability by ignoring the variability of interest rate risk, when in fact it was varying. If we incorporated into the model recognition of the variability of interest rate risk, then the appearance of unexplainable variations of velocity disappeared.

The Divisia index tracks the theoretically exact aggregate, measuring monetary-service flow. But for some purposes the economic capital stock is relevant, especially when investigating wealth effects of policy on the economy. The economic stock of money (ESM), as defined by Barnett (1991), is provided in appendix B in this book's part II as equation

---

function is weakened. The separability assumption also is a source of the well-known equity premium puzzle, by which CCAPM under-corrects for risk. Barnett and Wu's (2005) extension to intertemporal nonseparability is provided in section D.7 of this book's appendix D.

(B.5).[15] Comparing the Divisia monetary aggregate flow with the ESM is analogous to comparing the services of a rented apartment during a month, with the services of a purchased condominium during its useful lifetime. Clearly, the rent to use the apartment for one month will be less than the price to buy the condominium. The monetary velocity issue described above was about the service flow, analogous to renting an apartment; but in the rest of this section, the issue is about the capital stock, analogous to buying the apartment as a condominium and using it for multiple years. The relevant theory for measuring the economic capital stock of money is the subject of appendix B. As in the finance field's capital-asset-pricing theory, the value of the capital stock is the discounted present value of the service flow produced by the stock.

During the late 1980s and early 1990s concern grew about substitution among monetary assets and stock and bond mutual funds, which are not within the monetary aggregates. The FRB staff considered the possibility of incorporating stock and bond mutual funds into the monetary aggregates.[16] Barnett and Zhou (1994a) used the formulas discussed above to investigate the problem. The figures supplied in figures 3.16 through 3.19 are from that paper. The dotted line is the simple-sum monetary aggregate, which Barnett (1991) proved is equal to the sum of the economic capital stock of money and the discounted, expected, investment return from the components.[17] The simple-sum monetary aggregate measures a joint product, the sum of the discounted investment yield and the discounted monetary-service flow. That proof is provided in appendix B as equation (B.17).

The economic capital stock of money is the monetary stock relevant to macroeconomic theory. Hence we should concentrate on the solid lines in those figures. Note that figure 3.17 displays nearly parallel paths, so the growth rate is about the same for the simple-sum aggregate or the economic stock of money. That figure is for M2+, which was the FRB staff's proposed, extended aggregate, adding stock and bond mutual funds to M2. But note in figure 3.16 that the gap between the two graphs is decreasing, producing a slower rate of growth for the simple-sum aggregate than for the economic stock of money.

---

15. The extension of that economic capital stock formula to risk is available as equation (B.10) in appendix B in this book's part II, and has been implemented empirically by Barnett, Chae, and Keating (2006).

16. See Collins and Edwards (1994) and Orphanides, Reid, and Small (1994).

17. Computation of the capital stock of money requires modeling expectations. In that early paper, Barnett and Zhou (1994a) used martingale expectations, rather than the more recent approach of Barnett, Chae, and Keating (2006) using VAR forecasting. When martingale expectations are used, the index is called CE.

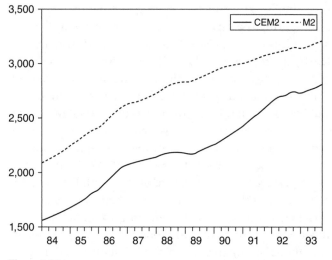

Figure 3.16
M2 joint product and economic capital stock of money. M2 = simple-sum joint product;
CEM2 = economic capital stock part of the joint product. Billions of dollars plotted against
year.

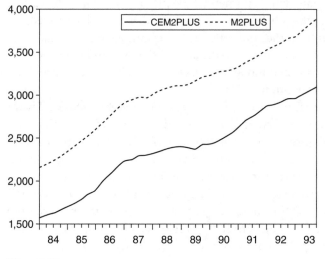

Figure 3.17
M2+ joint product and economic capital stock of money. M2+ = simple-sum joint product; CEM2+ = economic capital stock part of the joint product. Billions of dollars plotted
against year.

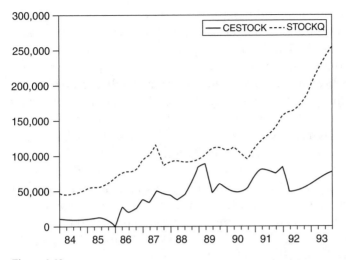

Figure 3.18
Common-stock mutual-funds joint product and their economic capital stock. StockQ = simple-sum joint product; CEstock = economic capital stock part of the joint product. Billions of dollars plotted against year.

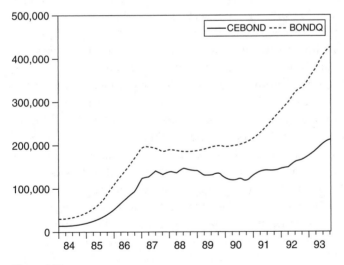

Figure 3.19
Bond mutual funds joint product and their economic capital stock. BondQ = simple-sum joint product; CEbond = economic capital stock part of the joint product. Billions of dollars plotted against year.

The reason can be found in figures 3.18 and 3.19, which use a solid line to display the monetary (i.e., liquidity) services from stock and bond mutual funds. The figures use a dotted line for the simple-sum valuation of those funds, where again the simple sum measures a joint product: the discounted investment yield plus the discounted service flow. Hence the gap between the two lines is the amount motivated by investment yield. Clearly, those gaps had been growing. But it is precisely that gap which does *not* measure monetary services. By adding the value of stock and bond mutual funds into figure 3.16 to get figure 3.17, the growth rate error of the simple-sum aggregate is offset by adding in more assets providing nonmonetary services. Rather than trying to stabilize the error gap by adding in more and more nonmonetary services, the correct solution would have been to remove the entire error gap by using the solid line in figure 3.16 (or figure 3.17). The solid line measures the actual capital stock of money.

I was invited to present these results at a conference at the Federal Reserve Bank of St. Louis. I asked the audience the following question: Would you consider a Ferrari sports car to be a means of transportation or a source of recreation? Clearly, the price of a Ferrari is too high, if valued solely for its transportation services, and the Ferrari cannot be solely for recreation, since Ferraris are seen on public highways. Ferraris must be a joint product providing both kinds of services. The same has been true of money, since many monetary assets began yielding interest long ago. Two motives exist for holding money: monetary services, such as liquidity, and investment return, such as interest. Investment return is not a monetary service. Otherwise, money would have to include the entire capital stock of the country.

The FRB's staff had observed something was going wrong with its official simple-sum monetary aggregates. Since nothing was going wrong with the Divisia monetary aggregates, we can see clearly what the source of the problem was. The error gap between the Divisia capital stock and the simple-sum monetary aggregate was narrowing, so the growth rates of the two aggregates were diverging. The error gap is caused by the monetary investment motive, which was declining as people increasingly moved funds out of money and into stock and bond mutual funds. The proposed response by the Board's staff was to stabilize the gap by bringing in stock and bond mutual funds.

A long history exists of this sort of mistaken approach, by which more and more sources of error were brought into the monetary aggregates in an attempt to stabilize the error component. The right solution is to remove the error gap. Reputable index number theory does exactly that, as with the Divisia monetary aggregates or their discounted, economic capital stock.

3.5   The Y2K Computer Bug: 1999 to 2000

The next major concern about monetary aggregates and monetary policy arose at the end of 1999. The financial press became highly critical of the Fed for what was perceived to be a large, inflationary surge in the monetary base. Recall that the monetary base is the sum of currency in the economy and bank reserves. Changes in the monetary base can be viewed as the output produced by the Fed's open market operations and hence is a primary measure of monetary policy actions. While this interpretation is true, the monetary base is nevertheless a highly defective measure of the effect of monetary policy on the economy, since the base adds together two measures having very different effects on the economy. Currency is dollar-for-dollar pure money. But only a fraction of bank deposit accounts is held as bank reserves. Hence checking accounts are a multiple of bank reserves; and bank account deposits, such as checking accounts, provide monetary services. Variations of bank reserves have a much more powerful "multiplier" effect on the economy than variations of currency, which reflect little more than the need for cash in retail businesses.

Changes in the monetary base are excellent measures of changes in the Fed's balance sheet and thereby of the Fed's open market operations. But the defects of the monetary base, as a measure of the consequences of policy for the economy, are well illustrated by the Great Depression of the 1930s. During that period the monetary base steadily grew, as might appear to reflect excellent policy. But the money supply crashed, since bank failures caused the destruction of bank deposits as a multiplier of the decline in the banks' reserves. Clearly, the crash in money supply was a far more accurate measure of the effects of monetary policy than the steady rise in the monetary base during the Depression.

Near the end of 1999, the reason for the alarming press commentaries is clear from figure 3.20.[18] But the reason was not valid, since the cause

---

18. The data is from the St. Louis Federal Reserve Bank's "adjusted" monetary base. According to its website, the St. Louis Fed "adjusts the monetary base for changes in the demand for base money due to changes in statutory reserve requirement ratios within a given structure of reserve requirements (where the structure defines the types of deposits that are reservable, perhaps by class or type of depository institution), conditional on an assumed model of depository institutions' demand for base money."

Adjusted monetary base

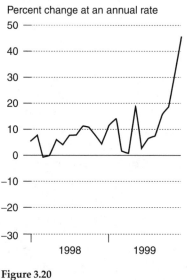

Figure 3.20
Monetary base surge.

was again a problem with the data. The so-called Y2K computer bug was expected to cause temporary problems with computers throughout the world, including at banks. Consequently many depositors, including me, withdrew funds from their checking accounts and moved them into cash. While the decrease in deposits thereby produced an equal increase in currency demand, the decrease in deposits produced a smaller decline in reserves because of the multiplier from reserves to deposits. The result was a surge in the monetary base, even though the cause was a harmless, temporary dollar-for-dollar transfer of funds from demand deposits into cash. In addition many bankers feared the computer bug and increased their vault cash as a precaution, with the encouragement of the Federal Reserve. In one such case a banker drove to the St. Louis Fed and filled the trunk of his Cadillac with currency, fearing he would not have enough. A few days later, he returned the cash. Those transfers of funds had little effect on economic liquidity. Once the computer bug was resolved, people put their withdrawn cash back into deposits, and banks returned their excess cash to the Fed, as is seen from figure 3.21.

The Federal Reserve seemed to recognize the fallacy in the alarmist articles in the press. At the time, I called some of my friends at the Fed and explained that the change in the monetary base was not a reflection of Fed actions on the supply side, but instead was produced by the

Adjusted monetary base

Percent change at an annual rate

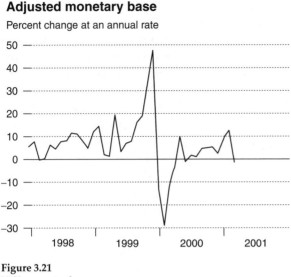

Figure 3.21
Y2K computer bug.

demand-side actions of depositors worried about the Y2K bug scare. I recommended the Fed ignore the press criticism and not clamp down on the money supply, since the surge in the monetary base would not translate into increased money supply and hence would not produce inflation. The Fed economists I called all agreed with me and said the Fed already understood. Clearly the Fed was right, but again the public (or at least the press) had become confused by the Federal Reserve data.

3.6   Conclusion

Once upon a time long ago, when monetary assets in the monetary aggregates were limited to cash plus checking accounts, yielding no interest and accepted as means of payment, simple-sum monetary aggregation was consistent with the principles of economic measurement. The Divisia quantity index correctly becomes the simple sum, when the prices of all goods within the aggregate are always equal to each other, since the goods then must be one-for-one perfect substitutes. In the case of monetary aggregation, equal prices mean equal user-cost prices, which can occur only if the interest rates paid on all component assets are equal to each other. Since the rate of interest paid on currency is zero, monetary aggregates validly can be simple sums, only if no interest is paid on any assets within the aggregate.

But those days are long gone, and many monetary assets included in central bank monetary aggregates pay interest. Simple-sum monetary aggregation severely overweights the monetary services of interest-bearing monetary assets, such as certificates of deposit (CDs). By failing to convert to reputable monetary aggregation procedures, *the Federal Reserve Board has contaminated the economics literature, misled the public, produced fundamental misperceptions about the abilities of the central bank, and taken away from itself a valuable tool that would have permitted it to make better policy decisions.* As financial markets have become more sophisticated, and more and more interest-bearing money market instruments have evolved, the problem has become progressively worse.

4 Current Policy Problems

4.1 European ECB Data

In 2002, I was approached by the European Central Bank in Frankfurt, Germany, for assistance in producing Divisia monetary aggregates for the European Monetary Union (the EMU, also called the "euro area" or the "euro zone"). I gave a seminar there and then was employed as a consultant to work out the relevant theory. I traveled there a few times in 2002 to 2003 to meet with the relevant people and to assist in producing a Divisia database for the EMU. The opportunity presented interesting, theoretical problems I had not previously addressed. In addition, the inertia produced by a long-established history had not yet become as entrenched as at older central banks. The ECB seemed very receptive to doing it right despite, as explained to me, the political constraints within Europe.[1]

The most challenging theoretical problem was extending the Divisia monetary aggregates to the case of multilateral aggregation, by which money could be aggregated first within countries and then over countries. That two-stage aggregation would permit the distribution effects of policy across countries to be tracked, where "distribution effects" are different effects within different countries. This ability was

---

1. For example, it was explained to me that much German money in Luxembourg, French money in Monaco, and Italian money in Switzerland are in banks that will not reveal the country of origin of the depositors and treat those deposits as domestic. As a result the data on money supply in individual countries are distorted. I was told that these data distortions are politically untouchable and are motived by tax evasion. I also was informed French banks were paying a savings-deposit interest rate exceeding that available to residents in other countries of the EMU, while residents of other countries are not permitted to deposit money in those accounts in France. This violates the intended "convergence" objectives of the EMU. But that violation also was untouchable, since the higher interest rate was subsidized by French income taxes to encourage savings within France.

particularly important in merging the current euro data with the older national currencies prior to the euro. In the United States the Fed gives little consideration to the differential effects of policy across different states. Fed data normally are supplied only for the entire country in aggregate. Because of the high mobility of Americans, all speaking the same language and all being within the same country, changes in relative regional prosperities are viewed as reasons for Americans to move to the states where the best opportunities exist.

But in Europe, where protection of the separate cultures of the countries is valued, the ECB cannot ignore differential "distribution effects" of its policy. My resulting theory for multilateral Divisia monetary aggregation was published in the 2004 ECB Working Paper 260, available on the website of the European Central Bank. A more tightly written, more formal, *Journal of Econometrics* version subsequently appeared in Barnett (2007). Much of that multilateral aggregation theory, equally relevant for other multi-country economic unions, is provided in appendix C.

During my last visit to the European Central Bank, one of their economists, who had assisted in setting up the Divisia database, printed out some figures using those data. Those figures are collected together and reproduced as figure 4.1, exactly as provided to me. The plots are for three of the countries in the EMU. I don't recall the countries. The plots on the right-hand side are of monetary velocity in those three countries, plotted against an interest rate or the user-cost price. Note that velocity increases with interest rates and user costs, exactly as demand-for-money theory would suggest. Clearly, the Divisia data were working very well.[2]

I had no way of knowing to whom the database was being made available, since the ECB, unlike the Bank of England and the National Bank of Poland, was not making the data available outside the central bank. Recently I was invited to give a seminar at the Bank of Greece in Athens, on May 26, 2010. Of course my seminar had a lot to say about the mysterious ECB Divisia data, if they existed anymore at all. To

---

2. I have not been asked to assist in working out the extensions to incorporate exchange rate risk among the old currencies or among the euro- and the foreign-denominated bank accounts sometimes held by EMU residents. As a result the ECB Divisia data probably do not include the risk extension, which evidently is not a major concern. The theory for that extension to risk, which could be incorporated into multilateral aggregation, is now available from Barnett and Wu (2005). The need for risk adjustment in monetary aggregation was first made clear in Poterba and Rotemberg (1987). Appendix D deals with that subject.

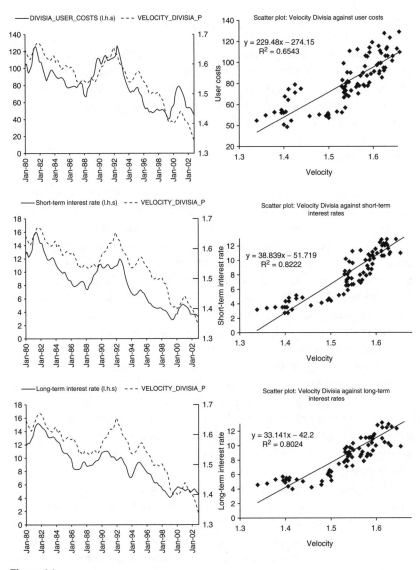

Figure 4.1
European Central Bank monetary velocity. Figures exactly as provided to me.

my astonishment, a high-ranking officer of the Bank of Greece, who sometimes sat on the ECB's Governing Council, informed me of the following: the Divisia monetary aggregate data are provided to the ECB Governing Council at its policy meetings along with analysis of its implications for policy. Yet the data are not provided to the public, and the public has not been informed Divisia monetary aggregates exist for the EMU. This is policy transparency?

4.2   The Most Recent Data: Would You Believe This?

Highly relevant recent research on the subject of this book is in Barnett, Chauvet, and Tierney (2009), which uses an area of time-series econometric research beyond the scope of this book.[3] What that research does is to remove the common trend movement of multiple data paths to reveal the data variations specific and unique to each. The resulting extracted part, specific to a data series, is called the "idiosyncratic term." The approach is used to provide pairwise comparisons of Divisia versus simple-sum monetary aggregates quarterly from 1960:2 to 2005:4.

Figure 4.2 below is from that paper. The figure displays the idiosyncratic terms specific to Divisia M3 and simple-sum M3. The shaded areas are the time periods declared officially to have been recessions by the National Bureau of Economic Research (NBER). That figure and the associated published paper not only compare Divisia with simple sum over time but also over the business cycle and across high and low inflation and interest rate phases. Information about monetary growth becomes particularly relevant for policy makers, when inflation enters a high-growth phase or the economy begins to weaken. Compare Divisia M3's idiosyncratic downward spikes in figure 4.2 with simple-sum M3's idiosyncratic behavior, and then compare the relative predictive ability of the two extracted idiosyncratic terms with respect to NBER recessions. Figure 4.2 speaks for itself and clearly identifies the value of Divisia data in explaining unemployment and higher interest periods. The data, available at the time the paper was produced, was from the early 1960s to the date that the St. Louis Fed froze the Divisia data in

---

3. It is a latent-factor Markov-switching approach, which separates out common dynamics from idiosyncratic terms. The dynamic factor measures the common cyclical movements underlying the observable variables. The idiosyncratic term captures movements peculiar to each index. In that paper, we introduced the connection between the state-space time-series approach to assessing measurement error and the aggregation-theoretic concept, with emphasis on the relevancy to monetary aggregation and monetary policy.

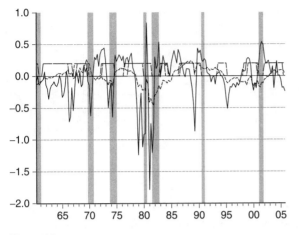

Figure 4.2
Idiosyncratic terms for M3 (dashed line) and Divisia M3 growth (solid line), high interest rate phases and high inflation phases (horizontal flat dashed), and NBER recessions (shaded posts). Units of billions of dollars plotted against the year.

2006—at the start of the real-estate bubble collapse.[4] The behavior of Divisia follows much more closely the expected behavior predicted by monetary theory across high and low interest rates and around recessions. Divisia is much to be preferred to simple sum.

Consider these most recent results along with the many others surveyed in this book, and also keep in mind the relevant aggregation theory, based solidly on microeconomic aggregation theory. You might find it worthwhile to compare those empirical and theoretical results with the most recent behavior of the Fed's reputed approach to monetary policy. That approach, although not officially adopted, is the "Taylor rule," which does not use money at all, not even as a long-run anchor.[5] Monetary policy without money? That might seem to be puzzling to you, perhaps even negligent. The Taylor rule provides a target range for the federal-funds interest rate, which then is supposed to be kept within

---

4. Barnett and Chauvet (2011b) subsequently pursued that approach further to look more closely at the data since 1987 in their figure 24 and since 1999 in their figure 25. Again the high explanatory power of money growth is lost, when the monetary aggregates are improperly constructed as simple sum, but very clear when constructed as Divisia indexes.
5. The Taylor rule equation is intended to put upward pressure on interest rates as inflation increases and downward pressure on interest rates as unemployment (or more formally the "output gap") increases, with the net effect on interest rates depending upon the formula's weighting on the two pressures. The output gap is the difference between the output of the economy and what it would have been at full employment.

Federal-funds rate and inflation targets

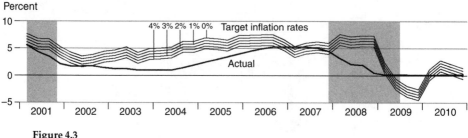

Figure 4.3
Taylor rule federal-funds rate

that range. The range is produced in a manner designed to take into account inflation and unemployment, but in a manner making no use at all of monetary quantity data. During the Great Recession, the federal-funds rate was nearly zero for many months—hardly an effective tool to stimulate the economy further. In fact, during the years of the Great Recession, Federal Reserve policy was the most volatile in its history, while the federal-funds rate hardly varied at all. As an indicator of Fed policy, the federal-funds rate, contrary to official pronouncements, was a nearly useless indicator of monetary policy.

But prior to the time that the federal-funds rate became nearly zero, we can look at what the Taylor rule was saying about policy. Figure 4.3 is reproduced from the St. Louis Fed's publication, *Monetary Trends*. That figure displays the Taylor rule range for the federal-funds rate target along with the actual federal-funds interest rate, where the actual funds rate is the dark solid line.[6] Notice the actual interest rate was off target for more than three successive years. Yet the associated "Taylor principle" was largely credited by Ben S. Bernanke with the success of the Great Moderation. He was very clear about that view in his speech at the meetings of the Eastern Economic Association, in Washington, DC, on February 20, 2004.[7]

---

6. This figure is not from a Federal Reserve Board publication, since the Board does not have an "official" federal-funds rate range. But this chart, published by the Federal Reserve Bank of St. Louis, is the closest I could come to finding a Federal Reserve defined target range for its funds rate. Clearly, it also is the closest that the St. Louis Fed could come.
7. In that speech Bernanke stated very clearly that improved monetary policy-making should be credited for much of the improved economic performance during the Great Moderation. However, his emphasis was less clearly on the full Taylor rule than on the Taylor principle, which is a derivable implication of the Taylor rule. The Taylor rule produces the Taylor principle, when the coefficient is positive on the gap between the inflation rate and the desired inflation rate. The Taylor rule conclusion then is that the real interest

To an economist, figure 4.3 would be self-explanatory. But if you feel you need further explanation, this paragraph presents it. The dark line shows the actual path of the federal-funds interest rate, as the Fed conducted monetary policy between 1999 and 2008. The other lines show paths for that funds rate under implied objectives for monetary policy, as if the goal of monetary policy had been an inflation rate between 0 and 4 percent. The top line represents an objective of zero inflation for policy, and the lowest of the five lines represents a policy objective of 4 percent inflation. The actual path of the federal-funds rate, between 2003 and 2006, lies below the lowest of the five lines, and the gap appears to be several percentage points during this interval. We are left to draw one of several conclusions: (1) the Taylor rule does not describe the Fed's approach to monetary policy, (2) the Fed made a series of policy errors over a number of years, or (3) during this period the Fed abandoned its commitment to price stability and implicitly allowed its target for the inflation rate to rise to somewhere in the range of 6 to 8 percent. Whatever the explanation might be, this episode reveals one glaring instance where transparency—in the form of publication of competently produced monetary statistics—would have allowed the Congress and the public to be more acutely aware of the consequences of the Fed's overly stimulative policy actions.

This book has documented the fact that the "paradoxes," which had dominated monetary economics research for over three decades, are not paradoxes at all. They are just consequences of the use of the official simple-sum monetary aggregate data. But perhaps we now have a real paradox: the evident "instability" of the Taylor rule, which makes no use of monetary data. Perhaps the literature on monetary paradoxes has been looking in the wrong places.

As documented in this book, monetary policy and monetary research have been plagued by bad monetary aggregates, resulting from simple-sum aggregation. In addition we have shown that the puzzles since the early 1970s were produced by simple-sum aggregation and would have gone away, if reputable index-number formulas had been used. With so much history and evidence and so much research documenting the data problems, central banks might be expected now to be taking more care to provide high-quality data, consistent with economic theory.

---

rate should not be allowed to fall during periods of rising actual or expected inflation. But this book finds little evidence of significantly improved monetary policy over the past forty years, or reason to credit such improved policy for the Great Moderation.

Billions of dollars

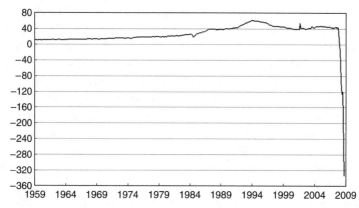

Figure 4.4
Nonborrowed reserves of depository institutions (BOGNONBR). Source: Board of Governors of the Federal Reserve System.

If that is what you would expect, then look at figure 4.4, which was downloaded from the St. Louis Fed's website and is produced from official FRB data. Recall from section 3.3 of chapter 3 that Volcker's Monetarist Experiment used nonborrowed reserves as the instrument of policy. Hence it is particularly interesting to look at figure 4.4, which displays official, recent data on nonborrowed reserves from the Federal Reserve Board. As mentioned in section 2.7.5 of chapter 2, good reason exists to look at this recent data very carefully.

To make the implications of that figure clear, let us provide some formal definitions:

Definition 5 *"Total reserves" are the sum of all borrowed and nonborrowed bank reserves.*

Definition 6 *"Borrowed reserves" are those funds held by banks in reserve, but borrowed by banks for that purpose.*

What else could total reserves and borrowed reserves possibly mean? It follows immediately from elementary logic and definition 5 that nonborrowed reserves cannot be negative, since borrowed reserves in definition 6 cannot possibly exceed total reserves. Clearly, everything included in borrowed reserves must be held by banks in reserves, and everything contained in nonborrowed reserves must also be held by banks in reserves. Hence neither borrowed reserves nor nonborrowed reserves can possibly exceed total reserves. For nonborrowed reserves

Billions of dollars

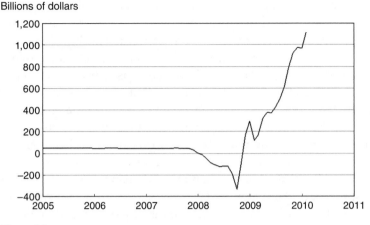

Figure 4.5
Updated nonborrowed reserves of depository institutions (BOGNONBR). Source: Board of Governors of the Federal Reserve System.

to be negative would be an oxymoron. They certainly never were, when being used by Paul Volcker as his instrument of policy during the period of the monetarist experiment.

Now look again at figure 4.4. Observe that nonborrowed reserves crashed to about minus 50 billion dollars during early months of the financial crisis. Nonborrowed reserves subsequently recovered to positive values, as seen in figure 4.5, but that is beside the point. How can anyone take seriously nonborrowed reserves data that became negative? The Fed's explanation is banks' new auction borrowing from the Federal Reserve is included in nonborrowed reserves, even though those borrowings need not be reserves at all. According to this data, the instrument of monetary policy during Volcker's Monetarist Experiment period was recently driven to very negative values, although impossible by the logical definition of nonborrowed reserves. Clearly, Fed data on nonborrowed reserves are terrible measures of bank reserves not borrowed.[8]

We might hope that perhaps this example of extremely bad accounting is the exception to the rule, so other Fed data can be trusted. Sad to say, that is not the case. Consider, for example, the monetary aggregate,

---

8. The Fed's justification is that under recent operating procedures, including "sterilizing loans" by selling bonds to keep the federal-funds rate close to target, accounting for bank borrowing held as reserves has become very difficult. While this justification may not be a problem for the Fed's own recent policy procedures, the resulting published data can be severely misleading to the public.

M1, which contains currency and demand deposits. This monetary aggregate is important since its components are legal means of payment. But to avoid reserve requirements on regular checking accounts, banks are "sweeping" a large fraction of demand deposits into money-market-deposit savings accounts. I have previously discussed sweeps in less detail in section 2.7.5 of chapter 2. Banks have complete data on their demand deposits, since they need to service them and to do so as checking accounts, not as savings accounts. But to camouflage the evasion of reserve requirements on checking accounts, banks report sweeps to the Federal Reserve as being in money-market deposit savings accounts (MMDAs), rather than in the demand-deposit checking accounts. But since the swept funds are serviced as fully checkable demand deposits, their liquidity services to the economy are those of demand deposits. The sweeps are just an accounting trick. By subtracting sweeps from demand deposits, banks are severely biasing downward the data on demand deposit services. Demand deposits, not MMDAs, are in the Fed's M1 monetary aggregate, as supplied to the public and the Congress. As a result M1 is severely biased downward.[9]

Checking account "demand deposits" data are thereby under reported by about 50 percent, rendering M1 monetary aggregate data nearly useless. The Federal Reserve is fully capable of requiring banks to provide the correct data on demand deposits, including the amounts swept. In fact the Board might have those data on its protected "reserves file," which is not made public. Recall that the last time someone on the FRB's staff provided data to the public from the reserves file, that person was hunted down by the FBI and fired.

Also recall the Fed has terminated reporting the broad monetary aggregates, M3 and L. During decades of increasingly sophisticated monetary instruments and money markets, the private sector of the economy needs increasing quantity and quality of data about financial instruments. What has the Fed done? The exact opposite! Some of the most liquid money-market assets are no longer considered to provide liquidity to the economy and thereby are completely excluded from "money," including negotiable certificates of deposit, commercial

---

9. It might appear that the damage to monetary aggregation from misclassification of sweeps is offset by using the broader monetary aggregate, M2, since simple sum M2 includes MMDA's as well as regular checking accounts. The sweeps improperly removed from checking accounts are added back into the MMDAs in the sum. But checking accounts and MMDA's are not perfect substitutes and are not treated as such in properly weighted monetary aggregates, such as Divisia M2. The misclassification of sweeps damages all properly constructed monetary aggregates.

paper, banker's acceptances, and Treasure bills, while demand-deposit checking accounts are undervalued by about 50 percent. Is it surprising that banks, Wall Street professionals, home buyers, and almost everyone else were unable accurately to assess the risks they were taking and instead became entranced with "the Maestro," from whom unreasonable expectations arose?

4.3 The Current Crisis

4.3.1 Prior to April 14, 2006
The highly leveraged investment, borrowing, and lending, which led up to the current crisis, were not irrational—relative to the widespread views about the presumably tamed business cycle. Clearly, the financial crisis and Great Recession are not consistent with the views that produced the high-risk behavior precipitating the crisis. The primary objective of this book is not to emphasize that policy errors contributed to the crisis, although this book does provide substantial evidence that policy was disturbingly less effective than might have been hoped. In fact, the primary objective of this book is to suggest that poor Federal Reserve data unnecessarily complicated private decision-making and interfered with the abilities of the private sector to recognize the extent of the systemic risk existing at the time. That is the primary message.

Nevertheless, relevant evidence most definitely does exist about possible policy errors. In particular, monetary policy in recent decades might have been more expansionary than was realized by the Federal Reserve and thereby might have fed the bubbles. Also policy more recently might have been more contractionary than realized by the Federal Reserve at the start of the crisis. During those periods of time, the evidence was not clear, largely as a result of the Fed's data limitations, most conspicuously the lack of availability of the Divisia monetary aggregates since April 14, 2006 until very recently. Nevertheless, we feel it is worthwhile providing the evidence we had at those times. In accordance with the design of this book to provide results in chronological order, and relative to the data availability at the time, we continue in that manner now.

There is a strain of thought that maintains the current US financial crisis was prompted by excessive money creation fueling the bubbles. Evidence exists supporting that point of view. The process started in early 2001 when money supply was increased substantially to minimize the economic recession begun in March of that year. However,

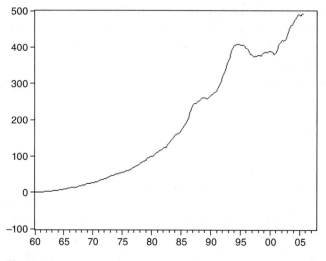

Figure 4.6
Deviation of the Divisia M1 monetary aggregate (MSI1) from the common trend shared by the simple-sum M1 monetary aggregate and its corresponding Divisia monetary aggregate. Units in billions of dollars, relative to 1960. The deviation was set equal to zero in 1960. Source: Board of Governors of the Federal Reserve System.

in contrast with previous recessions, money supply growth remained expansionary for over three years after the recession's end in November 2001. How long the policy remained expansionary depends on the monetary aggregate used. Monetary expansion led to both speculation and leveraging, especially in housing-sector lending. This monetary expansion is argued to have made it possible for marginal borrowers to obtain loans with lower collateral values. When money creation slowed, housing prices began to decline, leading many to own negative equity and inducing a wave of defaults and foreclosures. If this were the case, what would have motivated the policy that had this outcome?

We see no reason to believe that the Fed would have adopted, as a goal, the creation of "excessive" money growth. Had the Fed known the amount of money circulating in the economy was excessive and could generate an asset bubble, monetary policy could have been reverted long before it was. We review in figure 4.6 the data on money supply, as measured by simple-sum M1 and by the corresponding Divisia monetary aggregate, using the St. Louis Fed's Divisia MSI M1 aggregate for this period. In figure 4.7 the data at the M2 level of aggregation is provided. These figures plot deviations from the common trend shared by the two monetary indexes, with the deviation normalized to equal

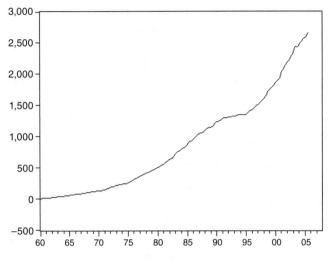

Figure 4.7
Deviation of the Divisia M2 monetary aggregate (MSI2) from the common trend shared by the simple-sum M2 monetary aggregate and its corresponding Divisia monetary aggregate. Units in billions of dollars, relative to 1960. The deviation was set equal to zero in 1960. Source: Board of Governors of the Federal Reserve System.

zero in 1960.[10] The Divisia monetary-aggregates' growth rates were increasingly higher than those of the simple sums, a trend that started most conspicuously in the late 1980s and continued until the end of the sample, available to us at the time of the study. In figure 4.6 the level of the MSI (Divisia) M1 index was about 500 billion dollars higher in 2005 than the common trend, relative to the difference that existed in 1960. While the deviation had increased by 100 billion dollars during the 20 years from 1960 to 1980, that deviation increased by an additional 400 billion dollars during the next 25 years from 1980 to 2005. In figure 4.7 the level of the MSI (Divisia) M2 index was about 2,500 billion dollars higher in 2005 than the common trend, relative to the difference in 1960.

---

10. I am indebted to Marcelle Chauvet for producing and supplying those two figures. The data she used are the data that were available at the time this plot was produced, and are the data that were online from the St. Louis Fed at the time this book was complete. The revised MSI data were not yet available at that time and had not yet been made public at the time of completion of this book. Judging the difference of the Divisia data relative to the common trend is consistent with the use of the idiosyncratic term in her work on figure 4.2, as is consistent with the modern state-space factor-analysis approach to time-series inference. While comparison with the common trend may seem excessively complicated to noneconomists, the approach has become standard in state-space econometric time series for reasons beyond the scope of this book.

While the deviation had increased by 500 billion dollars during the 20 years from 1960 to 1980, that deviation increased by an additional 2 *trillion dollars* during the next 25 years from 1980 to 2005. This rise in the difference between the simple-sum and Divisia indexes' growth rates could have distorted perceptions of monetary policy by inducing underestimation of the real amount of money available in the economy, as correctly measured by the Divisia index.[11] *The Federal Reserve could have been feeding the asset bubbles without the Fed's being aware of it.*

4.3.2 Subsequent to April 14, 2006

The evidence provided above suggests there may be some truth to the view that the recent bubble economy was accommodated by years of excessively expansionary monetary policy. Since all bubbles eventually burst, the subsequent problems may have been unavoidable. Whether or not that view is correct, it is interesting to ask what broke the bubble, even if it eventually would have burst anyway. Inspection of Fed data provides relevant information.

By conventional measures, the Fed has been easing its monetary policy stance by reducing its target value for the federal-funds interest rate from over 4 percent at the start of the crisis to the level of near zero within the Great Recession. Has the Fed thereby been engaging in stimulative actions to economic activity? Low interest rates do not an expansionary monetary policy make.[12]

It is helpful to illustrate the problem with a different central bank activity: sterilized exchange rate intervention. When the Fed decides to intervene in foreign exchange markets, its foreign desk swaps dollar-denominated assets for assets denominated in a foreign currency. Left unchecked at this point, the reserves of the US banking system (and the US money supply) would change, as would the market value of the federal-funds interest rate. To sterilize the foreign exchange transaction, the domestic desk of the Fed, in a subsequent operation, either

---

11. We have no way of knowing the pattern of the broader aggregates, M3 and L, since collection of both has been terminated by the Federal Reserve. Regarding M1, the method of aggregation is not the only problem. For example, there are the serious issues regarding sweeps. See, for example, Jones, Dutkowsky, and Elger (2005). But to the degree that policy may have been influenced by M1 growth, the relevant index to evaluate policy intent is the official Federal Reserve Board simple-sum index, unadjusted for sweeps or for other problems.

12. If you are not a native English speaker, this sentence structure may appear to be in error, as was pointed out to me by many of the manuscript's readers. But it is a common usage, which began in 1546 with John Heywood's *Proverbs*, including "one swallow does not a summer make." Earlier usages of that sentence structure appeared in Greek over 2,500 years ago in Aristophanes and Aesop.

Billions of dollars

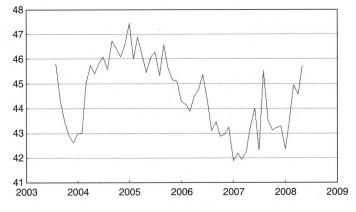

Figure 4.8
Total reserves until very recently, adjusted for changes in reserve requirements (TRARR).
Source: Board of Governors of the Federal Reserve System.

buys or sells US Treasuries in a magnitude sufficient to offset the impact
of the foreign desk's activity and thereby keeps the US money supply,
the federal-funds rate, and the reserves of the US banking system unchanged. On net, two things are accomplished by these offsetting transactions by the Fed's foreign and domestic desks: creating the symbolic
gesture of "doing something" about the dollar's value and exposing the
US taxpayer to potential losses, if subsequent changes in the exchange
rate cause losses in the market value of the foreign assets now on the
Fed's books.

Similarly much Fed activity early in the crisis, including its role in
bailouts, was sterilized and had little effect on bank reserves.[13] To illustrate the point, the Federal Reserve chart, reproduced in figure 4.8,
shows the total amount of reserves in the US banking system during
the five years leading up to and entering the crisis. Note that reserves—
the raw material from which loans and spending are created—were

---

13. I am indebted to Steve Hanke for the following further explanation, which he documented with a graph he provided to me. The Federal Reserve introduced the TAF ("term
auction facility") in December 2007. Any Fed credit created through the TAF, or through
other newly instituted means, was initially counteracted or "sterilized" by sales of US
Treasury securities, until mid-2008. Treasuries declined, while other Fed credit increased,
but the overall total remained pretty much unchanged until the Lehman Brothers bank-
ruptcy. The total assets of the Fed did not change significantly until after the Lehman bank-
ruptcy, and then they soared from around $920 billion to over $2,000 billion within a few
weeks. The Fed was already making substantial loans prior to the Lehman episode, but the
Fed's overall balance sheet was kept under control through the "sterilizing" sales of Treasuries. The intent was to prevent TAF loans from affecting the stance of monetary policy.

lower in mid-2008 than in August of 2003! But changes in the funds rate are usually interpreted in the media as the product of Fed policy actions. According to that view, if the funds rate declines, the decline must be the result of an expansionary monetary policy action. Missing from this analysis is the other side of the reserves market: those who demand reserves have some ability to affect the price—namely the federal-funds interest rate—at which reserves trade. Those demanders are banks, which see the demand for reserves rise and fall along with the demand for loans. When the demand for loans falls, the demand for reserves by banks declines. Hence the federal-funds rate can decline because of declines in the demands for loans and reserves, without the Fed taking any policy action. While a decline in the funds rate is usually interpreted as "evidence" of an easy policy stance, the real signal in the market may be the economy is weakening. As David Laidler, at the University of Western Ontario, has pointed out, this appears to be what happened in Japan during the 1990s. The Bank of Japan thought its monetary policy was "easy," because interest rates were low. The Japanese economy did not begin its recovery, after a decade of stagnation, until the quantity of money began to expand.

The Great Depression and the recent history of Japan's long stagnation reveal that low interest rates *per se* are ambiguous indicators of the relative ease of monetary policy. The missing ingredient is the flow of bank reserves, the ultimate source of credit from which all other lending ultimately grows. For better or for worse, intentional or unintentional, herein may lie the pin that pricked the recent bubble. But I need to qualify this conclusion. If Federal Reserve data were produced in a manner that permits clear interpretation of policy implications, I would not need to hedge on the interpretation of figure 4.8. As currently defined by the Fed, "total reserves" equal the sum of bank reserve balances and "service-related balances." While decline in bank reserve balances can be interpreted to be contractionary on the economy, the policy consequences of service-related balances is far less clear. As a result the policy implications of a decline in total reserves are ambiguous. You want to know what "service-related balances" are? Don't ask.[14]

---

14. Even Federal Reserve staff economists often become uncomfortable about such questions of accounting "details." If you are an advocate of the monetary base, the complications are even worse. The Board has three different definitions of the monetary base, depending on whether or not the data are adjusted for the effect of changes in statutory reserve requirements, and whether or not the data are seasonally adjusted. Oh, and of course, those messy service-related balances are also within the base that includes total reserves, not just bank reserve balances.

Billions of dollars

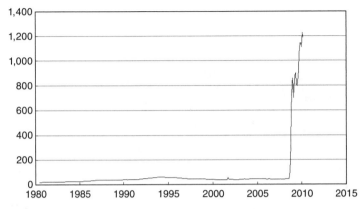

Figure 4.9
Total reserves including recent surge, adjusted for changes in reserve requirements (TRARR). Source: Board of Governors of the Federal Reserve System.

Subsequent to the Fed's publication of the discouraging figure 4.8 chart, which displays declining bank reserves from 2005 to 2008, an enormous surge of reserves was injected into the banking system. That injection operated through the Fed's lender-of-last-resort function at its discount window, as well as through the new credit facilities, such as the Primary Dealer Credit Facility and Term Auction Facility, and also through the long overdue payment of interest on reserves—an important new reform that provides an incentive for banks to increase their holdings of reserves.[15] See the Federal Reserve chart, reproduced in figure 4.9, regarding the astonishing surge in reserves. Although uncertainty in financial markets remained high, the dramatic injection of reserves by the Fed seemed encouraging.[16] *The official Federal Reserve Board data leave us with a feeling of ambiguity and uncertainty about monetary policy in recent years.*

In contrast, let us look at the Bank of England (BOE) data. As explained above, the BOE officially provides to the public the Divisia

---

15. There is no question that payment of interest on required reserves is long overdue, at least so long as reserve requirements continue to exist. The payment of interest on excess reserves is more controversial. Why should the federal government be paying interest to banks for not lending? Why was this incentive not-to-lend begun during a credit crunch, while the Fed was pumping reserves into the system with the opposite objective? To my way of thinking, the interest rate paid on involuntary required reserves should be higher than on excess reserves.
16. That surge was at least partially motivated by a shortage in Treasury bonds available to the Federal Reserve for sterilization.

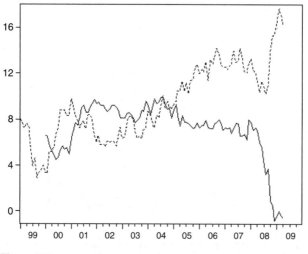

Figure 4.10
Percentage growth rate in M4 simple sum (solid line) and M4 Divisia aggregate (dashed line) for the United Kingdom

monetary aggregate for a broad aggregate, M4—exactly what a central bank should do. Since the BOE is one of the world's few central banks publishing Divisia money officially, looking at UK data is especially interesting. As the current recession developed, the BOE adopted a policy of "quantitative easing," focusing on expanding the supply of monetary services rather than lowering interest rates, which already were at very low levels. Following that change in policy, little evidence appeared of positive consequences. While this puzzled many, who were following the BOE's simple-sum monetary aggregates, figure 4.10 displays simple sum M4 and Divisia M4, both from the official BOE source. Clearly, Divisia M4 reflects a tightening of policy, rather than the intended loosening, implied by simple sum M4. For further details of this phenomenon, see Rayton and Pavlyk (2010). With these data officially available at the BOE and to the public, policy has adapted and the gap is closing.

4.3.3   The Revised MSI Data
As stated above, the Divisia monetary aggregates data for the United States, called the MSI (monetary services index) by the St. Louis Fed, were frozen at the start of the troubles in the real estate market in 2006 and remained frozen during the financial crisis and the Great Recession

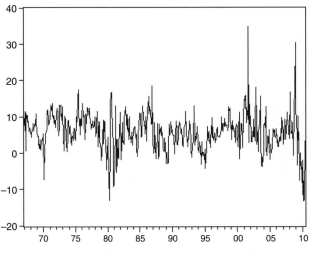

Figure 4.11
Annualized monthly growth rates of the United States: MSI Divisia over forty years for the broadest available monetary aggregate

with no MSI updates published during that period. The data revisions in MSI's Divisia index most certainly did not need to take five years to complete. At the time of delivery of this book's manuscript to MIT Press, the revised Divisia data were available within the St. Louis Fed, but withheld from the public. Nevertheless, graphs using the newly revised data were provided to me by Marcelle Chauvet, who had access to those data as a coauthor with the economists maintaining the data at the St. Louis Fed.[17]

What was made available to me by Professor Chauvet is in figure 4.11, exactly as provided to me for the entire time period during which the data were available. The figure plots the monthly growth rate of the Divisia monetary aggregate for the broadest available aggregate, called ALL, which is M2 plus institutional money market funds.[18] Notice the disturbing decline in money growth rate during the past two years.[19] This clearly demonstrates the importance of data on properly measured

---

17. Marcelle Chauvet at the University of California-Riverside produced and provided the plots to me with permission to include them in this book. She had access to the revised St. Louis Fed data for her research.
18. The discontinued Divisia M3 or Divisia L monetary aggregates would be more informative. The Federal Reserve's discontinuation of M3 data is particularly incomprehensible.
19. The growth rate is annualized to be the rate of growth per year during each month.

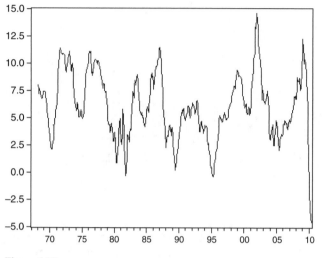

Figure 4.12
Year over year growth rates of MSI Divisia during forty years for the broadest available monetary aggregate

money growth, instead of interest rates. While interest rates were very low during those two years, money was very tight, as shown by Divisia growth—declining to negative levels. The money growth rate recently had declined to minus 10 percent per year, but seems to be recovering.[20] The last time this happened was during the Monetarist Experiment period leading up to the recession that followed. As we have seen in section 3.2 of chapter 3, that recession was produced by distortions in the target used by the Federal Reserve, as a result of simple-sum aggregation.

While monthly growth rates are informative about current policy, smoothing those data by computing "year-over-year" growth rates can also be useful. Instead of computing growth rate in monetary services during a month, the year-over-year growth rate computes the growth rate from the same month last year to the current month this year. Such year-over-year growth rates are commonly used in the retail business as a means of adjusting for seasonal effects. Figure 4.12 provides the year-over-year growth rates. While that figure does smooth some of

---

20. The precipitous decline to minus 10 percent is disappointing, in light of the enormous positive surge in reserves. There is no simple explanation for this failure of the normal transmission mechanism of monetary policy, but Federal Reserve payment of interest on excess reserves may have been a contributing factor.

the high-frequency oscillations, the resulting information about current monetary tightness is even more disturbing than the figure 4.11 monthly growth-rate information. *The monetary tightening, leading into the financial crisis and recession, is the largest and most precipitous that has occurred over the entire 42-year period for which the data were available—from 1968 to 2010!*

4.4   Conclusion

As the IMF, the BOE, the National Bank of Poland, the Bank of Israel, the Bank of Japan, and the ECB have moved to improve their data quality in recent years, and as the need for competently produced data has increased with the explosion in financial instrument complexity, it would be comforting to be able to say that Fed data quality and quantity, along with policy transparency, also have been increasing. Unfortunately, that is not what has happened. Data quality from the FRB has gotten worse—much worse. We have seen in this chapter that competently produced data provide evidence that Fed policy fueled the bubbles preceding the financial crisis. That best-practice data also show, after the real estate bubble broke, that monetary policy became more contractionary than indicated by interest rates, and thereby likely aggravated the severity of what followed.

Here are the facts. (1) Years of published research have demonstrated that Divisia M3, or even better the broader Divisia L, were the most informative monetary aggregate. By terminating publication of the severely distorted and thereby useless simple-sum M3 and L aggregates, the Federal Reserve has eliminated availability of many of the consolidated, seasonally adjusted, monthly component quantities and their interest rates needed to facilitate direct production of Divisia M3 and Divisia L. The Fed "threw the baby out with the bath water."[21] (2) The publication of checking-account deposits as post-sweep deposits, to cover up reserve requirement evasion, is a scandal. (3) The publication of negative nonborrowed reserves is an oxymoron. (4) While the St. Louis Fed computes Divisia monetary aggregates, using the remaining components still available from the Board, the Board does not supply those aggregates in its official releases. (5) Finally, the Divisia data contain disturbing explanatory power about repeated Fed policy

---

21. This is actually a German proverb, "das Kind mit dem Bade ausschütten," going back to 1512.

errors, leading up to and including the most recent. Transparency? Not a chance.

At this point, I have provided the book's empirical research along with an informal discussion of the relevant theory. Part II provides the formal economic theory for the benefit of the professionals having the relevant mathematical background. You now have the evidence. Should monetary policy be credited with producing the Great Moderation, such that the Great Moderation could reasonably have been viewed to be permanent? Do you see any reason to believe that monetary policy had improved during the Great Moderation? I find—none.

It is now time to conclude.

5 Summary and Conclusion

It is well to recall the warning of Josiah Stamp, once both director of the Bank of England and president of the Royal Statistical Society. The statistics governments relied on were, he observed, ultimately derived from the records of the village night watchman, "who just put down whatever he damn pleased."
—(John Kay, *The Financial Times*, April 5, 2011.)

Most of the puzzles and paradoxes that have evolved in the monetary economics literature, since the early 1970s, were produced by the simple-sum monetary aggregates, which are provided officially by many central banks, including the Federal Reserve. Those puzzles and paradoxes are resolved by use of proper aggregation-theoretic monetary aggregates. Except for the Bank of England's data, the National Bank of Poland's data, and Bank of Israel data, official central bank data provided to the public throughout the world have not significantly improved. Nevertheless, better data do exist, available only internally within some of those central banks, such as the Divisia monetary aggregates produced by the European Central Bank for the use of its Governing Council and the Bank of Japan Divisia data provided only to its executives. Some central banks make the better data available publicly, but only unofficially, such as the Divisia (MSI) money supply data provided by the St. Louis Federal Reserve Bank, but not included by the Federal Reserve Board in its official releases. As mentioned in section 2.6 of chapter 2, official or unofficial Divisia monetary aggregates data are available for over 37 countries, and that number of countries is increasing rapidly, as can be seen on the website of the Center for Financial Stability in New York City.

Researchers should be cautious about the use of official central bank data in research. This book documents the fact that the economics profession, financial firms, borrowers, lenders, and the central banks themselves have repeatedly been misled by poor central bank monetary data over the past half century. A primary objective of this book is to show that poor Fed data unnecessarily complicated private decision-making and interfered with the abilities of the private sector to recognize the extent of the systemic risk existing during the years leading up to the financial crisis and the Great Recession. A secondary objective is to provide evidence that the Fed itself has made repeated policy errors, best explained by use of its own poor data.

If you are looking for simple answers to difficult questions or support for a particular political ideology, you bought the wrong book. I wrote this book for those who want to deepen their understanding of what has happened, including how it evolved over thirty years, and why it happened. But here is one clear statement. The Federal Reserve Board has "gotten it wrong." In contrast, there is at least one major central bank that has "gotten it right": the Bank of England. This fact has been recognized by the IMF, in the most recent edition of its *Monetary and Financial Statistics: Compilation Guide*.[1] Remember what Paul Revere said on April 18, 1775: "The British are coming! The British are coming!"[2] You are wondering why the BOE, the National Bank of Poland, and the Bank of Israel are getting it right, while the FRB is getting it wrong? Excellent question. That is the right question to ask. Keep asking.

Books about the financial crisis and the Great Recession commonly display "20/20 hindsight." To avoid any such appearances, I have delayed until the end of part I the display of new data in figures 4.11 and 4.12. Those two figures can be viewed as providing a "punch line" to the book, although that punch line is far from funny. To grasp the message of the book, all of the figures need to be kept in mind. The other figures intentionally contain only the data which existed and had been published at the time period being discussed. None of those figures or data have been revised, updated, or extended for this book. I have reprinted those figures exactly as available and published at the time. The sole exceptions are figures 4.6 and 4.7, which have not previously been published, but are based on data available at the time. In short, this book presents the history as it occurred with whatever information was available at the time. No hindsight was needed to "get it right." Then why did the Fed "get it wrong"? If you have read this book carefully, you know the answer.

---

1. I am indebted to Steve Hanke for bringing the IMF's publication to my attention.
2. Historians now believe what he said was: "The regulars are coming. The regulars are coming."

Some commonly held views need to be rethought, since many such views were based on data disconnected from relevant theory. For example, the views on the Great Moderation should be reconsidered, at least relative to the current crisis and the role of Fed's monetary policy. I find no reason to believe the moderation in the business cycle during the two decades prior to the crisis had any appreciable connection with improved monetary policy, or that any such significant improvements in Fed monetary policy arose over that time period. In particular, I believe the increased risk-taking, which produced the recent financial crisis, resulted from a misperception of cyclical systemic risk, based on unreasonable expectations of Fed monetary policy. If the FRB had been supplying best-practice financial data, the truth would have been evident all along.

I do not take a position on what produced the Great Moderation or on whether it will reappear after the current crisis ends. But the likelihood of the current crisis did not figure into the expectations of those who now are viewed as having taken excessive risk. I am not comfortable with the widespread view that the source of the crisis is the "greed" of some of the country's most sophisticated people, many of whom were themselves victims of the misperceptions. I similarly do not believe Fed policy was intentionally and knowingly too expansionary during the evolution of the bubbles preceding the current crisis, or intentionally and knowingly excessively contractionary as the bubbles burst. The Federal Reserve was doing the best it could with the tools and inadequate data it was itself producing and providing, under very difficult circumstances. But I do find substantial evidence supporting the view that the risk misperceptions and poor decisions in the private and public sectors of the economy, including decisions at the Fed itself, were influenced by poor data, inconsistent with modern aggregation and index number theory.[3] In fact the published research papers this book cites and uses have been warning of those misperceptions throughout the more than two decades of the Great Moderation. The recent economic consequences are easily understood in that context.

When asked why some central banks, including the FRB, continue to produce and distribute data inconsistent with reputable index-number and aggregation theory, I never provide a direct answer to that question. Since I am not responsible for those central banks' "getting it wrong," I do not consider it appropriate for me to reply to such questions. But if you have read section 2.7 of chapter 2, you might have reached your own conclusions. If not, then you might be interested in the views of

---

3. Also see Chari, Christiano, and Kehoe (2008).

Belongia (2009), previously assistant vice president of the St. Louis Federal Reserve Bank and economic adviser to the bank's president. In that paper, he proposed the following explanation, which I paraphrase:

If the Fed produces data of poor quality, it accomplishes two things: (1) it cannot be held accountable for policy mistakes, because the world is more mysterious, and hence more decisions must be left to the Fed's "discretion." This has a long history in the "misbehaving" money-supply data; and (2) if the money-supply data are "misbehaving," they become less useful, if not useless, as a monitoring device on the Fed's actions. If you want to have maximum discretion to act according to your own ideology and escape accountability for the mistakes you make as a result of exercising that discretion, publishing scientifically misleading/unreliable/misbehaving data supports that objective.[4]

If Belongia's view seems puzzling, I strongly suggest that you read Hanke and Sekerke (2002), "A Shroud of Secrecy." Personally I feel no obligation to rationalize the Fed's data production, over which I have no control. But I will say this: Belongia's theory is not inconsistent with any of the observations provided in this book, most notably section 2.7 of chapter 2.

The book discusses what needs to be done to prevent these problems from arising again in the future. The source of the problems ultimately is to be found in a principal agent problem unresolved in the mechanism design of the Federal Reserve System. The decline in dissent in the years leading up to the financial crisis strongly correlates with the growing misperception of declining systemic risk.[5] Lack of dissent is not healthy in a democracy and fails to recognize the inherent principal agent problem. In addition, limited dissent increases the pressure on the central bank governors always to be right, since errors in central bank decisions have greatest negative impact on the economy, when public risk exposure is greatest, as when public confidence in policy is unrealistically high.

Dependence on the decisions of the Federal Reserve System is likely to grow in the future, because the prior 1951 "Accord," separating Fed

---

4. In paraphrasing this position in Belongia (2009), I also benefitted from private correspondence with him about his views, which are based on public choice theory.

5. For example, the SOMC did not meet during much of the time leading up to the Great Recession, despite the fact that the St. Louis Fed had frozen its Divisia monetary aggregates database and the FRB had stopped publishing its official M3 monetary aggregate, at a critical time leading up to the current crisis. But such complacency is now declining. One of the two founders of the SOMC, Allan Meltzer, in his testimony on July 8, 2009 before the Subcommittee on Monetary Policy, House Committee on Financial Services, was highly critical of Fed policy. For example, he stated that "I do not know of any clear examples in which the Federal Reserve acted in advance to head off a crisis or a series of banking or financial failures."

monetary policy from the Treasury's fiscal policy, has been compromised. The Federal Reserve and the Treasury now are coordinating monetary and fiscal policy. For example, during the financial crisis a transfer occurred of 500 billion dollars of Treasury securities to the balance sheet of the Federal Reserve. This book takes no positions on such matters but emphasizes the importance of having the highest possible levels of competence at the Federal Reserve, including high competence and professionalism in data production and the highest possible level of transparency, as the complexity of Fed policy and of financial instruments and markets continues to grow. Has the Federal Reserve been doing well in those areas? The answer to that question could not be clearer. The answer is—no.

Since I am not an expert in political science or economic mechanism design, I am not providing explicit recommendations for Federal Reserve System reform, with one exception. I propose that the Fed create its own data bureau, the Bureau of Financial Statistics (BFS), along the lines of the Labor Department's BLS or the Commerce Department's BEA. Since the information provided by such a bureau would best be provided as a public good, a private source could not adequately serve that purpose without access to funds from public or private grants. Such data bureaus value employment of professionals in economic measurement. Expertise in those areas currently is spread very thinly throughout the Federal Reserve System. If the Fed does not deal with this conspicuous need in a professional manner, then sooner or later an independent financial data institute should be authorized by the Congress to "get it right," on the ground that the Federal Reserve's failures in this area reflect a conflict of interests between the Fed's policy authority and the Fed's reporting of data.

If the needed financial data bureau is moved outside the Federal Reserve, a logical choice would be the Office of Financial Research (OFR), newly created by the Dodd–Frank Act. Clearly, the problems with the Fed's monitoring of systemic risk have not escaped the attention of the Congress, as evidenced by its creation of the OFR. But similar conflict of interests could be associated with the OFR's authority to recommend regulatory actions dealing with systemic risk. Hence, if macro data gathering and construction are moved to within the OFR, then an autonomous BFS, without policy recommendation authority, should be created within the OFR.

Creation of a BFS would be a step in the right direction, but would be far from a complete solution. With the growing complexity of financial instruments and markets, a need exists for growing availability of data and improving quality of data from all relevant sources. A need also exists for careful changes in regulations to deal with the growing complexities of financial markets, since information availability is likely never to be entirely adequate. This book has concentrated on the conspicuous relevance of Federal Reserve data. But many other information sources need to improve, both public and private, such as the FDIC, Moody's Investors Service, the SEC, and the NBER. A promising step in the right direction has recently been taken by creation of the independent, nonprofit Center for Financial Stability (CFS), through which I plan to be providing new data and analysis as Director of Advances in Monetary and Financial Measurement (AMFM). Domestic and international Divisia monetary aggregates data, plus eventually much more, will appear in the AMFM section of the CFS website at www.CenterforFinancialStability.org.

Macroeconomics, by its very definition, must make simplifying assumptions not inherent to microeconomic theory. But some oversimplifications, while making analysis and policy formulation much easier, can produce fundamental misperceptions. Such oversimplifications had a role in the excessive risk taking in recent years by some of the otherwise most sophisticated investors, lenders, and borrowers in the country. This book does not argue that anything is wrong with mainstream economic theory. On the contrary, a message of this book is that *not enough* mainstream economic theory was being used in policy design and data reporting in recent years.[6] In particular, aggregation theory, which is a specialized area of economic theory, should not be marginalized to avoid its mathematical complexity in applied economics research and central bank policy design.[7] Measurement is critically important in any science. In economics, the foundations of measurement are aggregation and index number theory. How else does one get from microeconomics to macroeconomics, if not by aggregation?

Divisia quantity indexes inherently are no more complicated or mysterious than the Laspeyres or Paasche price indexes known to everyone,

---

6. Austrian School economists are fond of criticizing the mainstream of the economics profession for "scientism," used as a negative term characterizing the conformity of views among many mainstream economists. The term blames that conformity on overuse of the scientific method. Yes, there is a problem of appeal to consensus views. But that phenomenon is not a result of excessive use of the scientific method. That conformity results from attempts to circumvent the scientific method and its logical discipline on research through oversimplification. The solution is more science, not less.

7. There is a deeper problem: nonlinearity. The complexities associated with aggregation and index number theory are associated with the nonlinearity that results when goods are not perfect substitutes. But linearization in macroeconomics extends into all areas of the field, not just into aggregation theory.

even if not by those names. In theory the only significant difference is that Laspeyres and Paasche index numbers provide first-order approximations, while Divisia (or Fisher-ideal) index numbers provide second-order approximations. The Labor Department's CPI is a Laspeyres index and is reported regularly on the national news. The Commerce Department's implicit price deflator was, for many years, a Paasche index, but has been converted to a Fisher-ideal index. Yet few users of the CPI or of the implicit price deflator concern themselves with the aggregation-theoretic foundations of Laspeyres, Paasche, or Fisher-ideal index numbers. Rather such users have become accustomed to treating each index as a statistical price aggregate with properties learned from experience, as is also the case with the National Accounts. When was the last time you heard about the complicated formula for the CPI reported on TV, when the percentage change in that inflation index was being reported?

If users were to become accustomed to the Divisia monetary aggregates and their historical behavior, the aggregation-theoretic source of the Divisia monetary aggregates would become a matter of interest only to specialists in aggregation theory. But until experience with the Divisia aggregates becomes widely distributed over potential users, the theoretical considerations presented in this book are likely to remain the most readily accessible source of interpretive information about the behavior of the Divisia monetary aggregates.

This book seeks to make a central point about the sources of the recent financial crisis and the Great Recession. Much has been written on that subject, and many explanations proposed. I agree with all of them. Most amount to accurate reporting of facts, such as observations about the explosion of fraud that evolved and grew during the years leading up to the crisis. I do not comment explicitly on the subject of "greed," since that word has no definition in the peer-reviewed journal literature in economics. A position on that subject would be outside my area of professional expertise. But most of the literature imputing the crisis to "greed" is closely related to the literature connecting the crisis with fraud; so greed may not warrant separate commentary, except among attorneys, who draw a clear distinction between the two words.

While the existing literature on the crisis primarily documents what happened, that literature also contains a degree of "name calling." Homeowners are accused of "greed" in buying into the housing bubble; banks and mortgage companies are accused of intentionally and irrationally deceiving borrowers in a manner ultimately undermining their own financial solvency; economists and the economics profession are accused of incompetence and selling out to the Federal Reserve; the SEC and the Division of Supervision and Regulation of the FRB are accused of negligence or worse; and investors along with Wall Street firms are accused of all sorts of irrational conspiracies, potentially against their own self-interests. Such "name calling" is outside the field of economics and therefore is not a suitable subject for this book. This book is based on the tools and expertise that exist within the economics profession.

While I do not disagree with any of the published facts on the explosion of fraud and do not comment on any of the "rock throwing," I do ask some questions. *Why did this all evolve?* Is fraud a new invention? Was greed a new discovery? Did the IQs and/or rationalities of homeowners, bankers, Wall Street professionals, and economists decline? Did the securitization of risk through credit default swaps (CDS) appear out of nowhere for no reason? The buyers of CDS were among the world's most sophisticated investors. Did they blindly fail to investigate the risks they were taking? The oldest Wall Street firms, which had survived the Great Depression, increased their leverage to heights never before seen in their histories, not even during the 1920s with far less regulation. Why did those firms "underprice" risk? Was it a conspiracy by the Trilateral Commission or the United Nations in the interests of "world government"? Of course, not!

The growth of the view that systemic risk had declined, as the Great Moderation progressed, was in proportion to the increase in private risk-taking. That increased private risk-taking was thereby viewed as prudent in a world of declining systemic risk. The source was a fundamental mistake—the widely held view that the Great Moderation, which had lasted for over two decades, was permanent and could be imputed to improved monetary policy. The view was wrong, and the Fed's lack of transparency had a great deal to do with that misperception, both within the economics profession and outside of it.

The economics profession has much to say about misperceptions. In economic theory the expectations of private economic agents are produced conditionally upon the information available to them (their "information sets"). *If the economy is damaged by ill-advised expectations, the first place to look is the available information on which the expectations were based.* If there are problems with that information, the cure is to remedy the source of the problem. If the cost of improving on information quality and availability exceeds the benefit, the remaining remedy is increased regulation. The objective of such regulation is to prevent behavior from drifting off in ways that would not have occurred, if consumers and firms had been better informed. This book documents that information supplied by the Fed has been inadequate and often inconsistent with best-practice economic measurement procedures—at a time when the need for more and better data was increasing with the growth in the complexity of securities and financial markets. Under those circumstances, more and better regulation was needed but was lacking. However, the involuntary constraints on behavior by increased regulation are usually not preferable to remedies inducing improved voluntary behavior, when remedies of the cause are available at reasonable cost.

It is tempting to conclude that the Federal Reserve has been producing inferior data simply by innocent mistake. But this is clearly not true. The Fed does not employ hundreds of stupid economists. The FRB's staff is fully aware of the fact that negative value of nonborrowed reserves is an oxymoron, making the Federal Reserve look silly. The Fed's staff is fully aware of the fact that publishing checking account data post-sweeps, to cover up reserve-requirement evasion by banks, grossly underestimates checking account services and severely distorts M1. The Federal Reserve's staff is fully aware of my Divisia monetary aggregates, since I first published the relevant theory, while I was employed on the Board's staff. The Board's staff also is fully aware of the fact that the St. Louis Fed is "doing it right" with its MSI Divisia aggregates, while the Board's staff continues to "do it wrong."

Do the economists on the Federal Reserve Board's staff not know they are "doing it wrong"? Of course, they know. They correctly use aggregation theory and index number to produce their industrial production index. So why are those economists producing such poor financial data in flagrant violation of basic principles of index number theory, aggregation theory, and elementary accounting? They are rationally pursuing their bureaucracies' self-interests. Organizations subject to oversight often, and rationally, do the same. Policy makers who care about appearing successful have an interest in limiting and controlling the data that reflect on their performance. Belongia's (2009) forcefully stated views are highly relevant in this regard. An obvious conflict of interests exists in Federal Reserve production of data. Fed policy failures are periodically inevitable in its complex role within the economy. Why should the Fed wish to make it easier for the Congress, the public, and the economics profession to criticize the Fed for those failures?

An element of human nature leads to confirmation bias. Even well-intentioned policy makers might miss evidence at odds with their world views. If you were in a high level position on the Board's staff, you would do the same. Economic mechanism design, political-science formal theory, public choice, and institutional economics, which recognize the consequences of such problems, have become sophisticated fields. Incentive compatibility problems are not exclusive to organizations subject to public oversight. Consider the way in which Enron's management treated its stockholders. Establishing incentive compatibility in large organizations is far from trivial. Experts in mechanism design should look carefully at the differences in the institutional structures of the Federal Reserve System, the Bank of England, the National Bank of Poland, the Bank of Israel, the International Monetary Fund, the Bank of Japan, and the European Central Bank. The differences among those institutions' performances in data production and transparency are not random events, and the sources of those differences need to be understood.

Leading up to the financial crisis, the decisions of many homeowners, bankers, economists, and investors were based on misperceptions about systemic risk. It is not my intention to suggest that each of them was reading FRB data releases and was directly misled by distorted or inadequate Fed data. No professional economist would view the effects of information "shocks" to operate in that manner. Undoubtedly, the vast majority of economic agents, harmed by the financial crisis and the Great Recession, were not personally following that data, and many such consumers and firms likely did not even know the data existed. In economic theory, the economic system is highly sensitive to information shocks, which transmit themselves throughout the economy in complex manners, involving markets, the media, and the publications of economists. In fact, when incomplete contingent claims markets exist, as obviously always is the case, even entirely irrelevant information shocks are capable of heavily impacting the economic system's dynamics. Such irrelevant shocks are called "sunspots" in modern economic theory.[8]

As Barnett and Chauvet (2011a) found and this book summarizes in figure 4.2, most recessions in the past fifty years were preceded by more contractionary monetary policy than was indicated by the official simple-sum monetary aggregates. Monetary aggregates produced in accordance with reputable economic measurement practices grew at rates generally lower than the growth rates of the Fed's official monetary aggregates prior to those recessions, but at higher rates than the official aggregates since the mid-1980s. Monetary policy was more contractionary than likely intended before the 2001 recession and more expansionary

---

8. See, for example, Cass and Shell (1983). There is a related economics literature on self-fulfilling prophecies.

than likely intended during the subsequent recovery, thereby feeding the bubbles leading to the financial crisis. This book provides a series of examples, in chronological order, of policy errors and misperceptions associated with the Fed's monetary data. This sequence of examples paints a grim picture. The most damaging consequences of the bad data were the growing misperceptions about the abilities of the Federal Reserve, "the Maestro," and the "Greenspan put." While supplying bad data may have been in the best interests of the Federal Reserve, the resulting confusion and poorly informed decision-making were not in the public interest, and the world has been paying a heavy price.

Leading up to the recent financial crisis and Great Recession, low-quality and inadequate Federal Reserve data not only fed the risk misperceptions of the public, the financial industry, and the economics profession but also likely contributed to policy errors by the Federal Reserve itself. The official data underestimated the degree to which the Federal Reserve was feeding the bubbles leading up to the financial crisis. Then as the crisis began, the liquidity of the economy crashed to negative rates of flow, as the long suppressed Divisia aggregate data now show. That precipitous liquidity decline is the most extreme during the forty years for which the Divisia data are available. That monetary crash is undoubtedly the reason the financial crisis turned into the Great Recession and is a clear indication of how deceptive interest rate information can be. Interest rates during that period were down to near zero. Those low interest rates and the increase in interest-yielding bank reserves were widely interpreted as reflecting loose, expansionary monetary policy, while the Divisia data were correctly showing the exact opposite. Was there an easily available policy solution that could have been used by the Federal Reserve? Maybe yes. Maybe no. But regardless of your views on that subject, one thing is clear. The public had the right to know.

At this point, I wish to repeat a statement that appears in section 2.3 of chapter 2. I am not a dogmatic advocate of any "ism," whether it be monetarism, new-monetarism, Keynesianism, new-Keynesianism, post-Keynesianism, Austrianism, institutionalism, or Marxism.[9] Controversy exists within the profession about the role money should play in policy. Should money be a target, a long-run anchor, or an indicator? It is not the purpose of this book to weigh in on those matters. But this is clear: money matters! I do not know of a single central bank

---

9. I fully agree with monetarists that the money supply provides important information about the economy. But unlike monetarists, I have never published a proposal for any particular monetary rule. The economy is an extraordinarily complex dynamical system, and I do not presume to advocate an optimal approach to monetary policy.

anywhere in the world that does not compute and publish at least one monetary aggregate. Is this just a coincidence? In the United States, Section 2a of the Federal Reserve Act is unambiguous about the importance of central-bank money and credit creation, as quoted in section 2.3 of chapter 2.

What about hyperinflation, periodically appearing when a country's national debt becomes so high that regular taxation is inadequate to pay the interest on the debt? Interest rates are extremely high during hyperinflations, since no one then is willing to lend money except at extremely high interest rates. Suppose that no one is willing to lend money denominated in the domestic currency. How would you set an interest rate to end a hyperinflation? A million percent? A hundred million percent? Does anyone seriously believe the seigniorage tax is irrelevant to explaining such hyperinflations? The seigniorage tax is the "printing of money," often to make interest payments on the national debt. A large literature exists on intentional, seigniorage-maximizing hyperinflations, the ultimate "taxation without representation."[10] The tax base for the seigniorage tax is real money balances. Would you believe that Greece's financial crisis is unrelated to loss of the drachma, which Greece was able to "print," in favor of the euro, which is not under the country's control?[11]

This book does not presume to advocate a monetary policy rule, approach, or design. I am an advocate of professional scientific standards for economic measurement. The economy responds strongly to the information available to private economic agents, governmental policy makers, and academic researchers. With the increasing sophistication of financial markets and securities, a need exists for more and better information. Inadequate, distorted, and fraudulent information are damaging to the economy as a whole, not just to those who personally make direct use of that information. We all have now witnessed the shockingly dark economic consequences of "getting it wrong."

Indeed this is the Information Age. The sooner that fact is fully recognized—and prioritized—the better off we all will be.

---

10. "No taxation without representation" was, of course, a rallying cry associated with the origins of the American Revolution. The slogan was coined by Reverend Jonathan Mayhew in a sermon in Boston in 1750. In 1765, James Otis in Boston was famously associated with the phrase, "taxation without representation is tyranny." But the sentiment had its origins in England itself during the English Civil War of 1642 to 1651.

11. See, for example, Easterly, Mauro, and Schimdt-Hebbel (1995).

II Mathematical Appendixes

A   Monetary Aggregation Theory under Perfect Certainty

This appendix contains the theory that is central to the research that produced part I of this book. The other appendixes provide extensions to the fundamental theory contained in this primary appendix.

A.1   Introduction

The economic statistics that the government issues every week should come with a warning sticker: User beware. In the midst of the greatest information explosion in history, the government is pumping out a stream of statistics that are nothing but myths and misinformation.

—Michael J. Mandel, "The Real Truth about the Economy: Are Government Statistics So Much Pulp Fiction? Take a Look," *Business Week* cover story, November 7, 1994, pp. 110–18

In recent decades there has been a resurgence of interest in index-number theory, resulting from discoveries that the properties of index numbers can be directly related to the properties of the underlying aggregator functions that they represent. The underlying functions—production functions and utility functions—are the building blocks of economic theory, and the study of relationships among these functions and index-number formulas has been referred to by Samuelson and Swamy (1974) as the economic theory of index numbers.

The use of economic index-number theory was introduced into monetary theory by Barnett (1980a, 1981a, b). His merger of economic index-number theory with monetary theory was based on the use of Diewert's unifying approach to producing "superlative" approximations to the exact aggregates from consumer demand theory, along with the earlier approaches of Divisia (1925, 1926a, b) and Theil (1967).

As a result Barnett's approach produces a Diewert-superlative measure of the monetary services flow perceived to be received by consumers from their monetary asset portfolio. However, aggregation and index-number theory are highly developed in production theory as well as in consumer demand theory. Substantial literatures exist on aggregation over factor inputs demanded by firms, aggregation over multiple product outputs produced by firms, and aggregation over individual firms and consumers. In addition substantial literatures exist on exact measurement of value added by firms and of technical change by firms. All of these literatures are potentially relevant to closing a cleared money market in an exact aggregation-theoretic monetary aggregate. This appendix establishes the relationship between monetary theory and all of the above-listed areas of aggregation and index-number theory. These results are relevant to building and using theoretical or empirical macroeconomic models possessing an aggregated money market.

The demand for money is both by firms and consumers. Hence we present the aggregation and index-number theory relevant to demand by firms as well as by consumers. The supply of money is partially produced by financial intermediaries. As a result we present the aggregation and index-number theory relevant to aggregation over the multiple outputs of such financial firms. Because there has been considerable technological change in the banking industry in recent years, a theory relevant to measuring technological change within a financial firm is presented. In addition, because the impact of changes in outside money on the economy is likely to depend on value added by financial intermediaries, the theoretical and approximation approaches relevant to measuring value added by such firms are also presented.

In this appendix the models of monetary asset demand by consumers and by firms, as well as the model of monetary asset supply by financial intermediaries, are based on commonly used neoclassical formulations. In addition the results in the aggregation and index-number theories used in this appendix are well established and widely known in their respective literatures. Besides surveying the relevant results from those literatures, the primary objective of this appendix is algebraically to formulate and manipulate the presented theories of monetary consumption, factor demand, and production in a manner that provides immediate direct relevancy to the existing results in the literatures on aggregation and index-number theory. A primary source for the theory in this appendix is Barnett (1987).

Because a government sector is not introduced, the financial firm, the consumer, and the manufacturing firm modeled herein are not embedded in a closed macroeconomic model. The reason is that the results surveyed and developed here are applicable to macroeconomic modeling, regardless of the nature of the model's transmission mechanism or of any policy implications that might be suggested by a full macroeconomic model. There are as many ways to embed these results into a macroeconomic model as there are ways to build a macroeconomic model.

This appendix deals with demand and supply for flows, as is normal in economic general equilibrium theory. But in some cases, wealth effects are relevant. In such cases, the discounted present value of flows becomes relevant. Appendix B provides those theoretical results. Also this appendix does not consider multilateral aggregation, as would be needed in a multicountry economic union. That extension is provided in appendix C. Appendixes A, B, and C assume perfect certainty or risk neutrality regarding contemporaneous interest rates. Appendix D extends to the case of risk aversion, when interest rates paid during the current period are not realized until the end of the period, so are random at the start of the period, at which the portfolio allocation decision is made.

In microeconomics the famous "diamonds versus water" paradox is in almost all textbooks, but nevertheless is often a source of misunderstanding. Since economic aggregation and index-number theories are derived from neoclassical microeconomics, analogous misunderstands sometimes appear from people not familiar with the relevant theory provided in these appendixes. Examples of those misunderstandings and the correct interpretations are provided in appendix E.

A.2   Consumer Demand for Monetary Assets

A.2.1   Finite Planning Horizon
The following variables are used in consumer c's decision problem, formulated in period t for periods $t, t + 1, \ldots, s, \ldots, t + T$, where T is the number of periods in the consumer's planning horizon:

x_s = vector of planned consumption of goods and services during period s;

p_s = vector of goods' and services' expected prices and of durable goods' expected rental prices during period s;

$\mathbf{m}_s$ = vector of planned real balances of monetary assets during period s;

$\mathbf{r}_s$ = vector of expected nominal holding period yields of monetary assets;

A_s = planned holdings of the benchmark asset during period s;

R_s = expected one-period holding yield on the benchmark asset during period s;

L_s = planned labor supply during period s;

$\bar{L}_t = k - L_s$ = planned leisure demand during period s, where k = total hours available per period;

w_s = the expected wage rate during period s; and

I_s = other expected income (government transfer payments, profits of owned firms, etc.) during period s.

The benchmark asset is defined to provide no services other than its yield R_s, which motivates holding of the asset solely as a means of accumulating wealth. As a result, R_s is the maximum expected holding period yield in the economy in period s, and the benchmark asset is held to transfer wealth between multiperiod planning horizons, rather than to provide liquidity or other services.

The consumer's intertemporal utility function in period t is[1]

$$u_t = u_t(\mathbf{m}_t, \ldots, \mathbf{m}_{t+T}; \bar{L}_t, \ldots, \bar{L}_{t+T}; \mathbf{x}_t, \ldots, \mathbf{x}_{t+T}; A_{t+T}). \tag{A.1}$$

We assume that u_t is blockwise weakly separable as follows:

$$u_t = U_t(u(\mathbf{m}_t), u_{t+1}(\mathbf{m}_{t+1}), \ldots, u_{t+T}(\mathbf{m}_{t+T}); \bar{L}_t, \ldots, \bar{L}_{t+T};$$

$$v(\mathbf{x}_t), v_{t+1}(\mathbf{x}_{t+1}), \ldots, v_{t+T}(\mathbf{x}_{t+T}); A_{t+T}). \tag{A.2}$$

The functions $u, u_{t+1}, \ldots, u_{t+T}, v, v_{t+1}, \ldots, v_{t+T}$ are called category subutility functions. Then, dual to the functions v and $v_s (s = t+1, \ldots, t+T)$, there exist current and planned true cost of living indexes, p_t^* and $p_s^* (s = t+1, \ldots, t+T)$, that can be used to deflate nominal to real values.

---

1. Regarding the existence of this derived utility function into which the consumer's transactions technology has been absorbed, see Arrow and Hahn (1971), Phlips and Spinnewyn (1982), and Samuelson and Sato (1984). In the general case, the derived utility function containing money could also include prices of consumer goods. Additional assumptions, which are implicitly made here, limit that price dependency to the price level deflator used to deflate nominal to real balances of money in the derived utility function. To my knowledge, no one has ever empirically investigated dependency of the derived utility function on relative prices of consumer goods.

Assuming continuous replanning at each t, the consumer's decision is to choose $(\mathbf{m}_t, \ldots, \mathbf{m}_{t+T}, \bar{L}_t, \ldots, \bar{L}_{t+T}; \mathbf{x}_t, \ldots, \mathbf{x}_{t+T}; A_{t+T})$ to maximize u_t subject to the $T + 1$ budget constraints

$$\mathbf{p}_s'\mathbf{x}_s = w_s L_s + \sum_{i=1}^{n}[(1 + r_{i,s-1})p_{s-1}^* m_{i,s-1} - p_s^* m_{is}]$$

$$+ [(1 + R_{s-1})p_{s-1}^* A_{s-1} - p_s^* A_s] + I_s \tag{A.3}$$

for $s = t, t + 1, \ldots, t + T$ and with $\bar{L}_s = k - L_s$. The consumer's initial nominal wealth in period t is $\sum_{i=1}^{n}(1 + r_{i,t-1})p_{t-1}^* m_{i,t-1} + (1 + R_{t-1})p_{t-1}^* A_{t-1}$.

Let $(\mathbf{m}_t^*, \ldots, \mathbf{m}_{t+T}^*, \bar{L}_t^*, \ldots, \bar{L}_{t+T}^*; \mathbf{x}_t^*, \ldots, \mathbf{x}_{t+T}^*; A_{t+T}^*)$ be the solution to that constrained optimization problem. Following the procedures in Barnett (1980a, 1981a), it then can be shown that $\mathbf{m}_t^*$ is also the solution for $\mathbf{m}_t$ to the following current period conditional decision:

maximize $u(\mathbf{m}_t)$ subject to $\boldsymbol{\pi}_t'\mathbf{m}_t = y_t$, $\tag{A.4}$

where $\boldsymbol{\pi}_t = (\pi_{1t}, \ldots, \pi_{nt})'$ is the vector of monetary asset nominal user costs,

$$\pi_{it} = \frac{p_t^*(R_t - r_{it})}{1 + R_t}, \tag{A.5}$$

and $y_t = \boldsymbol{\pi}_t'\mathbf{m}_t^*$. We could convert from the nominal user costs, $\boldsymbol{\pi}_t$, to the real user costs, $\boldsymbol{\pi}_t^*$, by dividing the budget constraint of decision (A.4) by p_t^* to obtain

maximize $u(\mathbf{m}_t)$ subject to $\boldsymbol{\pi}_t^{*'}\mathbf{m}_t = y_t^*$, $\tag{A.6}$

where $y_t^* = y_t / p_t^*$ and $\boldsymbol{\pi}_t^* = \boldsymbol{\pi}_t / p_t^*$. The function u is assumed to be monotonically increasing and strictly concave. Decision problem (A.6) is in the form of a conventional consumer decision problem, and hence the literature on aggregation theory and index-number theory for consumers is immediately available.

A.2.2 Infinite Planning Horizon
In this section, the consumer's decision problem is reformulated using an infinite planning horizon. The same current-period conditional decision problem (A.6) is acquired. As a result the existing literature on aggregation and index-number theory will remain relevant.

Replace the finite planning horizon intertemporal utility function (A.2) by the infinite horizon intertemporally separable utility function

$$u_t = \sum_{s=t}^{\infty} \left(\frac{1}{1+\xi} \right)^{s-t} U(u(\mathbf{m}_s), \bar{L}_s, \mathbf{x}_s), \tag{A.7}$$

where ξ is the consumer's subjective rate of time preference, assumed to be constant to assure Strotz consistent planning.[2] The consumer selects the sequence $(\mathbf{m}_s, \bar{L}_s, \mathbf{x}_s), s = t, t+1, \ldots$, to maximize (A.7) subject to the sequence of constraints (3) for $s = t, t+1, \ldots$. The upper limit $t + T$ to the planning horizon no longer exists. Again R_s must exceed r_{is} for all i, because A_s is not in the utility function and hence would not otherwise be held.

Construct the Lagrangian, Λ, and differentiate with respect to $A_t, \mathbf{x}_t$, and $\mathbf{m}_t$ to acquire the following first-order conditions for constrained maximization at t:

$$\frac{\partial \Lambda}{\partial A_t} = -\lambda_t + \lambda_{t+1}(1 + R_t) = 0, \tag{A.8}$$

$$\frac{\partial \Lambda}{\partial x_{it}} = \frac{\partial U}{\partial x_{it}} - \lambda_t p_{it} = 0, \tag{A.9}$$

$$\frac{\partial \Lambda}{\partial m_{it}} = \frac{\partial U}{\partial m_{it}} - \lambda_t p_i^* + \lambda_{t+1} p_i^*(1 + r_{it}) = 0, \tag{A.10}$$

where λ_t and λ_{t+1} are two of the Lagrange multipliers in the sequence $(\lambda_t, \lambda_{t+1}, \lambda_{t+2}, \ldots)$ of Lagrange multipliers in Λ. Substituting (A.8) into (A.10) to eliminate λ_{t+1}, we obtain

$$\frac{\partial U}{\partial m_{it}} = \lambda_t \pi_{it}, \tag{A.11}$$

where π_{it} is as in (A.5).

Hence, from (A.11), we have that

$$\frac{\partial U / \partial m_{it}}{\partial U / \partial m_{jt}} = \frac{\pi_{it}}{\pi_{jt}}, \tag{A.12}$$

or

$$\frac{\partial U / \partial m_{it}}{\partial U / \partial m_{jt}} = \frac{\pi_{it}^*}{\pi_{jt}^*}. \tag{A.13}$$

---

2. The same current-period conditional decision would result, if ξ were not constant. As a result Strotz consistency produces no loss in generality in these aggregation-theoretic results. If intertemporal separability were not assumed, expectations could be endogenized through rational expectations, as in Attfield and Browning (1985).

Now for $s = t, t + 1, \ldots$, let $(\mathbf{m}_s^*, \overline{L}_s^*, \mathbf{x}_s^*)$ maximize (A.7) subject to (A.3), and let

$$y_t^* = \boldsymbol{\pi}_t^{*\prime} \mathbf{m}_t^*. \tag{A.14}$$

Then the first-order conditions for the solution to problem (A.6) are (A.13) and (A.14). Hence $\mathbf{m}_s^*$ solves problem (A.6). As a result we again find that we can use the conventional neoclassical decision (A.6), and thereby all of the existing literature on aggregation over goods consumed.

A.2.3 Income Taxes

The results in sections A.2.1 and A.2.2 do not explicitly incorporate taxes. Nevertheless all of those results would remain valid, if we convert to after-tax yields as follows. Let τ_t be the consumer's marginal tax rate on interest earned from the benchmark asset, and let τ_{it} be the consumer's marginal tax rate on monetary asset i. Then the nominal user cost (A.5) becomes

$$\pi_{it} = p_t^* \frac{R_t(1 - \tau_t) - r_{it}(1 - \tau_{it})}{1 + R_t(1 - \tau_t)}, \tag{A.5a}$$

which in turn becomes

$$\pi_{it} = p_t^* \frac{(R_t - r_{it})(1 - \tau_{it})}{1 + R_t(1 - \tau_t)}, \tag{A.5b}$$

if $\tau_{it} = \tau_t$ for all i, so that all marginal tax rates are equal.

In the latter case, we can return to using (A.5) instead of (A.5b) to acquire $\pi_{it}^* = \pi_{it} / p_t^*$, when $\boldsymbol{\pi}_t^*$ is to be used in decision (A.6). To do so, we need only replace y_t^* by $[1 + R_t(1 - \tau_t)]y_t^* / [(1 - \tau_t)(1 + R_t)]$, since we then would only have multiplied both sides of the budget constraint of (A.6) by $[1 + R_t(1 - \tau_t)] / [(1 - \tau_t)(1 + R_t)]$.

A.3 Supply of Monetary Assets by Financial Intermediaries

Monetary assets are generally either primary securities, such as currency or Treasury bills, or assets produced through the financial intermediation of financial firms. In this section, we develop a model of production by financial intermediaries under perfect certainty. It will be shown that the model can be manipulated into the conventional neoclassical form of production by a multiproduct firm. As a result the existing literature on output aggregation becomes immediately applicable to the construction of a neoclassical money supply function for aggregated money.

Consider a financial intermediary that makes only one kind of loan, yielding R_t, and produces (through financial intermediation) a vector μ_t of real balances of monetary assets. The firm uses c_t real units of excess reserves, in the form of currency, as a factor of production in producing μ_t during period t. We treat monetary assets produced by financial intermediation to be outputs of financial intermediaries, and we thereby implicitly assume that the user costs of such assets are positive.[3]

Real balances such as μ_t and c_t are defined to equal nominal balances divided by p_t^*, which was defined in section A.2.1 of this appendix. The firm also uses the vector L_t of labor quantities and the vector z_t of other factor quantities. The vector of reserve requirements is k_t, where k_{it} is the reserve requirement applicable to μ_{it} and $0 \le k_{it} \le 1$ for all i.

The firm's efficient production technology is defined by the transformation function $F(\mu_t, z_t, L_t, c_t; k_t) = 0$. The firm's technology can be equivalently defined by its efficient production set (also called the production possibility efficient set)

$$S(k_t) = \{(\mu_t, z_t, L_t, c_t) = 0 : F(\mu_t, z_t, L_t, c_t; k_t) = 0\} \tag{A.15}$$

or by its production correspondence F, defined such that

$$G(z_t, L_t, c_t; k_t) = \{\mu_t \ge 0 : (\mu_t, z_t, L_t, c_t) \in S(k_t)\}. \tag{A.16}$$

If $(z_t, L_t) = 0$, then no financial intermediation takes place, no value added exists, and no loans are made. In short, in that case the firm is acting as a vault, so that all of $\sum_i p_t^* \mu_{it}$ is reserves, and hence excess reserves are $p_t^* c_t = \sum_i \mu_{it}(1 - k_{it}) p_t^*$.

The transformation function, F, is strictly quasiconvex in (μ_t, z_t, L_t, c_t). In addition $\partial F / \partial L_{it} < 0, \partial F / \partial z_{it} < 0$, and $\partial F / \partial c_t < 0$ because L_t, z_t, and c_t are inputs. Conversely, $\partial F / \partial \mu_{it} > 0$ because μ_t are outputs. If the user cost of μ_{it} were negative for some $i = j$, then $\partial F / \partial \mu_{jt}$ would become nonpositive because μ_{jt} would become an input. In that probably rare case, μ_{jt} could be removed from μ_t and treated as a component of z_t. All factors z_t are purchased at the start of period t for use during period t, and the firm must pay for those factors at the start of the period. The

---

3. Hancock (1985, 1986) postulates that some such assets can be inputs to financial intermediaries, if the corresponding user costs are negative. That possibility is not excluded by the formulation presented below, although in this appendix the probably unusual case of negative user costs is not explicitly discussed.

exception is labor, L_t, which receives its wages at the end of the period t for labor quantities supplied to the firm during period t. Interest on produced monetary assets μ_t is paid at the end of the period, and interest on loans outstanding during period t is received at the end of period t.

Because our model contains only one kind of primary market loan yielding R_t, the federal funds rate must therefore also equal R_t. However, the discount rate, being regulated, can differ from R_t. Let R_t^d be the discount rate during period t, and define $\bar{R}_t = \min\{R_t, R_t^d\}$. We assume that required reserves are never borrowed from the Federal Reserve, but could be borrowed in the federal funds market. The assumption of "perfect moral suasion" easily could be removed. Excess reserves can be borrowed from either source. As a result, if $R_t^d < R_t$, then all excess reserves will be borrowed from the Federal Reserve, and there are no free reserves. If $R_t^d > R_t$, then there is no borrowing from the Federal Reserve, and free reserves equal excess reserves. In addition, in that case the percentage of excess reserves borrowed from the federal funds market is indeterminate because the opportunity cost of not lending free reserves at R_t is equal to the cost of borrowing free reserves from the federal funds market at R_t. For the same reason, the percentage of required reserves borrowed in the federal funds market is indeterminate in both cases. If $R_t^d = R_t$, then all of the following are indeterminate: the percentage of required reserves or of excess reserves borrowed in the federal funds market, the percentage of excess reserves borrowed from the Federal Reserve, and the level of free reserves.

We now proceed to determine the level of variable profits at the end of period t. Suppose that $R_t = R_t^d$, so that $\bar{R}_t = R_t$. Then variable revenue from loans is

$$\left(\sum_i \mu_{it} p_t^* - \sum_i k_{it} \mu_{it} p_t^* - c_t p_t^* - \mathbf{q}_t' \mathbf{z}_t \right) R_t, \tag{A.17}$$

where $\mathbf{q}_t$ is the price of the factors, $\mathbf{z}_t$. If z_{it} is a durable variable factor, then q_{it} is its user cost. However, if $R_t > R_t^d$, so that $\bar{R}_t = R_t^d$, then variable revenue from loans is

$$\left(\sum_i \mu_{it} p_t^* - \sum_i k_{it} \mu_{it} p_t^* - \mathbf{q}_t' \mathbf{z}_t \right) R_t - c_t p_t^* R_t^d. \tag{A.18}$$

Hence, in either case, variable revenue from loans is

$$\left[\sum_i (1 - k_{it}) \mu_{it} p_t^* - c_t p_t^* - \mathbf{q}_t' \mathbf{z}_t \right] R_t + c_t p_t^* (R_t - \bar{R}_t). \tag{A.19}$$

Variable cost that must be paid out of variable revenue is

$$\sum_i \mu_{it} p_t^* \rho_{it} + \mathbf{q}_t' \mathbf{z}_t + \mathbf{w}_t' \mathbf{L}_t, \tag{A.20}$$

where $\mathbf{w}_t$ is the vector of wage rates corresponding to labor quantities, $\mathbf{L}_t$, and ρ_t is the vector of yields paid by the firm on μ_t. Observe that $\mathbf{w}_t' \mathbf{L}_t$ appears in (A.20), but not in (A.19), because $\mathbf{w}_t' \mathbf{L}_t$ is not paid until the end of the period and therefore is not subtracted out of loan quantities placed at the beginning of the period.

Variable profit received at the end of period t is acquired by subtracting (A.20) from (A.19). Observe that fixed factors, including financial capital, are not relevant to the determination of variable profit. If we then divide by $1 + R_t$ in order to discount variable profits to the beginning of period t, we find that the present value of period t variable profits is

$$P(\mu_t, \mathbf{z}_t, \mathbf{L}_t, c_t; p_t^*, \mathbf{q}_t, R_t, R_t^d, \rho_t, \mathbf{w}_t, \mathbf{k}_t) = \frac{\mu_t' \gamma_t - \mathbf{q}_t' \mathbf{z}_t - \mathbf{L}_t' \mathbf{w}_t}{1 + R_t} - \gamma_{ot} c_t, \tag{A.21}$$

where the nominal user-cost price of produced monetary asset μ_{it} is

$$\gamma_{it} = p_t^* \frac{(1 - k_{it}) R_t - \rho_{it}}{1 + R_t} \tag{A.22}$$

and the nominal user cost price of excess reserves is

$$\gamma_{ot} = p_t^* \frac{\overline{R}_t}{1 + R_t}. \tag{A.23}$$

The corresponding real user costs are γ_t / p_t^* and γ_{ot} / p_t^*.[4]

If we write the vector of all variable factor quantities as $\alpha_t = (\mathbf{z}_t', \mathbf{L}_t', c_t)'$ and the vector of corresponding factor prices as $\beta_t = (\mathbf{q}_t', \mathbf{w}_t' / (1 + R_t), \gamma_{ot})'$, it becomes evident that variable profits take the conventional form

$$P_t = \mu_t' \gamma_t - \alpha_t' \beta_t, \tag{A.24}$$

and the firm's variable profit maximization problem takes the conventional form of selecting $(\mu_t, \alpha_t) \in S(\mathbf{k}_t)$ to maximize (A.24). Hence the existing literature on output aggregation for multiproduct firms becomes immediately applicable to aggregation over the produced

---

4. Observe that those derived user-cost formulas, after some manipulation, become equivalent to those used by Hancock (1985, 1986), although her method of measuring the discount rate is not consistent with the theory above that produced results (A.22) and (A.23). She also incorporated explicit transactions costs into the formula.

monetary assets μ_t and to measuring value-added and technological change in financial intermediation.

A.3.1 Properties of the Model

Observe that variable revenue can be written in the form

$$\mu_t' \gamma_t = \mu_t' \pi_t^b - \frac{p_t^* R_t \mathbf{k}_t' \mu_t}{1 + R_t}, \tag{A.25}$$

where

$$\pi_{it}^b = p_t^* \frac{R_t - \rho_{it}}{1 + R_t} \tag{A.26}$$

has the same form as the monetary asset user-cost formula (A.5) for consumers' π_{it}. Clearly, π_{it}^b in (A.26) would equal γ_{it} if $\mathbf{k}_t = \mathbf{0}$. As a result it is evident that $p_t^* R_t \mathbf{k}_t' \mu_t / (1 + R_t)$ is the present value (at the beginning of the period) of the tax $p_t^* R_t \mathbf{k}_t' \mu_t$ "paid" by the financial intermediary (at the end of the period) as a result of the existence of reserve requirements. The tax is the forgone interest on uninvested required reserves. If used with recent data, this formula would have to be modified to incorporate payment of interest on reserves. There still is an implicit tax on required reserves, so long as the interest rate paid on required reserves is less than the loan rate that can be earned by making bank loans. In fact interest now is being paid even on voluntary bank holding of excess reserves, decreasing the opportunity cost of excess reserves and thereby decreasing the optimal solution for bank lending. In this chapter we do not introduce those modifications, since most of the data on bank behavior precedes the recent introduction of interest payment on reserves.

The solution to the firm's variable profit-maximization problem is its factor demand functions for $\alpha_t = (\mathbf{z}_t', \mathbf{L}_t', c_t)'$ and its supply functions for its multiple products μ_t. Derived demand is thereby produced for high-powered (base) money. That derived demand, in real terms, is

$$h_t = c_t + \sum_i k_{it} \mu_{it}. \tag{A.27}$$

The financial firm's nominal demand for high-powered money is $p_t^* h_t$.

Stockholder capital (net worth) is a fixed factor during period t and hence does not enter the variable cost. Since stockholder capital is not reservable, all stockholder capital will go into loans at yield, R_t. If capital is paid the competitive rate of return, then all of the yield on the investment of stockholder capital will be paid to stockholders as dividends and hence will not affect either total or variable economic profits. However, the investment of stockholder capital will augment total accounting profits and will contribute to the total stock of loans in the economy.

A.3.2   Separability of Technology

If the user costs γ_t all moved proportionally, then we could use Hicksian aggregation to aggregate over the firm's joint monetary supplies, μ_t. But since that proportionality assumption is not typically reasonable for monetary asset user costs, aggregation over outputs is possible only if outputs are separable from inputs in the financial firm's technology. Hence, in order to establish the existence of an output aggregate, we will assume that there exist functions f and H such that

$$F(\mu_t, z_t, L_t, c_t; k_t) = H(f(\mu_t; k_t), z_t, L_t, c_t). \tag{A.28}$$

It seems likely that k_t would enter F only through f, as in (A.28). However, this analysis could easily be extended to the case where k_t also enters H as independent arguments.

There will exist a function g such that

$$f(\mu_t; k_t) = g(z_t, L_t, c_t) \tag{A.29}$$

is the solution for $f(\mu_t; k_t)$ to

$$H(f(\mu_t; k_t), z_t, L_t, c_t) = 0. \tag{A.30}$$

The function $f(\mu_t; k_t)$ is called the factor requirements function, because it equals the right-hand side of (A.29), which is the minimum amount of aggregate input required to produce the vector, μ_t. The function, $g(z_t, L_t, c_t)$, is the production function, because it equals the left-hand side of (A.29), which is the maximum amount of aggregate output that can be produced from the inputs, (z_t, L_t, c_t). Hence f is both the factor requirements function and the outputs aggregator function, while g is both the output production function and the inputs aggregator function.

We assume that f is convex and linearly homogeneous in μ_t. In addition it follows—from our assumptions on the derivatives of the transformation function F—that g is monotonically increasing in all of its arguments and that f is monotonically increasing in μ_t. We assume that g is locally strictly concave in a neighborhood of the solution to the first-order conditions for variable profit maximization. In addition it follows—from the strict quasiconvexity of the transformation function, F—that g is globally strictly quasiconcave.

A.4 Demand for Monetary Assets by Manufacturing Firms

Besides consumer demand for monetary assets, there is demand for monetary assets by manufacturing firms. I here define "manufacturing firms" to be any nonfinancial firms, including firms that produce personal services other than financial services. This section formulates the decision problem of such a manufacturing firm when monetary assets enter the firm's production function. The firm is assumed to maximize the present value of its profits flow subject to its technology. The firm's intertemporal technology, over its T-period planning horizon, is defined by its transformation function

$$\Omega(\delta_t, \ldots, \delta_{t+T}, \varepsilon_t, \ldots, \varepsilon_{t+T}, \kappa_t, \ldots, \kappa_{t+T}) = 0, \tag{A.31}$$

where for $t \le s \le t + T$,

$\delta_s =$ vector of planned production of output quantities

during period s,

$\varepsilon_s =$ vector of planned real balances of monetary assets held

during period s, and

$\kappa_s =$ vector of planned use of other factors during period s.

The firm's technology can equivalently be defined by its efficient production set

$$\Gamma = \{(\delta_t, \ldots, \delta_{t+T}, \varepsilon_t, \ldots, \varepsilon_{t+T}, \kappa_t, \ldots, \kappa_{t+T}): \tag{A.32}$$

$$\Omega(\delta_t, \ldots, \delta_{t+T}, \varepsilon_t, \ldots, \varepsilon_{t+T}, \kappa_t, \ldots, \kappa_{t+T}) = 0\}.$$

The transformation function Ω is assumed to be strictly quasiconvex. In addition $\partial\Omega/\partial\delta_{is} > 0$, $\partial\Omega/\partial\varepsilon_{is} < 0$, and $\partial\Omega/\partial\kappa_{is} < 0$.

The firm's decision problem is formulated in period t for periods t, $t + 1, \ldots, s, \ldots, t + T$, where T is the number of periods in the firm's planning horizon. During period s the firm's profits are

$$\Psi_s = \delta_s'\mathbf{v}_s - \kappa_s'\zeta_s + \sum_i[(1 + r_{i,s-1})p_{s-1}^*\varepsilon_{i,s-1} - p_s^*\varepsilon_{is}], \tag{A.33}$$

where

$\mathbf{v}_s$ = vector of output expected prices, and

$\boldsymbol{\zeta}_s$ = vector of expected prices of the factors, $\boldsymbol{\kappa}_s$.

To simplify the notation, we assume that consumers and manufacturing firms have access to the same monetary assets, so the expected nominal holding period yields on $\boldsymbol{\varepsilon}_s$ can be viewed as being $\mathbf{r}_s$ (defined in section A.2.1). Real balances ε_t are defined to equal nominal balances divided by p_t^* (also defined in section A.2.1).[5]

The discounted present value of the firm's profit flow during the $T + 1$ periods plus the discounted present value of the firm's monetary asset portfolio at the end of the planning horizon is

$$\Psi_t^* + \sum_{s=t}^{t+T}\left(\frac{\Psi_s}{\theta_s}\right) + \left(\frac{1}{\theta_{t+T+1}}\right)\sum_i p_{t+T}^* \varepsilon_{i,t+T}(1 + r_{i,t+T}) \tag{A.34}$$

where the discount factor is θ_s, such that $\theta_s = 1.0$ for $s = t$ and

$$\theta_s = \prod_{a=t}^{s-1}(1 + R_a) \qquad \text{for } t + 1 \le s \le t + T + 1.$$

We now substitute (A.33) into (A.34) and rearrange the terms, grouping together those terms with common time subscripts. The result is

$$\Psi_t^* = \sum_{s=t}^{t+T}\delta_s'\bar{\mathbf{v}}_s - \sum_{s=t}^{t+T}\boldsymbol{\kappa}_s'\bar{\boldsymbol{\zeta}}_s - \sum_{s=t}^{t+T}\boldsymbol{\varepsilon}_s'\boldsymbol{\eta}_s + \sum_{i=1}^{n}(1 + r_{i,t-1})p_{t-1}^*\varepsilon_{i,t-1}, \tag{A.35}$$

where $\bar{\mathbf{v}}_s = \mathbf{v}_s/\theta_s$ and $\bar{\boldsymbol{\zeta}}_s = \boldsymbol{\zeta}_s/\theta_s$ are the discounted present values of the prices $\mathbf{v}_s$ and $\boldsymbol{\zeta}_s$, respectively, and where the user cost of ε_{is} is

$$\eta_{is} = \frac{p_s^*}{\theta_s} - \frac{(1 + r_{is})p_s^*}{\theta_{s+1}}. \tag{A.36}$$

Because $\sum_{i=1}^{n}(1 + r_{i,t-1})p_{t-1}^*\varepsilon_{i,t-1}$ is wealth endowed from the previous planning horizon, that contribution to present wealth is fixed. Hence the discounted present value of variable profits is

---

5. This definition is greatly simplifying because it permits use of the same price index, p_t^*, for the manufacturing firm as for the consumer. We do the same thing with the financial firm's output in the next section. Thus the same price deflator applies to consumer monetary asset demand, manufacturing firm monetary factor demand, and financial firm output demand. Unfortunately, this assumption is not based on solid theoretical foundations; in principle, a different price deflator should be used in each of the three cases. Our only defense is that perhaps the three theoretically correct deflators may not differ that much. However, our deflator is theoretically correct only for the consumer, since we produced p_t^* from consumer duality theory. For rigorous treatment of firm input and output deflators, see Fisher and Shell (1972, essay 2; 1998).

$$\Psi_{vt}^* = \sum_{s=t}^{t+T} \delta_s' \overline{v}_s \; - \sum_{s}^{t+T} \kappa_s' \overline{\zeta}_s - \sum_{s=t}^{t+T} \varepsilon_s' \eta_s,$$ (A.37)

which is in conventional form. In addition, the user cost η_{is} in the current period $s = t$ is

$$\eta_{it} = p_t^* \frac{R_t - r_{it}}{1 + R_t},$$ (A.38)

which is in familiar form (see equations A.4 and A.26). With the conventional decision problem of maximizing variable profit (A.37) subject to (A.31), we have immediate access to the existing literature on aggregation over factors of production, enabling us to aggregate over monetary assets ε_t demanded by the manufacturing firm.

The approach used above to derive the user-cost formula η_{is} is analogous to that used for physical capital by Diewert (1980a, p. 47). The same result would be acquired from the approach of Coen and Hickman (1970, p. 298), because the first-order conditions for maximization of (A.37) subject to (A.31) include the condition that the marginal rate of substitution between ε_{is} and ε_{js} be $-\eta_{is}/\eta_{js}$. Using the observations of Diewert (1980a, pp. 478–79), extension of the results above to include taxes is straightforward. See Coen and Hickman (1970, p. 299) for discussion of the approaches to dealing with such further potential complications as differences between borrowing and lending rates, the existence of more than one lending rate, differences in taxation rates, risk-induced dependency on debt/equity ratios, and so on. The extension of the result above to an infinite planning horizon is immediate by allowing $T \to \infty$ in (A.35).

A.4.1 Separability of Technology

For the same reason discussed in (A.16), we require that technology be separable, although here separability will be assumed in current monetary assets used as inputs (by the manufacturing firm) rather than in monetary assets produced as outputs (by the financial intermediary). In particular, we assume that there exist functions a and B such that

$$\Omega(\delta_t, \ldots, \delta_{t+T}, \varepsilon_t, \ldots, \varepsilon_{t+T}, \kappa_t, \ldots, \kappa_{t+T})$$

$$= B(\delta_t, \ldots, \delta_{t+T}, a(\varepsilon_t), \varepsilon_{t+1}, \ldots, \varepsilon_{t+T}, \kappa_t, \ldots, \kappa_{t+T}).$$ (A.39)

In that case the function $a(\varepsilon_t)$ is called a category subproduction function.

Let $(\delta_t^*, \ldots, \delta_{t+T}^*, \varepsilon_t^*, \ldots, \varepsilon_{t+T}^*, \kappa_t^*, \ldots, \kappa_{t+T}^*)$ be the solution to maximizing (A.37) subject to (A.31), and let $b_t = \varepsilon_t^{*'}\eta_t$. Then it follows that ε_t^* must also be the solution for ε_t to the current period conditional decision:

$$\text{maximize } a(\varepsilon_t) \text{ subject to } \eta_t'\varepsilon_t = b_t, \tag{A.40}$$

which is in the same form as (A.4) for the consumer. In addition, if we divide both sides of the constraint in (A.40) by p_t^*, then we obtain the following decision, which is in the same form as (A.6):

$$\text{maximize } a(\varepsilon_t) \text{ subject to } \eta_t^{*'}\varepsilon_t = b_t^*, \tag{A.41}$$

where $\eta_t^* = \eta_t/p_t^*$ and $b_t^* = b_t/p_t^*$. The function $a(\varepsilon_t)$ is assumed to be monotonically increasing and strictly concave in ε_t. The large literature in aggregation and index-number theory based on the conventional consumer decision, of form (A.6), is immediately applicable to decision (A.41) and hence to aggregation over ε_t.

Numerous simplifying assumptions were made in sections A.2, A.3, and A.4 of this appendix. Although these assumptions are common in the conventional neoclassical literature, extension of these results to include, for example, uncertainty and differences in taxation rates would be useful. A list of areas needing such extensions in the conventional approach can be found in Diewert (1980b, p. 265).

A.5 Aggregation Theory under Homogeneity

The theory of aggregation over goods directly produces unique, exact results when the aggregator function is linearly homogeneous. In that case the growth rates of the aggregation-theoretic price and quantity aggregates are independent of selected reference levels for utility, prices, or quantities. In addition the dual quantity and price aggregates then behave in a manner indistinguishable from that of an elementary good. In this section we discuss that most elegant of situations. In section A.6 of this appendix, we present recent theory relevant to aggregation in the nonhomothetic case.

A.5.1 The Consumer
Here we seek to produce the exact aggregation-theoretic aggregate over the monetary asset quantities $\mathbf{m}_t$ of this appendix's section A.2. As shown in Barnett (1980a, 1981b), the exact quantity aggregate is the level of indirect (i.e., optimized) utility

$$M_t^c = \max\{u(\mathbf{m}_t): \pi_t'\mathbf{m}_t = y_t\}, \tag{A.42}$$

so u is the aggregator function that we assume to be linearly homogeneous in this section. Dual to any exact quantity aggregate, there exists a unique price aggregate, which aggregates over the prices of the goods. Hence there must exist an exact nominal price aggregate over the user costs, π_t, and there must also exist the corresponding real (user-cost) price aggregate over π_t^*. As shown in Barnett (1980a, 1981b), the consumer behaves relative to the dual pair of exact quantity and price aggregates as if they were the quantity and price of an elementary good. As a result the exact aggregate is empirically indistinguishable from an elementary good.

One of the properties that an exact dual pair of price and quantity aggregates satisfies is Fisher's "factor reversal" test, which states that the product of an exact quantity aggregate and its dual exact price aggregate must equal actual expenditure on the components. Hence, if $\Pi^c(\pi_t)$ is the exact user-cost aggregate dual to M_t^c, then $\Pi^c(\pi_t)$ must satisfy

$$\Pi^c(\pi_t) = \frac{y_t}{M_t^c}. \tag{A.43}$$

Since (A.43) produces a unique solution for $\Pi^c(\pi_t)$, we could use (A.43) to define $\Pi^c(\pi_t)$. In addition, if we replace M_t^c by the indirect utility function that is defined by (A.42) and use the linear homogeneity of u, we can show that $\Pi_t^c = \Pi^c(\pi_t)$ defined by (A.43) does indeed depend only on π_t, and not on $\mathbf{m}_t$ or y_t. See Barnett (1983a, 1987) for a version of that proof. The conclusion produced by that proof can be written in the form

$$\Pi^c(\pi_t) = [\max_{\mathbf{m}_t}\{u(\mathbf{m}_t): \pi_t'\mathbf{m}_t = 1\}]^{-1}, \tag{A.44}$$

which clearly depends only on π_t.

Although (A.43) provides a valid definition of $\Pi^c(\pi_t)$, a direct definition (not produced indirectly through M_t^c and Fisher's factor reversal test) is more informative and often more useful. The direct definition depends on the cost (or expenditure) function, E, defined by

$$E(u_0, \pi_t) = \min_{\mathbf{m}_t}\{\pi_t'\mathbf{m}_t : u(\mathbf{m}_t) = u_0\}, \tag{A.45}$$

which equivalently can be acquired by solving the indirect utility function equation (A.42) for y as a function of $u_0 = M_t^c$ and π_t. It can be proved (e.g., see Shephard 1970, p. 144) that

$$\Pi^c(\pi_t) = E(1, \pi_t) = \min_{\mathbf{m}_t}\{\pi_t'\mathbf{m}_t : u(\mathbf{m}_t) = 1\}, \tag{A.46}$$

which is often called the unit cost or price function. The unit-cost function is the minimum cost of attaining unit utility level for $u(\mathbf{m}_t)$ at given user-cost prices $\boldsymbol{\pi}_t$. Clearly, (A.46) depends only on $\boldsymbol{\pi}_t$. Hence by (A.43) and (A.46) we see that $\Pi^c(\boldsymbol{\pi}_t) = y_t / M_t^c = E(1, \boldsymbol{\pi}_t)$.

Equation (A.46) is the most informative expression for $\Pi^c(\boldsymbol{\pi}_t)$. For example, it is immediately evident from (A.46) that Π^c is linearly homogeneous in $\boldsymbol{\pi}_t$. Hence the real user-cost aggregate is $\Pi_t^{c*} = \Pi^c(\boldsymbol{\pi}_t/p_t^*) = \Pi^c(\boldsymbol{\pi}_t)/p_t^*$. In addition we can see from (A.46) that (M_t^c, Π_t^c) must satisfy Fisher's factor reversal test. The demonstration of that result follows. Observe first that

$$M_t^c \min_{\mathbf{m}_t}\{\boldsymbol{\pi}_t'\mathbf{m}_t : u(\mathbf{m}_t) = 1\} = \min_{\mathbf{m}_t}\{\boldsymbol{\pi}_t'(M_t^c\mathbf{m}_t) : M_t^c u(\mathbf{m}_t) = M_t^c\}$$
$$= \min_{\mathbf{m}_t}\{\boldsymbol{\pi}_t'(M_t^c\mathbf{m}_t) : u(M_t^c\mathbf{m}_t) = M_t^c\}, \tag{A.47}$$

where the last equality follows from the linear homogeneity of u. If we let $\hat{\mathbf{m}}_t = M_t^c\mathbf{m}_t$, then

$$M_t^c \min_{\mathbf{m}_t}\{\boldsymbol{\pi}_t'\mathbf{m}_t : u(\mathbf{m}_t) = 1\} = \min_{\hat{\mathbf{m}}_t}\{\boldsymbol{\pi}_t'\hat{\mathbf{m}}_t : u(\hat{\mathbf{m}}_t) = M_t^c\}. \tag{A.48}$$

Hence, by (A.46), we obtain from (A.48) that

$$M_t^c \Pi_t^c = \min_{\hat{\mathbf{m}}_t}\{\boldsymbol{\pi}_t'\hat{\mathbf{m}}_t : u(\hat{\mathbf{m}}_t) = M_t^c\}. \tag{A.49}$$

However, expenditure minimization (at the optimized value M_t^c of utility) is a necessary condition for utility maximization. Hence the right-hand side of (A.49) will be actual expenditure on the services of $\mathbf{m}_t$, and therefore (A.49) is Fisher's factor reversal test. A more formal proof, not explicitly including monetary assets, is available in Shephard (1970, p. 93).

In addition, (A.42) and (A.46) provide easy interpretations of (M_t^c, Π_t^c). From (A.42), we see that M_t^c is the consumer's optimized utility level from monetary assets held during period t. Hence M_t^c is the consumer's perceived service flow from his selected $\mathbf{m}_t$. In order similarly to interpret Π_t^c, observe from (A.45) and (A.49) that $E(M_t^c, \boldsymbol{\pi}_t) = M_t^c \Pi_t^c$. Differentiating both sides with respect to M_t^c, we see immediately that

$$\Pi_t^c = \frac{\partial E(M_t^c, \boldsymbol{\pi}_t)}{\partial M_t^c}. \tag{A.50}$$

Hence Π_t^c is the marginal cost to the consumer of consuming another unit of aggregate monetary services, M_t^c.

It is interesting to observe that we could work in reverse to derive (A.46) from Fisher's factor reversal test, (A.49). In particular, if we *define* Π_t^c by (A.49), we could then use (A.48) to acquire (A.46) as a conclusion. Alternatively, we could start with (A.49) and simply let $M_t^c = 1$ to acquire (A.46) immediately.

The duality between M_t^c and Π_t^c is evident from (A.42) and (A.46), which use dual decision problems. In addition the duality between M_t^c and Π_t^c permits us to get back and forth between them easily. The indirect method would be through (A.43). But we also can derive either M_t^c or Π_t^c directly in terms of the other. As can be seen from (A.42), the quantity aggregator function is u, because M_t^c is equal to M_t^c when $\mathbf{m}_t^*$ is the consumer's chosen (constrained utility-maximizing) choice for $\mathbf{m}_t$. Hence we see immediately that we can derive the user-cost price aggregate directly from the corresponding quantity aggregator function from either (A.44) or (A.46). Conversely, the quantity aggregate $M_t^c = u(\mathbf{m}_t^*)$ can be derived directly from the price aggregator function, Π^c, because

$$u(\mathbf{m}_t^*) = \left[\max_{\pi \geq 0}\{\Pi^c(\boldsymbol{\pi}) : \boldsymbol{\pi}'\mathbf{m}_t^* = 1\}\right]^{-1}. \tag{A.51}$$

See Diewert (1981, eq. 4).

We now have the fundamental aggregation-theoretic tools for aggregating over goods within the decision of a consumer. The reason that M_t^c and Π_t^c are called exact aggregates is that (M_t^c, Π_t^c) can be used to decompose the consumer's decision into a two-stage budgeting process. In the first stage, M_t^c is treated as an elementary good with price Π_t^c within the intertemporal utility maximization decision. In particular, M_t^c appears in place of $u(\mathbf{m}_t)$ within the intertemporal utility function, U_t. Having solved for M_t^c in the first stage, the consumer then solves for $\mathbf{m}_t$ from the second-stage decision (A.4), with y_t determined from $M_t^c \Pi_t^c$. For all possible nonnegative values of prices and wealth, the two-stage decision will produce the same solution as the original complete decision defined in section A.2.1 or A.2.2 of this appendix. Hence (M_t^c, Π_t^c) are behaviorally indistinguishable from the quantity and price of an elementary good. The details of the two-stage budgeting theorem are available in Barnett (1980a, 1981b) and Green (1964, thm. 4).

A.5.2   The Manufacturing Firm
Since the decision problems (A.6) and (A.41) are in the same form, the aggregation theory in section A.5.1 for consumer demand for monetary

assets is immediately applicable to aggregation over monetary assets demanded by a manufacturing firm. The only change is in the interpretation of the quantity aggregator function. With a consumer, the quantity aggregator function is the category subutility function, u. With a manufacturing firm, the quantity aggregator function is the category subproduction function, $a(\varepsilon_t)$. Clearly, the quantity aggregator function in both cases is the objective function of the corresponding conditional decision problem, (A.6) or (A.41).

In the case of demand by a manufacturing firm, however, a particularly interesting interpretation of the derivable two-stage budgeting process is available, as has been observed by Blackorby, Primont, and Russell (1978, p. 210). Restating their interpretation of separable factor demand in terms of monetary asset demand, the following becomes available under our assumptions. Instead of maximizing profits directly in a single joint decision, the firm can produce the same optimum solution by decentralizing its monetary portfolio decisions to a financial "division" or department, which is instructed to maximize its financial services with a fixed allocated budget, b_t. In other words, the financial division is asked to select its monetary portfolio, ε_t, by solving decision problem (A.40). In order for that decentralized decision to be solvable, the firm's corporate office must be able to determine the optimal level of monetary expenditure b_t to be supplied to the financial division before it solves problem (A.40). It can be shown that the firm can produce that correct prior solution for b_t from its first-stage decision problem. That first-stage decision requires knowledge of the firm's exact monetary user-cost aggregate $\Pi_t^f = \Pi^f(\eta_t)$, which can be acquired by the financial division from the right-hand side of (A.44) or of (A.46), when the symbols (functions or variables) from the consumer's decision are replaced in the obvious manner by the corresponding symbols from the firm's decision. That correspondence between symbols is the one acquired by replacing decision (A.6) with decision (A.41).

In summary, the firm could operate in the following decentralized manner. The financial division uses (A.44) or (A.46) to acquire Π_t^f, which the financial division supplies to the firm's corporate office. The corporate office then solves the firm's first-stage decision to acquire the profit-maximizing budget b_t to be allocated to financial services. Having received b_t, the financial division then selects the optimal portfolio of monetary assets ε_t by solving problem (A.40) to maximize monetary services M_t^f available from the fixed budget. The result is exact profit maximization by the firm. The resulting exact monetary quantity aggregate, as with the consumer, is (A.42)—with the obvious change of symbols between consumers and firms. Observe that the monetary quantity aggregate M_t^f is the optimized level of the financial division's objective function, and hence is the optimized monetary asset service flow.

In the above decentralized two-stage decision, we have identified the second-stage decision to be decision problem (A.40), which is solved conditionally upon b_t. However, we have not formally defined the first-stage ("corporate office") decision, which is needed to determine the profit maximizing portfolio services budget, b_t. That first-stage decision is to select $(\delta_t^*, \ldots, \delta_{t+T}^*, M_t^f, \varepsilon_{t+1}^*, \ldots, \varepsilon_{t+T}^*, \kappa_t^*, \ldots, \kappa_{t+T}^*)$ to maximize the discounted present value of variable profits

$$\Psi_t^* = \sum_{s=t}^{t+T} \delta_s' \bar{v}_s - \sum_s^{t+T} \kappa_s' \bar{\zeta}_s - \sum_{s=t}^{t+T} \varepsilon_s' \eta_s - M_t^f \Pi_t^f, \tag{A.52}$$

subject to

$$B(\delta_t, \ldots, \delta_{t+T}, M_t^f, \varepsilon_{t+1}, \ldots, \varepsilon_{t+T}, \kappa_t, \ldots, \kappa_{t+T}) = 0. \tag{A.53}$$

Having solved that decision, involving the aggregated quantity M_t^f and price Π_t^f, the optimal budget for financial services is immediately available as $b_t = M_t^f \Pi_t^f$.

The consumer's two-stage decision can be interpreted in an analogous manner, but with the quantity aggregator function u viewed as the consumer's transactions technology. The fact that two-stage decentralization is possible, and that it always produces the firm's profit-maximizing solution for all values, is easily proved when the two-stage decision is restated in a different form. Since that result previously has been proved only for single-output firms, we now provide the proof for multiple-output firms. The proof is a straightforward extension of Shephard's (1970, pp. 144–46) result with a single-output technology. In this section we assume that the second-stage decision (the financial division's decision) is to minimize cost at fixed output of monetary services. Hence the corporate office, after solving the first-stage decision, supplies M_t^f to the financial division, which then minimizes cost subject to $a(\varepsilon_t) = M_t^f$. In our previous equivalent interpretation, the corporate office supplies $b_t = M_t^f \Pi_t^f$ to the financial division, which then maximizes $a(\varepsilon_t)$ subject to the condition that cost cannot exceed b_t.

We need the firm's full intertemporal variable cost function

$$C(\delta_t, \ldots, \delta_{t+T}, \overline{\zeta}_t, \ldots, \overline{\zeta}_{t+T}, \eta_t, \ldots, \eta_{t+T}) = \min_{(\varepsilon_t, \ldots, \varepsilon_{t+T}, \kappa_t, \ldots, \kappa_{t+T})}$$

$$\left\{ \sum_{s=t}^{t+T} \kappa_s' \overline{\zeta}_s - \sum_{s=t}^{t+T} \varepsilon_s' \eta_s : B(\delta_t, \ldots, \delta_{t+T}, a(\varepsilon_{t+1}), \varepsilon_t, \ldots, \varepsilon_{t+T}, \kappa_t, \ldots, \kappa_{t+T}) = 0 \right\} \tag{A.54}$$

Observe that (A.54) is acquired by minimizing all of the firm's variable factor costs. In contrast, the sub–cost function, $E(a_0, \eta_t)$, defined by the production analogue to (A.45), is acquired by minimizing only the firm's monetary service costs. In particular, that sub–cost function is

$$E(a_0, \eta_t) = \min_{\varepsilon_t} \{ \eta_t' \varepsilon_t : a(\varepsilon_t) = a_0 \}. \tag{A.55}$$

Let

$$\delta = (\delta_t', \ldots, \delta_{t+T}')', \overline{\zeta} = (\overline{\zeta}_t', \ldots, \overline{\zeta}_{t+T}')', \eta = (\eta_t', \ldots, \eta_{t+T}')',$$

$$\kappa = (\kappa_t', \ldots, \kappa_{t+T}')', \varepsilon = (\varepsilon_t', \ldots, \varepsilon_{t+T}')', \text{ and } \overline{v} = (\overline{v}_t', \ldots, \overline{v}_{t+T}')'.$$

We now prove the following theorem, which is needed to prove the consistency of the two-stage decision.

Theorem 1   *The firm's full cost function can be written as*

$$C(\delta, \overline{\zeta}, \eta) = \min_{(\kappa, a_0, \varepsilon_{t+1}, \ldots, \varepsilon_{t+T})}$$

$$\left\{ \kappa' \overline{\zeta} + E(a_0, \eta_t) + \sum_{s=t+1}^{t+T} \varepsilon_s' \eta_s : B(\delta, a_0, \varepsilon_{t+1}, \ldots, \varepsilon_{t+T}, \kappa) = 0 \right\}.$$

Proof   Define $(\kappa^*, \varepsilon^*)$ to solve the minimization problem in (A.54), so that

$$C(\delta, \overline{\zeta}, \eta) = \kappa^{*\prime} \overline{\zeta} + \varepsilon^{*\prime} \eta \tag{A.56}$$

with

$$B(\delta, a(\varepsilon_t^*), \varepsilon_{t+1}^*, \ldots, \varepsilon_{t+T}^*, \kappa^*) = 0; \tag{A.57}$$

and define $(\hat{\kappa}, \hat{a}_0, \hat{\varepsilon}_{t+1}, \ldots, \hat{\varepsilon}_{t+T})$, such that

$$\min_{(\kappa, a_0, \varepsilon_{t+1}, \ldots, \varepsilon_{t+T})} \left\{ \kappa' \overline{\zeta} + E(a_0, \eta_t) + \sum_{s=t+1}^{t+T} \varepsilon_s' \eta_s : B(\delta, a_0, \varepsilon_{t+1}, \ldots, \varepsilon_{t+T}, \kappa) = 0 \right\} =$$

$$\hat{\kappa}' \overline{\zeta} + E(\hat{a}_0, \eta_t) + \sum_{s=t+1}^{t+T} \hat{\varepsilon}_s' \eta_s \tag{A.58}$$

with

$$B(\delta, \hat{a}_0, \hat{\varepsilon}_{t+1}, \ldots, \hat{\varepsilon}_{t+T}, \hat{\kappa}_t) = 0,$$ (A.59)

but suppose that

$$\kappa^{*'}\overline{\zeta} + \varepsilon^{*'}\eta \neq \hat{\kappa}'\overline{\zeta} + E(\hat{a}_0, \eta_t) + \sum_{s=t+1}^{t+T} \hat{\varepsilon}'_s \eta_s.$$ (A.60)

Define ε_t to solve the minimization problem in (A.55), when $a_0 = \hat{a}_0$, so that

$$E(\hat{a}_0, \eta_t) = \eta'_t \hat{\varepsilon}_t$$ (A.61)

with

$$a(\hat{\varepsilon}_t) = \hat{a}_0.$$ (A.62)

Then, by (A.59) and (A.62), we have that

$$B(\delta, a(\hat{\varepsilon}_t), \hat{\varepsilon}_{t+1}, \ldots, \hat{\varepsilon}_{t+T}, \hat{\kappa}_t) = 0,$$ (A.63)

so $(\hat{\kappa}, \hat{\varepsilon}_t, \hat{\varepsilon}_{t+1}, \ldots, \hat{\varepsilon}_{t+T})$ is feasible for the minimization problem in (A.54). Hence, by the definition of $(\kappa^*, \varepsilon^*)$, we see that

$$\kappa^{*'}\overline{\zeta} + \varepsilon_t^{*'}\eta_t + \sum_{s=t+1}^{t+T} \varepsilon_t^{*'}\eta_s < \hat{\kappa}'\overline{\zeta} + \hat{\varepsilon}'_t\eta_t + \sum_{s=t+1}^{t+T} \hat{\varepsilon}'_s\eta_s.$$ (A.64)

Let $a_0^* = a(\varepsilon_t^*)$. Then, by (A.57), we have that

$$B(\delta, a_0^*, \varepsilon_{t+1}^*, \ldots, \varepsilon_{t+T}^*, \kappa^*) = 0,$$

so $(\kappa^*, a_0^*, \varepsilon_{t+1}^*, \ldots, \varepsilon_{t+T}^*)$ is feasible for the minimization problem in (A.58). But by (A.54), ε_t^* must minimize $\eta'_t\varepsilon_t$ subject to

$$B(\delta, a(\varepsilon_t), \varepsilon_{t+1}^*, \ldots, \varepsilon_{t+T}^*, \kappa^*) = 0.$$ (A.65)

Also, by the monotonicity of B in $a(\varepsilon_t)$ and by (A.57), it follows that (A.65) is true if and only if $a_0^* = a(\varepsilon_t)$. Hence ε_t^* must minimize $\eta'_t\varepsilon_t$ subject to $a_0^* = a(\varepsilon_t)$, which is the minimization problem in (A.55). So

$$E(a_0^*, \eta_t) = \eta'_t\varepsilon_t^*.$$ (A.66)

By the feasibility of $(\kappa^*, a_0^*, \varepsilon_{t+1}^*, \ldots, \varepsilon_{t+T}^*)$ in the minimization problem in (A.58) and by the definition of $(\hat{\kappa}, \hat{\varepsilon}_t, \hat{\varepsilon}_{t+1}, \ldots, \hat{\varepsilon}_{t+T})$, it follows that

$$\hat{\kappa}'\overline{\zeta} + E(\hat{a}_0, \eta_t) + \sum_{s=t+1}^{t+T} \hat{\varepsilon}'_s\eta_s < \kappa^{*'}\overline{\zeta} + E(a_0^*, \eta_t) + \sum_{s=t+1}^{t+T} \hat{\varepsilon}'_s\eta_s.$$

Combining that result with (A.61) and (A.66), we contradict (A.64). ∎

Producing the firm's decentralized two-stage decision problem is now straightforward. First observe from the production analogue of (A.49) that

$$\Pi_t^f(\mathbf{\eta}_t)a_0 = E(a_0, \mathbf{\eta}_t),$$

which is just Fisher's factor reversal test. From theorem 1 we therefore have that

$$C(\mathbf{\delta}, \overline{\mathbf{\zeta}}, \mathbf{\eta}) = \min_{(\mathbf{\kappa}, a_0, \mathbf{\varepsilon}_{t+1}, \ldots, \mathbf{\varepsilon}_{t+T})} \qquad \text{(A.67)}$$
$$\geq \left\{ \mathbf{\kappa}'\overline{\mathbf{\zeta}} + E(a_0, \mathbf{\eta}_t) + \sum_{s=t+1}^{t+T} \mathbf{\varepsilon}_s'\mathbf{\eta}_s : B(\mathbf{\delta}, a_0, \mathbf{\varepsilon}_{t+1}, \ldots, \mathbf{\varepsilon}_{t+T}, \mathbf{\kappa}) = 0 \right\}.$$

The firm maximizes profits by solving for the output levels, $\mathbf{\delta}$, to maximize $\mathbf{\delta}'v - C(\mathbf{\delta}, \overline{\mathbf{\zeta}}, \mathbf{\eta})$. Hence it follows from (A.67) that the firm can maximize profits by selecting $(\mathbf{\delta}^*, \mathbf{\kappa}^*, a_0^*, \mathbf{\varepsilon}_{t+1}^*, \ldots, \mathbf{\varepsilon}_{t+T}^*)$ to

$$\text{maximize } \mathbf{\delta}'v - \mathbf{\kappa}'\overline{\mathbf{\zeta}} - \Pi_t^f(\mathbf{\eta}_t)a_0 - \sum_{s=t+1}^{t+T} \mathbf{\varepsilon}_s'\mathbf{\eta}_s \text{ subject to}$$

$$B(\mathbf{\delta}, a_0, \mathbf{\varepsilon}_{t+1}, \ldots, \mathbf{\varepsilon}_{t+T}, \mathbf{\kappa}) = 0, \qquad \text{(A.68)}$$

which is the first-stage decision.

In the second stage the firm's corporate office instructs the financial division to purchase a_0^* quantity units of monetary services at minimum cost. The financial division then selects the monetary asset portfolio $\mathbf{\varepsilon}_0^*$ to solve the decision problem on the right-hand side of (A.55) with a_0 set at a_0^*. At this point the firm has optimally solved its full profit-maximization problem, because $(\mathbf{\delta}^*, \mathbf{\kappa}^*, \mathbf{\varepsilon}_t^*, \mathbf{\varepsilon}_{t+1}^*, \ldots, \mathbf{\varepsilon}_{t+T}^*)$ is the profit-maximizing input–output vector.

Recall that a necessary condition for profit maximization is that $\mathbf{\varepsilon}_t^*$ solve problem (A.32). Hence it follows from the production analogue of (A.42) that the firm's solution value for $a_0^* = a(\mathbf{\varepsilon}_t^*)$ must equal its exact monetary quantity aggregate

$$M_t^f = \max \{a(\mathbf{\varepsilon}_t) : \mathbf{\eta}_t'\mathbf{\varepsilon}_t = b_t\}. \qquad \text{(A.69)}$$

The corresponding exact economic price aggregate clearly is $\Pi_t^f(\mathbf{\eta}_t)$.

The above two-stage decomposition of the firm's profit-maximization decision provides the reason for defining M_t^f and $\Pi_t^f(\mathbf{\eta}_t)$ to be the firm's exact monetary quantity and price aggregates. However, that decomposition can also be used as a means for estimating the firm's technology in two stages. See Fuss (1977).

A.5.3 The Financial Intermediary

The aggregation theory relevant to aggregating over the outputs of the multiproduct financial firm is analogous to that for aggregation over the financial inputs of the manufacturing firm, but with the manufacturing firm's cost function replaced by the financial firm's revenue (or "benefit") function. In this manner we can produce a two-stage decision for the financial intermediary. In the first stage the firm solves for profit-maximizing factor demands and the profit-maximizing level of aggregate financial assets produced. In the second stage, the revenue-maximizing vector of individual financial asset quantities supplied is determined at fixed aggregate financial asset quantity supplied.

To display that decomposition of the firm's profit-maximization decision, we start by defining the relevant revenue functions. The financial firm's revenue function is

$$R^*(\alpha_t, \gamma_t; \kappa_t) = \max_{\mu_t}\{\mu_t'\gamma_t : f(\mu_t; k_t) = g(\alpha_t)\}, \tag{A.70}$$

which is the revenue function analogue of the manufacturing firm's cost function, (A.54). The firm selects α_t to maximize variable profits

$$P_t = R^*(\alpha_t, \gamma_t; k_t) - \alpha_t'\beta_t. \tag{A.71}$$

However, by Shephard's (1970, p. 251) proposition 83, it follows that there exists a linearly homogeneous output price aggregator function Γ such that

$$R^*(\alpha_t, \gamma_t; k_t) = \Gamma(\gamma_t)g(\alpha_t). \tag{A.72}$$

Hence the financial firm's variable profits can alternatively be written as

$$P_t = \Gamma(\gamma_t)g(\alpha_t) - \alpha_t'\beta_t. \tag{A.73}$$

The firm's first-stage decision is to select α_t^* to maximize (A.73). Substituting the optimized input vector, α_t^*, into $g(\alpha_t)$, the firm can compute the optimum aggregate monetary asset quantity supplied, M_t^b. In stage two of the decentralized decision, M_t^b is substituted into (A.70) to replace $g(\alpha_t)$, and the maximization problem in (A.70) is solved to acquire the optimum vector of individual monetary assets μ_t produced. Observe that the intermediary's supply function for its monetary aggregate is produced from stage one alone.

Clearly, the exact economic output quantity aggregate for the financial firm is

$$M_t^b = f(\mu_t^*; k_t), \tag{A.74}$$

when μ_t^* is the profit-maximizing vector of monetary assets produced; the corresponding output price aggregate is

$$\Gamma_t^b = \Gamma(\gamma_t). \tag{A.75}$$

Fisher's output reversal test states that $M_t^b \Gamma_t^b$ must equal actual revenue from production of μ_t^*. That condition is satisfied as a result of (A.70), (A.72), and the fact that $f(\mu_t^*; k_t)$ must equal $g(\alpha_t)$ at $\alpha_t = \alpha_t^*$. Also observe from (A.70) and (A.72), with $g(\alpha_t)$ set equal to 1.0, that the output price aggregate is equal to

$$\Gamma(\gamma_t) = \max_{\mu_t}\{\mu_t'\gamma_t : f(\mu_t; k_t)\} = 1\}, \tag{A.76}$$

which is the unit revenue function. The unit revenue function is the maximum revenue that can be acquired from the production of one unit of the output monetary aggregate, $M_t^b = f(\mu_t; k_t)$. The linear homogeneity of Γ is clear from (A.76). In addition the unit revenue function is convex and increasing in γ_t.

It is easily shown that—instead of maximizing $\mu_t'\gamma_t$ subject to

$$f(\mu_t; k_t) = g(a_t^*)$$

to acquire the stage-two solution for μ_t^*—we could equivalently define the stage-two decision to be the selection of μ_t^* to minimize the aggregate factor requirement $f(\mu_t; k_t)$ subject to

$$\mu_t'\gamma_t = \Gamma(\gamma_t)g(\alpha_t^*).$$

As a result we can rewrite (A.74) to obtain

$$M_t^b = \min_{\mu_t}\{f(\mu_t; k_t) : \mu_t'\gamma_t = \Gamma(\gamma_t)g(\alpha_t^*)\}, \tag{A.77}$$

while our earlier statement of the stage-two decision produces the equivalent result that

$$M_t^b \Gamma(\gamma_t) = \max_{\mu_t}\{\mu_t'\gamma_t : f(\mu_t; k_t) = g(\alpha_t^*)\}. \tag{A.78}$$

Comparing (A.76) and (A.77), we can see the clear duality between the decision problems. As usual, the exact quantity and price aggregates of economic theory are true duals.

Equation (A.76) defines the unit revenue (output price aggregator) function in terms of the factor requirement (output quantity aggregator) function. The converse is also possible as a result of the fact that

$$f(\boldsymbol{\mu}_t^*; \mathbf{k}_t) = \left[\min_{\boldsymbol{\gamma}_t \geq 0} \{ \Gamma(\boldsymbol{\gamma}_t) : \boldsymbol{\mu}_t^{*'} \boldsymbol{\gamma}_t = 1 \} \right]^{-1},$$

which is the output analogue to (A.51).

A.5.4 Summary of Aggregator Functions

The aggregation theory presented above demonstrates that a unique correct monetary quantity and price aggregator function exists for each of the three economic agents (the consumer, the manufacturing firm, and the financial intermediary), when the aggregator function is linearly homogeneous. We summarize below the aggregator function found in each case.

In the consumer case, the monetary quantity aggregate is given by (A.42). If $\mathbf{m}_t^*$ is the consumer's optimal portfolio, which solves the decision problem on the right-hand side of (A.42), we see that the exact monetary quantity aggregate is $M_t^c = u(\mathbf{m}_t^*)$. So u is the monetary quantity aggregator function. The corresponding dual user-cost price aggregate is given by $\Pi^c(\boldsymbol{\pi}_t)$, defined in (A.46), where Π^c is the unit cost function dual to the category utility function u. So the price aggregator function is the unit cost function.

In the case of the manufacturing firm, the exact monetary quantity aggregate is given by (A.69). Hence, if $\boldsymbol{\varepsilon}_t^*$ is the firm's optimal portfolio that solves the decision problem on the right-hand side of (A.69), then the firm's exact monetary quantity aggregate is $M_t^f = a(\boldsymbol{\varepsilon}_t^*)$. So the category production function a is the monetary quantity aggregator function. The corresponding dual user-cost price aggregate is given by $\Pi^f(\boldsymbol{\eta}_t)$, where Π^f is the unit cost function dual to the category production function a. So the price aggregator function again is the unit cost function.

In the case of the financial intermediary, the exact monetary quantity aggregate is given by (A.74), (A.77), or (A.78). Hence, if $\boldsymbol{\mu}_t^*$ is the firm's profit-maximizing vector of monetary assets produced, then $M_t^b = f(\boldsymbol{\mu}_t^*; \mathbf{k}_t)$ is the firm's exact monetary supply quantity aggregate. So the input requirement function, f, is the firm's monetary quantity aggregator function. The corresponding dual monetary price aggregate is $\Gamma(\boldsymbol{\gamma}_t)$, defined in (A.76). So the financial intermediary's output price aggregator function is its unit function, Γ.

A.5.5 Subaggregation

In section A.5.4 we provided a single monetary quantity aggregator function for each economic agent. This quantity aggregate in each case aggregates over all of the monetary assets demanded or supplied by the economic agent. However, exact subaggregates also exist, if the quantity aggregator functions in section A.5.4 are weakly separable in a subvector of the monetary assets demanded or supplied, and if those subfunctions are linearly homogeneous. The resulting weakly separable subfunction is an exact aggregator function over its subvector of monetary asset components, and the corresponding unit cost or unit revenue function is the dual user-cost price aggregate. By nesting weakly separable blocks within weakly separable blocks, a hierarchy of nested exact aggregates can be produced. See Barnett (1980a, 1981b) for the construction of such a hierarchy of exact monetary assets for a representative consumer.

The two-stage decision described above can be extended into an n-stage decision for an n-level hierarchy of nested monetary aggregates. The fact that the n-stage decision produces the optimal solution for the economic agent can be proved from induction, using the results for the corresponding two-stage decision. The theory of multistage recursive aggregation has been developed in detail by Blackorby, Primont, and Russell (1978).

By nesting weakly separable blocks within weakly separable blocks to produce recursive subaggregation, the consumer's utility function produces a "utility tree" (e.g., see Barnett 1980a, 1981b). The analogous structure for the manufacturing firm's production function is a "production tree." In that case the firm can optimize factor intensities within branches and then optimize between subset intensities conditionally upon the fixed preselected intensities within branches (e.g., see Berndt and Christensen 1973). Whenever a quantity aggregator function is weakly separable into subfunctions, the subfunctions are quantity aggregator functions at a lower level of aggregation. If those subfunctions are linearly homogeneous, then the price (unit cost or unit revenue) function is also correspondingly weakly separable. The resulting subfunctions of the price function are the price (unit cost or unit revenue) functions dual to the corresponding quantity aggregator functions (see Diewert 1980a). Hence all of the quantity and price aggregator functions are easily produced at all applicable levels of aggregation.

A.6   Index-Number Theory under Homogeneity

The results in section A.5 provide unique exact economic aggregator functions for aggregating over monetary assets demanded or supplied by each of the three classes of economic agents. Each of the resulting monetary quantity aggregates depends only on the component monetary asset quantities and the form of the aggregator function. To use such an aggregate, it is necessary to select a parameterized econometric specification for the aggregator function and estimate its parameters. Estimating aggregator functions and exploring their properties plays an important role in the aggregation theory literature. For many purposes, however, the most useful aggregates are those produced without the need to estimate unknown parameters. In that case nonparametric approximations to the unknown aggregator functions are needed. The production of such nonparametric approximations is the subject of index-number theory.

Index-number theory eliminates the need to estimate unknown parameters by using both prices and quantities simultaneously, along with approximation techniques often resembling revealed preference theory, in order to estimate economic quantity aggregates that depend only on quantities and not prices. Similarly index-number theory uses both prices and quantities simultaneously in order to approximate economic price aggregates that depend only on prices and not quantities.

A.6.1   The Consumer and Manufacturing Firm

Solution of the decision problem (A.6) is a necessary condition (with the appropriate selection of notation) for optimal portfolio choice for either the consumer or the manufacturing firm, and the exact monetary aggregate is the optimized value of the objective function in either case. Hence the approximation theory relevant to producing a nonparametric approximation to the exact aggregate is the same in both. Therefore we present the index-number theory only for the consumer in this section. The corresponding results for the manufacturing firm could be acquired immediately by changing notation in the obvious way.

If $\mathbf{m}_t^*$ is acquired by solving (A.6), then $u(\mathbf{m}_t^*)$ is the exact monetary aggregate, M_t^c. In continuous time, $M_t^c = u(\mathbf{m}_t^*)$ can be tracked without error (see Barnett 1983b for a proof) by the Divisia index, which provides M_t^c as the solution to the differential equation

$$d \log \frac{M_t^c}{dt} = \sum_i s_{it} d \log \frac{m_{it}^*}{dt}, \tag{A.79}$$

where $s_{it} = \pi_{it} m_{it}^* / y_t = \pi_{it}^* m_{it}^* / y_t^*$ is the ith asset's share in expenditure on the total portfolio's service flow. Note that $\mathbf{m}_t^*$ in (A.79) must continually solve (A.6) for (A.79) to hold.

In continuous time, under our assumptions the Divisia index is perfect. There is no remainder term in its approximation (e.g., see Hulten 1973), regardless of the form of the unknown function u. In discrete time, however, many different approximations to (A.79) are possible, because $\mathbf{s}_t = (s_{1t}, \ldots, s_{nt})'$ need not be constant during any given time interval. With annual data, differences between such approximations can be substantial. The most popular discrete time approximation to the Divisia index is the Törnqvist–Theil approximation (often called the Törnqvist index), which is just the Simpson's rule approximation:

$$\log M_t^c - \log M_{t-1}^c = \sum_i \bar{s}_{it} (\log m_{it}^* - \log m_{i,t-1}^*), \qquad (A.80)$$

where $\bar{s}_{it} = (s_{it} + s_{i,t-1})/2$. By using the Simpson's rule average shares, $\mathbf{s}_t^* = (\bar{s}_{1t}, \ldots, \bar{s}_{nt})'$, the index (A.80) has obvious appeal as a discrete time approximation to the Divisia index (A.79). Hence in discrete time we will call (A.80) simply the Divisia index.

A very compelling reason has appeared for using (A.80) as the discrete time approximation to the Divisia index. Diewert (1976) has defined a class of index numbers, called "superlative" index numbers, which have particular appeal in producing discrete time approximations to $M_t^c = u(\mathbf{m}_t^*)$. Diewert defines a superlative index number to be one that is exactly correct for some quadratic approximation to u. The discrete Divisia index (A.80) is in the superlative class, because it is exact for the translog specification for u. The translog is quadratic in the logarithms. As a result, if the translog specification is not exactly correct, then the discrete Divisia index (A.80) has a third-order remainder term in the changes, since quadratic approximations possess third-order remainder terms. With weekly or monthly monetary asset data, the Divisia index (A.80) is accurate to within three decimal places, which is smaller than the data's round off error (see Barnett 1980a).

The Fisher-ideal index is another popular element of Diewert's superlative class, and was proposed for use with monetary data, along with the Divisia index, by Barnett (1980a, 1981b). The Fisher-ideal index is exact for the square root of the quadratic specification for u. Usually the Fisher-ideal and Divisia indexes are identical with monetary data (to within round off error).[6] Nevertheless, on theoretical grounds the

---

6. An exception is when a new asset is introduced. Special procedures, involving the imputation of a reservation price, are needed in that case. See Diewert (1980a, sec. 8.6). Special procedures are additionally needed to deal with seasonality. See Diewert (1980a, sec. 8.7).

Divisia index is now the preferred selection from the superlative class by index-number theorists, largely as a result of its uniquely attractive properties in the nonhomothetic case (to be discussed in section A.8 below).

When the quantity aggregate, M_t^c, is acquired from the Divisia index, the dual user-cost price index, called the implicit Divisia price index, is acquired from Fisher's factor reversal test $\Pi_t^c = y_t / M_t^c$. Since relative user costs usually vary more than relative quantities, use of the Divisia index to produce the quantity aggregate, with the price aggregate produced from factor reversal, is preferable to the converse (see Allen and Diewert 1981). When M_t^c is produced from the discrete Divisia index, it is easily shown that the implicit Divisia price index, produced from factor reversal, is superlative in the Diewert sense.

A.6.2   The Financial Intermediary

The financial intermediary's output aggregation is produced from a decision that does not have the same form as the decision that produced the Divisia index for the consumer or manufacturing firm. Monetary output aggregation is produced by solving the financial intermediary's second-stage decision for μ_t^* and substituting it into f to acquire $M_t^b = f(\mu_t^*; \mathbf{k}_t)$. That second-stage decision is to select μ_t to

$$\text{maximize } \mu_t' \gamma_t \text{ subject to } f(\mu_t; \mathbf{k}_t) = M_t^b. \tag{A.81}$$

The following theorem proves that the Divisia index tracks M_t^b without error in continuous time, so long as μ_t^* is continually selected to solve (A.81) at each instant, t.

Theorem 2   *If μ_t^* solves (A.81) continually at each instant $t \in T_0$, then for every $t \in T_0$,*

$$\frac{d \log M_t^b}{dt} = \sum_i s_{it}^b \frac{d \log \mu_{it}^*}{dt},$$

where the ith asset's share in the financial intermediary's revenue from production of monetary services is $s_{it}^b = \gamma_{it}\mu_{it}^* / \gamma_t'\mu_t^*$.

Proof   The first-order conditions for solution to (A.81) are

$$\gamma_{it} = -\lambda \frac{\partial f}{\partial \mu_{it}} \tag{A.82}$$

and $f(\mu_t^*; \mathbf{k}_t) = M_t^b$, where λ is the Lagrange multiplier.

Compute the total differential of f to acquire

$$df(\mathbf{\mu}_t; \mathbf{k}_t) = \sum_i \frac{\partial f}{\partial \mu_{it}} d\mu_{it}.$$

Substitute (A.82) to find, at $\mathbf{\mu}_t = \mathbf{\mu}_t^*$, that

$$\lambda df(\mathbf{\mu}_t^*; \mathbf{k}_t) = -\sum_i \gamma_{it} d\mu_{it}^*. \tag{A.83}$$

But by summing (A.82) over i and solving for λ, we have that

$$\lambda = -\frac{\mathbf{\mu}_t^{*\prime} \mathbf{\gamma}_t}{\mathbf{\mu}_t^{*\prime} \partial f / \partial \mathbf{\mu}_t}. \tag{A.84}$$

Substitute (A.84) into (A.83) and rearrange to obtain

$$d \log f(\mathbf{\mu}_t^*; \mathbf{k}_t) = \frac{\mathbf{\mu}_t^{*\prime} \partial f / \partial \mathbf{\mu}_t}{f(\mathbf{\mu}_t^*; \mathbf{k}_t)} \sum_i \frac{\gamma_{it}}{\mathbf{\mu}_t^{*\prime} \mathbf{\gamma}_t} d\mu_{it}. \tag{A.85}$$

But since f is linearly homogeneous in $\mathbf{\mu}_t$, we have from Euler's equation that

$$\mathbf{\mu}_t^{*\prime} \frac{\partial f}{\partial \mathbf{\mu}_t} = f(\mathbf{\mu}_t^*; \mathbf{k}_t). \tag{A.86}$$

Substituting (A.86) into (A.85), we obtain

$$\frac{d \log f(\mathbf{\mu}_t^*; \mathbf{k}_t)}{dt} = \sum_i s_{it}^b \frac{d \log \mu_{it}^*}{dt},$$

where $s_{it}^b = \gamma_{it} \mu_{it}^* / \mathbf{\gamma}' \mathbf{\mu}_t^*$.   ∎

Hence the Divisia index is equally as applicable to aggregating over the monetary assets produced by the financial intermediary as over the monetary assets purchased by the consumer or manufacturing firm. In addition Simpson's rule again produces the Törnqvist–Theil discrete time approximation

$$\log M_t^b - \log M_{t-1}^b = \sum_i \bar{s}_{it}^b (\log \mu_{it}^* - \log \mu_{i,t-1}^*), \tag{A.87}$$

where $\bar{s}_{it}^b = (s_{it}^b + s_{i,t-1}^b)/2$. Furthermore, if the input requirement function f is translog, then the discrete Divisia index (A.87) is exact in discrete time (see Diewert 1976, p. 125). Hence (A.87) is a superlative index number. The reason for preferring the Divisia index over the other superlative indexes will be evident from the nonhomothetic case below.

While the Divisia monetary quantity index takes the same form for all three economic agents, the financial firm's monetary output aggregate nevertheless is distinguishable from the monetary aggregates for the consumer or manufacturing firm, because only the financial intermediary's aggregate depends on reserve requirements, $\mathbf{k}_t$. The financial intermediary's monetary asset user costs, $\mathbf{\gamma}_t$, each depend directly in (A.22) on the "reserve requirement tax" produced by nonzero $\mathbf{k}_t$ with no interest paid on required reserves. But the financial intermediary's monetary quantity aggregator function, f, also depends on $\mathbf{k}_t$. Hence the Divisia quantity index for the financial intermediary depends on $\mathbf{k}_t$ both through the effect on $\mathbf{\gamma}_t$ and also on $f(\mathbf{\mu}_t; \mathbf{k}_t)$, which the Divisia index seeks to track. As a result the Divisia monetary quantity index for the financial intermediaries tends to internalize the effects of changes in reserve requirements.

Having produced the output quantity aggregate from the Divisia index, the dual price aggregate is produced from output reversal,

$$\Gamma_t = \frac{\mathbf{\mu}_t^{*\prime} \mathbf{\gamma}_t}{M_t^b}. \tag{A.88}$$

The user-cost price index produced in that manner is called the implicit Divisia price index. The resulting price index is superlative in the Diewert sense, as is easily shown from (A.88) and the fact that M_t^b is superlative.

A.7   Aggregation Theory without Homotheticity

As we have seen in sections A.4 and A.5 above, aggregation theory and index-number theory provide readily derived results, when aggregator functions are linearly homogeneous. However, linear homogeneity is a strong assumption, especially for a consumer. As a result, despite the elegance of the theory produced under linear homogeneity, extension of aggregation and index-number theory to the nonhomothetic case can be very important empirically. As concluded by Samuelson and Swamy (1974, p. 592):

Empirical experience is abundant that the Santa Claus hypothesis of homotheticity in tastes and in technical change is quite unrealistic. Therefore, we must not be bemused by the undoubted elegances and richness of the homothetic theory. Nor should we shoot the honest theorist who points out to us the unavoidable truth that in nonhomothetic cases of realistic life, one must not expect to be able to make the naive measurements that untutored common sense always longs for; we must accept the sad facts of life, and be grateful for the more complicated procedures economic theory devises.

This section deals with the most promising of those more complicated procedures devised by economic theory.

The quantity and price aggregates presented in previous sections were produced from duality theory under the assumption that the category utility (or production) function defined over the component quantities is linearly homogeneous. However, in recent years it has been shown in the literature on duality theory that the quantity and price aggregates produced under that homogeneity assumption are special cases of a more general pair of dual functions that are applicable without any homotheticity assumptions on tastes or technology. This section provides the more general aggregation theory, as it applies to the three economic agents postulated in sections A.2, A.3, and A.4.

A.7.1 The Consumer and the Manufacturing Firm

As we have seen in the homogeneous case, the monetary aggregation theory applicable to the manufacturing firm is identical to that of the consumer, since the decision problems producing the aggregates are identical. All of the monetary aggregation theory for both economic agents is produced by the second-stage decision problem (A.4). The conditional portfolio decision (A.4) for the consumer is converted to the manufacturing firm's conditional portfolio decision (A.40) by a simple change of notation. Hence in this section we will use (A.4) with the understanding that the appropriate change of notation would be used, if our results were applied to the manufacturing firm rather than the consumer. However, we now no longer assume that u is linearly homogeneous, or even homothetic.

As we have seen, under linear homogeneity of u, the quantity aggregator function is the category subutility function u itself. However, if u is not linearly homogeneous, u clearly cannot serve the role of the quantity aggregator function, because a quantity aggregator function that is not linearly homogeneous does not make sense. If every component quantity is growing at the same rate, then any sensible quantity aggregate would have to grow at that same rate. But that is the definition of linear homogeneity. Hence the theoretically appropriate quantity aggregator function should be linearly homogeneous in the component quantities $\mathbf{m}_t$, and should reduce to the category subutility function, u, in the special case of linearly homogeneous u. The corresponding price aggregator function should be the true dual to the quantity aggregator function, should be linearly homogeneous in the component prices, and should reduce to the unit cost function (A.46) in the case of linearly homogeneous category subutility u. It has been shown in recent literature that the duals that best serve those purposes are the distance function at fixed utility level (as the quantity aggregate) and the cost function at fixed utility level (as the dual price aggregate). When normalized to equal one at base-period prices and utility, the result is the aggregation-theoretic Malmquist quantity index and the Konüs true-cost-of-living index, respectively.

Before we can present these results, we must define the distance function, $d(u_0, \mathbf{m}_t)$, at u_0. That function can be defined in implicit form to be the solution to the equation

$$u\left[\frac{\mathbf{m}_t}{d(u_0, \mathbf{m}_t)}\right] = u_0 \tag{A.89}$$

for preselected fixed reference utility level, u_0. The equivalent direct definition is

$$d(u_0, \mathbf{m}_t) = \max_{\kappa}\left\{\kappa : u\left(\frac{\mathbf{m}_t}{\kappa}\right) = u_0\right\}.$$

Equation (A.89) has an interesting geometric interpretation. We see that $d(u_0, \mathbf{m}_t)$ is the factor by which $\mathbf{m}_t$ must be deflated to reduce (or increase) the utility level to the fixed reference level u_0. In other words, we move along the direction of the $\mathbf{m}_t$ vector until we intersect the isoquant, $u(\mathbf{m}_t) = u_0$; then $d(u_0, \mathbf{m}_t)$ measures how far that intersection point is from the point, $\mathbf{m}_t$. While (A.89) defines the distance function in terms of the utility function, we also can do the converse, since the utility function is the solution for u to $d(u, \mathbf{m}_t) = 1$.

The distance function (at fixed u_0) is indeed linearly homogeneous, monotonically increasing and strictly concave in $\mathbf{m}_t$, even when u is not linearly homogeneous. Hence, when u is linearly homogeneous, u has exactly the same properties that d always has, regardless of whether or not u is linearly homogeneous. In addition, when u actually is linearly homogeneous, the distance function becomes proportional to the utility function. Hence, when u is linear homogeneous, the quantity aggregate produced from the distance function will always grow at exactly the same rate as the quantity aggregate $u(\mathbf{m}_t^*)$, which we already have derived in the case of linearly homogeneous u. This fact is easily seen by observing that linear homogeneity of u implies that $u(\mathbf{m}_t)/d(u_0,\mathbf{m}_t) = u(\mathbf{m}_t/d(u_0,\mathbf{m}_t))$, which equals u_0 by (A.89). Hence $d(u_0,\mathbf{m}_t) = u(\mathbf{m}_t)/u_0$, which is proportional to $u(\mathbf{m}_t)$ at fixed u_0.

In order to acquire the dual price aggregate, we need only observe the following two relationships, which follow from equations (A.92) and (A.93) in Deaton and Muellbauer (1980, p. 55):

$$d(u_0,\mathbf{m}_t) = \min_{\pi_t}\{\pi_t'\mathbf{m}_t : E(u_0,\pi_t) = 1\} \tag{A.90}$$

and

$$E(u_0,\pi_t) = \min_{\mathbf{m}_t}\{\pi_t'\mathbf{m}_t : d(u_0,\mathbf{m}_t) = 1\}. \tag{A.91}$$

Equations (A.90) and (A.91) demonstrate that the distance function d and the cost function E are duals. As we therefore might expect, the price aggregate in general is the cost function, as a function of π_t, at fixed reference utility level u_0.

At fixed reference u_0, the cost function has all of the correct properties for a price aggregator function, including linear homogeneity in π_t. In addition the cost function is monotonically increasing and concave in π_t. Hence, regardless of whether or not u is linearly homogeneous, the cost function has all of the same properties that the unit cost function has when u is linearly homogeneous. In addition, if category subutility really is linearly homogeneous, we get the same price aggregate growth rates by using the cost function as we did in section A.5 above, when we used the unit-cost function, since the two functions are then proportional to each other. That result follows from (A.48) by setting M_t^c equal to u_0; the proportionality constant becomes u_0. Observe that both the exact quantity aggregate produced by the distance function and the exact price aggregate produced by the cost function are entirely ordinal, because each is invariant to monotonic transformations of utility.

In order for the duality defined in (A.90) and (A.91) to be perfect, we also need the distance and cost functions to satisfy factor reversal, when consumer decisions are made optimally. Gorman (1976) has shown this to be the case. Following earlier work by Afriat, Gorman defines the price vector π_t and the quantity vector $\mathbf{m}_t$ to be "conjugate" at category subutility level u_0, if the cheapest way to reach u_0 at prices π_t is a vector proportional to $\mathbf{m}_t$. Gorman proved that if $\bar{\pi}_t$ and $\bar{\mathbf{m}}_t$ are conjugates in that sense, then

$$M^c(\bar{\mathbf{m}}_t;u_0)\Pi^c(\bar{\pi}_t;u_0) = \bar{\mathbf{m}}_t'\bar{\pi}_t, \tag{A.92}$$

where the exact monetary aggregate is

$$M^c(\mathbf{m}_t; u_0) = d(u_0, \mathbf{m}_t),\tag{A.93}$$

and the exact dual monetary user-cost aggregate is

$$\Pi^c(\boldsymbol{\pi}_t; u_0) = E(u_0, \boldsymbol{\pi}_t).\tag{A.94}$$

Clearly, (A.92) is factor reversal at $(\bar{\mathbf{m}}_t, \bar{\boldsymbol{\pi}}_t)$.

In aggregation theory, exact economic aggregates are converted to exact economic indexes by dividing by a base period value of the aggregate. The natural ways thereby to convert (A.93) and (A.94) into exact economic indexes are

$$M^{mc}(\mathbf{m}_{t_2}, \mathbf{m}_{t_1}; u_0) = \frac{d(u_0, \mathbf{m}_{t_2})}{d(u_0, \mathbf{m}_{t_1})}\tag{A.95}$$

and

$$\Pi^{kc}(\boldsymbol{\pi}_{t_2}, \boldsymbol{\pi}_{t_1}; u_0) = \frac{E(u_0, \boldsymbol{\pi}_{t_2})}{E(u_0, \boldsymbol{\pi}_{t_1})}.\tag{A.96}$$

The price index $\Pi^{kc}(\boldsymbol{\pi}_{t_2}, \boldsymbol{\pi}_{t_1}; u_0)$ is the famous Konüs (1924) true-cost-of-living index. The dual quantity index $M^{mc}(\mathbf{m}_{t_2}, \mathbf{m}_{t_1}; u_0)$ is the Malmquist index, proposed in consumer theory by Malmquist (1953) and later in producer theory by Moorsteen (1961).

At this point, it is clear why the case of linear homogeneity of u is so important. Without linear homogeneity of utility, the exact quantity and price aggregator functions M^{mc} and Π^{kc}, although unique and based on very elegant duality theory, nevertheless depend on a reference utility level, u_0; the index provides no information about how to choose the reference utility level. The base period need not be t_1 or t_2. Hence the aggregation theory is equally applicable for any selection of u_0. It can be shown that M^{mc} and Π^{kc} are independent of u_0, if and only if category utility is linearly homogeneous (see Diewert 1981, sec. 3). Otherwise, the exact economic monetary quantity and price aggregates depend on the reference utility surface relative to which the indexes are defined.

Although the Konüs true-cost-of-living index has long been recognized to be the correct price index in economic aggregation theory, recognition that the Malmquist quantity index is the correct dual quantity index has been more recent. Previously, the quantity index commonly viewed to be exact was the Allen index

$$M^{ac}(\mathbf{m}_{t_2}, \mathbf{m}_{t_1}; \boldsymbol{\pi}_0) = \frac{E(u(\mathbf{m}_{t_2}); \boldsymbol{\pi}_0)}{E(u(\mathbf{m}_{t_1}); \boldsymbol{\pi}_0)},\tag{A.97}$$

whereas the Malmquist quantity index depends on an undefined value for u_0, the Allen quantity index depends on an undefined value for the reference user-cost price vector, π_0, which need not be the prices at either t_2 or t_1. Although the Allen index is now primarily of historical interest only, we nevertheless will see that our choice of a statistical (nonparametric) quantity index number will be the same, regardless of whether it is viewed to be an approximation to the exact parametric Malmquist index or to the Allen index. It is also interesting to observe than in the case of linearly homogeneous utility, the Malmquist and Allen indexes are equal.

A.7.2 The Financial Intermediary

As may be expected from our results in the homogeneous case, the results in section A.7.1 above for the consumer and manufacturing firm apply also to aggregation of financial intermediary output with a non-homogeneous factor requirement function, if we replace the cost function by its output analogue, the revenue function, and if we replace the category subutility function, u (or $a(\varepsilon_t)$ for the manufacturing firm), by its output analogue, the factor requirements function.

By analogy to (A.89), define the financial firm's output distance function implicitly to be the value of $D(\mu_t, \alpha_t; k_t)$ that solves

$$f\left(\frac{\mu_t}{D(\mu_t, \alpha_t; k_t)}; k_t\right) = g(\alpha_0), \tag{A.98}$$

for preselected reference input vector α_0. The equivalent direct definition is

$$D(\mu_t, \alpha_t; k_t) = \min_{\kappa}\left\{\kappa : f\left(\frac{\mu_t}{\kappa}; k_t\right) \le g(\alpha_0)\right\}.$$

Then the exact monetary quantity output aggregate for the financial intermediary is

$$M^b(\mu_t; \alpha_0, k_t) = D(\mu_t, \alpha_t; k_t), \tag{A.99}$$

and the corresponding Malmquist economic output quantity index is

$$M^{mb}(\mu_{t_2}, \mu_{t_1}; \alpha_0, k_t) = \frac{D(\mu_{t_2}, \alpha_0; k_t)}{D(\mu_{t_1}, \alpha_0; k_t)}. \tag{A.100}$$

The corresponding dual Konüs monetary output price index is produced by replacing the cost function in section A.7.1 by its output analogue, the revenue function (A.70). Hence the true output price aggregate is

$$\Gamma(\gamma_t; \alpha_0, \mathbf{k}_t) = R^*(\alpha_0, \gamma_t; \mathbf{k}_t), \tag{A.101}$$

and the corresponding Konüs true financial output price aggregate is

$$\Gamma^k(\gamma_{t_2}, \gamma_{t_1}; \alpha_0, \mathbf{k}_t) = \frac{R^*(\alpha_0, \gamma_{t_2}; \mathbf{k}_t)}{R^*(\alpha_0, \gamma_{t_1}; \mathbf{k}_t)}. \tag{A.102}$$

Again, we find that in the case of nonhomogeneity (of f), the exact economic output price and quantity aggregates and indexes depend on an undefined choice. In this case that choice is of the reference input vector, α_0. The dependency on α_0 disappears if and only if the factor requirement function is linearly homogeneous, in which case the results above reduce to those in section A.5.3.

The duality results analogous to (A.90) and (A.91) are

$$D(\mu_t, \alpha_t; \mathbf{k}_t) = \max_{\gamma_t} \{\gamma_t' \mu_t : R^*(\alpha_0, \gamma_t; \mathbf{k}_t) = 1\} \tag{A.103}$$

and

$$R^*(\alpha_0, \gamma_t; \mathbf{k}_t) = \max_{\mu_t} \{\gamma_t' \mu_t : D(\mu_t, \alpha_0; \mathbf{k}_t) = 1\}. \tag{A.104}$$

A.8   Index-Number Theory under Nonhomogeneity

There are a number of published approaches to producing nonparametric approximations to the Malmquist or Allen quantity index. Yet virtually all of them result in selection of the discrete (Törnqvist) Divisia index. It is in fact the nonhomogeneous case where the Divisia index stands out as being the uniquely best element of Diewert's superlative class. When Denny asked whether it is possible to acquire superlative indexes other than the Divisia in the nonhomothetic case, Diewert (1980c, p. 538) replied: "My answer is that it may be possible, but I have not been able to do it." Subsequently Caves, Christensen, and Diewert (1982b, p. 1411) proved that the (discrete) Divisia index "is superlative in a considerably more general sense than shown by Diewert. We are not aware of other indexes that can be shown to be superlative in this more general sense."

A.8.1   The Consumer and the Manufacturing Firm

Perhaps the first rigorously proved theoretical results on nonparametric approximation in the nonhomothetic case are those of Theil (1968) and

Kloek (1967). Their result produces the following conclusion in our case. Suppose that $\mathbf{m}_{t_i}$ is the consumer's utility-maximizing monetary asset portfolio at user-cost prices, $\boldsymbol{\pi}_{t_i}$, and at expenditure, $\boldsymbol{\pi}'_{t_i}\mathbf{m}_{t_i}$, (with i = 1 or 2), and let $\boldsymbol{\pi}_0$ be the vector having $(\pi_{t_1 k}\pi_{t_2 k})^{1/2}$ as its kth component. Then the (discrete) Divisia index provides a second-order approximation to the Allen quantity index, (97).

More recently Diewert (1976, pp. 123–24) has proved that the discrete Divisia index is exact for the Malmquist quantity index, (A.95), under a specific choice for the distance function and the reference utility level. In our case those assumptions would be that: the distance function, d, is generalized translog; $\mathbf{m}_{t_i}$ is the consumer's utility-maximizing monetary asset portfolio at user-cost prices, $\boldsymbol{\pi}_{t_i}$, and at expenditure, $\boldsymbol{\pi}'_{t_i}\mathbf{m}_{t_i}$, (with i = 1 or 2); and the reference utility level, u_0, is $(u_1 u_2)^{1/2}$, where $u_1 = u(\mathbf{m}_{t_1})$ and $u_2 = u(\mathbf{m}_{t_2})$. Since the translog specification can produce a second-order approximation to any distance function, we see that the Divisia index produces a second-order approximation to any Malmquist quantity index, if the reference utility level is selected in accordance with Diewert's theorem.

In addition it has recently been shown that the Divisia index is not only exact for a generalized translog distance function, but remains appropriate even when tastes or technology are changing over time. The Divisia index is a chained index that measures changes relative to the previous period, rather than relative to a fixed base period. As a result it has always been believed that the Divisia index would work well with shifting tastes or technology, since chained indexes adjust rapidly to the latest form of a shifting aggregator function. However, Caves, Christensen, and Diewert (1982a, b) have recently found a precise relationship between the Divisia quantity index and a shifting aggregator function. In particular, their result shows that, if u shifts between periods t_1 or t_2 then the Divisia index accurately produces the log change in aggregate consumption (or factor demand, for the manufacturing firm) of monetary services by the consumer, if the distance function is generalized translog in both periods t_1 or t_2, such that the second-order terms in $\mathbf{m}(t)$ have the same coefficients in both periods. The result does not require constancy of the remaining coefficients or homotheticity of u.

Any of the results above can be used to prove that the implicit Divisia user-cost price index, produced from the Divisia quantity index and factor reversal, possesses the same approximation properties relative to the Konüs true-cost-of-living index that the Divisia quantity index possesses relative to the Malmquist (or Allen) quantity index. Also the results imputed above to consumer monetary portfolio aggregation clearly are immediately applicable to manufacturing firm monetary portfolio demand. We need only replace the consumer's category subutility function u with the manufacturing firm's category subproduction function, a.

A.8.2   The Financial Intermediary

All the results described in section A.8.1 are equally applicable to providing nonparametric ("statistical") approximations to the financial intermediary's monetary asset output Malmquist quantity index, (A.100), and its dual Konüs user-cost price aggregate, (A.102). All that is needed is to replace the input distance function, d, by the output distance function, D, and the cost function, E, by the revenue function R^* (see Diewert 1976, p. 125, 1980a, p. 463; Caves, Christensen, and Diewert 1982b, sec. 3).

A.8.3   Subaggregation

In section A.5.5 we discussed the theory of exact subaggregation in economic aggregation theory. The resulting utility or production tree can produce recursive aggregation over increasingly broad aggregates—for example, from Divisia M1, to Divisia M2, to Divisia M3, to Divisia L. However, the aggregation theory is in terms of exact aggregator functions, recursively nested. The question naturally arises as to whether statistical index numbers, such as the Divisia index, can be nested within each other to produce Divisia indexes of Divisia indexes at successively higher levels of aggregation.

If, for example, Divisia indexes of Divisia indexes are Divisia indexes of the original components, then the Divisia index would be called consistent in aggregation. A statistical index that has the property of consistency in aggregation is the Vartia (1976) index. However, the Vartia quantity index has the extremely unattractive property of not being invariant to rescaling of the prices in either period. Similarly the Vartia price index does not increase at the same rate as second-period prices, when all second-period prices are inflated by a common rate. The Vartia index is also not a superlative index. However, the Divisia index is almost consistent in aggregation, since the Divisia index of Divisia indexes differs from the Divisia index over the original components only by an error of the third order. These results apply in discrete time, regardless of whether the category subutility or category subproduction function is linearly homogeneous.

Of course, in continuous time the Divisia index is exactly consistent in aggregation in the homogeneous case, since the Divisia index then is exact at all levels of aggregation for any aggregator function. There are no remainder terms.

A.9 Aggregation over Consumers and Firms

The aggregation theory presented above is for individual decision makers: one consumer, one manufacturing firm, or one financial intermediary. We have not discussed aggregation over individual decision makers, although a large literature exists on the subject. In this section we cite a few of the more useful results in that literature, and present one particularly interesting result that is specific to the Divisia index.

The subject of aggregation over consumers has been heavily researched, and the results are well known. The most important of those results are surveyed in Barnett (1983a, b) and will not be repeated here. Two different literatures exist on aggregation over firms. One literature resembles that for aggregation over consumers, but a more specialized literature exists on the derivation of production transformation surfaces for an industry or the entire economy. Sato (1975) has provided an excellent survey of that early literature. One of his more interesting results (1975, p. 283) is that a constant-returns-to-scale economywide production function exists if there is a social utility function. As a result aggregation over consumers can produce perfect aggregation over firms. Other results on aggregation over firms are surveyed in Diewert (1980a, pp. 464–70). Particularly useful results are those of Bliss (1975, p. 146) and Debreu (1959, p. 45), who found that if all firms are competitive profit maximizers, then the group of firms can be treated as a single firm maximizing profits subject to the sum of the individual firm's production sets. That result provides a very simple means of aggregating over firms.

All of the theory presented above is directly linked to deterministic microeconomic and aggregation theory. However, the Divisia index can be acquired in another manner, one that easily permits aggregation over goods, consumers, and firms jointly. This approach, called the atomistic approach and championed by Theil (1967) and Clements and Izan (1984), treats the expenditure weights in the Divisia index as the probabilities of drawing the corresponding quantity log changes. Then the Divisia quantity index is just the mean of the distribution of log changes. To see how easily we can thereby also aggregate jointly over economic agents, consider the case of demand for monetary assets by the consumer and the manufacturing firm. In continuous time the consumer's Divisia monetary quantity index from (A.79) can be written in differential form as

$$d \log M_t^c = \sum_i s_{it}^c d \log m_{it}^*, \qquad (A.105)$$

where the share weights, $s_{it}^c = \pi_{it} m_{it}^* / \pi_t' m_t^*$, can be interpreted as the probability of drawing $d \log m_{it}^*$ in a random sampling from the population of monetary asset growth rates at t by consumer i. The analogous Divisia index for the manufacturing firm is

$$d \log M_t^f = \sum_i s_{it}^f d \log \eta_{it}, \qquad (A.106)$$

where $s_{it}^f = \eta_{it} \varepsilon_{it} / \eta_t' \varepsilon_t$,

Now let Π_t^c be the implicit Divisia user-cost aggregate produced from M_t^c and factor reversal, and let Π_t^f be the implicit Divisia user-cost aggregate produced from M_t^f and factor reversal. Let $W_t^f = \Pi_t^f M_t^f / (\Pi_t^f M_t^f + \Pi_t^c M_t^c)$ and $W_t^c = \Pi_t^c M_t^c / (\Pi_t^f M_t^f + \Pi_t^c M_t^c)$. Then the shares (W_t^f, W_t^c) can be interpreted as probabilities, so that we can define the Divisia quantity M_t^{fc} aggregated over both the firm and consumer by

$$d \log M_t^{fc} = W^f d \log M_t^f + W^c d \log M_t^c. \qquad (A.107)$$

Substituting (A.105) and (A.106) into (A.107), we find that

$$d \log M_t^{fc} = \sum_i \frac{\eta_{it} \varepsilon_{it}}{\Pi_t^f M_t^f + \Pi_t^c M_t^c} d \log \eta_{it} \qquad (A.108)$$

Clearly, (A.108) is itself a Divisia index, since

$$\sum_i \frac{\eta_{it} \varepsilon_{it}}{\Pi_t^f M_t^f + \Pi_t^c M_t^c} + \sum_i \frac{\pi_{it} m_{it}}{\Pi_t^f M_t^f + \Pi_t^c M_t^c} = 1,$$

so (A.108) is a share-weighted average of log changes. But (A.108) aggregates simultaneously over monetary assets demanded by both the consumer and the manufacturing firm. This procedure is equally applicable to aggregation over monetary assets demanded by many consumers and firms. The approach is most advantageously used to aggregate over monetary assets demanded by different pre-aggregated groups of asset holders (firms, rich consumers, other consumers, etc.), when the ability to decompose the aggregate into the group subaggregates could be useful. Prior aggregation within the groups could be in accordance with the methods mentioned earlier in this section.

A.10 Technical Change

It has frequently been argued that substantial technical change occurred in the banking industry over the past decade. The potential existence of technological innovation in that industry has sometimes been viewed as a complicating factor in financial modeling and in monetary policy. However, aggregation theory and index-number theory are directly relevant to measuring technical change. In fact, a long literature exists on that subject. This section discusses some of those results that are most relevant to measuring technical change in the banking industry. The discussion is in terms of the technology of the financial intermediary.

When technical change is possible, the financial intermediary's production function is

$$M_t^b = g(\alpha_t, t), \tag{A.109}$$

where α_t is the vector of factor inputs and

$$M_t^b = f(\mu_t; \mathbf{k}_t) \tag{A.110}$$

is the exact economic quantity aggregate over monetary asset outputs, μ_t. Technical change in production of aggregate monetary output is thereby equivalent to a shift in technology in (A.109) over time, so $g(\alpha_t, t)$ must have time as an argument. In accordance with Ohta's (1974) definition, the primal (as opposed to dual) rate of change of total factor productivity is

$$\left. \frac{\partial \log g(\alpha_t, t)}{\partial t} \right|_{\alpha_t},$$

which measures the rate of disembodied technical change.

Consider first the simplest case, which is neutral technological progress. Then there must exist a function $\varphi(t)$ of time, such that (A.109) can be written

$$M_t^b = \varphi(t) g(\alpha_t), \tag{A.111}$$

with variation in $\varphi(t)$ producing parallel translations of isoquants. In discrete time, according to Ohta's definition, the rate of disembodied technical change is the log change of (A.111) with α_t held constant:

$$(\log M_{t+1}^b - \log M_t^b)|_{\alpha_t} = \log\left(\frac{\varphi(t+1)}{\varphi(t)}\right). \tag{A.112}$$

Substituting (A.111) into (A.112), we obtain

$$(\log M_{t+1}^b - \log M_t^b)|_{\alpha_t} = \log\left(\frac{M_{t+1}^b}{M_t^b}\right) - \log\left(\frac{g(\alpha_{t+1})}{g(\alpha_t)}\right) \tag{A.113}$$

If the input aggregator function (or output production function) g is linearly homogeneous, then

$$\log\left(\frac{g(\alpha_{t+1})}{g(\alpha_t)}\right) = \log g(\alpha_{t+1}) - \log g(\alpha_t) \tag{A.114}$$

can be measured by the discrete Divisia index over growth rates of input quantities, α_t. Since the index is superlative, the error is third order. If the output aggregator function, f, is also linearly homogeneous, then

$$\log\left(\frac{M_{t+1}^b}{M_t^b}\right) = \log M_{t+1}^b - \log M_t^b \tag{A.115}$$

can be measured by the discrete Divisia index over growth rates of output quantities, μ_t. Hence we can see from (A.113), (A.114), and (A.115) that the rate of technical change can be measured by the difference between two Divisia indexes, one aggregating over growth rates of output quantities and the other aggregating over growth rates of input quantities. In continuous time the result measures the total rate of disembodied technical change exactly. If f and g are both translog, then the result is also exact in discrete time.

Sometimes $\varphi(t) - 1$ is treated as the rate of technical progress. In that case there is said to be technical progress if $\varphi(t) > 0$, or technical regress if $\varphi(t) < 0$. Clearly, from (A.111) we see that $\varphi(t)$ can be computed from the ratio of the output Divisia index level to the input Divisia index level.

Since we explicitly assumed output separability, when we defined the technology of the financial intermediary in section A.3, we do so in the derivation above as well. However, it is worth observing that the result can be adapted to the case of nonseparability (see Diewert 1976, pp. 127–29). The results also can be generalized to the case of nonhomothetic g and f; see Caves, Christensen, and Diewert (1982a, b). In that case technical progress is defined in terms of Malmquist input and output indexes. When the distance functions used to define the Malmquist input and output indexes are translog, the rate of technological change again is measured exactly in terms of Divisia input and output indexes.

For a discussion of nonneutral technical change, see Jorgenson and Lau (1975). In that case the Divisia index still measures aggregate monetary output by the financial intermediary (regardless of the technical progress), but measurement of the technical progress itself requires estimation of the firm's technology, containing an index of technological change.

A.11   Value Added

In monetary theory, outside money plays an important role because outside (or high-powered, or base) money is net wealth, whereas the potential wealth effect of inside money is often viewed as offset by equal liabilities corresponding to each such asset. Although outside money certainly is uniquely important in many ways, it seems worth observing that there is value added produced by the banking industry. So long as primary factors of production other than base money are employed in that industry, the banking industry produces net services that were not embodied in the industry's employment of outside money. In this section, I discuss the measurement of value added for our financial intermediary.

Partition the financial intermediary's input vector α_t so that $\alpha_t = (\alpha'_{1t}, \alpha'_{2t})'$, where α_{1t} is quantities of primary inputs (e.g., labor, capital, and land) and α_{2t} is quantities of intermediate inputs (e.g., materials). Partition the factor-price vector correspondingly, so that $\beta_t = (\beta'_{1t}, \beta'_{2t})'$. Then the financial intermediary's technology can be written as

$$M_t^b = g(\alpha_{1t}, \alpha_{2t}). \tag{A.116}$$

Let the firm's maximum variable profit level at given α_{1t} be

$$V_t = V(\alpha_{1t}, \beta_{2t}, \gamma_t), \tag{A.117}$$

which is the firm's variable profit function conditional upon α_{1t}. As a function of α_{1t} at fixed prices, V has all of the usual properties of a neoclassical production function. Sato (1975) calls

$$V_{t_0,t_1} = \frac{V(\alpha_{1t_0}, \beta_2^*, \gamma^*)}{V(\alpha_{1t_1}, \beta_2^*, \gamma^*)} \tag{A.118}$$

the true index of real value added, which depends on the selection of the reference prices, (β_2^*, γ^*).

In order to provide a nonparametric (statistical) approximation to (A.118), assume constant returns to scale. Also assume that V is translog and select (β_2^*, γ^*) to be the geometric means of those prices in periods t_0 and t_1. Diewert (1980a, p. 459) then has shown that (A.118) equals the discrete Divisia quantity index for aggregating over the primary inputs.

The need to select the reference prices (β_2^*, γ^*) becomes unnecessary, if and only if g is separable, so that (A.116) can be written

$$M_t^b = G(\zeta(\alpha_{1t}), \alpha_{2t}). \tag{A.119}$$

In that case, V can be written

$$V_t = V_1(\alpha_{1t})V_2(\beta_{2t}, \gamma_t). \tag{A.120}$$

Clearly,

$$V_{t_0,t_1} = \frac{V_1(\alpha_{1t_0})}{V_1(\alpha_{1t_1})}, \tag{A.121}$$

which does not depend on reference prices. The function V_1 has all of the properties of a conventional neoclassical production function. However, in this case $\zeta(\alpha_{1t})$ is a category subproduction function, so we can more directly define the value-added index to be

$$V_{t_0,t_1}^* = \frac{\zeta(\alpha_{1t_0})}{\zeta(\alpha_{1t_1})}. \tag{A.122}$$

If ζ is translog, then the discrete Divisia index is exact for either (A.121) or (A.122). So the discrete Divisia index provides a second-order approximation for V_{t_0,t_1} or V_{t_0,t_1}^* for any ζ. In continuous time the Divisia index is always exact for $\zeta(\alpha_{1t})$, which is value added. Clearly, high-powered money is all value added, if and only if α_{1t} contains only high-powered money.

The source of the term "value added" can be found in the accounting conventions for measuring value added. The accounting convention, called "double deflation," requires the very restrictive assumption that (A.119) can be written in the form

$$M_t^b = \zeta_1(\alpha_{1t}) + \zeta_2(\alpha_{2t}). \tag{A.123}$$

Clearly, $\zeta_1(\alpha_{1t})$ is value added, since it is added to $\zeta_2(\alpha_{2t})$ to get M_t^b. In that case Sims (1969) has proved that value added is measured exactly by a Divisia index.

A.12 Macroeconomic and General Equilibrium Theory

In terms of its relationship with final targets of policy, the demand-side Divisia monetary aggregates are the most relevant. Those aggregates measure the economy's monetary service flows, as perceived by the users of monetary assets. As a result it might seem that we would be interested only in the consumer and manufacturing firm whose decisions are analogous and pose little difficulty. This convenient situation would arise, for example, if we were seeking monetary aggregates to be used as indicators. Frequently, however, money plays a more complex role in economics. For example, a money market appears in most macroeconomic models and in many recent general equilibrium models. Policy simulations with macroeconometric models usually require a modeled money market. In addition targeting a monetary aggregate, perhaps as a long-run "anchor," would require information about the supply function for the aggregate. All of these objectives would be facilitated if the supply-side Divisia monetary aggregates from the financial firm, along with the transmission mechanism from central bank instruments, were incorporated into a full model of the economy. Producing a cleared money market in a Divisia monetary aggregate, along with a transmission mechanism operating through that market, is an objective toward which the research above could tend. However, much research remains before such a closed model could be constructed with full aggregation-theoretic microfoundations.

If a model included only a demand-side Divisia monetary aggregate, then closing a complete model would require modeling the supply of every component in the Divisia monetary aggregate. Market clearing then would occur at the level of disaggregated component quantities, which then could be substituted into the Divisia demand monetary aggregate. While the resulting aggregate could be informative and useful, much of the potential simplification is lost by the need to produce completely disaggregated supply functions. However, incorporating both supply and demand aggregates in a model—which would be needed to produce a market for an aggregate—has been given very little consideration in aggregation theory. Many difficult issues arise. What do we do if the financial firm's technology is separable in different blockings of monetary assets from those that appear in the consumer's utility function or the manufacturing firm's technology? How do we deal with the fact that currency and primary monetary securities appear as components of the consumer's and manufacturing firm's monetary demand aggregate, but not as components of the financial firm's monetary output aggregate? What happens to the ability to close the money market if homotheticity applies on one side of the money market while nonhomotheticity requires use of a Malmquist index on the other side of the market?

One potential problem is immediately evident from the results in prior sections. The user-cost prices of monetary assets produced by the financial intermediary are different from those for the consumer (or manufacturing firm). The reason is the existence of reserve requirements, which produce an implicit tax on financial intermediaries. The tax does not affect the user cost of the same assets for consumers or manufacturing firms. Income taxes produce similar "wedges" between user costs on the supply and demand sides of the money markets. As a result, even when the markets for every component are cleared, the Divisia demand and corresponding Divisia supply aggregate need not be equal, because the different user costs can produce different weights, although all corresponding component quantities nevertheless may be equal.

Another potential problem is that in some macroeconomic models monetary wealth, rather than monetary service flow, is relevant. This could be the case, for example, in producing an argument of a consumption function. Then it is necessary to compute the expected discounted present value of the service flow, in accordance with the formula provided in appendix B to this book. The expected service flow in a future period is measured by its expected Divisia index. For a discussion of the appropriate use of capital stocks and capital service flows, see Usher (1980, pp. 17–18).

Regarding the possibility of a regulatory wedge, the following two figures illustrate the problem in general equilibrium. It should be observed that the demand-side Divisia monetary aggregate, measuring perceived service flows received by financial asset holders, can be slightly different from the supply-side Divisia monetary aggregate, measuring service flows produced by financial intermediaries. The reason is the regulatory wedge resulting from non–interest-bearing

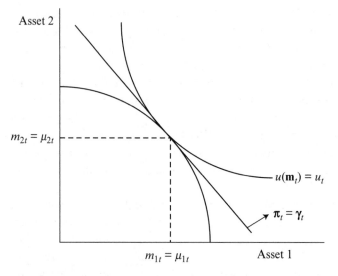

Figure A.1
Financial general equilibrium without required reserves

required reserves. That wedge produces a difference between demand-side and supply-side user-cost prices and thereby can produce a small difference between the demand-side and supply-side Divisia aggregates.

When there are no required reserves and hence no regulatory wedge, the general equilibrium looks like part I's figure 3.1 in the two-asset case, with the usual separating hyperplane determining the user-cost prices, which are the same on both sides of the market. The production possibility surface between deposit types 1 and 2 is for a financial intermediary, while the indifference curve is for a depositor allocating funds over the two asset types.

While this separating-hyperplane general equilibrium diagram is elementary, it assumes that the same prices and user costs are seen on both sides of the market. But when non–interest-bearing required reserves exist, the forgone investment return to banks is an implicit tax on banks and produces a regulatory wedge between the demand and supply side, as shown in the last term on the right-hand side of equation (A.25). It was shown by Barnett (1987) that under those circumstances, the user cost of supplied financial services by banks is not equal to the demand-side user-cost price, (A.5), but rather is equation (A.22). Note that this supply-side user cost, (A.22), is equal to the demand-side formula, (A.5), when required reserve ratios, $k_{it} = 0$.

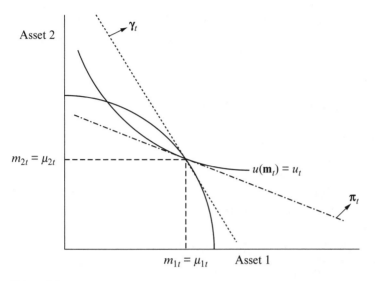

Figure A.2
Financial equilibrium with positive required reserves

The resulting general equilibrium diagram, with the regulatory wedge, is displayed in figure A.2. Notice that one tangency determines the supply-side prices, while the other tangency produces the demand-side prices, with the angle between the two straight lines being the "regulatory wedge." Observe that the demand equals the supply for each of the component assets, 1 and 2.

Although the component demands and supplies are equal to each other, the failure of tangency between the production possibility curve and the indifference curve at the equilibrium results in a wedge between the growth rates of aggregate demand and supply services, as reflected in the fact that the user-cost prices in the Divisia index are not the same in the demand- and the supply-side aggregates. To determine whether this wedge might provide a reason to compute and track the Divisia monetary supply aggregate, as well as the more common demand-side Divisia monetary aggregate, Barnett, Hinich, and Weber (1986) conducted a detailed spectral analysis in the frequency domain. They found that the effect of the wedge was negligible, except in the very short run, and the difference between Divisia demand and Divisia supply monetary aggregates is trivial compared with the difference between simple-sum monetary aggregation and Divisia demand monetary aggregation, even in the very short run.

This appendix does not embed our three economic agents (along with a government sector) into a full closed model, since that objective is a subject for future research. Below are some partial results in that direction.

A.12.1   The Utility Production Function

The supply of money function used in monetary theory often has not been a neoclassical supply function, in the traditional sense. Instead, the supply of money function often has been an equilibrium condition or reduced-form equation relating money to the monetary base through a multiplier. For example, such a function has played a central role in much of the literature produced by the Shadow Open Market Committee.

As seen from our model of the financial intermediary, the relationship between such an equation and monetary production technology is not clear. Although high-powered money is a factor of production for the financial intermediary, the total monetary base (which also includes currency held by the consumer and manufacturing firm) does not appear in the financial intermediary's decision. In addition, as described above, the demand Divisia aggregate need not exactly equal the corresponding supply Divisia aggregate, even in complete general equilibrium.

Nevertheless, a straightforward interpretation can be given to the conventional multiplier-type money "supply" function as a utility production function. As defined by Samuelson (1968), a utility production function is acquired by replacing the quantities in a utility function by their reduced-form equations. By applying that procedure to the consumer's monetary category subutility function and analogously to the manufacturing firm's monetary category subproduction function, equations can be produced describing the equilibrium monetary service flows as functions of exogenous variables, including central bank instruments.

In continuous time, Sato (1975, p. 283) has shown that the left-hand side of a utility production function can be measured exactly by a Divisia index.

A.12.2   Velocity Function

The aggregation theory provided above can be used to derive the velocity function. Assuming intertemporal separability of the utility function in (A.2), we can produce a current period category utility function of the form, $\chi(u(\mathbf{m}_t), v(\mathbf{x}_t), \overline{L}_t)$, with leisure being weakly separable from goods and monetary assets. Then a consistent current period conditional decision can be defined. That decision is to select $(\mathbf{m}_t, \mathbf{x}_t, \overline{L}_t)$ to

$$\text{maximize } \chi(u(\mathbf{m}_t), v(\mathbf{x}_t), \overline{L}_t) \text{ subject to } \boldsymbol{\pi}_t'\mathbf{m}_t + \mathbf{p}_t'\mathbf{x}_t + w_t\overline{L}_t = Y_t, \qquad (A.124)$$

where Y_t is total current period expenditure on goods, monetary services, and leisure. The variable, Y_t, is preallocated from a prior-stage intertemporal allocation decision.

However, decision (A.124) can itself be solved in two stages. The first stage is to solve for $(M_t^c, X_t, \overline{L}_t)$ to

$$\text{maximize } \chi(M_t^c, X_t, \overline{L}_t) \text{ subject to } M_t^c \Pi_t^c + p_t^* X_t + w_t \overline{L}_t = Y_t, \qquad (A.125)$$

where X_t is the goods quantity aggregate over $\mathbf{x}_t$. The solution function for M_t^c will be of the form

$$M_t^c = \Psi(Y_t, \Pi_t^c, p_t^*, w_t). \qquad (A.126)$$

If χ is linearly homogeneous, then (A.126) can be written in the form

$$M_t^c = Y_t \Phi(\Pi_t^c, p_t^*, w_t) \qquad (A.127)$$

or

$$M_t^c [\Phi(\Pi_t^c, p_t^*, w_t)]^{-1} = Y_t, \qquad (A.128)$$

so that $[\Phi(\Pi_t^c, p_t^*, w_t)]^{-1}$ is velocity relative to the "income" variable, Y_t.

For some purposes it would be useful to solve (A.125) conditionally on $\overline{L}_t$ with $w_t\overline{L}_t$ subtracted from both sides of the constraint in (A.125). Then the income variable would become $Y_t^* = Y_t - w_t\overline{L}_t$, and w_t would not appear as a variable in velocity. Moreover χ could be the current period utility function for a representative consumer under the conditions for aggregation over consumers. Since the second-stage decision for the manufacturing firm is analogous to that for the consumer, (A.128) could be produced even after aggregation over consumers and manufacturing firms jointly.

It is particularly interesting to observe that the velocity function depends only on the tastes of consumers and the technology of manufacturing firms. The velocity function does not depend on the technology of the financial firm, or on Federal Reserve policy, or on the money multipliers. As a result the velocity function is not affected by structural change in the banking sector. In contrast, the velocity of the monetary base depends jointly on money demand and money supply, and hence is affected by structural change in the banking industry.

When applying the aggregation and index-number theory presented in this appendix to produce macroeconomic results, such as the results above on velocity, it is critically important to ensure that the behavioral theory on which the index numbers are based is consistent with one's model. Many examples of such inconsistency exist in the literature on monetary aggregation. For example, the official simple-sum monetary aggregates are consistent with aggregation theory, if and only if the components are indistinguishable perfect substitutes. Yet many models in which the official aggregates are used are structured in a manner inconsistent with that assumption.

In addition to the severely defective simple-sum monetary aggregates, another example is the aggregate, M_Q, proposed by Spindt, which uses the Fisher ideal index to produce a monetary aggregate and a velocity aggregate. However, turnover rates—rather than the user-cost prices appearing in the usual Fisher-ideal index—are treated as dual to quantities. The theory on which Spindt's aggregates are based is presented in Spindt (1985). Nevertheless, it is easily seen from the theory in sections A.5 and A.6 above that his results are consistent with the relevant index-number theory (including Diewert's 1976 theory, used by Spindt), only if economic agents solve one of the following two possible decision problems:

select $\mathbf{m}_t$ to maximize $M(\mathbf{m}_t)$ subject to $\mathbf{m}_t'\bar{\mathbf{v}}_t = p_t^* X_t$ (A.129)

or

select $\bar{\mathbf{v}}_t$ to maximize $V(\bar{\mathbf{v}}_t)$ subject to $\mathbf{m}_t'\bar{\mathbf{v}}_t = p_t^* X_t$,   (A.130)

where $\bar{\mathbf{v}}_t$ is the vector of turnover rates corresponding to the vector of monetary asset quantities, $\mathbf{m}_t$. The resulting monetary aggregate is $M(\mathbf{m}_t)$ and the resulting velocity aggregate is $V(\bar{\mathbf{v}}_t)$. Either of these two behavioral hypotheses would be consistent with Spindt's use of index-number theory. In addition, if either of those two decision problems is applicable, and if M and V are linearly homogeneous, it follows from factor reversal that $M(\mathbf{m}_t)V(\bar{\mathbf{v}}_t) = p_t^* X_t$, which is the "quantity equation."

However, it is not at all clear how either of those two decisions could be embedded in a sensible way into a jointly rational decision over goods and monetary assets (for either a consumer or firm) under any kind of separability assumption. In addition, if (A.129) is solved, then $\bar{\mathbf{v}}_t$ must be treated as exogenous to the decision maker. Alternatively, if (A.130) is solved, then $\mathbf{m}_t$ must be treated as exogenous to the decision maker. Neither possibility is reasonable, since both turnover rates, $\bar{v}_t$, and monetary asset quantities demanded, $\mathbf{m}_t$, are selected by monetary asset holders.

The source of this problem in Spindt's work is the fact that he used Diewert's (1976) result that the Fisher ideal index is exact for the square root quadratic aggregator function; but Spindt overlooked the fact that Diewert's proof applies only for optimizing behavior. With the use of turnover rates rather than user costs, the optimizing behavior required for use of Diewert's theorem must be either (A.129) or (A.130).

Without rigorous internally consistent behavioral theory, a Fisher-ideal index in monetary quantities and turnover rates (as opposed to the prices, which fall directly out of the existing aggregation and index-number theory) is just an arbitrary combination of component quantities and turnover rates. An infinite number of such functions of monetary quantities and turnover rates exist, and they can produce any arbitrary growth rate for the aggregate from the same component data. As a result M_Q is entirely arbitrary. In short, rolling one's own index number, without access to the hundred-year-old cumulative literature on quantity and price (not turnover rate) indexes, is a hazardous venture.

A.13   Aggregation Error from Simple-Sum Aggregation

Figure A.3 displays the magnitude of the aggregation error and policy slackness produced by the use of the simple-sum monetary aggregates. Suppose that there are two monetary assets over which the central bank aggregates, and the quantity of each of the two component assets is $m_{1t} = y_1$ and $m_{2t} = y_2$. Suppose that the central bank reports, as data, that the value of the simple-sum monetary aggregates is M_{ss}. The information content of that reported variable level is contained in the fact that the two components must be somewhere along the figure A.3 hyperplane, $y_1 + y_2 = M_{ss}$, or more formally that the components are in the set A:

$$A = \{(y_1, y_2): y_1 + y_2 = M_{ss}\}. \tag{A.131}$$

Assume that the utility function, $u(y_1, y_2)$, is linearly homogeneous. But according to equation (A.42), the actual value of the service flow from those asset holdings is $u(y_1, y_2)$, which is thereby the correct monetary quantity aggregate. Consequently the information content of the feasible set, A, regarding the monetary service flow is the information that the service flow is in the set E:

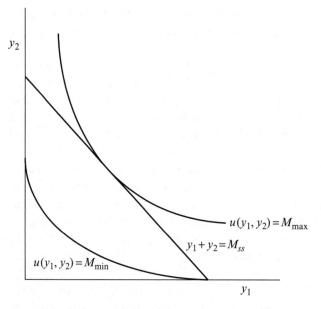

Figure A.3
Demand-side aggregation error range

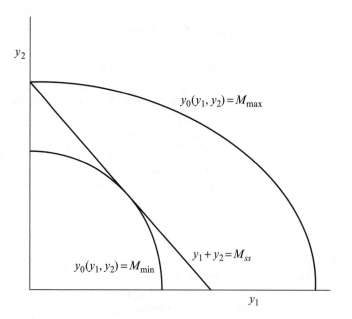

Figure A.4
Supply-side aggregation error range

$$E = \{u(y_1, y_2): (y_1, y_2) \in A\}. \tag{A.132}$$

Note that E is not a singleton. To see the magnitude of the slackness in that information, observe from figure A.3 that if the utility level (service flow) is M_{min}, then the indifference curve does touch the hyperplane, A, at its lower right corner. Hence that indifference curve cannot rule out the M_{ss} reported value of the simple-sum monetary aggregate, although a lower level of utility is ruled out, since indifference curves at lower utility levels cannot touch the hyperplane, A.

Now consider the higher utility level of M_{max} and its associated indifference curve in figure A.3. Observe that that indifference curve also does have a point in common with the hyperplane, A, at the tangency. But higher levels of utility are ruled out, since their indifference curves cannot touch the hyperplane, A. Hence the information about the monetary service flow, provided by the reported value of the simple-sum aggregate, M_{ss}, is the interval

$$E = [M_{min}, M_{max}]. \tag{A.133}$$

The supply-side aggregation is analogous, but the lines of constant supplied service flow for financial firms are production possibility curves, not indifference curves, as follows from equation (A.74). The resulting display of the information content of the simple-sum aggregate is in figure A.4, with the analogous conclusions. To make the figure easy to understand, the same symbols are used as in figure A.3, with the exception of the replacement of the utility aggregator function, u, with production aggregator function, y_0, where $M_t^b = f(\mu_t^*; k_t) = y_0(y_1, y_2)$.

A.14 Conclusion

This appendix has provided much of the modern aggregation theory relevant to producing rigorous microeconomic foundations for monetary economics and macroeconomics. This aggregation theory is central to the empirical results provided in part I of this book. Extensions to this fundamental theory are provided in the following appendixes.

B Discounted Capital Stock of Money with Risk Neutrality

This appendix provides the derivation of the economic capital stock of money, as the discounted expected value of the monetary service flow. While general equilibrium theory deals with demand and supply for flows, wealth effects depend on capital stock.

B.1 Introduction

In appendix A, when we were concentrating on the demand and supply for flows, we needed only to work with conditional current period models under the assumption of intertemporal separability. But since the discounted present value of the future flows depends on the entire intertemporal decision, we now return to the consumer's full intertemporal decision.

The relevant utility function is equation (A.2) in appendix A subject to the $T + 1$ budget constraints in equation (A.3) in appendix A. To be able to deal with the full intertemporal decision, we now need the Fisherine wealth constraint acquired by combining all of the $T + 1$ flow of funds constraints, (A.3), in appendix A The procedure resembles the Bellman method for solving dynamic programming problems, since it starts at the end of the decision and works backward. In particular, first solve (A.3) in appendix A for the benchmark asset quantity, A_s, and write the resulting equation for each s between t and $t + T$. Then back-substitute for A_s, starting from A_{t+T}, and working down to A_t, always substituting the lower subscripted equation into the next higher one. The result is the following discounted wealth allocation constraint, permitting the full intertemporal allocation decision to be to maximize (A.2) in appendix A subject to this one wealth constraint:

$$\sum_{s=t}^{t+T}\left(\frac{\mathbf{p}_s'}{\varpi_s}\right)\mathbf{x}_s + \sum_{s=t}^{t+T}\sum_{i=1}^{n}\left[\frac{p_s^*}{\varpi_\sigma} - \frac{p_s^*(1+r_{is})}{\varpi_{s+1}}\right]m_{is} + \sum_{i=1}^{n}\frac{p_{s+T}^*(1+r_{i,t+T})}{\varpi_{t+T+1}}m_{i,t+T} + \frac{p_{s+T}^*}{\rho_{s+T}}A_{t+T}$$

$$\tag{B.1}$$

$$= \sum_{s=t}^{t+T}\left(\frac{w_s}{\varpi_s}\right)L + \sum_{i=1}^{n}(1+r_{i,t-1})p_{t-1}^*m_{i,t-1} + (1+R_{t-1})A_{t-1}p_{t-1}^*.$$

From that factorization of the intertemporal constraint, we see immediately from (B.1) that the forward user cost of the services of the monetary asset, m_{it}, in period s is

$$\pi_{is} = \frac{p_s^*}{\varpi_s} - \frac{p_s^*(1+r_{is})}{\varpi_{s+1}}, \tag{B.2}$$

where the discount rate for period s is

$$\varpi_s = \begin{cases} 1 & \text{for } s=t, \\ \prod_{u=t}^{s-1}(1+R_u) & \text{for } s>t. \end{cases} \tag{B.3}$$

It follows from (B.2) that the current-period nominal user cost of monetary asset, m_{it}, is

$$\pi_{it} = p_t^*\frac{R_t - r_{it}}{1+R_t}, \tag{B.4}$$

while the corresponding real user cost of monetary asset, m_{it}, is $\pi_{it}^r = \pi_{it}/p_t^*$. Note that (B.4) is in accordance with appendix A's equation (A.5), which we now have formally derived.

B.2   Economic Stock of Money (ESM) under Perfect Foresight

The economic stock of money (ESM), as defined by Barnett (1991) under perfect foresight, follows immediately from the manner in which monetary assets are found to enter the derived wealth constraint, (B.1). As a result the formula for the economic stock of money under perfect foresight is

$$V_t = \sum_{s=t}^{\infty}\sum_{i=1}^{n}\left[\frac{p_s^*}{\varpi_s} - \frac{p_s^*(1+r_{is})}{\varpi_{s+1}}\right]m_{is}. \tag{B.5}$$

The economic stock of money is thereby found to be the discounted present value of expenditure flow on the services of all monetary assets, with each asset priced at its user cost. Let M_{is} be the nominal balance of monetary asset i in period s, so that $M_{is} = p_s^* m_{is}$. Using the definition in equation (B.3), V_t becomes

$$V_t = \sum_{s=t}^{\infty} \sum_{i=1}^{n} \left[\frac{R_s - r_{is}}{\prod_{u=t}^{s}(1 + R_u)} \right] M_{is}. \tag{B.6}$$

A mathematically equivalent alternative form of (B.6) can be derived from quantity and user-cost flow aggregates, discounted to present value. Dual to any exact quantity flow aggregate, a unique price aggregate exists. The price aggregate equals the minimum cost of consuming one unit of the quantity aggregate. Let $\Pi_t = \Pi(\boldsymbol{\pi}_t)$ be the nominal user cost aggregate that is dual to the exact, real monetary quantity aggregate, $M_t = M(\mathbf{m}_t)$. By Fisher's factor reversal, the product of the quantity and user cost price aggregate must equal expenditure on the components, so that

$$(TE)_s = \sum_{i=1}^{n} m_{is} \pi_{is} = M(\mathbf{m}_s) \Pi(\boldsymbol{\pi}_s), \tag{B.7}$$

where $(TE)_s$ is total nominal expenditure on the monetary services of all monetary components. Alternatively, instead of using real quantities and nominal user costs, we can use nominal quantities and real user costs to acquire

$$(TE)_s = \sum_{i=1}^{n} M_{is} \pi_{is}^r = M(\mathbf{M}_s) \Pi(\boldsymbol{\pi}_s^r), \tag{B.8}$$

where $\pi_{is}^r = \pi_{is} / p_s^* = (R_s - r_{is}) / (1 + R_s)$ is the real user cost of monetary asset i in period s, while $\mathbf{M}_s = (M_{1s}, \ldots, M_{ns})'$ is the vector of nominal balances and $\boldsymbol{\pi}_s^r = (\pi_{1s}^r, \ldots, \pi_{ns}^r)' = \boldsymbol{\pi}_s / p_s^*$ is the vector of real user costs. Since M is the aggregator function, $M(\mathbf{M}_s)$ is aggregate nominal balances and is a scalar.

Therefore V_t can be rewritten as follows:

$$V_t = \sum_{s=t}^{\infty} \sum_{i=1}^{n} \left[\left(M_{is} \frac{R_s - r_{is}}{1 + R_s} \right) \frac{1}{\varpi_s} \right] = \sum_{s=t}^{\infty} \left[M(\mathbf{m}_s) \Pi(\boldsymbol{\pi}_s) \frac{1}{\varpi_s} \right] = \sum_{s=t}^{\infty} \frac{(TE)_s}{\varpi_s}. \tag{B.9}$$

Note that equation (B.9) provides a connection between the Divisia aggregate flow index, $M(\mathbf{m}_s)$, and the discounted money stock, V_t. Also observe that the formula contains a time-varying discount rate.

B.3   Extension to Risk

The theory reviewed above assumes perfect foresight. It has been shown by Barnett (1995) and Barnett, Liu, and Jensen (1997) that all of the results on user costs and on Divisia aggregation, including (B.2) and (B.4), along with the Divisia indexes, (A.79) and (A.80) in appendix A, carry over to risk neutrality, so long as all random interest rates and prices are replaced by their expectations. Under risk aversion, a "beta"-type correction for risk aversion is shown in appendix D to appear in those formulas. The further extension to intertemporal nonseparability also is contained in that appendix. The derivations under risk aversion do not use the discounted Fisherine wealth constraint (B.1) but rather are produced from the Euler equations, which solve the stochastic dynamic programming problem of maximizing expected intertemporally separable utility, subject to the sequence of random flow-of-funds constraints (A.3) in appendix A.[1]

We introduce the expectations operator, E_t, to designate expectations conditional on all information available at current period t. In accordance with consumption-based capital asset-pricing theory (e.g., see Blanchard and Fischer (1989, p. 292), the general formula for the economic capital stock of money under risk becomes

$$V_t = E_t \left[\sum_{s=t}^{\infty} \xi_s (TE)_s \right],$$
(B.10)

where ξ_s is the subjectively discounted intertemporal rate of substitution between consumption of goods in current period t and in future period s, and is a generalization of the subjective discounting in equation (A.7) in appendix A. In general, ξ_s is random and can be correlated with current and future values of $(TE)_s$. Assuming maximization of expected intertemporal utility subject to the sequence of flow of funds equations (A.3) in appendix A, Barnett (1995) and Barnett, Liu, and Jensen (1997) have derived the relevant Euler equations for ξ_s under intertemporal separability. If we further assume risk neutrality, as in Blanchard and Fischer (1989, p. 294), it follows that

$$V_t = E_t \left[\sum_{s=t}^{\infty} \frac{(TE)_s}{\varpi_s} \right],$$
(B.11)

---

1. Under risk, equation (B.1) is a state-contingent random constraint. Neither (B.1) nor its expectation is used in Bellman's method for solving and is not useful in producing the extension to risk aversion in Barnett (1995) and Barnett, Liu, and Jensen (1997).

which becomes (B.9) under perfect foresight. Results relevant to extending to risk aversion are provided in appendix D to this book.

B.4 CE and Simple Sum as Special Cases of the ESM

B.4.1 The CE Index

Rotemberg (1991) and Rotemberg, Driscoll, and Poterba (1995) introduced the currency equivalent index (CE index),

$$V_t^{CE} = \sum_{i=1}^{n} \left[\frac{(R_t - r_{it})}{R_t} \right] M_{it}, \tag{B.12}$$

as a flow index under assumptions stronger than needed to derive the Divisia monetary flow index. But Barnett (1991) proved that the CE index can be interpreted to be a stock index, rather than a flow index, and is therefore called the Rotemberg money stock in that paper. In particular, he showed that the CE index is a special case of the ESM, (B.11), under the assumption of martingale expectations, in addition to the assumption of risk neutrality.

Following Barnett's proof, assume that M_{it}, r_{it}, and R_t follow martingale processes. Then we can see from (B.6) that under risk neutrality equation (B.11) can be rewritten as

$$V_t = \sum_{i=1}^{n} \sum_{s=t}^{\infty} \left[\frac{R_t - r_{it}}{(1 + R_t)^{s-t+1}} \right] M_{it}, \tag{B.13}$$

so that

$$V_t = \sum_{i=1}^{n} \left[\frac{(R_t - r_{it})}{R_t} \right] M_{it} = V_t^{CE}. \tag{B.14}$$

This shows that the CE index is a special case of the economic stock of money, when the conditional expectation of the future value of each variable is equal to its current value.

From equation (B.13) under martingale expectations, we furthermore can show that the CE index is proportional to the Divisia current-period monetary flow aggregate, as follows:

$$V_t^{CE} = \sum_{s=t}^{\infty} \sum_{i=1}^{n} \left[\left(\frac{R_t - r_{it}}{(1 + R_t)} M_{it} \right) \frac{1}{(1 + R_t)^{s-t}} \right]$$

$$= \sum_{s=t}^{\infty} \frac{M(\mathbf{m}_t) \Pi(\pi_s)}{(1 + R_t)^{s-t}} = \sum_{s=t}^{\infty} \frac{(TE)_t}{(1 + R_t)^{s-t}}. \tag{B.15}$$

B.4.2   The Simple-Sum (SSI) Index

We define the simple-sum aggregate, V_t^{SSI}, by

$$V_t^{SSI} = \sum_{i=1}^{n} M_{it}. \tag{B.16}$$

As a flow index, this index requires that all monetary components be perfect substitutes, so that linear aggregation is possible, and furthermore that the coefficients in the resulting linear quantity aggregator function be equal for all components. But we also can acquire that index as a stock index of a joint product under the assumption of martingale expectations, since it then follows that

$$V_t^{SSI} = \sum_{i=1}^{n} \left[\frac{(R_t - r_{it})}{R_t} \right] M_{it} + \sum_{i=1}^{n} \left[\frac{r_{it}}{R_t} \right] M_{it} = V_t^{CE} + IY_t, \tag{B.17}$$

where $IY_t = \sum_{i=1}^{n} [r_{it} / R_t] M_{it}$ is the discounted investment yield part of the simple-sum aggregate and V_t^{CE} is the discounted monetary service flow part.

Hence the simple-sum monetary aggregate, treated as a stock index, is the stock of a joint product, consisting of the discounted monetary service flow and the discounted investment yield flow. For the SSI to be valid as an economic money capital stock measure, all monetary assets must yield no interest. Clearly, investment yield cannot be viewed as a monetary service, or the entire capital stock of the country would have to be counted as part of the money stock, so the investment yield part, IY_t, must be removed. The simple-sum monetary aggregates confound together the discounted monetary service flow and the nonmonetary investment-motivated yield. The simple-sum aggregates will overestimate the actual monetary stock by the amount of the discounted nonmonetary services. Furthermore the magnitude of the simple-sum aggregates' upward bias will increase, as more interest-bearing monetary assets are introduced into the monetary aggregates.

Under martingale expectations and the assumption that all monetary assets yield zero interest, it follows that

$$V_t = V_t^{CE} = V_t^{SSI}. \tag{B.18}$$

In short, the ESM is the general formula for measuring money stock and fully nests the CE and the SSI as special cases. As financial innovation and deregulation of financial intermediation have progressed, the assumption that all monetary assets yield zero interest rates has become increasingly unrealistic.

B.5   Measurement of the Economic Stock of Money

The previous section showed that the economic monetary stock provides a general capital stock formula nesting the currency equivalent (CE) index and the simple-sum index as special cases. Each of these results requires martingale expectations, and the simple-sum result further requires that every monetary asset pay a nominal return of zero. Empirical results using those assumptions and that theory are available in Barnett and Zhou (1994a). More recently Barnett, Chae, and Keating (2006) have shown how the ESM can be computed without making either of those restrictive assumptions, but retaining the assumption of risk neutrality. They propose and apply three methods of approximating V_t. The first two linearize the function in terms of expected future variables, and the third imposes a set of convenient covariance restrictions. Appendix D to this book provides extensions to the case of risk aversion.

C Multilateral Aggregation within a Multicountry Economic Union

Appendix A provides the fundamental theory needed to measure monetary services flows within a country. In that theory the distribution effects of policy over regions of the country are not considered. But in an economic union, such as the European Monetary Union (EMU), the central bank cannot ignore differential distribution effects over countries. In a single country, the central bank can argue that residents of disadvantaged states, provinces, or regions could move to geographical areas that benefit from the monetary policy. In a multicountry economic union, countries seek to protect their cultures and rarely favor evolution of a uniform homogeneous population throughout the union. When there is a need to track distribution effects over countries, as well as the aggregate effects over the economic union, there is a need to extend the single country theory of appendix A to multilateral aggregation. Multilateral aggregation theory permits aggregation within countries and then aggregation over countries, with the ability to monitor second-moment dispersion of policy over countries. This appendix provides the extension of monetary aggregation theory to multilateral aggregation.

C.1 Introduction

This appendix derives the fundamental theory for measuring monetary service flows aggregated within and then over countries for a multi-country area. The appendix develops three increasingly restrictive approaches: (1) the heterogeneous-agents approach, (2) the multilateral representative-agent approach, and (3) the unilateral representative-agent approach. These results were produced at the request of the European Central Bank (ECB) for the purpose of supporting construction of its Divisia monetary aggregates database, with convergence from the most general to the more restrictive approaches that is expected as economic convergence within the area proceeds. This theory permits monitoring the effects of policy over a multicountry area, while also monitoring the distribution effects of policy among the countries. The theory is equally as relevant to constructing a multilateral Divisia database for other multicountry economic union. This appendix is based on the ECB Working Paper, Barnett (2003), and the subsequent published article in the *Journal of Econometrics*, Barnett (2007).

With the growth of "free trade" economic and political unions, such as the North American Free Trade Agreement (NAFTA) and the European Union, and more profoundly the growth of economic monetary unions, such as the EMU, an increasing amount of research effort has focused on index-number-theoretic measurement problems associated with economic modeling and the conduct of macroeconomic policy in such economic unions.[1] The need for internally consistent recursive aggregation over monetary data within and over countries is central to the objectives of that research. For those purposes this research, unlike prior research on this subject, was conducted in a manner that produces direct, multilateral extensions of the available closed-economy results.

The purpose of this appendix is to extend the theory of appendix A to the multicountry case in a form that would be applicable to economic unions, both prior to and after the introduction of a common currency. Progress toward convergence within economic unions occurs gradually. For that reason the results are produced under a sequence of increasingly strong assumptions, beginning with (1) a heterogeneous-agents approach applicable to the past under reasonable assumptions, and then progressing to (2) a new multilateral representative-agent approach applicable to an economic union under reasonable convergence assumptions, and finally to (3) a unilateral representative-agent approach requiring very strong assumptions, perhaps relevant to the very distant future, if at all.

---

1. See, for example, M. M. G. Fase and C. C. A. Winder (1994), Spencer (1997), Wesche (1997), Fase (2000), Beyer, Doornik, and Hendry (2001), Stracca (2001), and Reimers (2002). Two approaches to international aggregation have been proposed and applied by other researchers. One has been called the direct approach and the other the indirect approach. We show that the direct approach implies the existence of our most restrictive, unilateral representative agent, which requires assumptions that we consider to be very strong. The alternative indirect approach uses Divisia aggregation within countries and then ad hoc weighting of those within-country indexes to aggregate over countries. The indirect approach produces a result that is disconnected from theory and does not produce nesting of the multilateral or unilateral representative-agent approaches.

At some date following the introduction of a common currency, the heterogeneous-agents approach could become mathematically equivalent to the multilateral representative-agent approach, since the assumptions necessary for equivalence of the two approaches are reasonably related to the long-run objectives of economic monetary unions. But the far more restrictive unilateral representative-agent approach requires very strong assumptions. In particular, the unilateral representative-agent approach would require convergence of inflation rates and interest rates across countries and would imply demographic convergence to a homogeneous population, such that the country of residence of a consumer would become irrelevant to the unilateral representative agent's decisions. In the case of the EMU, the unilateral representative-agent approach could represent full convergence to a "United States of Europe." The unilateral representative-agent approach is strictly nested within the multilateral representative-agent approach, while the multilateral representative-agent approach is strictly nested within the heterogeneous-agents approach having the weakest assumptions of the three approaches.

This appendix's extensions of my earlier work produced a number of unexpected innovations, including the need for simultaneous use of two different consumer price indexes for internal consistency of the theory. The current appendix is intended to solve the central theoretical problems associated with monetary aggregation over countries.

The purposes and objectives of this research in the multicountry case are analogous to the purposes and objectives of monetary and financial aggregation and index number theory in the single country case. Data construction and measurement procedures imply the theory that can rationalize those procedures. Unless that implied theory is internally consistent with the theory used in applications of those data in modeling and policy, the data and its applications are incoherent. Such internal inconsistencies can produce the appearance of structural change, when there has been none.[2]

C.2   Definition of Variables

We define an "economic union" to be any multicountry area within which multilateral measurement and policy are relevant. Whether or

---

2. This phenomenon has been called the "Barnett critique" by Chrystal and MacDonald (1994) and Belongia and Ireland (2010).

not a common currency exists within the area is not part of this definition, but is relevant to the choice among assumptions we introduce. In practice, the identification of an economic union is usually by political treaty. But in economic theory, existence of such an area can be defined by a weak separability clustering condition, which need not imply the existence of a political treaty or an "optimal currency area."[3] All results are in continuous time. Certainty equivalence is assumed within the decisions of each consumer, as would be attained under risk neutrality by replacing contemporaneously random rates of return by their expectations. Appendix D develops the theory for extension of appendixes A, B, and C to the case of risk aversion, which becomes particularly relevant when there is exchange rate risk, as between different country's interest rates within an economic union not having a single common currency. Examples would be the European Union, since only the EMU countries have the euro, or the EMU countries prior to their acquiring the euro.

Let K be the number of countries in the economic union. We let $p_k^* = p_k^*(\mathbf{p}_k)$ be the true cost of living index in country $k \in \{1, \ldots, K\}$, where $\mathbf{p}_k = \mathbf{p}_k(t)$ is the vector of prices of consumer goods at time t and $\mathbf{x}_k = \mathbf{x}_k(t)$ is the vector of per capita real rates of consumption of those goods in country k at time t. Let $H_k = H_k(t)$ be the population of country k at time t, and let m_{kji} be the nominal per capita holdings of asset type i located or purchased in country j but owned by economic agents in country k. The holdings are per capita relative to country k's own population, H_k. We present all results in per capita form, since the per capita variables are the ones that are needed in demand functions at the aggregate level. In addition the correlation with inflation tends to be in terms of per capita flows, since increases in monetary services that produce no change in per capita monetary services just accommodate population growth.

Assume that asset holders within the economic union also sometimes hold assets in Z countries that are outside the economic union. Let N_j be the number of asset types available within country, j, and let N be the total number of asset types available within all of the relevant countries, $j \in \{1, \ldots, K + Z\}$, where clearly $N \geq N_j$ for all $j \in \{1, \ldots, K + Z\}$. Then the subscripts of m_{kji} have range $k \in \{1, \ldots, K\}, j \in \{1, \ldots, K + Z\}, i \in \{1, \ldots, N\}$. We are not limiting i to be within $\{1, \ldots, N_j\}$, since we wish to associate a unique numerical value of i to each asset type, regardless of country j within which the asset is located. As a result for each (k, j) there will necessarily be zero values of m_{kji} for $N - N_j$ values

---

3. See Swofford (2000) and Drake, Mullineux, and Agung (1997).

of i. If countries j and k do not share the same currency, then nominal holdings are converted to units of country k's currency using the exchange rate between country k's and country j's currencies.[4] Then $m^*_{kji} = m_{kji}/p^*_k$ is the real per capita holdings of asset i located or purchased in country j but owned by economic agents in country k.

Let $r_{kji} = r_{kji}(t)$ be the holding period after-tax yield on asset i located or purchased in country j and owned by an economic agent in country k at instant of time t, where all asset rates of return are yield-curve adjusted to the same holding period (e.g., 30 days).[5] It is important to recognize that the subscript k identifies the country of residence of the asset holder, and not necessarily the country of location of the asset. Rates of return on foreign denominated assets owned by residents of country k are understood to be effective rates of return, net of the instantaneous expected percentage rate of change in the exchange rate between the domestic and foreign currency. At some time following the introduction of a common currency, the dependency of rates of return on k can be expected to end, and the dependency on j will be relevant only to holdings within the economic union of assets located in the Z countries outside the economic union. Hence at some time after the introduction of a common currency, it follows that r_{kji} will be independent of (j, k) for all $j, k \in \{1, \ldots, K\}$.

Let $R_k = R_k(t)$ be the benchmark rate of return in country k at instant of time t, where the benchmark rate of return is the rate of return received on a pure investment, providing no services other than its yield.[6] Then $\pi^*_{kji}(t) = R_k(t) - r_{kji}(t)$ is the real user-cost price of asset i located or purchased in country j and owned by residents of country k at time t, and $\pi_{kji} = p^*_k\pi^*_{kji}$ is the corresponding nominal user cost.[7] It does not

---

4. Similarly we assume that prices of consumer goods are converted to units of country k's currency. Since aggregation over consumer goods is not the primary subject of this appendix, our notation for consumer-goods quantities, expenditures, and prices is less formal than for monetary assets.

5. In most cases below, the adjustment for taxation will have no effect, unless the marginal tax rate is not the same on assets appearing in the numerator and denominator of the shares. See equations (A.5a) and (A.5b) in appendix A. The yield curve adjustment of rates of return of different maturities is acquired by subtracting from the asset's yield the country's Treasury security yield of the same maturity and then adding that yield differential onto the Treasury security yield of the chosen holding period. The same holding period should be used for all assets.

6. See the appendix and footnotes 17 and 28 to Barnett (2003), regarding construction of a proxy for the benchmark rate.

7. In discrete time it is necessary to discount to the beginning of the period all interest paid at the end of the period. This requires dividing nominal and real user costs by $1 + R_k$. This is the multilateral analogue of equation (A.5) in appendix A.

matter whether real or nominal interest rates are used, since the inflation rate conversion between nominal and real applies to both terms in
the user-cost formula and hence cancels out between the two terms.

Technically speaking, whenever m_{kji} is zero, as often will happen
when a particular asset type i is not available within country j, the user-
cost price should be the asset's reservation price in country j. But, in
practice, terms containing assets having zero quantity will drop out of
all of our formulas, except when the asset's quantity becomes nonzero
in the next period. In such cases the reservation price must be imputed
during the period preceding the innovation, and the new goods introduction procedure must be used.[8] Since such innovations are infre-
quent, it usually will not be necessary to impute a reservation price or
interest rate to asset holdings for which $m_{kji} = 0$.

We now define

$$\mathbf{m}_{kj}^* = (m_{kj1}^*, \ldots, m_{kji}^*, \ldots, m_{kjN}^*)',$$

$$\mathbf{m}_{kj} = (m_{kj1}, \ldots, m_{kji}, \ldots, m_{kjN})',$$

$$\mathbf{r}_{kj} = (r_{kj1}, \ldots, r_{kji}, \ldots, r_{kjN})',$$

$$\boldsymbol{\pi}_{kj}^* = (\pi_{kj1}^*, \ldots, \pi_{kji}^*, \ldots, \pi_{kjN}^*)',$$

$$\boldsymbol{\pi}_{kj} = (\pi_{kj1}, \ldots, \pi_{kji}, \ldots, \pi_{kjN})',$$

and let

$$\mathbf{m}_k^* = (\mathbf{m}_{k1}^*, \ldots, \mathbf{m}_{kj}^*, \ldots, \mathbf{m}_{k,K+Z}^*)',$$

$$\mathbf{m}_k = (\mathbf{m}_{k1}, \ldots, \mathbf{m}_{kj}, \ldots, \mathbf{m}_{k,K+Z})',$$

$$\mathbf{r}_k = (\mathbf{r}_{k1}, \ldots, \mathbf{r}_{kj}, \ldots, \mathbf{r}_{k,K+Z})',$$

$$\boldsymbol{\pi}_k^* = (\boldsymbol{\pi}_{k1}^*, \ldots, \boldsymbol{\pi}_{kj}^*, \ldots, \boldsymbol{\pi}_{k,K+Z}^*)',$$

$$\boldsymbol{\pi}_k = (\boldsymbol{\pi}_{k1}, \ldots, \boldsymbol{\pi}_{kj}, \ldots, \boldsymbol{\pi}_{k,K+Z})'.$$

C.3 Aggregation within Countries

Aggregation within countries uses the existing theory presented in appendix A and developed by Barnett (1980a, b, 1987). That theory uses
the economic approach to index number theory and assumes the existence of a representative agent within each country. To avoid the unnecessary imputation of reservation prices to assets not being held by
residents of country k, we will restrict most of our computations to the

---

8. For the new goods introduction procedure, see Anderson, Jones, and Nesmith (1997,
pp. 77–78) and footnote 6 in Appendix A of this book.

index set $S_k = \{(j, i): m_{kji} > 0, j \in \{1, \ldots, K + Z\}, i \in \{1, \ldots, N\}\}$ for all $k \in \{1, \ldots, K\}$.

Definition 1   *Within each country $k \in \{1, \ldots, K\}$, define the monetary real user-cost price aggregate, Π_k^*, the monetary nominal user-cost price aggregate, Π_k, the real per capita monetary services aggregate, M_k^*, and the nominal per capita monetary services aggregate, M_k, by the following Divisia indexes:*

$d \log \Pi_k^* = \sum_{(j,i)\in S_k} w_{kji} d \log \pi_{kji}^*,$

$d \log \Pi_k = \sum_{(j,i)\in S_k} w_{kji} d \log \pi_{kji},$

$d \log M_k^* = \sum_{(j,i)\in S_k} w_{kji} d \log m_{kji}^*,$

$d \log M_k = \sum_{(j,i)\in S_k} w_{kji} d \log m_{kji},$

where

$$w_{kji} = \frac{\pi_{kji} m_{kji}^*}{\pi_k' \mathbf{m}_k^*} = \frac{\pi_{kji}^* m_{kji}^*}{\pi_k^{*'} \mathbf{m}_k^*} = \frac{(R_k - r_{kji})m_{kji}^*}{\sum_{(j,i)\in S_k}(R_k - r_{kji})m_{kji}^*} = \frac{(R_k - r_{kji})m_{kji}}{\sum_{(j,i)\in S_k}(R_k - r_{kji})m_{kji}}.$$

Observe that $0 \le w_{kji} \le 1$ for all $k \in \{1, \ldots, K\}, j \in \{1, \ldots, K + Z\}$, and $i \in \{1, \ldots, N\}$. Also observe that $\sum_{(j,i)\in S_k} w_{kji} = 1$ for all $k \in \{1, \ldots, K\}$. Hence the shares, w_{kji}, have the properties of a probability distribution for each $k \in \{1, \ldots, K\}$, and we could interpret our Divisia indexes above as Divisia growth rate means. But since it is convenient to assume the existence of a representative agent within each country, the statistical interpretation as a mean is not necessary. We instead can appeal to the Divisia index's known ability to track the aggregator function of the country's representative consumer.

The following result relating nominal to real values follows immediately.

Lemma 1 $M_k = M_k^* p_k^*$ and $\Pi_k = \Pi_k^* p_k^*$.

Proof   The proof follows from the known linear homogeneity of the Divisia index.   ∎

C.4   Aggregation over Countries

Our heterogeneous-agents approach to aggregation over countries is based on the stochastic convergence approach to aggregation, championed by Theil (1967) and developed further by Barnett (1979a, b, 1981, ch. 2). This approach not only can be used to aggregate over heterogeneous consumers but also jointly over consumers and firms. Hence the approach is not only a heterogeneous-consumers approach, but more generally is a true heterogeneous-agents approach. See section A.9 of appendix A to this book along with Barnett and Serletis (2000, ch. 9). By assuming the existence of a representative agent within each country, and treating those representative agents as heterogeneous agents, we produce a heterogeneous-countries approach to aggregation over countries.

In aggregating within an economic union, this approach implies that the countries' characteristics, such as cultures, tastes, and languages, , were sampled from underlying theoretical populations consistent with the climates, histories, resources, geographies, neighboring population characteristics, and so forth. All time-varying variables then become stochastic processes. Each Divisia index aggregating over component stochastic processes becomes the sample mean of realizations of those stochastic processes, and thereby an estimate of the mean function of the underlying unknown population stochastic process. The distributions of those stochastic processes are derived distributions induced by the random sampling from country characteristics. The derived empirical distributions of the countries' solution stochastic-process growth rates impute probabilities to countries equal to their relevant expenditure shares in expenditure within the economic union.

Let e_k be the exchange rate of country k's currency relative to a market basket of currencies, such as the ecu (European currency unit), where e_k is defined in units of the market basket currency per unit of country k's currency. When extending the data backward to before the introduction of a common currency, the exchange rates can play an important role in our results.

The stochastic convergence approach to aggregation over heterogeneous agents has traditionally been based more on statistical theory than on economic theory. But a rigorous connection with economic theory has been provided by Barnett (1979a). We use that interpretation in our heterogeneous-agents approach, as we now explain.

Consider a possible country with representative consumer c, having utility function, $U_c = U_c[u_c(\mathbf{m}_c^*), g_c(\mathbf{x}_c)]$. Assume that the differences in tastes across possible countries can be explained in terms of a vector of taste-determining variables, ϕ_c. The dimension of the vector of taste-determining variables must be finite, but otherwise is irrelevant to the theory.[9] Then there must exist functions U, u, and g, such that

9. The assumption of finite dimensionality of ϕ_c is only for notational convenience. Without that assumption, ϕ_c could not be written as a vector. A sequence or continuum of taste-determining variables would not alter any of our conclusions, but would complicate the notation.

$$U_c = U_c[u_c(\mathbf{m}_c^*), g_c(\mathbf{x}_c)] = U[u(\mathbf{m}_c^*, \boldsymbol{\phi}_c), g(\mathbf{x}_c, \boldsymbol{\phi}_c), \boldsymbol{\phi}_c]$$

for all possible countries' tastes, $\boldsymbol{\phi}_c$. Although U, u, and g are fixed functions, the random vector $\boldsymbol{\phi}_c$ of taste-determining variables causes U_c, u_c, and g_c to become random functions, reflecting the possible variations of tastes and their probabilities, conditionally on their given environmental, demographic, historical, resource, and other factors in the economic union.

Assume that each possible country c's representative consumer solves the following decision problem for $(\mathbf{m}_c^*, \mathbf{x}_c)$ at each instant of time t:

maximize $U[u(\mathbf{m}_c^*, \boldsymbol{\phi}_c), g(\mathbf{x}_c, \boldsymbol{\phi}_c), \boldsymbol{\phi}_c]$

subject to $\mathbf{m}_c^{*\prime} \boldsymbol{\phi}_c + \mathbf{x}_c' \mathbf{p}_c = I_c$.

Assume that the countries and their representative agents are about to be drawn from the theoretically possible populations, but have not yet been drawn. Assume that there is an infinite number of possible countries in the economic union, so that there exists a continuous joint distribution of the random variables $(I_c, \mathbf{p}_c, e_c, \boldsymbol{\pi}_c, \boldsymbol{\phi}_c)$ at any time t. We assume that $\boldsymbol{\phi}_c$ is sampled at birth and does not change during lifetimes, so that $\boldsymbol{\phi}_c$ is not time dependent. But $\{I_c(t), \mathbf{p}_c(t), e_c(t), \boldsymbol{\pi}_c(t)\}$ are stochastic processes. Hence at any time t we can write the theoretical population distribution function of $\{I_c(t), \mathbf{p}_c(t), e_c(t), \boldsymbol{\pi}_c(t), \boldsymbol{\phi}_c\}$ at t as F_t. With distributions derived from F_t, it follows that at any t, the following are random variables:

$d\log(p_c^* e_c)$, $d\log(M_c e_c)$, $d\log(M_c^*)$, $d\log(\Pi_c e_c)$, and $d\log(\Pi_c^*)$.

Using the derived distribution of those random variables, we can define their theoretical population means by $\theta_1 = E[d\log(p_c^* e_c)]$, $\theta_2 = E[d\log(M_c e_c)]$, $\theta_3 = E[d\log(M_c^*)]$, $\theta_4 = E[d\log(\Pi_c e_c)]$, and $\theta_5 = E[d\log(\Pi_c^*)]$, where $(\theta_1, \theta_2, \theta_3, \theta_4, \theta_5) = (\theta_1(t), \theta_2(t), \theta_3(t), \theta_4(t), \theta_5(t))$ is a nonstochastic function of time. Now consider sampling from the theoretical population K times to draw the $k \in \{1, \ldots, K\}$ actual countries. The countries are assumed to have representative consumers having characteristics that are produced from the continuous theoretical population distribution, F_t, at t.

Definition 2   *Let $s_k = H_k / \sum_{\kappa=1}^K H_\kappa$ be country k's fraction of total economic union population. Define the kth country's expenditure share, W_k, of the economic union's monetary service flow by*

$$W_k = \frac{M_k^* \Pi_k^* p_k^* e_k s_k}{\sum_{\kappa=1}^{K} M_\kappa^* \Pi_\kappa^* p_\kappa^* e_\kappa s_\kappa} = \frac{M_k \Pi_k^* e_k s_k}{\sum_{\kappa=1}^{K} M_\kappa \Pi_\kappa^* e_\kappa s_\kappa} = \frac{M_k^* \Pi_k e_k s_k}{\sum_{\kappa=1}^{K} M_\kappa^* \Pi_\kappa e_\kappa s_\kappa}. \tag{C.1}$$

The fact that this definition is in terms of total national expenditure shares, rather than per capita shares, is evident from the fact that

$$\frac{M_k^* \Pi_k^* p_k^* e_k s_k}{\sum_{\kappa=1}^{K} M_\kappa^* \Pi_\kappa^* p_\kappa^* e_\kappa s_\kappa} = \frac{M_k^* \Pi_k^* p_k^* e_k H_k}{\sum_{\kappa=1}^{K} M_\kappa^* \Pi_\kappa^* p_\kappa^* e_\kappa H_\kappa}.$$

Observe that $0 \leq W_k \leq 1$ for all k, and $\sum_{k=1}^{K} W_k = 1$. We thereby can treat $\{W_1, \ldots, W_K\}$ as a probability distribution in computing the following Divisia means by our stochastic heterogeneous-countries approach to aggregation over countries.

Definition 3 *Aggregating over countries, define the monetary-sector-weighted Divisia consumer price index, $p^* = p^*(t)$, by*

$$d \log p^* = \sum_{k=1}^{K} W_k d \log (p_k^* e_k). \tag{C.2}$$

Definition 4 *Define the economic union's nominal, M, and real, M^*, per capita monetary service flows by*

$$d \log M = \sum_{k=1}^{K} W_k d \log (s_k M_k e_k)$$

and

$$d \log M^* = \sum_{k=1}^{K} W_k d \log (s_k M_k^*).$$

Definition 5 *Define the economic union's nominal, Π, and real, Π^*, monetary user-cost prices by*

$$d \log \Pi = \sum_{k=1}^{K} W_k d \log (\Pi_k e_k)$$

and

$$d \log \Pi^* = \sum_{k=1}^{K} W_k d \log (\Pi_k^*).$$

When we draw from the derived population distributions, the frequency with which we draw the growth rates, $d \log p_k^* e_k$, $d \log(s_k M_k e_k)$, $d \log(s_k M_k^*)$, $d \log(\Pi_k e_k)$, and $d \log(\Pi_k^*)$, is W_k. From Khinchine's theorem, assuming independent sampling, we find that $d \log p^*$, $d \log M$, $d \log M^*$, $d \log \Pi$, and $d \log \Pi^*$ are sample means of distributions having population means equal to $\theta_1(t)$, $\theta_2(t)$, $\theta_3(t)$, $\theta_4(t)$, and $\theta_5(t)$, respectively. In addition, $d \log p^*$, $d \log M$, $d \log M^*$, $d \log \Pi$, and $d \log \Pi^*$ converge in probability as $K \to \infty$ to $\theta_1(t)$, $\theta_2(t)$, $\theta_3(t)$, $\theta_4(t)$, and $\theta_5(t)$, respectively. It is this convergence to theoretical population properties that accounts for this aggregation approach's name, "the stochastic convergence approach," in Barnett (1979a).

Observe that there is no assumption that a representative agent exists over countries. We assume in this heterogeneous-agents approach only that representative agents exist within countries. Aggregation over countries is defined to be estimation of the moments of the stochastic processes generated by sampling from the underlying theoretical population that produces the countries' representative agents. When in later sections we consider the existence of multilateral and unilateral representative agents over countries, we add strong assumptions about the *realized* tastes after sampling from the theoretical population.

In summary, the perspective from which our heterogeneous-agents approach is produced is prior to the drawing from the theoretical distribution, so that random variables have not yet been realized and all dynamic solution paths are stochastic processes induced by the randomness of $\{I_c(t), \mathbf{p}_c(t), e_c(t), \boldsymbol{\pi}_c(t), \boldsymbol{\phi}_c\}$. No assumptions are made about the precise form in which realized tastes relate to each other across countries. The heterogeneous-agents approach tracks aggregator functions within countries. But this approach does not require assumptions sufficient for the existence of microeconomic aggregator functions over countries. After aggregating over countries, this approach tracks moments of aggregate stochastic processes and is interpreted relative to the underlying population distributions.

In contrast, our multilateral and unilateral representative-agent approaches add assumptions regarding the functional relationship among realized tastes of countries already in existence, and seek to track the realized aggregator function over countries. Under those additional assumptions producing the existence of an aggregator function over the economic union, the heterogeneous-agents approach reduces to the multilateral representative-agent approach as a special case. Although the two approaches have different interpretations, because of the difference in perspective regarding prior versus post sampling, the multilateral economic-agent approach is nevertheless mathematically a nested special case of the heterogeneous-agents approach.

It is important to recognize the following proof's dependence on the definition of p^* in equation (C.2), with the share weights determined by definition 2. If any other weights, such as consumption-expenditure share or GDP weights, had been used in defining p^*, then theorem 1 would not hold.

Theorem 1 $M = M^*p^*$ and $\Pi = \Pi^*p^*$.

Proof   The method of proof is proof by contradiction. First consider M, and suppose that $M \neq M^*p^*$. Then

$$d \log M \neq d \log(M^*p^*) = d \log M^* + d \log p^*.$$

So by lemma 1,

$$\sum_{k=1}^{K} W_k d \log(s_k M_k e_k) \neq \sum_{k=1}^{K} W_k d \log(s_k M_k / p_k^*) + d \log p^*$$

$$= \sum_{k=1}^{K} W_k d \log(s_k M_k) - \sum_{k=1}^{K} W_k d \log p_k^* + d \log p^*.$$

Hence

$$\sum_{k=1}^{K} W_k d \log(s_k M_k) \neq \sum_{k=1}^{K} W_k d \log(s_k M_k) - \sum_{k=1}^{K} W_k d \log p_k^* + d \log p^* - \sum_{k=1}^{K} W_k d \log e_k$$

$$= \sum_{k=1}^{K} W_k d \log(s_k M_k) - \sum_{k=1}^{K} W_k d \log(p_k^* e_k) + d \log p^*$$

$$= \sum_{k=1}^{K} W_k d \log(s_k M_k),$$

which is a contradiction. The last equality follows from equation (C.2) in definition 3.

Now consider Π, and suppose that $\Pi \neq \Pi^*p^*$. Then

$$d \log \Pi \neq d \log(\Pi^*p^*) = d \log \Pi^* + d \log p^*.$$

By definitions 3 and 5, it follows that

$$\sum_{k=1}^{K} W_k d \log(\Pi_k e_k) \neq \sum_{k=1}^{K} W_k d \log(\Pi_k^*) + \sum_{k=1}^{K} W_k d \log(p_k^* e_k).$$

Hence by lemma 1, we have that

$$\sum_{k=1}^{K} W_k d \log(\Pi_k^* p_k^* e_k) \neq \sum_{k=1}^{K} W_k d \log(\Pi_k^*) + \sum_{k=1}^{K} W_k d \log(p_k^* e_k),$$

or

$$\sum_{k=1}^{K} W_k d \log(\Pi_k^*) + \sum_{k=1}^{K} W_k d \log(p_k^* e_k) \neq \sum_{k=1}^{K} W_k d \log(\Pi_k^*) + \sum_{k=1}^{K} W_k d \log(p_k^* e_k),$$

which is a contradiction. ∎

The following theorem proves Fisher's factor reversal property for the monetary quantity and user-cost aggregates over countries. In particular, we prove that total expenditure on monetary services aggregated over countries is the same, whether computed from the product of the economic union's quantity and user-cost aggregates or from the sum of the products within countries. The multiplications by s_k convert to per capita values relative to total economic union population, while the within-country aggregates, M_k^*, remain per capita relative to each country's own population.

Theorem 2 $M^*\Pi = \sum_{k=1}^{K}(M_k^* s_k)\Pi_k e_k.$

Proof The method of proof is proof by contradiction. So assume that

$$d \log(M^*) + d \log(\Pi) \neq d \log\left(\sum_{k=1}^{K} M_k^* s_k \Pi_k e_k\right)$$

$$= \frac{d\left(\sum_{k=1}^{K} M_k^* s_k \Pi_k e_k\right)}{\sum_{k=1}^{K} M_k^* s_k \Pi_k e_k}.$$

Hence by definitions 4 and 5, it follows that

$$\sum_{k=1}^{K} W_k d \log(s_k M_k^*) + \sum_{k=1}^{K} W_k d \log(\Pi_k e_k) \neq \frac{d\left(\sum_{k=1}^{K} M_k^* s_k \Pi_k e_k\right)}{\sum_{k=1}^{K} M_k^* s_k \Pi_k e_k}.$$

Multiplying through by $\sum_{k=1}^{K} M_k^* s_k \Pi_k e_k$ and using definition 2, we get

$$\sum_{k=1}^{K} (M_k^* s_k \Pi_k e_k) d \log(M_k^* s_k) + \sum_{k=1}^{K} (M_k^* s_k \Pi_k e_k) d \log(\Pi_k e_k) \neq d\left(\sum_{k=1}^{K} M_k^* s_k \Pi_k e_k\right).$$

So

$$\sum_{k=1}^{K} (M_k^* s_k \Pi_k e_k) \frac{d(s_k M_k^*)}{s_k M_k^*} + \sum_{k=1}^{K} (M_k^* s_k \Pi_k e_k) \frac{d(\Pi_k e_k)}{\Pi_k e_k} \neq \sum_{k=1}^{K} d(M_k^* s_k \Pi_k e_k).$$

Hence

$$\sum_{k=1}^{K}(\Pi_k e_k)d(s_k M_k^*) + \sum_{k=1}^{K}(M_k^* s_k)d(\Pi_k e_k) \neq \sum_{k=1}^{K}d(M_k^* s_k \Pi_k e_k).$$

But taking the total differential of $M_k^* s_k \Pi_k e_k$, we have

$$d(M_k^* s_k \Pi_k e_k) = (\Pi_k e_k)d(M_k^* s_k) + (M_k^* s_k)d(\Pi_k e_k),$$

so that

$$\sum_{k=1}^{K}(\Pi_k e_k)d(s_k M_k^*) + \sum_{k=1}^{K}(M_k^* s_k)d(\Pi_k e_k) \neq \sum_{k=1}^{K}(\Pi_k e_k)d(s_k M_k^*) + \sum_{k=1}^{K}(M_k^* s_k)d(\Pi_k e_k),$$

which is a contradiction.   ∎

C.5   Special Cases

We now consider some special cases of our results. First we consider the case of purchasing power parity. While the purchasing power parity assumption is not applicable to many economic unions, this special case is useful in understanding the forms of the more general formulas we have derived without purchasing power parity and could be useful in applying this theory to other economic unions in which purchasing power parity may apply.

C.5.1   Purchasing Power Parity

Definition 6   *We define $E = \{e_k : k = 1, \ldots, K\}$ to satisfy purchasing power parity, if $p_j^*/p_i^* = e_i/e_j$ for all countries $i, j \in \{1, \ldots, K\}$. Under this definition, it equivalently follows that there exists a price, p^0, such that $p^0 = p_i^* e_i = p_j^* e_j$ for all $i, j \in \{1, \ldots, K\}$.*

Theorem 3   If E satisfies purchasing power parity, then

$$W_k = \frac{M_k^* \Pi_k^* s_k}{\sum_{\kappa=1}^{K} M_\kappa^* \Pi_\kappa^* s_\kappa}.\tag{C.3}$$

Proof   See the ECB working paper, Barnett (2003).   ∎

Theorem 4   If E satisfies purchasing power parity, then

$$d \log p^* = d \log(p_k^* e_k)\tag{C.4}$$

for all countries, $k \in \{1, \ldots, K\}$.

Proof   See the ECB working paper, Barnett (2003).   ∎

Compare (C.3) with (C.1), and (C.4) with (C.2), to see the sources of the complications in (C.1) and (C.2) caused by violations of purchasing power parity.

C.5.2   Multilateral Representative Agent over the Economic Union

This section defines the concept of a multilateral representative agent. The next section defines a unilateral representative agent over countries to be a representative agent who considers the same goods in different countries to be perfect substitutes, regardless of the country of residence of the purchaser or the country within which the good or asset is acquired. The existence of a unilateral representative agent has been implicit in the existing studies using the "direct method" of aggregation over monetary assets in the euro area. As I will show, the existence of a unilateral representative agent requires extremely strong assumptions. Without a homogeneous culture and the vast population migrations that could produce that uniformity, this assumption will not apply. The existence of a multilateral representative agent requires far more reasonable assumptions.

If tastes across countries do converge in the distant future, the convergence is more likely to be toward a homogeneous multilateral representative agent, rather than toward a unilateral representative agent. A homogeneous multilateral representative agent recognizes the existence of country specific tastes but equates those tastes across countries. A unilateral representative agent does not recognize the relevancy of countries at all and thereby does not recognize the existence of country specific tastes. Country specific utility functions cannot be factored out of the economic union's tastes (i.e., weak separability of country tastes fails); and the country subscripts, j and k, disappear from the decision of the unilateral representative agent. The allocation of goods across countries is indeterminate in that case.

C.5.3   Multilateral Representative Agent with Heterogeneous Tastes

We begin by defining relevant assumptions and produce the theory of a multilateral representative agent. We show that the existence of a multilateral representative agent is a special case of our heterogeneous-countries theory. We further show that a homogeneous multilateral representative agent exists under stronger assumptions.

As described in the previous section, our representative-agent approach for aggregating over countries treats countries as already realized, so that variables and functions no longer are random. Hence we can consider realized functional structure aggregated over realized countries. The following assumption is needed, and begins to become weak only after the introduction of a common currency.

Assumption 1 *Suppose that there is convergence over the economic union in the following sense. Let there exist $R = R(t)$ such that $R_k = R(t)$ for all $k \in \{1, \ldots, K\}$ and all t.*

The existence of a representative agent is necessary and sufficient for the nonexistence of distribution effects.[10] Distribution effects introduce second moments and possibly higher order moments into demand functions aggregated over consumers. The existence of such second and higher order moments in the macroeconomy can cause policy to influence distributions of income and wealth across consumers. Assumption 1 rules out certain possible distribution effects. Additional assumptions ruling out other sources of distribution effects will be needed as we consider further special cases.

By its definition, the benchmark asset, unlike "monetary" assets, provides no services other than its investment rate of return, and hence cannot enter the utility function of an infinitely lived representative agent.[11] Therefore differences in tastes across countries play no role in decisions regarding benchmark asset holdings by a representative agent within the economic union. For that reason the existence of a common benchmark rate for all countries is necessary for a representative agent over countries. A representative agent within the economic union would hold only the highest yielding of the possible benchmark assets. This conclusion is not necessary in our (thereby more general) heterogeneous-countries approach.

By assumption 1, we also can consider the following stronger assumption. We assume that all K countries have already been drawn from their theoretical population of potential countries. Then the tastes of the representative consumers in each country are realized and are no longer random. The following assumption produces the existence of aggregator functions, (U, V, G), over the individual realized countries' tastes, (u_k, g_k) for $k \in \{1, \ldots, K\}$.

Assumption 2a *Suppose that there exists a representative consumer over the economic union. Within that representative agent's intertemporal utility*

---

10. See Gorman (1953).
11. See equation (A.7) in Appendix A. In the finite planning horizon case, the benchmark asset enters utility only in the terminal period to produce a savings motive to endow the next planning horizon.

function, assume that $(\mathbf{m}_1^*(t), \ldots, \mathbf{m}_K^*(t), \mathbf{x}_1(t), \ldots, \mathbf{x}_K(t))$ *is intertemporally weakly separable from* $(\mathbf{m}_1^*(\tau), \ldots, \mathbf{m}_K^*(\tau), \mathbf{x}_1(\tau), \ldots, \mathbf{x}_K(\tau))$ *for all* $t \neq \tau$, *and also assume that monetary assets are weakly separable from consumer goods.*

As defined in section C.1, $\mathbf{x}_k$ is the vector of instantaneous per capita goods consumption rates in country k relative to the population of country k. Then $s_k \mathbf{x}_k$ is the per capita real consumption vector relative to total economic union population, $H = \sum_{k=1}^K H_k$. Since contemporaneous consumption of goods and services is weakly separable from future consumption, a contemporaneous category utility function exists of the form

$$U = U[\breve{V}(s_1 \mathbf{m}_1^*, \ldots, s_K \mathbf{m}_K^*), \breve{G}(s_1 \mathbf{x}_1, \ldots, s_K \mathbf{x}_K)], \tag{C.5a}$$

where $\breve{V}$ and $\breve{G}$ are linearly homogeneous.

Assumption 2b *Suppose further that consumption of monetary assets and goods are weakly separable among countries, so that the contemporaneous utility function has the blockwise weakly separable form*

$$U = U\{V[s_1 u_1(\mathbf{m}_1^*), \ldots, s_K u_K(\mathbf{m}_K^*)], G[s_1 g_1(\mathbf{x}_1), \ldots, s_K g_K(\mathbf{x}_K)]\}. \tag{C.5b}$$

Assume that the functions V, G, u_k, *and* g_k *do not change over time and are linearly homogeneous for all* $k \in \{1, \ldots, K\}$.[12]

The dependency of u_k and g_k on k permits heterogeneity of tastes across countries. In the next subsection, we will explore the special case of homogeneity of tastes across countries. As in our heterogeneous-agents approach, the subscript k identifies the country of residence of the owner of the asset and not necessarily the country within which the asset is purchased or located. Hence equation (C.5b) requires that the tastes which determine the utility functions, u_k and g_k, are those of the residents of country k, regardless of the country within which the residents have deposited their assets. Note that equation (C.5a) does not require that tastes of consumer's residing in country k exist independently of the tastes of consumers residing in other countries. The existence of stable country-specific tastes, u_k and g_k, exist only under the stronger assumption (C.5b).

Equation (C.5b) could equivalently be written as

$$U = U\{V[u_1(s_1 \mathbf{m}_1^*), \ldots, u_K(s_K \mathbf{m}_K^*)], G[g_1(s_1 \mathbf{x}_1), \ldots, g_K(s_K \mathbf{x}_K)]\},$$

---

12. The assumption that the functions do not move over time does not preclude subjective discounting of future utility within the integrand of the intertemporal utility integral.

because of the linear homogeneity of the utility functions, u_k and g_k. But the form of equation (C.5b) is preferable because it makes clear our ability to aggregate first within countries to acquire the within-country monetary aggregates, $M_k^* = u_k(\mathbf{m}_k^*)$, and the within-country consumer goods aggregates, $X_k = g_k(\mathbf{x}_k)$. Note that M_k^* and X_k are in per capita terms relative to country k's population. We then can aggregate over countries to acquire the economic union's monetary aggregate over countries, $M^* = V[s_1 u_1(\mathbf{m}_1^*), \ldots, s_K u_K(\mathbf{m}_K^*)] = V[s_1 M_1^*, \ldots, s_K M_K^*]$, and the economic union's consumer goods aggregate over countries, $X = G[s_1 g_1(\mathbf{x}_1), \ldots, s_K g_K(\mathbf{x}_K)] = G[s_1 X_1, \ldots, s_K X_K]$. Note that M^* and X are in per capita terms relative to total economic union population. Our proofs below demonstrate the capability to aggregate recursively in that manner.

By assumptions 1, 2a, and 2b, we let $I = I(t)$ be the instantaneous rate of expenditure. It is budgeted to t by the representative consumer in a prior stage intertemporal allocation. Then we can define the following contemporaneous, conditional decision at instant of time t.

Decision 1   *Choose* $(\mathbf{m}_1^*, \ldots, \mathbf{m}_K^*, \mathbf{x}_1, \ldots, \mathbf{x}_K)$ *to maximize* $U\{V[s_1 u_1(\mathbf{m}_1^*), \ldots, s_K u_K(\mathbf{m}_K^*)], G[s_1 g_1(\mathbf{x}_1), \ldots, s_K g_K(\mathbf{x}_K)]\}$ *subject to*

$$\sum_{k=1}^{K} s_k \mathbf{m}_k^{*\prime} \boldsymbol{\pi}_k e_k + \sum_{k=1}^{K} s_k \mathbf{x}_k' \mathbf{p}_k e_k = I.$$

Definition 7   *We define a multilateral representative consumer to be an economic agent who solves decision 1 by assumptions 1, 2a, and 2b.*

Note that our definitions of real and nominal money balances have not changed from those in section C.1. Nominal balances owned by residents of country k are deflated by p_k^* to acquire real balances, where p_k^* is the unit cost function dual to the consumer goods quantity aggregator function, $g_k(\mathbf{x}_k)$, within country k. We are not yet accepting assumptions that would be sufficient for existence of a single consumer price index that could be used to deflate nominal balances within all countries in the economic union to real balances in those countries. Hence p_k^* is not independent of k. Our economic union consumer-goods price aggregate, p^*, is relevant to deflation of monetary balances only after monetary balances have been aggregated over countries.

Observe that assumption 1 does not require convergence of rates of return on all monetary assets across countries. To produce the multilateral representative consumer, assumption 1 requires only that consumers in all countries of the economic union have access to the same benchmark rate of return on pure investment. We now consider the implications of a multilateral representative agent. In the next section we then focus on the case of a unilateral representative agent, requiring the adoption of very strong assumptions.

The following lemmas now are immediate:

Lemma 2   *By assumptions 1, 2a, and 2b, the representative consumer's allocation of I(t) over goods and monetary services will solve decision 1.*

Proof   Follows from known results on two-stage budgeting, where the first stage is intertemporal. One need only redefine the variables in the continuous time analogue to sections A.2.1 and A.2.2 of appendix A.   ∎

Lemma 3   *By assumptions 1, 2a, and 2b, let $X_k = g_k(x_k)$ be the exact consumer goods per capita quantity aggregate over x_k for country k, relative to the population of country k, and let $X = G(s_1 X_1, ..., s_K X_K)$ be the exact consumer goods per capita quantity aggregate over countries, relative to total economic union population. Then p_k^* is the exact price dual to X_k, and P* is the exact price dual to X, where P* is defined such that*

$$d \log P^* = \sum_{k=1}^{K} \left(\frac{X_k p_k^* e_k}{\sum_{\kappa=1}^{K} X_\kappa p_\kappa^* e_\kappa} \right) d \log p_k^* e_k. \tag{C.6}$$

Proof   The result regarding p_k^* follows, since it was defined in section C.1 to be the true cost of living index of X_k. The result on P* follows by a proof analogous to that of theorem 2, since duality of P* and X implies, from factor reversal, that

$$XP^* = \sum_{k=1}^{K} X_k p_k^* e_k. \tag{C.7}$$

This equation accounts for the form of the share weights in equation (C.6).   ∎

Note that P*, defined by equation (C.6), and p*, defined by equation (C.2), are not the same. Both consumer price indexes are needed for different purposes, as we will discuss further below. Now consider the following decision, within which aggregation over consumer goods has already occurred:

Decision 2   *Now choose $(\mathbf{m}_1^*, ..., \mathbf{m}_K^*, X)$ to maximize $U\{V[s_1 u_1(\mathbf{m}_1^*), ..., s_K u_K(\mathbf{m}_K^*)], X\}$ subject to*

$$\sum_{k=1}^{K} s_k \mathbf{m}_k^{*\prime} \pi_k e_k + XP^* = I.$$

The following theorem establishes the connection between decisions 1 and 2:

Theorem 5   *By assumptions 1, 2a, and 2b, we let* $(\mathbf{m}_1^*, \ldots, \mathbf{m}_K^*, \mathbf{x}_1, \ldots, \mathbf{x}_K)$ *solve decision 1, and let X and P* be defined as in lemma 3. Then* $(\mathbf{m}_1^*, \ldots, \mathbf{m}_K^*, X)$ *will solve decision 2.*

Proof   The proof follows from lemma 3 and well-known results on two-stage budgeting.   ■

Theorem 5 permits us to concentrate on aggregation over monetary assets within countries and then over countries, while using a quantity and price aggregate for consumer goods. Theorem 5 also demonstrates our need for the *P** price index in the prior aggregation over consumer goods.

In decision 3 we next define a "second-stage" decision by which funds preallocated to monetary-services expenditure within the economic union are allocated over countries. In decision 4, we define a "third-stage" decision, by which funds preallocated to monetary-services expenditure within the each country are allocated over assets in the country.

Let Π_k for each $k \in \{1, \ldots, K\}$ be as in definition 1. We can then define the following decision:

Decision 3   *For given value of X, choose* $(M_1^*, \ldots, M_K^*)$ *to maximize* $V(s_1 M_1^*, \ldots, s_K M_K^*)$ *subject to*

$$\sum_{k=1}^{K} s_k M_k^* \Pi_k e_k = I - XP^*. \tag{C.8}$$

Decision 4   *For each* $k \in \{1, \ldots, K\}$ *choose* $\mathbf{m}_k^*$ *to maximize* $u_k(\mathbf{m}_k^*)$ *subject to*

$$\mathbf{m}_k^{*\prime} \pi_k = M_k^* \Pi_k.$$

The following two corollaries to theorem 5 relate to decisions 3 and 4.

Corollary 1 to theorem 5   *By assumptions 1, 2a, and 2b, let* $(\mathbf{m}_1^*, \ldots, \mathbf{m}_K^*, X)$ *solve decision 2. Define P* as in equation (6) and the vector of user costs* $\Pi = (\Pi_1, \ldots, \Pi_K)$ *as in definition 1. Then* $(M_1^*, \ldots, M_K^*)$ *will solve decision 3, where* $M_k^* = u_k(\mathbf{m}_k^*)$ *for all* $k \in \{1, \ldots, K\}$.

Proof   The proof follows from well-known results on two stage budgeting.   ■

Corollary 2 to theorem 5   *By assumptions 1, 2a, and 2b, let* $(\mathbf{m}_1^*, \ldots, \mathbf{m}_K^*,$ *X) solve decision 2, and let* $M_k^* = u_k(\mathbf{m}_k^*)$ *for all* $k \in \{1, \ldots, K\}$. *Define* Π_k *as in definition 1. Then* $\mathbf{m}_k^*$ *also will solve decision 4 for all* $k \in \{1, \ldots, K\}$.

Proof   The proof follows from well-known results on two-stage budgeting and a simple proof by contradiction. Suppose that $M_k^* = u_k(\mathbf{m}_k^*)$ but $\mathbf{m}_k^*$ does not solve decision 4 for all $k \in \{1, \ldots, K\}$. Then $(\mathbf{m}_1^*, \ldots, \mathbf{m}_K^*, X)$ cannot solve decision 2.   ∎

Decision 4 defines the representative consumers assumed to exist within countries in section C.3.2. By the assumptions in definition 7 for the existence of a multilateral representative consumer, corollary 2 to theorem 5 proves that the decisions of the representative consumers in section C.3.2 are nested as conditional decisions within the decision of the multilateral representative-consumer. Hence our results in section C.3.2 can be used to aggregate within countries, regardless of whether aggregation over countries is by our heterogeneous-countries approach or by our multilateral representative-consumer approach.

After the aggregation within countries is complete, corollary 1 to theorem 5 demonstrates that decision 3 can be used to aggregate over countries, if we accept the assumptions necessary for the existence of a multilateral representative agent. The monetary quantity aggregator function for aggregation over countries then is V, and a Divisia index can be used to track V in the usual manner. Observe that decision 4 would be unaffected, if the vector of within-country user costs π_k and the aggregate within-country user cost Π_k were changed to real user costs, since all that would be involved is the division of each constraint by p_k^*. Hence that constraint would continue to hold, if all values in the constraint were in real terms.

But observe that in decisions 2 and 3, the consumer price index, P^*, on the right-hand side of equation (C.8) is not the same as the consumer price index, p_k^*, needed to deflate the user costs on the left-hand side to real value. In addition the consumer price index, p_k^*, used to deflate each term on the left-hand side is different for each $k \in \{1, \ldots, K\}$. Hence the constraint would be broken, if all variables on both sides of the constraint were replaced by real values. This would amount to dividing each term by a different price index. Also recall that conversion of $\mathbf{m}_k^*$ to nominal balances requires multiplication by p_k^*, which is different for each country, k.

The following illustration can further clarify the need for two price indexes in modeling. Consider the following decision using the exact aggregates both over monetary assets and goods within the economic union.

Decision 5   *Choose (M*, X) to maximize U(M*, X) subject to M*Π + XP* = I.*

The solution will be of the form

$$
\begin{pmatrix} M^* \\ X \end{pmatrix} = D(I, \Pi, P^*) = D(I, \Pi^* p^*, P^*).
\tag{C.9a}
$$

But by lemma 1 and the homogeneity of degree zero of demand, we equivalently can write

$$
\begin{pmatrix} M^* \\ X \end{pmatrix} = D\left(\frac{I}{p^*}, \Pi^*, \frac{P^*}{p^*} \right),
\tag{C.9b}
$$

or

$$
\begin{pmatrix} M^* \\ X \end{pmatrix} = \hat{D}\left(\frac{I}{P^*}, \frac{\Pi^* p^*}{P^*} \right),
\tag{C.9c}
$$

where

$$
\hat{D}\left(\frac{I}{P^*}, \frac{\Pi^* p^*}{P^*} \right) = D\left(\frac{I}{P^*}, \frac{\Pi^* p^*}{P^*}, 1 \right).
$$

As can be seen from equations (C.9b) and (C.9c), there is no way to remove the simultaneous dependence of the solution demand function systems on the two price indexes, P^* and p^*. The form of the demand system in (C.9a) is in terms of nominal total expenditure ("income"), I. The form of the demand system in (C.9b) is in terms of real income relative to p^* aggregate prices. The form in (C.9c) is in terms of real income relative to P^* aggregate prices. None of the three possible forms results in either p^* or P^* canceling out. In addition lemma 1 requires that conversion of M^* to nominal balances must be relative to p^* prices.

The following theorem establishes the relationship between our heterogeneous-countries approach and our multilateral representative-agent approach.

Theorem 6   *Under assumptions 1, 2a, and 2b, let $(M_1^*, \ldots, M_K^*)$ solve decision 3, and let M^* be as defined in definition 4. Then*

$d \log M^* = d \log V(s_1 M_1^*, \ldots, s_K M_K^*).$

Proof   The proof follows from the exact tracking of the Divisia index in continuous time.   ∎

Our multilateral representative-agent theory produces conditions under which an economic (rather than statistical) monetary aggregate exists over countries. When an economic monetary aggregator function, V, exists over countries, theorem 6 shows that our quantity index number, M^*, introduced in definition 4, will exactly track the theoretical aggregate. In particular, we have demonstrated that our heterogeneous-agents approach for aggregating over countries reduces to the multilateral approach under assumptions 1, 2a, and 2b, since both approaches then produce the same monetary aggregate, M^*, over countries. In addition Π_k and Π_k^* defined in definition 5 will remain dual to M^*, since the proofs of theorems 1 and 2 remain valid by assumptions 1, 2a, and 2b.

We have demonstrated at all stages of aggregation that our multilateral representative-agent approach is nested within our heterogeneous-countries approach as a special case of assumptions 1, 2a, and 2b. Theorem 6 is the result at the level of aggregation over countries, while corollary 2 to theorem 5 is the result for aggregation within countries.

Also observe that since the proofs of theorems 1 and 2 remain valid under our additional assumptions in this section, it follows that we must continue to deflate nominal M aggregated over countries to real M^* using p^*, not P^*. The correct dual to aggregate real consumption X is P^*, which should be used to deflate nominal to real consumption expenditure. Regarding the computation of P^* and its possible use as an inflation target, see Diewert (2002). It is important to recognize that p^* and P^* both play important roles in this theory, and neither is an acceptable substitute for the other.[13] These conclusions hold in both our heterogeneous-countries approach and in the multilateral representative-agents special case acquired when the benchmark rate is the same for all countries in the economic union.

C.5.4   Multilateral Representative Agent with Homogeneous Tastes
Let us now proceed to the far more restrictive case of a homogeneous multilateral representative agent who imputes identical tastes to the

---

13. Although perhaps somewhat surprising, the need for two different consumer price indexes is not entirely without precedent. The theory that produces the relative price version of Theil's (1971, p. 578, eq. 6.19) Rotterdam consumer demand system model also requires two consumer price indexes: the Divisia price index with average share weights to deflate nominal income to real income and the Frisch consumer price index with marginal budget share weights to deflate nominal to real relative prices. But that Rotterdam model phenomenon has a different source.

residents of all countries in the economic union. An initial necessary assumption is assumption 1. As shown by theorem 7 below, the seeming paradox of the existence of two consumer price indexes—p^* to deflate nominal money balances to real balances and P^* to deflate nominal consumption expenditure to real aggregate consumption—disappears under the following additional important assumption.

Assumption 3   *Suppose that there is convergence over the economic union in the following strong sense. Let there exist $\hat{P} = \hat{P}(t)$ such that*

$$\frac{d}{dt}[\log(p_k^*(t)e_k(t))] = \frac{d}{dt}[\log \hat{P}(t)] \tag{C.10}$$

for all $k \in \{1, \ldots, K\}$ and all t.
    The following theorem is immediate:

Theorem 7   *By assumption 3, the following equation holds for all nonnegative $(e_1, \ldots, e_K)$ and all nonnegative $(p_1^*, \ldots, p_K^*)$:*

$$d \log p^*(p_1^* e_1, \ldots, p_K^* e_K) = d \log P^*(p_1^* e_1, \ldots, p_K^* e_K).$$

Proof   By equation (C.10), $d \log(p_k^* e_k) = d \log \hat{P}$ for all $k \in \{1, \ldots, K\}$ and all t. Hence $d \log p^* = d \log \hat{P}$ by equation (C.2), and $d \log P^* = d \log \hat{P}$ by equation (C.10). So $d \log p^* = d \log P^*$.   ∎

We now consider further the case of a homogeneous multilateral representative agent, but first we need the following lemma:

Lemma 4   *By assumptions 1, 2a, 2b, and 3, there exists g such that $g_k = g$ for all $k \in \{1, \ldots, K\}$, so that tastes for consumer goods are identical across countries.*

Proof   From equation (C.10) it follows that $d \log [p_k^*(t)e_k(t)] = d \log \hat{P}[\mathbf{p}_k(t)e_k(t)]$ for all $k \in \{1, \ldots, K\}$. Hence the same consumer-goods price aggregator function, $\hat{P}$, applies for all $k \in \{1, \ldots, K\}$. But the consumer-goods quantity aggregator function, g_k, is dual to the consumer-goods price aggregator function. So the consumer-goods quantity aggregator functions, g_k, must also be independent of k. ∎

To move further toward the existence of a homogeneous multilateral representative consumer, we also need the following assumption, which is analogous to assumption 3:

Assumption 4   *Suppose that convergence over the economic union results in the existence of $\hat{\Pi}$ such that*

$$\frac{d}{dt}[\log(\Pi_k(t)e_k(t))] = \frac{d}{dt}[\log \hat{\Pi}(t)]$$

for all $k \in \{1, \ldots, K\}$ and all t.

Clearly, by this assumption, it follows from definition 5 that $\hat{\Pi}(t) = \Pi(t)$ for all t. The following lemma depends heavily on assumption 4:

Lemma 5 *By assumptions 1, 2a, 2b, and 4, there exists u such that $u_k = u$ for all $k \in \{1, \ldots, K\}$, so that tastes for monetary services are identical across countries.*

Proof The proof is analogous to the proof of lemma 4. ∎

The form of decision 1 now is as follows:

Decision 1a *Choose $(\mathbf{m}_1^*, \ldots, \mathbf{m}_K^*, \mathbf{x}_1, \ldots, \mathbf{x}_K)$ to maximize $U\{V[s_1 u(\mathbf{m}_1^*), \ldots, s_K u(\mathbf{m}_K^*)], G[s_1 g(\mathbf{x}_1), \ldots, s_K g(\mathbf{x}_K)]\}$ subject to*

$$\sum_{k=1}^{K} s_k \mathbf{m}_k^{*\prime} \boldsymbol{\pi}_k e_k + \sum_{k=1}^{K} s_k \mathbf{x}_k' \mathbf{p}_k e_k = \mathbf{I}.$$

Observation 1 *By assumptions 1, 2a, 2b, 3, and 4, the solutions to decisions 1 and 1a will be the same, as is evident from lemmas 4 and 5. Because of the homogeneity of tastes across countries in decision 1a, we have the following definition.*

Definition 8 *We define a homogeneous multilateral representative agent to be an economic agent who solves decision 1a by assumptions 1, 2a, 2b, 3, and 4.*

Observe that despite the homogeneity of tastes across countries, the decision remains multilateral, as a result of the assumption of block-wise weak separability of tastes across countries. That separability assumption produces existence of within-country tastes, u, independent of consumption in other countries. The fact that the tastes are identical for all countries in the economic union does not negate the existence of those tastes, u.

In econometric studies there could be reason to investigate convergence of the general multilateral representative consumer toward the homogeneous multilateral representative agent. But for data construction purposes we see no advantage to adopting the homogeneous multilateral representative-agent model. The general multilateral representative-agent model can be used to construct aggregates recursively, first within countries and then across countries. When producing the aggregates within countries, there is not benefit to imposing uniformity of tastes across countries.

The next section explores the unilateral representative-agent model that would produce a large gain in data construction simplification, but only under a very strong assumption that is not likely to be reasonable within the near future, if ever.

C.5.5   Unilateral Representative Agent over the Economic Union

A unilateral representative agent considers the same goods and assets to be perfect substitutes, regardless of the country within which the goods and assets are purchased and regardless of the country within which the purchaser resides. By this assumption, our subscripts j and k will be irrelevant to the tastes of the unilateral representative agent. Only the subscript i will matter, since countries, and thereby country subscripts, will be irrelevant to the decision.

We no longer can accept assumption 2b; we will instead have to make a much stronger, but nonnested, assumption. Assumption 2b assumed weak separability among countries of residence of consumers. But a unilateral representative agent neither recognizes the country of residence of a consumer nor the country within which a good or asset was acquired. Hence tastes specific to a country no longer exist. It is important to recognize the fundamental difference between the homogeneous multilateral representative consumer and the unilateral representative consumer. The former imputes identical tastes to each country's residents but does recognize the existence of different countries and the existence of the identical tastes, u, within each country. But the unilateral representative consumer does not impute existence of weakly separable tastes to the residents of any country in the economic union.

Since we no longer can assume weak separability among countries, we will have to rewrite decision 1 as follows:

Decision 1b   *Choose* $(\mathbf{m}_1^*, \ldots, \mathbf{m}_K^*, \mathbf{x}_1, \ldots, \mathbf{x}_K)$ *to maximize* $U[\breve{V}(s_1\mathbf{m}_1^*, \ldots, s_K\mathbf{m}_K^*), \breve{G}(s_1\mathbf{x}_1, \ldots, s_K\mathbf{x}_K)]$ *subject to*

$$\sum_{k=1}^{K} s_k \mathbf{m}_k^{*\prime} \pi_k e_k + \sum_{k=1}^{K} s_k \mathbf{x}_k' \mathbf{p}_k e_k = I.$$

Hence we now replace assumption 2b with the following much stronger assumption, which is neither necessary nor sufficient for assumption 2b:

Assumption 5 Let $\mathbf{m}^* = \sum_{k=1}^{K}\sum_{j=1}^{K+Z} s_k\mathbf{m}^*_{kj}$, and $\mathbf{x} = \sum_{k=1}^{K} s_k\mathbf{x}_k$. Suppose that there exists linearly homogeneous $\hat{V}$ such that $\hat{V}(\mathbf{m}^*) = \breve{V}(s_1\mathbf{m}^*_1, \ldots, s_K\mathbf{m}^*_K)$, where $\breve{V}$ is as defined in equation (C.5a). Then for any i, all monetary assets of that type are perfect substitutes, regardless of the country within which they are located or the country in which the owner resides. Analogously for consumer goods, assume there exists $\hat{G}$ such that $\hat{G}(\mathbf{x}) = \breve{G}(s_1\mathbf{x}_1, \ldots, s_K\mathbf{x}_K)$, where $\breve{G}$ is as defined in equation (C.5a). Hence for any i, all consumer goods of that type are perfect substitutes, regardless of the country within which they are located or the country in which the owner resides. Further assume that there exist $\pi(t)$ and $p(t)$ such that $\pi_{kj}(t)e_k(t) = \pi(t)$ and $p_k(t)e_k(t) = p(t)$ for all $k \in \{1, \ldots, K\}$, $j \in \{1, \ldots, K + Z\}$, and all t.

The assumptions $\pi_{kj}(t)e_k(t) = \pi(t)$ and $\mathbf{p}_k(t)e_k(t) = \mathbf{p}(t)$ are needed to avoid corner solutions allocating no consumption to residents of some countries. Otherwise, with perfect substitutability across countries of residence, all consumption of each good by the unilateral representative agent would be allocated to residents of the country having the lowest price of that good. By assumption 5, decision 1b now becomes decision 1c, defined as follows:

Decision 1c Choose $(\mathbf{m}^*, \mathbf{x})$ to maximize $U[\hat{V}(\mathbf{m}^*), \hat{G}(\mathbf{x})]$

subject to $\mathbf{m}^{*\prime}\pi + \mathbf{x}'\mathbf{p} = I$.

The following theorem demonstrates that decision 1c is the decision of a unilateral representative consumer for the economic union:

Theorem 8 Let $(\mathbf{m}^*_1, \ldots, \mathbf{m}^*_K, \mathbf{x}_1, \ldots, \mathbf{x}_K)$ solve decision 1b, and let $\mathbf{m}^*$ and $\mathbf{x}$ be as defined in assumption 5. By assumptions 1, 2a, and 5, it follows that $\mathbf{m}^*$ and $\mathbf{x}$ will solve decision 1c.

Proof Observe that there is no need to include assumptions 3 or 4 in this theorem, since assumption 5 implies assumptions 3 and 4. The result follows directly from the theorem's assumptions and the definitions of $\mathbf{m}^*$ and $\mathbf{x}$. ∎

We thereby are led to the following definition:

Definition 9 By assumptions 1, 2a, and 5, we define a unilateral representative consumer to be an economic agent who solves decision 1c.

Note that a unilateral economic agent recognizes no differences in tastes among countries, either for the owner's country of residence or for the country within which the asset or good is located or purchased. But in a more fundamental sense, observe that in general, it is impossible to factor out of $\hat{V}(\mathbf{m}^*)$ or $\hat{G}(\mathbf{x})$ the consumption or asset holdings of residents of any country. Hence country-specific separable subfunction, u_k or g_k, does not exist, and hence separable tastes of residents of a country do not exist. In fact for any solution for $(\mathbf{m}^*, \mathbf{x})$ to decision 1c, the allocation of asset holdings and consumption expenditure to countries is indeterminate. Assumptions 3 and 4 have been omitted from theorem 8, because of redundancy with assumption 5. But assumption 2b, which also has been omitted, is not redundant but rather is omitted since it contradicts assumption 5. The unilateral representative agent exists under much stronger assumptions than the multilateral representative agent. But the unilateral representative agent is not a nested special case of the multilateral representative agent, whether in its general or homogeneous form.[14]

The multilateral representative-agent model of decision 1 is far more reasonable, requiring only assumptions 1, 2a, and 2b. But we see from theorem 6 that our heterogeneous-agents approach would produce the same results as the multilateral representative-agent theory, if the necessary conditions for existence of a multilateral representative agent were satisfied.

C.6   Interest Rate Aggregation

Since interest rates play important roles in policy, it could be useful to compute the interest rate aggregate that is dual to the Divisia monetary quantity index. We show that the correct interest rate aggregate is not the one in common use by central banks, and we view the commonly used interest rate aggregates to be unacceptable. In particular, we provide the correct formula for aggregating interest rates jointly over monetary assets and over countries.

Let $\bar{r}_k$ be the dual aggregate interest rate for country k. It follows from definition 1 and the definition of the vector of component user-cost

---

14. Decision 1c is the representative-agent model previously used in some studies to aggregate within the euro area. But the required convergence conditions, assumptions 1, 2a, and 5 and the implied assumptions 3 and 4, are clearly very strong, since they imply decision independence of the country of residence of purchasers and of the country of location of the purchase. Rather than requiring identical tastes of consumers among all countries in the economic union, as in the homogeneous multilateral representative-agent case, the unilateral representative-agent case implies nonexistence of separable tastes or cultures for any country, through irrelevancy of the location of the purchaser or of the purchased good or asset.

prices, π_k^*, that $R_k - \bar{r}_k = \Pi_k^*$, where $\Pi_k^* = \Pi_k^*(\pi_k^*)$. Hence $\bar{r}_k$ easily can be computed from $\bar{r}_k = R_k - \Pi_k^*$. In discrete time when $\pi_{ki}^* = (R_k - r_{ki})/(1 + R_k)$, it follows that $(R_k - \bar{r}_k)/(1 + R_k) = \Pi_k^*$, with $\bar{r}_k$ being computed by solving that equation.

After aggregating over countries, the interest rate dual to M^* is similarly easy to compute, if the same benchmark rate applies to all countries. In that case, which we believe not likely to be applicable prior to the introduction of a common currency, our heterogeneous-agents approach to aggregating over countries becomes mathematically equivalent to our multilateral representative-agent approach.

Let $R = R(t)$ be the common benchmark rate applying to all countries in the economic union, and let $\bar{r} = \bar{r}(t)$ be the interest rate aggregate dual to M^*. In continuous time, it follows that $R - \bar{r} = \Pi^*$, where $\Pi^* = \Pi^*(t) = \Pi^*(\Pi_1^*, \ldots, \Pi_K^*)$. Hence $\bar{r}$ easily can be computed from $\bar{r} = R - \Pi^*$. Analogously in discrete time, it follows that $(R - \bar{r})/(1 + R) = \Pi^*$, with $\bar{r}$ being computed by solving that equation.[15]

Note that our aggregation-theoretic interest rate aggregates are not the interest rate weighted averages often used in this literature.

C.7 Divisia Second Moments

Use of the stochastic approach to aggregation lends itself naturally to the computation of Divisia second moments, although in the sections above we have provided only the Divisia first moments. In this tradition the "Divisia index" is synonymous with the Divisia growth rate mean. The Divisia growth rate variance could be especially useful for exploring distribution effects of policy within an economic union and progress toward convergence. Some potentially useful Divisia growth rate variances are proposed below. Conversion of the continuous time formulas to their discrete time version is analogous to that available for the within-country Divisia quantity and user-cost growth rate variances in Barnett and Serletis (2000, p. 172, eqs. 4 and 7).

The Divisia growth rate variances could be especially useful when computed about the Divisia means of the following growth rates: (1) the monetary quantity growth rates, $d \log M$ and $d \log M^*$, in definition

---

15. In the heterogeneous-agents approach, there does not exist a common benchmark rate, which can be imputed to all countries. Under those circumstances, the aggregation theoretic method of producing the interest rate aggregate can be found in Barnett (2000, p. 278, eq. 5).

4, (2) the Divisia means of the user-cost price growth rates, $d \log \Pi$ and $d \log \Pi^*$, in definition 5, and (3) the inflation growth rate, $d \log p^*$, in equation (C.2) or the inflation growth rate, $d \log P^*$, in equation (C.6). Repeating those Divisia mean formulas and producing the analogous Divisia variances, we have the following formulas:

The Divisia growth rate means are in definitions 3, 4, and 5 and equation (C.6). The analogous Divisia growth rate variances are

$$K = \sum_{k=1}^{K} W_k [d \log(s_k M_k e_k) - d \log M]^2,$$

$$K^* = \sum_{k=1}^{K} W_k [d \log(s_k M_k^*) - d \log M^*]^2,$$

$$J = \sum_{k=1}^{K} W_k [d \log(\Pi_k e_k) - d \log \Pi]^2,$$

$$J^* = \sum_{k=1}^{K} W_k [d \log(\Pi_k^*) - d \log \Pi^*]^2,$$

$$G_M = \sum_{k=1}^{K} W_k [d \log p_k^* e_k - d \log p^*]^2,$$

$$G = \sum_{k=1}^{K} B_k [d \log p_k^* e_k - d \log P^*]^2.$$

An additional potentially useful Divisia growth rate variance is that of the monetary expenditure share growth rates $\Psi = \sum_{k=1}^{K} W_k [d \log W_k - d \log W]^2$, where $d \log W = \sum_{k=1}^{K} W_k d \log W_k$.

The Divisia monetary services growth rate variances, K and K^*, and the Divisia monetary-services expenditure-share growth rate variance, Ψ, are measures of the dispersion of monetary service growth rates across countries in nominal and real terms, respectively, while the Divisia inflation rate variances, G and G_M, are measures of the dispersion of inflation rates across countries. Increasing values of K, K^*, Ψ, and G over time are indications of growth in the distribution effects of monetary policy over the countries of the economic union. Decreases in K, K^*, Ψ, and G over time are indications of convergence toward more uniform effects of policy over the economic union. If variations in K, K^*, and Ψ tend to precede those of G, then there is an implication of causality. The converse could indicate that policy is accommodating other causal factors.

The Divisia growth rate variances, J and J^*, are measures of the progress of harmonization of financial markets over countries and hence are less directly connected with monetary policy and more directly connected with structural progress in the unification of money markets over the economic union.

C.8 Conclusion

The approach in appendix A applies to Divisia aggregation within countries and then the heterogeneous-countries approach to aggregation over countries. The stochastic approach to aggregation over countries lends itself naturally to computation of Divisia second moments. Computation of Divisia variance growth rates about the Divisia means is advocated across countries. Those Divisia second moments could provide useful information about the distribution effects of policy and about progress toward convergence over an economic union, such as the EMU.

This appendix also defines and produces the theory relevant to a third very restrictive case, called the unilateral representative-agent approach. This approach, which is implied by some early studies of euro area monetary aggregation, may be relevant to aggregation over states or provinces of a single country, but not likely for aggregation over different countries within an economic union.

With the heterogeneous countries or multilateral representative-agent approach, there is the need for two different consumer price indexes: one for use in deflating nominal to real monetary balances after aggregation over countries, and one for deflating nominal to real consumer-goods expenditure. The imputation of either index to both uses would produce a serious specification error. Only under the very restrictive homogeneous multilateral representative-agent assumptions or the even more restrictive unilateral representative-agent assumptions do the growth rates of the two consumer price indexes become equal.

The choice among the nested assumption structures for aggregation must be consistent with the assumptions made in producing the models, within which the data is to be used. In fact attainment of that internal consistency is the primary objective of index number and aggregation theory. Without that coherence among aggregator function structure and the econometric models within which aggregates are embedded, stable structure can appear to become unstable.

D Extension to Risk Aversion

Appendixes A, B, and C assume perfect certainty, perfect foresight, or risk neutrality, in accordance with the existing literature on index number theory. All of the prior literature on index number theory assumed that contemporaneous prices are known with certainty, and the conditional current-period decision is therefore under perfect certainty. But in discrete time, decisions are made at the beginning of periods, while interest rates are not paid until the end of period. When risk about the current-period interest rate is nonnegligible, as when high and subject to exchange rate risk, risk aversion can become relevant. The relevancy of risk to monetary aggregation theory was first pointed out by Poterba and Rotemberg (1987). Without availability of the extension of index number theory to risk, they advocated direct econometric estimation of aggregator functions within Euler equation. This appendix extends the field of index number theory to the case of risk aversion. The theory in this appendix is based on Barnett (1995), Barnett, Liu, and Jensen (1997), and Barnett and Wu (2005), whose work produced that fundamental extension by deriving index-number theory from Euler equations, rather than from the perfect-certainty first-order conditions.

D.1 Introduction

In the case of perfect certainty the Divisia index exactly tracks any aggregator function. This follows from the fact that the Divisia line integral is directly derivable from the first-order conditions for optimizing behavior. This result is especially well known in the case of consumer behavior, in which the Divisia index is derived directly from the total differential of the demand function, after substitution of the first-order conditions for maximizing utility subject to a budget constraint. However, the exact tracking property of the Divisia index also applies to the demand for monetary services by firms and the supply of produced monetary services by financial intermediaries. See appendix A.

Risk aversion is another story. The first-order conditions in the case of risk aversion are Euler equations. Since those are not the first-order conditions used in deriving the Divisia index under perfect certainty, the tracking ability of the unadjusted Divisia index is compromised. The degree to which the tracking ability degrades is a function of the degree of risk aversion and the amount of risk. In principle this problem could be solved by estimating the Euler equations by generalized method of moments and producing the estimated exact rational expectations monetary aggregator function, as first advocated by Poterba and Rotemberg (1987). This inference procedure is in accordance with the one widely advocated as the solution to the Lucas Critique and more recently also advocated as the solution to what Chrystal and MacDonald (1994, p. 76) and Belongia and Ireland (2010) have called the Barnett critique.[1] However estimation of aggregator functions, while in strict accordance with the principles of microeconomic aggregation theory, produces results that depend on the parametric specification of the aggregator function and the choice of econometric estimator for estimating the parameters of the aggregator.

Index-number theory exists precisely for the purpose of permitting specification-free, nonparametric tracking ability. The Divisia index is such a parameter free index number and hence depends only on data. While the Divisia index number is known to permit exact tracking for any economic aggregator function under perfect certainty, that index had never been extended to a statistical index number that will track exactly under risk aversion until appearance of the journal articles that are the basis for this appendix. To our knowledge, no nonparametric, statistical index numbers had ever previously been derived directly from Euler equations in a manner that retains tracking ability under risk. In this appendix we derive a statistical index number directly from the Euler equations. The resulting index number turns out to be an extension of the original Divisia index derived by François Divisia (1925, 1926a, b) under perfect certainty, such that our extended Divisia index remains exact under risk aversion and reduces to the usual Divisia

---

1. According to the Barnett critique, the appearance of structural shift can be produced from an inconsistency between the aggregator function, tracked by the index number used to produce the data, and the aggregator function, implied by the structural model within which the index number is used. The use of simple-sum monetary aggregates as variables within models is an extreme example.

index in the special case of perfect certainty. The derivation is analogous to that for the usual Divisia index, but our extended Divisia index is derived from the Euler equations that are the correct first-order conditions produced from rational behavior of economic agents under risk.

If additional assumptions are imposed, we find that the resulting generalized Divisia index has a direct connection with the capital asset-pricing model (CAPM) in finance. In a sense our theory is a simultaneous generalization of both the CAPM and of economic index number theory, since our theory contains both as nested special cases. In particular, CAPM deals with a two dimensional trade-off between expected return and risk, while the Divisia index deals with the two-dimensional trade-off between investment return and liquidity. Our generalized theory includes the three-dimensional trade-off among mean return, risk, and liquidity. The two well-known special cases are based on two-dimensional sections, which are orthogonal to each other, through the relevant three-dimensional space.

A particularly productive area of possible application of this new index number is monetary aggregation, since money market assets are characterized by substantially different degrees of each of the three characteristics: mean rate of return, risk, and liquidity, especially when the collection of money market assets include those subject to prepayment penalties, such as Series EE bonds and nonnegotiable certificates of deposit, and those subject to regulated low rates of return, such as currency.

When central banks first produced monetary aggregates, all of the components over which they aggregated yielded no interest. Hence there was perfect certainty about the rate of return on each component. In addition, since that rate of return was exactly zero for each component, the user costs were known to be the same for each component. Under those circumstances it is well known in aggregation theory that the correct method of aggregation is simple summation. But monetary assets no longer yield the same rates of return and cannot be viewed as perfect substitutes. In addition the interest yield is not a monetary service, so that the interest yield's capitalized value, while embedded in the value of the stock of such assets, is not part of the economic monetary stock. The capitalized value of the monetary service flow, net of that interest yield, is the economy's economic monetary stock. Furthermore, since interest is not paid in advance, there is some degree of uncertainty about that rate of return, which is needed to compute the forgone interest (user cost) of any interest-yielding monetary asset. These observations indicate that the ability to track a nonlinear aggregator function under risk is needed to be able to measure the economy's monetary service flow.

In the case of the current Federal Reserve monetary aggregates, the component assets yield rates of return having low variance and low correlation with consumption, and most Americans do not have bank accounts or own money market assets denominated in foreign currencies subject to exchange rate risk. As a result the ordinary Divisia index produced from perfect-certainty first-order conditions may be adequate to track monetary service flows within the United States, except during periods of unusually high risk and high interest rates. But in countries within which asset holders have substantial funds in foreign denominated money market assets, subject to exchange rate risk, the perfect certainty first-order conditions may not be suitable, and hence the ordinary Divisia monetary aggregates may not track well.

In its most general interpretation the objective of this appendix is to extend index number theory to apply to aggregation over goods for which contemporaneous prices are not known with certainty. Since the user-cost prices of financial assets depend on risky contemporaneous rates of return, aggregation over financial assets seems like an especially suitable area for application of risk-extended index number theory, and we will concentrate on that application of that theory in this appendix.

In this appendix we display the derivation of the CAPM-extended Divisia monetary index based on the derived utility function containing money. Arrow and Hahn (1971), among others, have shown that such a derived utility function exists for any explicit motive for holding money, so long as money has positive value in equilibrium.[2] As a result it should be observed that exactly the same result would be produced from any explicit motive for holding money, such as a model having a transactions technology constraint. Even the case of perfect substitution among components is a nested special case of the index derived below.

D.2   Consumer Demand for Monetary Assets

D.2.1   The Decision
In this section we formulate a representative consumer's stochastic decision problem over consumer goods and monetary assets. The

---

2. Although money may not exist in the elementary utility function, there exists a derived utility function that contains money, so long as money has positive value in equilibrium. See, for example, Arrow and Hahn (1971), Phlips and Spinnewyn (1982), Quirk and Saposnik (1968), Samuelson (1947), and Feenstra (1986). We implicitly are using that derived utility function.

consumer's decisions are made in discrete time over an infinite planning horizon for the time intervals, t, $t+1$, . . ., s, . . ., where t is the current time period. The variables used in defining the consumer's decision
are as follows: x_s = n-dimensional vector of real consumption of goods
and services during period s, p_s = n-dimensional vector of goods and
services prices and of durable goods rental prices during period s, a_s =
k-dimensional vector of real balances of monetary assets during period s, ρ_s = k-dimensional vector of nominal holding period yields of
monetary assets, A_s = holdings of the benchmark asset during period s,
R_s = the one-period holding yield on the benchmark asset during period
s, I_s = the sum of all other sources of income during period s, and p_s^* =
$p_s^*(\mathbf{p}_s)$ = the true cost of living index.

Define Y to be the consumer's survival set, assumed to be a compact
subset of the $(n + k + 2)$-dimensional nonnegative orthant. In accordance with equation (A.3) in appendix A, the consumer's consumption
possibility set, $S(s)$, for period s is

$$S(s) = \{(\mathbf{a}_s, \mathbf{x}_s, A_s) \in Y : \sum_{i=1}^{k} p_{is} x_{is} = \sum_{i=1}^{k} [(1 + \rho_{i,s-1}) p_{s-1}^* a_{i,s-1} - p_s^* a_{i,s}]$$

$$+ (1 + R_{s-1}) p_{s-1}^* A_{s-1} - p_s^* A_s + I_s\}.$$

Since equation (A.3) in appendix A is a flow of funds identity, it remains valid under risk, with some of its variables now being stochastic
processes. The benchmark asset, A_s, provides no services other than its
yield, R_s. As a result, the benchmark asset does not enter the consumer's
contemporaneous utility function, as previously observed in appendix
A's equation (A.7). The asset is held only as a means of accumulating
wealth. The consumer's subjective rate of time preference, ξ, is assumed
to be constant. The single period utility function, $u(\mathbf{a}_t, \mathbf{x}_t)$, is assumed to
be increasing and strictly quasiconcave.

The consumer's decision problem is the following:

Problem 1 *Choose the deterministic point $(\mathbf{a}_t, \mathbf{x}_t, A_t)$ and the stochastic process $(\mathbf{a}_s, \mathbf{x}_s, A_s)$, $s = t +1$, . . ., ∞, to maximize*

$$u(\mathbf{a}_t, \mathbf{x}_t) + E_t \left[\sum_{s=t+1}^{\infty} \left(\frac{1}{1+\xi} \right)^{s-t} u(\mathbf{a}_s, \mathbf{x}_s) \right] \tag{D.1}$$

*subject to $(\mathbf{a}_s, \mathbf{x}_s, A_s) \in S(s)$ for $s \geq t$, and also subject to the transversality
condition*

$$\lim_{s \to \infty} E_t \left(\frac{1}{1+\xi} \right)^{s-t} A_s = 0.$$

The transversality condition rules out perpetual borrowing at the benchmark rate, R_t.

D.2.2 Existence of a Monetary Aggregate for the Consumer

In order to ensure the existence of a monetary aggregate for the consumer, we partition the vector of monetary asset quantities, $\mathbf{a}_s$, such that $\mathbf{a}'_s = (\mathbf{m}'_s, \mathbf{h}'_s)$. We correspondingly partition the vector of interest rates of those assets, ρ_s, such that $\pi'_s = (\mathbf{r}'_s, \mathbf{i}'_s)$. We then assume that the utility function, u, is blockwise weakly separable in $\mathbf{m}_s$ and in $\mathbf{x}_s$ for some such partition of $\mathbf{a}_s$ and blockwise strongly separable in $\mathbf{h}_s$.[3] Hence there exist a monetary aggregator ("category utility") function, M, a consumer goods aggregator function, X, and utility functions, F and H, such that

$$u(\mathbf{m}_s, \mathbf{h}_s, \mathbf{x}_s) = F(M(\mathbf{m}_s), X(\mathbf{x}_s)) + H(\mathbf{h}_s), \tag{D.2}$$

and we define the implied utility function $V(\mathbf{m}_s, c_s)$ by $V(\mathbf{m}_s, c_s) = F(M(\mathbf{m}_s), c_s)$, where aggregate consumptions of goods is defined by $c_s = X(\mathbf{x}_s)$. Then it follows that the exact monetary aggregate is

$$M_s = M(\mathbf{m}_s). \tag{D.3}$$

We define the dimension of $\mathbf{m}_s$ to be k_1, and the dimension of $\mathbf{h}_s$ to be k_2, so that $k = k_1 + k_2$. The fact that blockwise weak separability is a necessary condition for exact aggregation is well known in the perfect certainty case and is equally relevant under risk.

   The Euler equations that will be of the most use to us below are those for monetary assets. Those Euler equations are

$$E_s \left[\frac{\partial V}{\partial m_{is}} - \rho \frac{p^*_s (R_s - r_{is})}{p^*_{s+1}} \frac{\partial V}{\partial c_{s+1}} \right] = 0 \tag{D.4a}$$

for $s \geq t$ and $i = 1, \ldots, k_1$, where $\rho = 1/(1+\xi)$ and where p^*_s is the exact price aggregate that is dual to the consumer goods quantity aggregate c_s.[4] Similarly we can acquire the Euler equation for the consumer-goods aggregate, c_s, rather than for each of its components. The resulting Euler equation for c_s is

---

3. The strong separability assumption is largely for expository convenience. Weak separability would be sufficient.

4. Assuming that X is linearly homogeneous, the exact price aggregator function is the unit cost function.

$$E_s\left[\frac{\partial V}{\partial c_s} - \rho\frac{p_s^*(1+R_s)}{p_{s+1}^*}\frac{\partial V}{\partial c_{s+1}}\right] = 0. \tag{D.4b}$$

For the formal derivation of (D.4a) and (D.4b), using Bellman's method, see Barnett (1995, sec. 2.3).

D.3 The Perfect-Certainty Case

In the perfect-certainty case, nonparametric index number theory is highly developed and is applicable to monetary aggregation. In the perfect-certainty case, we have seen in appendix A's equation (A.5), and more formally derived in appendix B's equation (B.4), that the contemporaneous real user cost of the services of m_{it} is π_{it}, where

$$\pi_{it} = \frac{R_t - r_{it}}{1 + R_t}. \tag{D.5}$$

The corresponding nominal user cost is $p_t^*\pi_{it}$, where we now are using the notation π_{it} for the real user cost, while the previous appendixes used that notation for the nominal user cost. It can be shown that the solution value of the exact monetary aggregate $M(\mathbf{m}_t)$ can be tracked without error in continuous time (see appendix A's equation A.79) by the Divisia index:

$$d \log M_t = \sum_{i=1}^{k_1} s_{it} d \log m_{it}, \tag{D.6}$$

where the user cost evaluated expenditure shares are $s_{it} = \pi_{it}m_{it}/\sum_{j=1}^{k_1}\pi_{jt}m_{jt}$. The flawless tracking ability of the index in the perfect-certainty case holds regardless of the form of the unknown aggregator function, M. However, under risk, the ability of equation (D.6) to track $M(\mathbf{m}_t)$ is compromised in continuous time and hence also in discrete time at all data sampling frequencies.

D.4 The New Generalized Divisia Index

D.4.1 The User Cost of Money under Risk Aversion

We now return to the Euler equations for optimal behavior of consumers under risk. Those Euler equations are displayed in equation (D.4a) for monetary assets and equation (D.4b) for consumer goods. Our objective is to find the formula for the user cost of monetary services in a form that is applicable to our model of decision under risk. The following definition for the contemporaneous user cost simply states that the real user cost price of a monetary asset is the marginal rate of substitution between those assets and consumer goods.

Definition 1   *The contemporaneous risk-adjusted real user cost price of the services of monetary asset i is Π_{it}, defined such that*

$$\Pi_{it} = \frac{\partial V / \partial m_{it}}{\partial V / \partial c_t}.$$

No expectations operators appear in that definition, since the marginal utilities at t are known with certainty in period t. Nevertheless, formula (D.5), which applies under perfect certainty, cannot be correct under risk, since the end-of-period interest rates in equation (D.5) are not known at the time that contemporaneous discrete time decisions are made at the start of the period, as first pointed out by Poterba and Rotemberg (1987). The right-hand side of equation (D.5) is stochastic, while definition 1 defines Π_{it} to be deterministic. In this section we derive the correct formula for the user cost defined by definition 1 under risk.

For notational convenience, we sometimes convert the nominal rates of return, r_{it} and R_t, to real total rates of return, $1 + r_{it}^*$ and $1 + R_t^*$, such that

$$1 + r_{it}^* = \frac{p_t^*(1 + r_{it})}{p_{t+1}^*} \quad \text{and} \quad 1 + R_t^* = \frac{p_t^*(1 + R_t)}{p_{t+1}^*}, \tag{D.7}$$

where r_{it}^* and R_t^*, defined in that manner, are called the real rates of excess return. Under this change of variables, Euler equations (D.4a) and (D.4b) become

$$\frac{\partial V}{\partial m_{it}} - \rho E_t \left[\left(R_t^* - r_{it}^* \right) \frac{\partial V}{\partial c_{t+1}} \right] = 0 \tag{D.8}$$

and

$$\frac{\partial V}{\partial c_t} - \rho E_t \left[\left(1 + R_t^* \right) \frac{\partial V}{\partial c_{t+1}} \right] = 0. \tag{D.9}$$

We now can prove our user-cost theorem under risk.

Theorem 1   *The risk-adjusted user cost of the services of monetary asset i is $\Pi_{it} = \pi_{it} + \psi_{it}$, where we now alter the definition of π_{it} to be*

$$\pi_{it} = \frac{E_t R_t - E_t r_{it}}{1 + E_t R_t}, \tag{D.10}$$

and where

$$\psi_{it} = \rho(1-\pi_{it})\frac{\text{Cov}[R_t^*,(\partial V/\partial c_{t+1})]}{\partial V/\partial c_t} - \rho\frac{\text{Cov}[r_{it}^*,(\partial V/\partial c_{t+1})]}{\partial V/\partial c_t}. \tag{D.11}$$

Proof Equation (D.8) can be rewritten for current period t to be

$$\frac{\partial V}{\partial m_{it}} = \rho E_t\left[(R_t^* - r_{it}^*)\frac{\partial V}{\partial c_{t+1}}\right]. \tag{D.12}$$

If the marginal utility and the interest rates in the expectation on the right-hand side of (D.12) were uncorrelated, we could write the expectation of the product as the product of the expectations. But under our assumption of weak separability in monetary assets, $\mathbf{m}_t$, the utility function V can be written in the form $V(\mathbf{m}_t, c_t) = F(M(\mathbf{m}_t), c_t)$, where the consumer is risk neutral, if and only if F is linear in $M_t = M(\mathbf{m}_t)$ and in c_t. Hence under risk neutrality, V must be linear in c_t, so that the marginal utility of consumption must be a constant. But without risk neutrality and the resulting constancy of the marginal utility of consumption, we have no reason to expect the interest rates and marginal utility on the right-hand side of (D.11) to be uncorrelated. The result is that (D.12) becomes

$$\frac{\partial V}{\partial m_{it}} = \rho E_t\left[\frac{\partial V}{\partial c_{t+1}}\right](E_t R_t^* - E_t r_{it}^*) + \rho\,\text{Cov}\left(R_t^*, \frac{\partial V}{\partial c_{t+1}}\right) - \rho\,\text{Cov}\left(r_{it}^*, \frac{\partial V}{\partial c_{t+1}}\right), \tag{D.13}$$

where the covariances would become zero, if we were to assume risk neutrality. Similarly, without risk neutrality, equation (D.9) becomes

$$\frac{\partial V}{\partial c_t} = \rho E_t\left[\frac{\partial V}{\partial c_{t+1}}\right] + \rho E_t\left[R_t^*\right]E_t\left[\frac{\partial V}{\partial c_{t+1}}\right] + \rho\,\text{Cov}\left(R_t^*, \frac{\partial V}{\partial c_{t+1}}\right). \tag{D.14}$$

By eliminating $\rho E_t[\partial V/\partial c_{t+1}]$ between equations (D.13) and (D.14), we get

$$\frac{\partial V}{\partial m_{it}} = (\pi_{it} + \psi_{it})\frac{\partial V}{\partial c_t}, \tag{D.15}$$

where

$$\pi_{it} = \frac{E_t R_t^* - E_t r_{it}^*}{1 + E_t R_t^*} \tag{D.16}$$

and

$$\psi_{it} = \rho(1 - \pi_{it})\frac{\text{Cov}[R_t^*, (\partial V/\partial c_{t+1})]}{\partial V/\partial c_t} - \rho\frac{\text{Cov}[r_{it}^*, (\partial V/\partial c_{t+1})]}{\partial V/\partial c_t}. \tag{D.17}$$

Using equation (D.7) to convert the real rates in equation (D.16) back to nominal rates, equation (D.16) becomes (D.10), while equation (D.17) is immediately identical to equation (D.11). Solving equation (D.15) for $\Pi_{it} = \pi_{it} + \psi_{it}$, theorem 1 follows from definition 1.   ∎

Under risk neutrality, the covariances in (D.17) would all be zero, since the utility function would be linear in consumption. Hence the user cost would reduce to π_{it}, as defined in equation (D.10). The following corollary is immediate:

Corollary 1 to theorem 1   *Under risk neutrality, the user-cost formula is the same as equation (D.5) in the perfect-certainty case, but with all interest rates replaced by their expectations.*

However, under risk aversion the utility function is strictly concave in consumption, so that marginal utility is inversely related to consumption. In principle, it is possible for the interest rate on a slightly risky investment to reduce the risk in the consumer's consumption stream, if that interest rate and consumption are negatively correlated. Because of the inverse relationship between consumption and marginal utility, we conclude that risk is decreased by an investment, if the rate of return is positively correlated with marginal utility. For monetary assets, with little or no principal risk and low volatility, the riskiness of the asset is likely to contribute relatively little to the riskiness of the household's consumption stream, and hence the sign of the covariance between the asset's rate of return and of the consumption stream is not easy to predict a priori. But with a very risky asset, such as common stock, it is far more likely that holding such a risky investment will increase risk, rather than decrease it. That occurs if the rate of return on the asset is positively correlated with consumption and thereby negatively correlated with marginal utility. This phenomenon is central to the consumption based capital asset pricing model (CCAPM).

Consider the interpretation of equation (D.11), which defines the adjustment for risk under risk aversion. Suppose that we normalize relative to $\partial V/\partial c_t$, so that we need not consider the denominator of equation (D.11). Now consider the second term on the right-hand side of equation (D.11). Suppose that the own rate of return on monetary asset i is positively correlated with the marginal utility of consumption of goods, so that holding that monetary asset decreases risk. Since holding the asset decreases the consumer's consumption risk, we should expect that the risk-adjusted user-cost price, $\Pi_{it} = \pi_{it} + \psi_{it}$, which the consumer would have to "pay" to hold that asset, would be decreased as that positive covariance increases, and that is precisely what the second term of equation (D.11) would do in that case. Conversely, if the covariance between the own rate of return and the marginal utility of consumption of goods is negative, so that holding the asset increases the risk of the consumer's consumption stream, the second term in equation (D.11) introduces a positive term into the risk-adjusted user cost $\Pi_{it} = \pi_{it} + \psi_{it}$ to reflect the increased cost of holding the asset as that covariance increases the consumer's risk. If the central bank were to introduce common stock or bond funds into monetary aggregates or other assets having substantial principal risk or foreign-denominated exchange rate risk, we should expect to find the latter case would apply to those assets.

Now consider the first term on the right-hand side of equation (D.11). The benchmark rate is the interest rate forgone by not holding the benchmark asset. If the benchmark rate decreases consumption risk through a positive covariance between the benchmark rate and the marginal utility of consumption of goods, then the opportunity cost of forgoing the benchmark asset yield, by holding monetary asset i instead, is increased. Hence we should expect that such a positive covariance should increase the risk adjusted user cost Π_{it}, as indeed is the effect of the first term of equation (D.11). Conversely, if that covariance is negative, so that holding the benchmark asset increases the consumer's risk, then forgoing the benchmark asset in favor of monetary asset i decreases risk and hence results in a subtraction from the risk adjusted user cost, Π_{it}, of holding asset i.

D.4.2   The Generalized Divisia Index under Risk Aversion

The ordinary Divisia index was derived by François Divisia from the first-order conditions for rational consumer behavior under perfect certainty. In the case of risk aversion, the first-order conditions are Euler equations, and we have found that those Euler equations for consumers can be put into the form (D.8), which we now use to derive a generalized Divisia index, as follows:

Theorem 2   *In the share equations,* $s_{it} = \pi_{it} m_{it} / \sum_{j=1}^{k_1} \pi_{jt} m_{jt}$, *replace the unadjusted user costs,* π_{it}, *defined by (D.5), by the risk-adjusted user costs,* Π_{it}, *defined by definition 1, to produce the adjusted shares,* $S_{it} = \Pi_{it} m_{it} / \sum_{j=1}^{k_1} \Pi_{jt} m_{jt}$. *By* *our weak separability assumption, $V(\mathbf{m}_t, c_t) = F(M(\mathbf{m}_t), c_t)$, and our assumption that the monetary aggregator function, M, is linearly homogeneous, the following generalized Divisia index is true under risk:*

$$d \log M_t = \sum_i S_{it} d \log m_{it}. \tag{D.18}$$

Proof   By our weak separability assumption, $V(\mathbf{m}_t, c_t) = F(M(\mathbf{m}_t), c_t)$, we have that

$$\frac{\partial V}{\partial m_{it}} = \frac{\partial F}{\partial M_t} \frac{\partial M_t}{\partial m_{it}}. \tag{D.19}$$

Substituting (D.15) into (D.19), we acquire

$$\frac{\partial M_t}{\partial m_{it}} = (\pi_{it} + \psi_{it}) \frac{\partial V / \partial c_t}{\partial F / \partial M_t}. \tag{D.20}$$

Since the total differential of $M_t = M(\mathbf{m}_t)$ is

$$dM_t = \sum_i \frac{\partial M}{\partial m_{it}} dm_{it}, \tag{D.21}$$

we can substitute (D.20) into (D.21) to get

$$dM_t = \frac{\partial V / \partial c_t}{\partial F / \partial M_t} \sum (\pi_{it} + \psi_{it}) dm_{it}. \tag{D.22}$$

Using the linear homogeneity of M, we have from Euler's theorem for homogeneous functions that

$$M_t = \sum_i \frac{\partial M}{\partial m_{it}} m_{it}. \tag{D.23}$$

Substituting (D.20) into (D.23), we acquire

$$M_t = \frac{\partial V / \partial c_t}{\partial F / \partial M_t} \sum (\pi_{it} + \psi_{it}) m_{it}. \tag{D.24}$$

Dividing (D.22) by (D.24), we get equation (D.18).   ∎

Hence we see that the exact tracking of the Divisia monetary index is not compromised by risk aversion, so long as the adjusted user costs, $\pi_{it} + \psi_{it}$, are used in computing the index. As we have observed, the adjusted user costs reduce to the usual user costs in the case of perfect certainty and our generalized Divisia index (D.18) reduces to the usual Divisia index (D.6). Similarly the risk-neutral case is acquired as the special case with $\psi_{it} = 0$, so that equation (D.16) serves as the user cost. In short, our generalized Divisia index (D.18) is a true generalization, in the sense that the risk-neutral and perfect-certainty cases are strictly nested special cases. Formally that conclusion is the following:

Corollary 1 to theorem 2   *Under risk neutrality, the generalized Divisia index (D.18) reduces to (D.6), where the user costs in the formula are defined by (D.16). Under perfect certainty, the user costs reduce to equation (D.5).*

The need for the generalization can be explained as follows. The consumer has a three-dimensional decision, in terms of asset characteristics. The monetary assets having nonzero own rates of return produce investment returns, contribute to risk, and provide liquidity services. Our objective is to track the nested utility function, $M(\mathbf{m}_t)$, which measures liquidity and is the true economic monetary aggregate. To do so, we must remove the other two motives: investment yield and risk aversion. While those two motives are relevant to savings and intertemporal substitution, we seek to track the liquidity flow alone. The ordinary Divisia monetary aggregate removes the investment motive and would track the liquidity services, if there were no risk. The generalized Divisia index removes both the investment motive and the aversion-to-risk motive to extract the liquidity service flow, when the data is produced by consumers, who are making decisions that involve a three-way trade-off among mean investment return, risk aversion, and liquidity service consumption.

D.5   The CCAPM Special Case

As a means of illustrating the nature of the risk adjustment, ψ_{it}, we consider a special case, based on the usual assumptions in CAPM theory of either quadratic utility or Gaussian stochastic processes. Direct empirical use of theorems 1 and 2, without any CAPM simplifications, would require availability of prior econometric estimates of the parameters of the utility function, V, and of the subjective rate of time discount. Under the usual CAPM assumptions, we show in this section that empirical use of theorems 1 and 2 would require prior estimation of only one property of the utility function: the degree of risk aversion, on which a large body of published information is available.

Consider first the following case of utility that is quadratic in consumption of goods, conditionally on the level of monetary asset service consumption:

Assumption 1 *Let V have the form*

$$V(\mathbf{m}_t, c_t) = F(M(\mathbf{m}_t), c_t) = A(M(\mathbf{m}_t))c_t - \frac{1}{2}B(M(\mathbf{m}_t))c_t^2, \qquad (D.25)$$

where A is a positive, increasing, concave function and B is a nonnegative, decreasing, convex function.

The alternative assumption is Gaussianity, as follows:

Assumption 2 *Let (r_{it}^*, c_{t+1}) be a bivariate Gaussian process for each asset, $i = 1, \ldots, k_1$.*

We also make the following conventional CAPM assumption:[5]

Assumption 3 *The benchmark rate process is deterministic or already risk adjusted, so that R_s^* is a risk-free rate for all $s \geq t$.*

Under this assumption it follows that $\mathrm{Cov}[R_t^*, (\partial V / \partial c_{t+1})]$ equals zero.

We define $H_{t+1} = H(M_{t+1}, c_{t+1})$ to be the well-known Arrow–Pratt measure of absolute risk aversion,

$$H(M_{t+1}, c_{t+1}) = \frac{-E_t[V'']}{E_t[V']}, \qquad (D.26)$$

where $V' = \partial V(\mathbf{m}_{t+1}, c_{t+1}) / \partial c_{t+1}$ and $V'' = \partial V^2(\mathbf{m}_{t+1}, c_{t+1}) / \partial c_{t+1}^2$. By this definition, risk aversion is measured relative to consumption risk, conditionally on the level of monetary services produced by $M_{t+1} = M(\mathbf{m}_t)$. Under risk aversion H_{t+1} is positive and increases as the degree of absolute risk aversion increases. The following lemma is central to our theorem 3:

Lemma 1 *By assumption 3 and either assumption 1 or assumption 2, the user-cost risk adjustment, ψ_{it}, defined by equation (D.11), reduces to*

$$\psi_{it} = \frac{1}{1 + R_t^*} H_{t+1} \mathrm{Cov}(r_{it}^*, c_{t+1}). \qquad (D.27)$$

---

5. It amounts to the assumption that the risk premium already has been extracted from the benchmark rate. In practice, this assumption is harmless, since the risk premia adjustments below are applied to all component assets before the benchmark rate is computed—usually as an upper envelope on the component rate paths. If other asset paths are also included among those used to produce the upper envelope, then this assumption requires that the same risk premia adjustments also be applied to those paths before the upper envelope is generated. Since the risk premia already have been extracted at the time that the envelope is produced, the benchmark rate automatically is risk adjusted.

Proof   Assuming that R_t^* is a risk-free rate for all $s \geq t$, equation (D.9) simplifies to

$$\frac{\partial V}{\partial c_t} = \rho(1 + R_t^*)E_t\left[\frac{\partial V}{\partial c_{t+1}}\right],$$ (D.28)

and the risk adjustment term (D.11) simplifies to

$$\psi_{it} = -\rho\frac{\mathrm{Cov}[r_{it}^*,(\partial V/\partial c_{t+1})]}{\partial V/\partial c_t}.$$ (D.29)

Substituting (D.28) into (D.29), we acquire

$$\psi_{it} = -\frac{1}{1 + R_t^*}\frac{\mathrm{Cov}[r_{it}^*,(\partial V/\partial c_{t+1})]}{E_t[\partial V/\partial c_{t+1}]}.$$ (D.30)

Consider first the case in which we accept assumption 1. Substituting the quadratic specification (D.25) into (D.30), we get

$$\psi_{it} = \frac{1}{1 + R_t^*}\left[\frac{-EV''}{EV'}\right]\mathrm{Cov}(r_{it}^*,c_{t+1}),$$ (D.31)

which under our definition of H_{t+1} is identical to (D.27). Now consider the alternative possibility of accepting assumption 2 instead of assumption 1. Applying Stein's lemma for bivariate normal distributions to equation (D.30), we again acquire (D.31) and thereby (D.27).[6]   ∎

Observe that equation (D.27) provides a CCAPM type result, since the risk adjustment term, ψ_{it}, is very much like the risk premium on a risky asset in CCAPM. In CCAPM, as in our model, compensation for risk is proportional to the covariance of the asset's return with consumption through the factor $\mathrm{Cov}(r_{it}^*,c_{t+1})$ in (D.27) and also to the degree of risk aversion, H_{t+1}, in (D.27).[7]

---

6. For Stein's lemma, see Stein (1981). Alternatively see Ingersoll (1987, p. 13, eq. 62) or Rubinstein (1976).

7. If own interest rates are positively correlated with consumption, (D.27) is positive, since H_{t+1} would be positive under risk aversion. Alternatively, if the asset's return is not sufficiently risky to dominate the direction of the net shocks to consumption from risk, the opposite could happen. The asset's rate of return could correlate negatively with the consumption stream in a manner tending to decrease the household's consumption risk, and hence (D.27) would be negative. In the CCAPM theory of finance, "beta" of a very risky asset is usually positive, where "beta" is defined to be $\beta_g = \mathrm{Cov}(r_{it}^*,c_{t+1})/\mathrm{Var}(c_{t+1})$. The subscript c in β_{ic} designates consumption based "beta," and the lack of a time subscript in the notation, β_{ic}, results from the assumption of stationarity of the interest rate and consump-

In effect, what the adjustment does for very risky rates is to remove the risk premium from $E_t r_{it}$ so that the adjusted user cost becomes positive. To see this more clearly, define $Z_t = H_{t+1} c_t$, where Z_t is a modified (time shifted) Arrow–Pratt relative risk aversion measure. Our theorem now follows immediately:

Theorem 3 *By the assumptions of lemma 1, we have*

$$\Pi_{it} = \frac{E_t R_t^* - (E_t r_{it}^* - \phi_{it})}{1 + E_t R_t^*}.$$ (D.32)

where

$$\phi_{it} = Z_t \text{Cov}\left(r_{it}^*, \frac{c_{t+1}}{c_t} \right).$$ (D.33)

Proof Substitute (D.27) and (D.10) into $\Pi_{it} = \pi_{it} + \psi_{it}$ and substitute $Z_t = H_{t+1} c_t$. ∎

As is evident from this theorem, the risk premium adjustment is ϕ_{it}, where c_{t+1}/c_t is a measure of the consumption growth rate. Hence the risk adjustment depends on relative risk aversion and the covariance between the consumption growth path c_{t+1}/c_t and the real rates of excess return, r_{it}^*. We see that the adjusted user cost, $\Pi_{it} = \pi_{it} + \psi_{it}$, can be written in the same form as the unadjusted user cost (D.10), if the benchmark rate is defined to be risk free and if the risk premium adjustment, ϕ_{it}, is subtracted out of the expected value of the real rates of excess return, r_{it}^*. As we have observed, that adjustment should be expected to decrease the expected own rate of return, if the asset is very risky and thereby contributes positively to consumption risk.

---

tion bivariate process. Clearly, the usual finance view of positive β_{ic} can hold, if and only if $\text{Cov}(r_{it}^*, c_{t+1})$ is positive.

This conclusion about the sign of the adjustment term, ψ_{it}, in the adjusted user cost, $\pi_{it} + \psi_{it}$, of very risky assets is especially revealing, when the benchmark rate is defined to be riskless, as we have just done. Consider the definition of the unadjusted user cost in equation (D.10). Since we now are assuming that the benchmark rate is defined to be the maximum available rate of return on a risk-free asset, we can conclude that the benchmark asset has no embedded liquidity premium and cannot be less than the own rate of return on any risk-free monetary asset i. Hence (D.10) is nonnegative, if monetary asset i is risk free. But suppose that consumers are risk averse and that monetary asset i is not risk free. Then $E_t r_{it}$ will contain a risk premium, despite the fact that R_t does not (or its risk premium has been removed). Hence the unadjusted user cost (D.10) could be negative. But, as we have just observed, ψ_{it} in this case will be positive, and we would expect it will be sufficiently positive to offset the possible negativity of the unadjusted user cost to produce positive value of the adjusted user cost, $\pi_{it} + \psi_{it}$.

D.6 The Magnitude of the Adjustment

In accordance with the large and growing literature on the equity premium puzzle, we should expect that ϕ_{it} would be small for most i. The equity premium puzzle issues with CCAPM do not go away with incorporation of assets with substantial rate of return risk.

One possible explanation of the surprisingly small risk adjustment terms, even with risky assets, may be aggregation over economic agents. In some sense, the risk adjustments may tend to cancel each other out across economic agents. In addition aggregate consumption includes everybody's consumption, but the own rates of return on assets are relevant only to those consumers who hold each of those assets. This possibility has been investigated with simulated data by Barnett, Liu, and Jensen (1997) who found that the risk adjustment is far more adequate with simulated data from a single consumer than for data aggregated over consumers. But we believe that a more promising explanation may be in the customary assumption of intertemporal separability of utility, since response to a change in an interest rate may not be fully reflected in contemporaneous change in consumption. Hence the contemporaneous covariance in the "beta" correction may not take full account of the effect of an interest change on life style. We now turn to weakening that assumption. We also extend to the case of multiple nonmonetary assets, rather than only the single benchmark asset.

D.7 Intertemporal Nonseparability

The small risk adjustments found by Barnett, Liu, and Jensen (1997) with data aggregated over consumers are mainly due to the very low contemporaneous covariance between asset returns and the growth rate of consumption. Under the standard power utility function and a reasonable value of the risk-aversion coefficient, the low contemporaneous covariance between asset returns and consumption growth implies that the impact of risk on the user cost of monetary assets is very small. This finding is closely related to those in the well-established literature on the equity premium puzzle (e.g., see Mehra and Prescott 1985), in which it is shown that consumption-based asset-pricing models with the standard power utility function usually fail to reconcile the observed large equity premium with the low covariance between the equity return and consumption growth. Many different approaches have been pursued in the literature to explain the equity premium puzzle. One successful approach is the use of more general utility functions, such as those with intertemporal nonseparability. For example, Campbell and Cochrane (1999) showed that, in an otherwise standard consumption-based asset-pricing model, intertemporal nonseparability induced by habit formation can produce large time-varying risk premia similar in magnitude to those observed in the data. This suggests that the CCAPM adjustment to the certainty-equivalent monetary-asset user costs can similarly be larger under a more general utility function than those used in Barnett, Liu, and Jensen (1997), who assumed a standard time-separable power utility function, as presented in the prior sections of this appendix.

We now extend the results to intertemporal nonseparability. Based on Barnett and Wu (2005), we show that the basic result of Barnett, Liu, and Jensen (1997) still holds under a more general utility function. But by allowing intertemporal nonseparability, our model can lead to substantial, and we believe accurate, CCAPM risk adjustment, even with a reasonable setting of the risk-aversion coefficient. We believe that the resulting correction is accurate, since the full impact of asset returns on consumption is not contemporaneous, but rather spread over time, as would result from intertemporal nonseparability of tastes. This fact has been well established in the finance literature regarding nonmonetary assets, and, as we will see below, the risk adjustment to the rates of return on nonmonetary assets plays an important role within the computation of risk adjustments for monetary assets. Hence, even if intertemporal separability from consumption were a reasonable assumption for monetary assets, the established intertemporal nonseparability of nonmonetary assets from consumption would contaminate the results on monetary assets, under the assumption of the conventional fully intertemporally separable CCAPM.

As in Barnett and Wu (2005), we also now extend the model to include multiple risky nonmonetary assets, which are the assets that provide no liquidity services, other than their rates of return. This extension is important for two reasons. First, it was shown by Barnett (2003) that the same risk-free benchmark rate cannot be imputed to multiple countries, except under strong assumptions on convergence across the countries. In the literature on optimal currency areas and monetary aggregation over countries within a monetary union, multiple risk-free benchmark assets can be necessary. Even within a single country that is subject to regional regulations and taxation, appendix C's convergence assumptions for the existence of a unique risk-free benchmark rate may not hold. Under those circumstances Barnett (2003, 2007) has shown that the theory, under perfect certainty, requires multiple benchmark rates of return and the imputation of an additional regional or country subscript to all monetary asset quantities and rates of return, to differentiate assets and rates of return by region or country. Second, the need to compute a unique risk-free benchmark rate of return, when theoretically relevant, presents difficult empirical and measurement problems. We rarely observe the theoretical risk-free asset (in real terms) in financial markets, and hence the risk-free benchmark rate of return is inherently an unobserved variable, which, at best, has been proxied. But we show that the relationship between the user cost of a monetary asset and a risky "benchmark" asset's rate of return holds for an arbitrary pair of a monetary and a risky nonmonetary asset. Because of this fundamental extension, our results on risk adjustment do not depend on the existence of a unique risk free rate or the ability to measure such a rate. This important extension remains relevant, even if all monetary asset rates of return are subject to low risk, since relevant candidates for the benchmark asset may all have risky rates of return.

In the asset-pricing literature, one of the most popular models is the capital asset-pricing model (CAPM) developed by Sharpe (1964) and Lintner (1965), among others. In CAPM, the risk premium on an individual asset is determined by the covariance of its excess rate of return with that of the market portfolio, or equivalently its "beta." The advantage of CAPM is that it circumvents the issue of unobservable marginal utility, and the resulting "beta" can easily be estimated. We show in this appendix that there also exists a similar "beta" that relates the user cost of an individual monetary asset to the user cost of the consumer's wealth portfolio.

The rest of this appendix is organized as follows. In the next section, we specify the representative consumer's intertemporal optimization problem, extended in a manner needed for this analysis with multiple nonmonetary assets. The main results are contained in section D.9, while section D.10 concludes.

D.8 Consumer's Nonseparable Optimization Problem

We use a setup similar to that section D.2. But we now assume that the representative consumer has an intertemporally nonseparable general utility function, $U(\mathbf{m}_t, c_t, c_{t-1}, \ldots, c_{t-n})$, defined over current and past consumption and a vector of L current-period monetary assets,

$\mathbf{m}_t = (m_{1,t}, m_{2,t}, \ldots, m_{L,t})'$. The consumer's holdings of nonmonetary assets, $\mathbf{k}_t = (k_{1,t}, k_{2,t}, \ldots, k_{K,t})'$, do not enter the utility function, since those assets are assumed to produce no services other than their investment rate of return. To ensure the existence of a monetary aggregate, we further assume that there exists a linearly homogeneous aggregator function, $M(\cdot)$, such that U can be written in the form

$$U(\mathbf{m}_t, c_t, c_{t-1}, \ldots, c_{t-n}) = V(M(\mathbf{m}_t), c_t, c_{t-1}, \ldots, c_{t-n}). \tag{D.34}$$

Given initial wealth, W_t, the consumer seeks to maximize expected lifetime utility function,

$$E_t \sum_{s=0}^{\infty} \beta^s U(\mathbf{m}_{t+s}, c_{t+s}, c_{t+s-1}, \ldots, c_{t+s-n}), \tag{D.35}$$

subject to the following budget constraints:

$$W_t = p_t^* c_t + \sum_{i=1}^{L} p_t^* m_{i,t} + \sum_{j=1}^{K} p_t^* k_{j,t} = p_t^* c_t + p_t^* A_t \tag{D.36}$$

and

$$W_{t+1} = \sum_{i=1}^{L} R_{i,t+1} p_t^* m_{i,t} + \sum_{j=1}^{K} \tilde{R}_{j,t+1} p_t^* k_{j,t} + Y_{t+1}, \tag{D.37}$$

where $\beta \in (0, 1)$ is the consumer's subjective discount factor, p_t^* is the true cost-of-living index, and $A_t = \sum_{i=1}^{L} m_{i,t} + \sum_{j=1}^{K} k_{j,t}$ is the real value of the asset portfolio. Nonmonetary asset j is defined to provide no services other than its gross rate of return, $\tilde{R}_{j,t+1}$, between periods t and $t+1$. Monetary asset i, having quantity, $m_{i,t}$, has a gross rate of return, $R_{i,t+1}$, between periods t and $t+1$, and does provide monetary services. At the beginning of each period, the consumer allocates wealth among consumption, c_t, investment in the monetary assets, $\mathbf{m}_t$, and investment in the nonmonetary assets, $\mathbf{k}_t$. The consumer's income from all other sources, received at the beginning of period $t+1$, is Y_{t+1}. If any of that income's source is labor income, then we assume that leisure is weakly separable from consumption of goods and holding of monetary assets, so that the function, U, exists and the decision exists, as a conditional decision problem. The consumer also is subject to the transversality condition

$$\lim_{s \to \infty} \beta^s p_t^* A_{t+s} = 0. \tag{D.38}$$

The equivalency of the two constraints, (D.36) and (D.37), with the single constraint used in section D.2.1's feasible set, $S(s)$, is easily seen by substituting equation (D.36) for period $t+1$ into equation (D.37) and solving for $p_t^* c_t$.

Define the value function of the consumer's optimization problem to be $H_t = H(W_t, c_{t-1}, \ldots, c_{t-n})$. Assuming the solution to the decision problem exists, we then have the Bellman equation

$$H_t = \sup_{(c_t, \mathbf{m}_t, \mathbf{k}_t)} E_t\{U(\mathbf{m}_t, c_t, c_{t-1}, \ldots, c_{t-n}) + \beta H_{t+1}\}, \qquad (D.39)$$

where the maximization is subject to the budget constraints, (D.36) and (D.37). The first-order conditions can be obtained as

$$\lambda_t = \beta E_t\left(\lambda_{t+1}\tilde{R}_{j,t+1}\frac{p_t^*}{p_{t+1}^*}\right) \qquad (D.40)$$

and

$$\frac{\partial U_t}{\partial m_{i,t}} = \lambda_t - \beta E_t\left(\lambda_{t+1}R_{i,t+1}\frac{p_t^*}{p_{t+1}^*}\right), \qquad (D.41)$$

where $U_t = U(\mathbf{m}_t, c_t, c_{t-1}, \ldots, c_{t-n})$ and $\lambda_t = E_t(\partial U_t/\partial c_t + \beta\partial U_{t+1}/\partial c_t + \ldots + \beta^n\partial U_{t+n}/\partial c_t)$. Note that λ_t is the expected present value of the marginal utility of consumption, c_t. In the standard case where the instantaneous utility function is time separable, λ_t reduces to $\partial U(\mathbf{m}_t, c_t)/\partial c_t$.

D.9 Extended Risk-Adjusted User Cost of Monetary Assets

D.9.1. The Theory
As in definition 1 we define the contemporaneous real user-cost price of the services of monetary asset i to be the ratio of the marginal utility of the monetary asset and the marginal utility of consumption, so that

$$\pi_{i,t} = \frac{\partial U_t/\partial m_{i,t}}{E_t[(\partial U_t/\partial c_t) + \beta(\partial U_{t+1}/\partial c_t) + \ldots + \beta^n(\partial U_{t+n}/\partial c_t)]} = \frac{\partial U_t/\partial m_{i,t}}{\lambda_t}. \quad (D.42)$$

We denote the vector of L monetary asset user costs by $\boldsymbol{\pi}_t = (\pi_{1,t}, \pi_{2,t}, \ldots, \pi_{L,t})'$. With the user costs defined as above, we can show that the solution value of the exact monetary aggregate, $M(\mathbf{m}_t)$, can be tracked accurately in continuous time by the generalized Divisia index, as provided in this appendix's theorem 2 and in the perfect-certainty special case in appendix A's equation (A.79). We now provide François Divisia's (1926) perfect-certainty proof again, but in a form that more clearly remains relevant under intertemporal nonseparability.

Lemma 2   Let $s_{i,t} = \pi_{i,t} m_{i,t} / \sum_{j=1}^{L} \pi_{j,t} m_{j,t}$ be the user-cost-evaluated expenditure share. Under the weak-separability assumption (D.34), we have for any linearly homogeneous monetary aggregator function, $M(\cdot)$, that

$$d \log M_t = \sum_{i=1}^{L} s_{i,t} d \log m_{i,t},$$ (D.43)

where $M_t = M(\mathbf{m}_t)$.

Proof   Under the assumption of contemporaneous monetary weak separability, we have

$$\frac{\partial U_t}{\partial m_{i,t}} = \frac{\partial V_t}{\partial M_t} \frac{\partial M_t}{\partial m_{i,t}},$$ (D.44)

where $V_t = V(M(\mathbf{m}_t), c_t, c_{t-1}, \ldots, c_{t-n})$. By the definition in (D.42) and equation (D.44), it then follows that

$$\frac{\partial M_t}{\partial m_{i,t}} = \pi_{i,t} \left(\frac{\lambda_t}{\partial V_t / \partial M_t} \right).$$ (D.45)

Taking the total differential of $M_t = M(\mathbf{m}_t)$ and using the result in (D.45), we obtain

$$dM_t = \left(\frac{\lambda_t}{\partial V_t / \partial M_t} \right) \sum_{i=1}^{L} \pi_{i,t} dm_{i,t} = \left(\frac{\lambda_t}{\partial V_t / \partial M_t} \right) \sum_{i=1}^{L} \pi_{i,t} m_{i,t} d \log m_{i,t}.$$ (D.46)

However, because of the linear homogeneity of $M_t = M(\mathbf{m}_t)$, it follows from (D.45) that

$$M_t = \sum_{i=1}^{L} \frac{\partial M_t}{\partial m_{i,t}} m_{i,t} = \left(\frac{\lambda_t}{\partial V_t / \partial M_t} \right) \sum_{i=1}^{L} \pi_{i,t} m_{i,t}.$$ (D.47)

The lemma therefore follows by dividing (D.46) by (D.47).   ∎

The exact price aggregate dual, $\Pi_t = \Pi(\boldsymbol{\pi}_t)$, to the monetary quantity aggregator function, $M_t = M(\mathbf{m}_t)$, is easily computed from factor reversal, $\Pi(\boldsymbol{\pi}_t) M(\mathbf{m}_t) = \sum_{i=1}^{L} \pi_{it} m_{it}$, so that

$$\Pi(\boldsymbol{\pi}_t) = \frac{\sum_{i=1}^{L} \pi_{it} m_{it}}{M(\mathbf{m}_t)}.$$

In continuous time, the user-cost price dual can be tracked without error by the Divisia user-cost price index

$$d \log \Pi_t = \sum_{i=1}^{L} s_{i,t} d \log \pi_{i,t}.$$

To get a more convenient expression for the user cost, $\pi_{i,t}$, we define the pricing kernel to be

$$Q_{t+1} = \beta \frac{\lambda_{t+1}}{\lambda_t}. \tag{D.48}$$

Recall that λ_t is the present value of the marginal utility of consumption at time t. Hence Q_{t+1} measures the marginal utility growth from t to $t+1$. For example, if the utility function (D.34) is time separable, we have that $Q_{t+1} = \beta\{[\partial U(\mathbf{m}_{t+1}, c_{t+1})/\partial c_{t+1}]/[\partial U(\mathbf{m}_t, c_t)/\partial c_t]\}$, which is the subjectively discounted marginal rate of substitution between consumption this period and consumption next period. Clearly, Q_{t+1} is positive, as required of marginal rates of substitution.

While the introduction of a pricing kernel is well understood in finance, the intent also should be no surprise to experts in index-number theory. The way in which statistical index numbers, depending on prices and quantities, track quantity aggregator functions, containing no prices, is through the substitution of first-order conditions to replace marginal utilities by functions of relevant prices. This substitution is particularly well known in the famous derivation of the Divisia index by François Divisia (1925, 1926a, b). In our case the intent, as applied below, is to replace Q_{t+1} by a function of relevant determinants of its value in asset market equilibrium. If we use the approximation that characterizes CAPM, then the pricing kernel, Q_{t+1}, would be a linear function of the rate of return on the consumer's asset portfolio, A_t.

Using (D.42) and (D.48), the first-order conditions (D.40) and (D.41) can alternatively be written as

$$0 = 1 - E_t(Q_{t+1} \tilde{r}_{j,t+1}), \tag{D.49}$$

$$\pi_{i,t} = 1 - E_t(Q_{t+1} r_{i,t+1}), \tag{D.50}$$

where $\tilde{r}_{j,t+1} = \tilde{R}_{j,t+1} p_t^* / p_{t+1}^*$ is the real gross rate of return on nonmonetary asset, $k_{j,t}$, and $r_{i,t+1} = R_{i,t+1} p_t^* / p_{t+1}^*$ is the real gross rate of return on monetary asset, $m_{i,t}$, which provides the consumer with liquidity service.

Equations (D.49) and (D.50) impose restrictions on asset returns. Equation (D.49) applies to the returns on all risky nonmonetary assets,

$k_{j,t}$ ($j = 1, \ldots, K$), in the usual manner. For monetary assets, equation (D.50) implies that the "deviation" from the usual Euler equation measures the user cost of that monetary asset. To obtain good measures of the user costs of monetary assets, the nonmonetary asset pricing within the asset portfolio's pricing kernel, Q_{t+1}, should be as accurate as possible. Otherwise, we would attribute any nonmonetary asset pricing errors to the monetary asset user costs in (D.50), as pointed out by Marshall (1997). From the Euler equations above, we can obtain the following theorem:

Theorem 4 *Given the real rate of return, $r_{i,t+1}$, on a monetary asset and the real rate of return, $\tilde{r}_{j,t+1}$, on an arbitrary nonmonetary asset, the risk-adjusted real user-cost price of the services of the monetary asset can be obtained as*

$$\pi_{i,t} = \frac{(1 + \omega_{i,t})E_t\tilde{r}_{j,t+1} - (1 + \omega_{j,t})E_t r_{i,t+1}}{E_t\tilde{r}_{j,t+1}}, \tag{D.51}$$

where

$$\omega_{i,t} = -\text{Cov}_t(Q_{t+1}, r_{i,t+1}) \tag{D.52}$$

and

$$\omega_{j,t} = -\text{Cov}_t(Q_{t+1}, \tilde{r}_{j,t+1}). \tag{D.53}$$

Proof From the Euler equation (D.49), we have

$$1 = E_t Q_{t+1} E_t \tilde{r}_{j,t+1} + \text{Cov}_t(Q_{t+1}, \tilde{r}_{j,t+1}), \tag{D.54}$$

and similarly from the Euler equation (D.50), we have

$$\pi_{i,t} = 1 - E_t Q_{t+1} E_t r_{i,t+1} - \text{Cov}_t(Q_{t+1}, r_{i,t+1}). \tag{D.55}$$

Note that (D.54) implies that

$$E_t Q_{t+1} = \frac{1 - \text{Cov}_t(Q_{t+1}, \tilde{r}_{j,t+1})}{E_t\tilde{r}_{j,t+1}}. \tag{D.56}$$

Hence theorem 4 follows by substituting $E_t Q_{t+1}$ into (D.55). ∎

Theorem 4 relates the user cost of a monetary asset to the rates of return on financial assets, which need not be risk free. It applies to an arbitrary pair of monetary and nonmonetary assets. In fact, observe that the left-hand side of equation (D.51) has no j subscript, even though there are j subscripts on the right-hand side. The left-hand side of (D.51) is invariant to the choice of nonmonetary asset used on the right-hand side, as a result of equation (D.56), which holds for all j, regardless of i. This result suggests that we can choose an arbitrary nonmonetary financial asset as the "benchmark" asset in calculating the user costs of the financial assets that provide monetary services, so long as we correctly compute the covariance, $\omega_{j,t}$, of the return on the nonmonetary asset with the pricing kernel.

Practical considerations in estimating that covariance could tend to discourage use of multiple benchmark assets. In particular, a biased estimate of $\omega_{j,t}$ for a nonmonetary asset j would similarly bias the user costs of all monetary assets, if that nonmonetary asset were used as the benchmark asset in computing all monetary asset user costs. Alternatively, if a different nonmonetary financial assets were used as the benchmark assets for each monetary asset, errors in measuring $\omega_{j,t}$, for different j's, could bias relative user costs of monetary assets.

Nevertheless, in theory it is not necessary to use the same benchmark asset j for the computation of the user cost of each monetary asset, i. In particular, we have the following corollary.

Corollary 1 to theorem 4   *Under uncertainty we can choose any nonmonetary asset as the "benchmark" asset, when computing the risk-adjusted user-cost prices of the services of monetary assets.*

Notice that theorem 4 does not require existence of a risk-free nonmonetary asset (in real terms). Since we rarely observe the rate of return on such an entirely illiquid asset in financial markets, our theorem generalizes theorem 3 in a very useful manner. Although a unique risk-free totally illiquid investment, having no secondary market, may exist in theory, corollary 1 frees us from the need to seek a proxy for its inherently unobservable rate of return.

If we were to impose the further assumption of perfect certainty on top of the other assumptions we have made above, there would be only one benchmark asset, and all of our results would reduce, as a special case, to those in appendix A. Without risk and with no monetary services provided by benchmark assets, arbitrage would assure that there could be only one benchmark asset.

To see the intuition of theorem 4, assume that one of the nonmonetary assets is risk free with *gross* real interest rate of r_t^f at time t. Further, as proved by Barnett (1978), the certainty-equivalent user cost, $\pi_{i,t}^e$, of a monetary asset, $m_{i,t}$, is

$$\pi_{i,t}^e = \frac{r_t^f - E_t r_{i,t+1}}{r_t^f}. \tag{D.57}$$

From equation (D.49), the first-order condition for r_t^f is

$$1 = E_t(Q_{t+1} r_t^f). \tag{D.58}$$

Hence we have, from the nonrandomness of r_t^f, that

$$E_t Q_{t+1} = \frac{1}{r_t^f}. \tag{D.59}$$

Replacing $E_t Q_{t+1}$ in (D.50) with $1/r_t^f$, we then have

$$\pi_{i,t} = \frac{r_t^f - E_t r_{i,t+1}}{r_t^f} + \omega_{i,t} = \pi_{i,t}^e + \omega_{i,t}, \tag{D.60}$$

where $\omega_{i,t} = -\text{Cov}_t(Q_{t+1}, r_{i,t+1})$. Therefore $\pi_{i,t}$ could be larger or smaller than the certainty-equivalent user cost, $\pi_{i,t}^e$, depending on the sign of the covariance between $r_{i,t+1}$ and Q_{t+1}. When the return on a monetary asset is positively correlated with the pricing kernel, Q_{t+1}, and thereby negatively correlated with the rate of return on the full portfolio of monetary and nonmonetary assets, the monetary asset's user cost will be adjusted downward from the certainty-equivalent user cost. Such assets offer a hedge against aggregate risk by paying off, when the full asset portfolio's rate of return is low. In contrast, when the return on a monetary asset is negatively correlated with the pricing kernel, Q_{t+1}, and thereby positively correlated with the rate of return on the full asset portfolio, the asset's user cost will be adjusted upward from the certainty-equivalent user cost, since such assets tend to pay off when the asset portfolio's rate of return is high. Such assets are very risky.

To calculate the risk adjustment, we need to compute the covariance between the asset return, $r_{i,t+1}$, and the pricing kernel, Q_{t+1}, which is unobservable. Consumption-based asset-pricing models allow us to relate Q_{t+1} to consumption growth through a specific utility function. But most utility functions have been shown not to be able to reconcile the aggregate consumption data with the observed stock returns and the interest rate. Kocherlakota (1996) provides an excellent survey on the equity premium puzzle literature.

With more general utility functions than used in previous empirical studies on monetary aggregation, we can use the theory in this paper to extend the existing empirical studies on the user costs of risky monetary assets, and thereby on the induced risk-adjusted Divisia monetary quantity and user-cost aggregates. Campbell and Cochrane (1999), among others, have shown that a habit-formation-based utility function with reasonable risk-aversion coefficient could produce large time-varying risk premia, similar in magnitude to those observed in the data. The risk adjustment for the user costs of monetary assets is intimately related to the determination of risk premia. As a result there is reason to believe that intertemporally nonseparable utility functions, such as the one in Campbell and Cochrane (1999), can produce larger risk adjustments to the certainty-equivalent user costs than the small adjustments found in Barnett, Liu, and Jensen (1997) with data aggregated over consumers and assuming intertemporal separability. The results could be particularly dramatic in open economy applications in which rates of return are subject to exchange rate risk.

There is a particularly important reason to use more general and flexible utility functions in computing the user costs of risky monetary assets. As discussed above, to obtain good measures of the user costs of monetary assets, we need to choose the pricing kernel, and hence the utility function, such that the pricing of nonmonetary assets within the kernel is as accurate as possible. Otherwise, the user costs of monetary assets would be contaminated by the pricing errors. Since standard utility functions are known to lead to erroneous estimates of nonmonetary–asset risk premia, the risk adjustments to the users cost of monetary assets with those utility functions are likely to be much less accurate than those with utility functions that have better empirical performance in matching the observed nonmonetary-asset risk premia.

D.9.2 Approximation to the Theory

All of the consumption-based asset-pricing models require us to make explicit assumptions about investors' utility functions. An alternative approach, which is commonly practiced in finance, is to approximate Q_{t+1} by some simple function of observable macroeconomic factors, which are believed to be closely related to investors' marginal utility growth. For example, the well-known CAPM (Sharpe 1964; Lintner 1965) approximates Q_{t+1} by a linear function of the rate of return on the market portfolio. Then the rate of return on any individual asset is linked to its covariance with the market rate of return. Fama and French (1992) include two additional factors, firm size and book-to-market value, and show that the three-factor model is able to capture the cross-sectional variation in average stock returns. Using stock returns, Chen, Roll, and Ross (1986) and Lamont (2000) try to identify macroeconomic variables as priced risk factors. Cochrane (2000) provides detailed discussion on the approximation of the pricing kernel Q_{t+1}.

We show that there also exists a similar CAPM-type relationship among user costs of risky monetary assets, under the assumption that Q_{t+1} is a linear function of the rate of return on a well-diversified wealth portfolio. Barnett and Wu (2005) argue that this simple specification of the pricing kernel, based on a long-standing tradition in finance, is a reasonable first step in the extension of Barnett, Liu, and Jensen (1997) to the case of intertemporal nonseparability. In the finance literature, the CAPM specification of the pricing kernel results from a special case of a linear factor-model decomposition of the first-order conditions, (D.49) and (D.50), under the assumption of quadratic utility or Gaussianity. Deeper specifications of the pricing kernel, as being proposed now in finance, might prove similarly advantageous in future extensions of our research.

Specifically, define $r_{A,t+1}$ to be the share-weighted rate of return on the consumer's asset portfolio, including both the monetary assets, $m_{i,t}$ ($i = 1, \ldots, L$), and the nonmonetary assets, $k_{j,t}(j = 1, \ldots, K)$. Then the traditional CAPM approximation to Q_{t+1} mentioned above is of the form, $Q_{t+1} = a_t - b_t r_{A,t+1}$, where a_t, and b_t can be time dependent.

Let $\phi_{i,t}$ and $\varphi_{j,t}$ denote the share of $m_{i,t}$ and $k_{j,t}$, respectively, in the portfolio's stock value, so that

$$\phi_{i,t} = \frac{m_{i,t}}{\sum_{j=1}^{L} m_{j,t} + \sum_{j=1}^{K} k_{j,t}} = \frac{m_{i,t}}{A_t}$$

and

$$\varphi_{j,t} = \frac{k_{j,t}}{\sum_{i=1}^{L} m_{i,t} + \sum_{i=1}^{K} k_{i,t}} = \frac{k_{j,t}}{A_t}.$$

Then, by construction, $r_{A,t+1} = \sum_{i=1}^{L} \phi_{i,t} r_{i,t+1} + \sum_{j=1}^{K} \varphi_{j,t} \tilde{r}_{j,t+1}$, where

$$\sum_{i=1}^{L} \phi_{i,t} + \sum_{j=1}^{K} \varphi_{j,t} = 1. \tag{D.61}$$

Multiplying (49) by $\varphi_{j,t}$ and (50) by $\phi_{i,t}$, we have

$$0 = \varphi_{j,t} - E_t(Q_{t+1} \varphi_{j,t} \tilde{r}_{j,t+1}) \tag{D.62}$$

and

$$\phi_{i,t} \pi_{i,t} = \phi_{i,t} - E_t(Q_{t+1} \phi_{i,t} r_{i,t+1}). \tag{D.63}$$

Summing (D.62) over j and (D.63) over i, adding the two summed equations together, and using the definition of $r_{A,t+1}$, we get

$$\sum_{i=1}^{L} \phi_{i,t} \pi_{i,t} = 1 - E_t(Q_{t+1} r_{A,t+1}).$$ (D.64)

Let $\Pi_{A,t} = \sum_{i=1}^{L} \phi_{i,t} \pi_{i,t} + \sum_{j=1}^{K} \varphi_{i,t} \tilde{\pi}_{j,t}$, where $\tilde{\pi}_{j,t}$ is the user cost of nonmonetary asset j. We define $\Pi_{A,t}$ to be the user cost of the consumer's asset wealth portfolio. But the user cost, $\tilde{\pi}_{j,t}$, of every nonmonetary asset is simply 0, as shown in (D.49), so equivalently $\Pi_{A,t} = \sum \phi_{i,t} \pi_{i,t}$. The reason is that consumers do not pay a price, in terms of forgone interest, for the monetary services of nonmonetary assets, since they provide no monetary services and provide only their investment rate of return. We can show that our definition of $\Pi_{A,t}$ is consistent with Fisher's factor reversal test, as follows:

Lemma 3 *The pair* $(A_t, \Pi_{A,t})$ *satisfies factor reversal, defined by*

$$\Pi_{A,t} A_t = \sum_{i=1}^{L} \pi_{i,t} m_{i,t} + \sum_{j=1}^{K} \tilde{\pi}_{j,t} k_{j,t}.$$

Since we know that $\tilde{\pi}_{j,t} = 0$ for all j, factor reversal equivalently can be written as

$$\Pi_{A,t} A_t = \sum_{i=1}^{L} \pi_{i,t} m_{i,t}.$$

The proof of the lemma is straightforward.

Proof By the definition of $\phi_{i,t}$, we have $m_{i,t} = \phi_{i,t} A_t$. Hence we have

$$\sum_{i=1}^{L} \pi_{i,t} m_{i,t} = \sum_{i=1}^{L} \pi_{i,t} \phi_{i,t} A_t = A_t \sum_{i=1}^{L} \pi_{i,t} \phi_{i,t} = A_t \Pi_{A,t},$$

which is our result. ∎

Observe that the wealth portfolio is different from the monetary services aggregate, $M(\mathbf{m}_t)$. The portfolio weights in the asset wealth stock are the market-value-based shares, while the growth rate weights in the monetary services flow aggregate are the user-cost-evaluated shares.

Suppose that one of the nonmonetary assets is (locally) risk-free with gross real interest rate, r_t^f. By substituting equation (D.57) for $\pi_{i,t}$ into the definition of $\Pi_{A,t}$, using the definition of $r_{A,t+1}$, and letting $r_t^f = E \tilde{r}_{j,t+1}$

for all j, it follows that the certainty equivalent user cost of the asset wealth portfolio is $\Pi_{A,t}^e = (r_t^f - E_t r_{A,t+1})/r_t^f$. We now can prove the following important theorem, as in Barnett and Wu (2005).

Theorem 5 *If one of the nonmonetary assets is (locally) risk free with gross real interest rate r_t^f, and if $Q_{t+1} = a_t - b_t r_{A,t+1}$, where $r_{A,t+1}$ is the gross real rate of return on the consumer's wealth portfolio, then the user cost of any monetary asset i is given by*

$$\pi_{i,t} - \pi_{i,t}^e = \beta_{i,t}(\Pi_{A,t} - \Pi_{A,t}^e), \tag{D.65}$$

where $\pi_{i,t}$ and $\Pi_{A,t}$ are the user costs of asset i and of the asset wealth portfolio, respectively, and $\pi_{i,t}^e = (r_t^f - E_t r_{i,t+1})/r_t^f$ and $\Pi_{A,t}^e = (r_t^f - E_t r_{A,t+1})/r_t^f$ are the certainty-equivalent user costs of asset i and the asset wealth portfolio, respectively. The "beta" of asset i in equation (D.65) is given by

$$\beta_{i,t} = \frac{\text{Cov}_t(r_{A,t+1}, r_{i,t+1})}{\text{Var}_t(r_{A,t+1})}. \tag{D.66}$$

Proof From (D.64) and the definition of $\Pi_{A,t}$, we have for the wealth portfolio that

$$\Pi_{A,t} = 1 - E_t Q_{t+1} E_t r_{A,t+1} - \text{Cov}_t(Q_{t+1}, r_{A,t+1}). \tag{D.67}$$

Given the risk-free rate r_t^f, we have that $E_t Q_{t+1} = 1/r_t^f$ from equation (D.59). Hence

$$\Pi_{A,t} = 1 - \frac{E_t r_{A,t+1}}{r_t^f} - \text{Cov}_t(Q_{t+1}, r_{A,t+1}) = \Pi_{A,t}^e - \text{Cov}_t(Q_{t+1}, r_{A,t+1}). \tag{D.68}$$

Using the assumption that $Q_{t+1} = a_t - b_t r_{A,t+1}$, so that $\text{Cov}_t(Q_{t+1}, r_{A,t+1}) = -b_t \text{Var}_t(r_{A,t+1})$, it follows that

$$\Pi_{A,t} = \Pi_{A,t}^e + b_t \text{Var}_t(r_{A,t+1}). \tag{D.69}$$

However, for any asset i we have from (D.60) and $Q_{t+1} = a_t - b_t r_{A,t+1}$ that

$$\pi_{i,t} = \pi_{i,t}^e - \text{Cov}_t(Q_{t+1}, r_{i,t+1}) = \pi_{i,t}^e + b_t \text{Cov}_t(r_{A,t+1}, r_{i,t+1}). \tag{D.70}$$

Hence, from equations (D.69) and (D.70), we can conclude that

$$\frac{\pi_{i,t} - \pi_{i,t}^e}{\Pi_{A,t} - \Pi_{A,t}^e} = \frac{\text{Cov}_t(r_{A,t+1}, r_{i,t+1})}{\text{Var}_t(r_{A,t+1})}, \tag{D.71}$$

and the theorem follows.   ∎

In the approximation, $Q_{t+1} = a_t - b_t r_{A,t+1}$, to the theoretical pricing kernel, Q_{t+1}, the reason for the minus sign is similar to the reason for the minus signs before the own rates of return within monetary asset user costs: the intent in the finance literature is to measure a "price," not a rate of return. In particular, with the minus sign in front of b_t and with b_t positive, we can interpret b_t in equations (D.69) and (D.70) as a "price" of risk. This interpretation can be seen from the fact that b_t measures the amount of risk premium added to the left-hand side per unit of covariance in (D.70) or variance in (D.69). Also recall that the pricing kernel itself, as a subjectively discounted marginal rate of substitution, should be positive. Hence the signs of a_t and b_t must both be positive, and a_t must be sufficiently large so that the pricing kernel is positive for all observed values of $r_{A,t+1}$.

Theorem 5 is very similar to the standard CAPM formula for asset returns. In CAPM theory the expected excess rate of return, $E_t r_{i,t+1} - r_t^f$, on an individual asset is determined by its covariance with the excess rate of return on the market portfolio, $E_t r_{M,t+1} - r_t^f$, in accordance with

$$E_t r_{i,t+1} - r_t^f = \beta_{i,t}(E_t r_{M,t+1} - r_t^f), \tag{D.72}$$

where $\beta_{i,t} = \mathrm{Cov}_t(r_{i,t+1} - r_t^f, r_{M,t+1} - r_t^f)/\mathrm{Var}_t(r_{M,t+1} - r_t^f)$.

This result implies that asset i's risk premium depends on its market portfolio risk exposure, which is measured by the "beta" of this asset. Our theorem shows that the risk adjustment to the certainty equivalent user cost of asset i is determined in that manner as well. The larger the "beta," through risk exposure to the wealth portfolio, the larger is the risk adjustment. User costs will be adjusted upward for those monetary assets whose rates of return are positively correlated with the return on the wealth portfolio, and conversely for those monetary assets whose returns are negatively correlated with the wealth portfolio. In particular, if we find that $\beta_{i,t}$ is very small for all the monetary assets under consideration, then the risk adjustment to the user cost is also very small. In that case the unadjusted Divisia monetary index would be a good proxy for the extended index in theorem 2.

Notice that theorem 5 is a conditional version of CAPM with time-varying risk premia. Lettau and Ludvigson (2001) have shown that a conditional version of CAPM performs much better empirically, in explaining the cross section of asset returns, than the unconditional CAPM. In fact, the unconditional CAPM is usually rejected in empirical tests (e.g., see Breeden, Gibbons, and Litzenberger 1989; Campbell 1996).

D.10   Conclusion

Simple-sum monetary aggregates treat monetary assets with different rates of return as perfect substitutes. Barnett (1978, 1980) showed that the Divisia index, with user-cost prices, is a more appropriate measure for monetary services, and derived the formula for the user cost of monetary asset services in the absence of uncertainty. Barnett, Liu, and Jensen (1997) extended the Divisia monetary quantity index to the case of uncertain returns and risk aversion. For risky monetary assets, however, the magnitude of the risk adjustment to the certainty-equivalent user cost is unclear. Using a standard time-separable power utility function, Barnett, Liu, and Jensen (1997) showed that the difference between the unadjusted Divisia index and the index extended for risk is usually small, when computed with data aggregated over consumers. However, this result could be a consequence of the same problem that causes the equity premium puzzle in the asset pricing literature. The consumption-based asset-pricing model with more general utility functions, most notably those that are intertemporally nonseparable, can better reproduce the large and time-varying risk premia observed in the data. We believe that similarly extended asset-pricing models can provide larger and more accurate CCAPM adjustment to the user costs of monetary assets than those found in Barnett, Liu, and Jensen (1997). Accordingly, Barnett and Wu (2005) extended the basic results in Barnett, Liu, and Jensen (1997) in that manner. This appendix provides a unified treatment of the theoretical results of Barnett, Liu, and Jensen (1997) and the more general results of Barnett and Wu (2005) under intertemporal nonseparability.

Another extension of the current results could be to introduce heterogeneous investors, as considered for the case of perfect certainty in appendix C and in Barnett (2007). This extension can be of particular importance in multicountry or multiregional applications, in which regional or country-specific heterogeneity cannot be ignored. In such cases regional or national subscripts must be introduced to differentiate goods and assets by location. With the possibility of regulatory and taxation differences across the heterogeneous groups, arbitrage cannot be assumed to remove the possibility of multiple benchmark assets, even under perfect certainty, except under special assumptions on institutional convergence.

E   The Middle Ground: Understanding Divisia Aggregation

Anyone who has read and understood appendixes A through D will have no misperceptions about the Divisia monetary index. But students and nonexperts, who see the index without first knowing the underlying theory, sometimes read into the index the wrong interpretations. This appendix is intended to clarify the economic interpretation of the Divisia monetary aggregates for readers who are not index-number-theory professionals. Particular emphasis is placed on the need for proper understanding of the Divisia weights and of their source in theory. Whereas part I of this book assumes little, if any, prior knowledge of economic theory, the first four appendixes in part II assume extensive knowledge of the relevant background in aggregation and index-number theory. This appendix E addresses a middle ground relevant to a large percentage of those who are potential users of the Divisia monetary aggregates, without being experts in aggregation and index-number theory.

E.1   Introduction

The purpose of this appendix is to present the underlying theory of Divisia monetary aggregation in a form that would permit a potential user to understand the aggregates without the need to acquire extensive prior background of aggregation theory and index-number theory, as can be found in appendixes A through D. In this appendix only knowledge of basic microeconomic theory is needed. While this appendix and most of this book emphasize the Divisia index formula for financial aggregation, the emphasis on the Divisia index is largely for expositional convenience. All other reputable index numbers, including the Fisher ideal, can be put into a form such that this appendix becomes equally as applicable (see Barnett and Choi 2008).

The issues addressed in this appendix are equally as applicable to the data produced by the Commerce Department's BEA, the Labor Department's BLS, and the Department of Agriculture. But those US governmental agencies have been applying index-number theory for so long that users of their data rarely ask to see the formulas that produced the data. Such concerns are left to the experts in index-number theory employed by those agencies. If the Federal Reserve Board had adopted index-number theory for aggregation, when monetary assets began yielding interest, potential users of the Divisia monetary aggregates would be equally as uninterested in the underlying aggregation formula as they are about the index-number formulas being used by other governmental agency in Washington, DC. But since that unfortunately did not happen, it is not unreasonable for economists without expertise in index-number theory and aggregation theory to want to acquire a basic understanding of the economics of Divisia monetary aggregation.

E.2 The Divisia Index

Difficulties in understanding the Divisia monetary aggregates can almost invariably be traced to misunderstandings of the Divisia "weights." In order to understand those weights, the source of the Divisia index number must be understood. The following discussion presents that source in terms of easily understood microeconomic theory. In particular, we now present a more detailed and transparent derivation of lemma 2 in section D.9.1 of appendix D.

Suppose that the economy's transactions technology (or the "representative consumer's" utility function) over monetary assets is $Q(\mathbf{x})$, where $\mathbf{x}$ is the vector of n component asset quantities. In aggregation theory $Q(\mathbf{x})$ then is the economic quantity aggregate. The aggregation theoretic procedure for selecting the n component assets, as a weakly separable cluster, is described in Barnett (1982).

Take the total differential of Q to get

$$dQ(\mathbf{x}) = \sum_{i=1}^{n} \frac{\partial Q}{\partial x_i} dx_i. \tag{E.1}$$

Since $\partial Q / \partial x_i$ contains the unknown parameters of the function, Q, we replace each of those marginal products (or marginal utilities) by $\lambda p_i = \partial Q / \partial x_i$, which is a first-order condition for expenditure constrained maximization of Q, where λ is the Lagrange multiplier and p_i is the user-cost price of asset i. We get

$$\frac{dQ(\mathbf{x})}{\lambda} = \sum_{i=1}^{n} p_i dx_i, \tag{E.2}$$

which has no unknown parameters on the right-hand side.

In order for a quantity aggregate to be useful, it must be linearly homogeneous. If there is one case in which the correct growth rate of an aggregate is entirely obvious, it is in the case where all components are growing at the same rate. As required by linear homogeneity, we should certainly expect that the quantity aggregate then would grow at that same rate. Hence we assume Q is linearly homogeneous.

Define $P(\mathbf{p})$ to be the dual price index, satisfying Fisher's factor reversal test, $P(\mathbf{p})Q(\mathbf{x}) = \mathbf{p}'\mathbf{x}$. In other words, define $P(\mathbf{p})$ to equal $\mathbf{p}'\mathbf{x}/Q(\mathbf{x})$, which can be shown to depend only on $\mathbf{p}$ when Q is linearly homogeneous. The proof replaces $Q(\mathbf{x})$ by the corresponding indirect utility function, factors $m = \mathbf{p}'\mathbf{x}$ out of the indirect utility function, and cancels m out of the numerator and denominator of the expression for $P(\mathbf{p})$. Then the following lemma holds.

Lemma 1 $\lambda = 1/P(\mathbf{p})$.

Proof   Let $m = \mathbf{p}'\mathbf{x}$, and let $\mathbf{x} = \mathbf{D}(m, \mathbf{p})$ be the solution to maximization of $Q(\mathbf{x})$ subject to $\mathbf{p}'\mathbf{x} = m$. By the linear homogeneity of $Q(\mathbf{x})$, we know that there must exist $\varphi(\mathbf{p})$ such that $\mathbf{D}(m, \mathbf{p}) = \varphi(\mathbf{p})m$. Substituting for $\mathbf{x}$ into $Q(\mathbf{x})$, we get

$$Q(\mathbf{x}) = Q(\varphi(\mathbf{p})m) = mQ(\varphi(\mathbf{p})). \tag{E.3}$$

Since $\lambda = \partial Q/\partial m$, we have from equation (E.3) that $\lambda = Q(\varphi(\mathbf{p}))$. In addition from $Q(\mathbf{x})P(\mathbf{p}) = m$ and from equation (E.3) we have that $P(\mathbf{p}) = 1/Q(\varphi(\mathbf{p}))$. Hence

$$\lambda = \frac{1}{P(\mathbf{p})}. \qquad\qquad\blacksquare$$

From equation (E.3) we therefore find that

$$P(\mathbf{p})dQ(\mathbf{x}) = \sum_{i=1}^{n} p_i dx_i. \tag{E.4}$$

Manipulating equation (E.4) algebraically to convert to growth rate (log change) form, we find that

$$d \log Q(\mathbf{x}) = \sum_{i=1}^{n} w_i d \log x_i, \tag{E.5}$$

where $w_i = p_i x_i / m$ is the ith asset's value share in total expenditure on monetary asset services. Equation (E.5) is the Divisia index in growth rate terms. In short, the growth rate of the Divisia index, $Q(\mathbf{x})$, is the share weighted average of the growth rates of the components. The index, as provided in appendix A, equation (A.79), was originated by the French economist, François Divisia (1925, 1926a, b).

To be able to use (E.5) with discrete-time economic data, we need a finite change approximation to (E.5). The Törnqvist–Theil approximation in equation (A.80) of appendix A is very accurate in discrete time. That approximation is explained in section A.6.1 of appendix A along with its relationship to equation (E.5). In brief, the Törnqvist–Theil approximation is exact for the translog aggregator function, as proved by Diewert (1976). Since the translog is a second-order approximation to any aggregator function, it follows that the Törnqvist–Theil approximation is a second-order approximation to the Divisia index, (E.5). The Divisia index (E.5) exactly tracks any aggregator function in continuous time, since (E.5) is directly derived from aggregation theory.

Finally, in order to be able to apply (E.5) to monetary aggregation, we need the user cost of each monetary asset. As in equation (A.5) of appendix A, Barnett (1978, 1980a) proved that the user cost of monetary asset i is

$$p_i = f(p^*, R)(R - r_i), \tag{E.6}$$

where $f(p^*, R) = p^* / (1 + R)$, p^* is the true cost-of-living index, r_i, is the own yield on asset i, and R is the maximum expected holding-period yield available in the economy.

Substituting (E.6) into (E.5), we see that $f(p^*, R)$ cancels out of the numerator and denominator of each share, and hence $f(p^*, R)$ does not appear in the Divisia index formula. As a result we could use the simpler form of the user-cost prices,

$$p_i = R - r_i. \tag{E.7}$$

Clearly, (E.7) is just the interest forgone (and therefore the opportunity cost) of holding asset i.

The Divisia monetary aggregates are acquired by using (E.7) for the user-cost prices in the Törnqvist–Theil discrete time.

E.3   The Weights

The most widely asked questions regarding the Divisia monetary aggregates relate to the "weights" and to the relationship between the weights and interest rates. In this section we consider that subject in light of the derivation in the last section.

If r_i is high, for example, as was the case for money market funds in the late 1970s, then p_i is low in (E.7). Hence, if the yield on money market funds were high and if the "weight" attached to money market funds in a monetary aggregate were its user cost, money market funds would have little influence on the aggregate. Observations of that sort have occasionally led to misunderstandings of the Divisia aggregates. However, the user costs are not the weights. As can be seen from (E.4), the prices weight the marginal component changes, dx_i, to get the dollar value of the marginal change in the aggregate, $P(\mathbf{p})dQ(\mathbf{x})$. This elementary fact, which follows directly from microeconomic theory, does not apply either to the growth rate or to the level of the quantity aggregate. In addition the role of prices in (E.4) applies only at the margin.

The role of prices at the margin should be no surprise, since the relationship between prices and marginal utilities or marginal products is well known. The fallacies that can arise from misinterpreting the role of prices in economics are also well known. For example, the familiar "diamonds and water paradox" illustrates that high price and therefore high marginal utility do not necessarily imply high utility. In fact, if a utility function is strictly concave, then marginal utility and total utility are inversely related. Hence, if we view $Q(\mathbf{x})$ as a utility function, we see that low user-cost price of money-market funds (and therefore low marginal utility, as reflected in equation E.4) does not imply low contribution of money market funds to total utility, $Q(\mathbf{x})$.

If we look at (E.5) rather than (E.4), we see the source of the common interpretation of the shares, w_i, as being the Divisia weights. This interpretation is useful, both because (E.5) does define the Divisia index and also because (E.5) illustrates that the shares weight the component growth rates to get the growth rate of the aggregate. Since the growth rates of monetary aggregates are the most closely watched properties of the aggregates' time paths, the Divisia share weights are important. But note that each share depends on all prices and all quantities. This observation further emphasizes the fact that the user-cost prices are not the weights. Without knowing the own price elasticity of demand for asset i, it is impossible to predict the direction of the change in w_i, when p_i increases. Hence high or rising p_i need not imply high or rising w_i. For example, if $Q(\mathbf{x})$ were Cobb–Douglas, then w_i would be independent of p_i.

As weights, the value shares are far more meaningful than the user costs. The user costs are prices. Every quantity index contains prices in its weights. The Laspeyres, Paasche, and Fisher-ideal quantity indexes all contain prices in their weights. Although each such index uses the same vector of prices, each index certainly does not have the same weights.

Nevertheless, the value shares, w_i, also need to be interpreted with care, when viewed as "weights." If understood clearly in terms of their role in weighting growth rates in (E.5), the shares are indeed weights. However, in common usage, the term "weight" frequently refers to the contribution of the level of a component to the level of the aggregate. The shares do not serve that role for the Divisia index. In fact, in the Divisia index and in general aggregation theory, no such level weights exist. When components are not perfect substitutes, economic aggregates always are nonlinear and therefore cannot be completely strongly separable ("additive"). Without additivity, the concept of weights in levels has no meaning.

To see this problem, suppose that the economic quantity aggregate, $Q(\mathbf{x})$, is completely additive, so that it can be written in the form

$$Q(\mathbf{x}) = \sum_{i=1}^{n} f_i(x_i) \tag{E.8}$$

for some f_i (i = 1, . . ., n). Then we equivalently can write

$$Q(\mathbf{x}) = \sum_{i=1}^{n} A_i(x_i)x_i, \tag{E.9}$$

where $A_i(x_i) = f_i(x_i)/x_i$ is the *average product* (or average utility) of asset (or good) *i*. Clearly, $A_i(x_i)$ also is the weight imputed to component quantity level, x_i, to get the level of the aggregate, $Q(\mathbf{x})$. Since the user costs measure *marginal products* (or marginal utilities), the user costs do not measure the aggregation theoretic level weights, $A_i(x_i)$. Furthermore, unless $Q(\mathbf{x})$ can be written in the form (E.8), $Q(\mathbf{x})$ *cannot* be written as a weighted average of component levels, as in (E.9). Yet most misunderstandings of the Divisia monetary aggregates result from viewing the user costs as the level weights, $A_i(x_i)$, in (E.9). Clearly, both (E.9) and therefore the resulting level weights, $A_i(x_i)$, usually do not exist, and, even when they do, the level weights, $A_i(x_i)$, do not equal the user costs. Furthermore the level weights do not equal the shares, w_i.

In short, misunderstandings of the Divisia monetary aggregates generally stem from confusing marginal products (or user costs) with average products (or level weights, when they exist) or with growth rate weights (or value shares). Understanding of the derivation and discussion above should permit potential users of the Divisia aggregates to avoid such easily made errors.

Finally, to summarize all of the above in one equation, we will solve the differential equation (E.5) for the level of the index, $Q(\mathbf{x})$. First we rewrite (E.5) as the explicit differential equation

$$\frac{d \log Q(\mathbf{x}(t))}{dt} = \sum_{i=1}^{n} w_i(t) \frac{d \log x_i(t)}{dt}, \tag{E.10}$$

where $\mathbf{x}(t)$, $t \in T$, is the time path of the asset quantities and $w_i(t)$, $t \in T$, is the time path of the ith value share. Clearly, $w_i(t) = p_i(t) x_i(t) / \mathbf{p}(t)' \mathbf{x}(t)$, where $\mathbf{p}(t)$, $t \in T$, is the time path of the user-cost prices.

Solving the differential equation (E.10) for $Q(t)$, we get

$$Q(t) = \exp \int_{\tau=0}^{\infty} \left[\sum_{i=1}^{\infty} w_i(\tau) \frac{d \log x_i(\tau)}{d\tau} \right] d\tau. \tag{E.11}$$

In discrete time we would use the Törnqvist–Theil approximation to the line integral (E.11). Inspecting (E.11), we see that $Q(t)$ does not have the simple linearly weighted form of (E.9). Reading "weights" into a deeply nonlinear function such as (E.11) clearly is a hazardous enterprise.

E.4 Is It a Quantity or Price Index?

A deeper understanding of the Divisia index is acquired when one realizes that the weights and even the user-cost prices are really not there at all. One should learn to see through the weights and user costs to the fact that the resulting index equals $Q(\mathbf{x})$, which depends only on quantities. Clearly, the only arguments of $Q(\mathbf{x})$ are the quantities, $\mathbf{x}$. No prices appear as arguments of Q. In short $Q(\mathbf{x})$ is a quantity index, not a price index.

The paradox that may appear to be evident from the appearance of prices on the right-hand side of (E.5) is easily explained through the derivation of (E.5) from (E.2). The prices were used to eliminate the marginal products from (E.2), so that no unknown parameters would exist in the index. However, the marginal products depend only on quantities, and hence the right-hand side of (E.5) continues to track the quantity aggregate on the left side exactly.

Once one has recognized the fact that the Divisia quantity index measures $Q(\mathbf{x})$, which contains no prices, one can see that the Divisia monetary aggregates can be controlled. Federal Reserve policy instruments affect the economy's equilibrium value for $Q(\mathbf{x})$, which measures a true structural economic variable. Since the Divisia monetary aggregates accurately measure $Q(\mathbf{x})$, a stable relationship can be expected to exist between Federal Reserve instruments (e.g., the monetary base or nonborrowed reserves) and the Divisia monetary aggregates. Since the simple-sum aggregates do not measure $Q(\mathbf{x})$, we cannot expect to find a stable relationship between Federal Reserve instruments and the simple-sum aggregates. These theoretical conjectures have been verified empirically repeatedly, as illustrated by figures 3.5 and 3.6 in part I of this book.

The prices in (E.5) affect $Q(\mathbf{x})$ only to the degree that changes in prices induce changes in component quantities, $\mathbf{x}$, affecting $Q(\mathbf{x})$. Similarly prices appear in revealed preference theory, despite the fact that the preferences being revealed are defined only over quantities. Nevertheless, if the Federal Reserve were to adopt the Divisia monetary aggregates as policy targets, it is conceivable that some aspects of the targeting and control procedures might require forecasting of the share weights, w_i ($i = 1, \ldots, n$), rather than direct forecasting of $Q(\mathbf{x})$. However, it would be preferable to treat the Divisia monetary aggregates themselves as elementary variables, and target or forecast them directly, rather than to operate indirectly through the weights. Such targeting in the short run would require deep understanding of the underlying theory and its nonlinear dynamics, but a long-run Divisia "anchor" for policy would require little more than a clear understanding of what it measures.

Since quantities and own prices tend to move in opposite directions along demand curves, value shares tend to be more stable over time than either prices or quantities alone. Hence the value shares can more easily be forecasted than either component quantities or prices alone. In fact a no-change extrapolation, which uses the current-period shares as next-period shares, is usually hard to beat. Hence even the simplest means of forecasting the Divisia share weights is likely to result in far less weighting error than the use of the greatly inaccurate simple-sum weighting scheme.

Finally the possibility of controlling the Divisia monetary aggregates as a long-run policy anchor would be facilitated by the existing institutional arrangements in the money markets. The simple-sum aggregates, at high levels of aggregation, heavily weight high yielding money substitutes, which typically are backed by either zero or low-reserve requirements. The Divisia monetary aggregates, however, frequently impute lower weights to such high yielding component assets. Hence the problems of controlling component assets having low reserve requirements are less serious for the Divisia than the simple-sum aggregates. When treated directly as an elementary variable, the Divisia quantity aggregates are more heavily reserve backed than the simple-sum aggregates computed over the same components.

But it should be emphasized that the validity of the Divisia monetary aggregates as measures of monetary service flows, as opposed to the simple-sum monetary aggregates, which are not validly based on reputable index-number theory, is unrelated to whether or not a monetary long-run target is adopted by the central bank. The Divisia monetary aggregates measure perceived service flow on the demand side, regardless of whether markets are or are not in equilibrium, so long as demanders are price takers. But an understanding of the index-number theory's implications for control of the monetary service flow should give pause to any proposal based on short-term active control of money, since control brings in both demand and supply. The dependency on general equilibrium theory means that short-term active control could require a sophisticated model of the transmission mechanism and of the economy. Use as an indicator, rather than as a short term target, requires far weaker assumptions. Use as a long-run anchor also is far less demanding on the central bank's abilities than short-term active control

E.5   Stocks versus Flows

The Divisia monetary aggregate over $\mathbf{x}$ measures $Q(\mathbf{x})$. With the prices, $\mathbf{p}$, measured as user costs rather than stock prices, $Q(\mathbf{x})$ measures the service flow produced by $\mathbf{x}$. The simple-sum aggregates measure the stock. This result also can be seen by exploring the mathematical relationship between (E.5) and the simple-sum aggregate.

To determine that relationship, we need only write $Q(\mathbf{x}(t)) = \sum_{i=1}^{n} x_i(t)$ and take the time derivative of $\log Q(\mathbf{x}(t))$ in continuous time. We find that we again get (E.10), but with the shares equaling $w_i^* = x_i / \sum_{j=1}^{n} x_j(t)$. Hence in continuous time the Divisia aggregates reduce to the simple-sum aggregates, when all prices are equal. That simple-sum special case can be acquired in one of two ways. One method would be to use $Q(\mathbf{x})$ as a service-flow measure under the assumption that all components are perfect substitutes in identical units. In that case all equilibrium user-cost prices would be equal. The other method would be to treat $Q(\mathbf{x})$ as an accounting (as opposed to economic) stock aggregate. In that case each monetary asset would be a "numéraire" good with price of one dollar. But as shown in appendix B, that latter approach measures the accounting stock of a joint product, not the capital stock of money.

The relationship between the Divisia aggregates and service flows can further be seen through the form of the user-cost prices, (E.7). The theory views the services of monetary assets as being of two types: investment services and other services, such as transactions services. At the margin, r_i fully values the investment services of asset i. The other marginal services are valued by $R - r_i$, which measures the potential investment services forgone by holding asset i at yield r_i when R was potentially available on an asset providing nothing but investment services. In cases of rate regulated assets, the own market yield, r_i, may not fully measure the asset's investment yield. An implicit rate of return then is needed.

E.6   Conclusion

This appendix derives the Divisia index. The discussion examined the concept of "weights" and has pointed out that level weights, as commonly defined, do not exist in this nonlinear context. As shown, the Divisia index is a quantity index that depends only on quantities. The simple-sum stock measure is special case of the Divisia service-flow index, when the user cost or price of all included assets is the same.

References

Abbott, W. J. 1960. A new measure of the money supply. *Federal Reserve Bulletin* 46: 1102–23.

Abrams, B. A. 2006. How Richard Nixon pressured Arthur Burns: Evidence from the Nixon tapes. *Journal of Economic Perspectives* 20: 177–88.

Acharya, D., and B. Kamaia. 2001. Simple sum vs. Divisia monetary aggregates: an empirical evaluation. *Economic and Political Weekly* 36:317–326.

Allen, R. C., and W. E. Diewert. 1981. Direct versus implicit superlative index number formulae. *Review of Economics and Statistics* 63: 430–35.

Anderson, R. G., and C. S. Gascon. 2011. A closer look: Assistance programs in the wake of the crisis. *Regional Economist* 19: 4–10.

Anderson, R. G., and B. E. Jones. 2011 (forthcoming). A comprehensive revision of the monetary services (Divisia) indexes for the United States. *Federal Reserve Bank of St. Louis Review*.

Anderson, R. G., and K. A. Kavajecz. 1994. A historical perspective on the Federal Reserve's monetary aggregates: Definition, construction and targeting. *Federal Reserve Bank of St. Louis Review* 76: 1–31.

Anderson, R. G., B. E. Jones, and T. Nesmith. 1997. Introduction to the St. Louis Monetary Services Index Project. *Federal Reserve Bank of St. Louis Review* 79: 25–29. Reprinted in W. A. Barnett and A. Serletis, eds. (2000), *The Theory of Monetary Aggregation*. Amsterdam: North Holland, app. A.2: 610–16.

Arrow, K. J., and G. H. Hahn. 1971. *General Competitive Analysis*. San Francisco: Holden-Day.

Asimov, I. 1980. *Joy Still Felt: The Autobiography of Isaac Asimov, 1954–1978*. Doubleday, Avon.

Attfield, C. L. F., and M. J. Browning. 1985. A differential demand system, rational expectations, and the life cycle hypothesis. *Econometrica* 53: 31–48.

Axilrod, S. H. 2009. *Inside the Fed*. Cambridge: MIT Press.

Azzimonti, M., E. de Francisco, and P. Krusell. 2008. Aggregation and aggregation. *European Economic Association* 6: 381–94.

Barnett, W. A. 1978. The user cost of money. *Economics Letter* 1: 145–49. Reprinted in W. A. Barnett and A. Serletis, eds. (2000), *The Theory of Monetary Aggregation*. North Holland: Amsterdam: North Holland, pp. 6–10.

Barnett, W. A. 1979a. Theoretical foundations for the Rotterdam model. *Review of Economic Studies* 46: 109–30.

Barnett, W. A. 1979b. The joint allocation of leisure and goods expenditure. *Econometrica* 45: 1117–36.

Barnett, W. A. 1980a. Economic monetary aggregates: An application of aggregation and index number theory. *Journal of Econometrics* 14: 11–48. Reprinted in W. A. Barnett and A. Serletis, eds. (2000), *The Theory of Monetary Aggregation*. Amsterdam: North Holland, pp. 6–10.

Barnett, W. A. 1980b. Economic monetary aggregates: Reply. *Journal of Econometrics* 14: 57–59.

Barnett, W. A. 1981a. *Consumer Demand and Labor Supply: Goods, Monetary Assets, and Time.* Amsterdam: North Holland.

Barnett, W. A. 1981b. The new monetary aggregates: A comment. *Journal of Money, Credit and Banking* 13: 485–89.

Barnett, W. A. 1982. The optimal level of monetary aggregation. *Journal of Money, Credit, and Banking* 14: 687–710. Reprinted in W. A. Barnett and A. Serletis, eds. (2000), *The Theory of Monetary Aggregation*. Amsterdam: North Holland, pp. 125–49.

Barnett, W. A. 1983a. New indices of money supply and the flexible Laurent demand system. *Journal of Business and Economic Statistics* 1: 7–23. Reprinted in W. A. Barnett and A. Serletis, eds. (2000), *The Theory of Monetary Aggregation*. Amsterdam: North Holland, pp. 325–59.

Barnett, W. A. 1983b. Understanding the new Divisia monetary aggregate. *Review of Public Data Use* 11: 349–55. Reprinted in W. A. Barnett and A. Serletis, eds. (2000), *The Theory of Monetary Aggregation*. Amsterdam: North Holland, pp. 100–108.

Barnett, W. A. 1984. Recent monetary policy and the Divisia monetary aggregates. *American Statistician* 38: 162–72. Reprinted in W. A. Barnett and A. Serletis, eds. (2000), *The Theory of Monetary Aggregation*. Amsterdam: North Holland, pp. 563–76.

Barnett, W. A. 1987. The microeconomic theory of monetary aggregation. In W. A. Barnett and K. Singleton, eds., *New Approaches to Monetary Economics*. Cambridge: Cambridge University Press. Reprinted in W. A. Barnett and A. Serletis, eds. (2000), *The Theory of Monetary Aggregation*. Amsterdam: North Holland, pp. 49–99.

Barnett, W. A. 1991. A reply to Julio J. Rotemberg. In M. T. Belongia, ed., *Monetary Policy on the 75th Anniversary of the Federal Reserve System*. Boston: Kluwer Academic, pp. 232–44. Reprinted in W. A. Barnett and A. Serletis, eds. (2000), *The Theory of Monetary Aggregation*. Amsterdam: North Holland, pp. 296–306.

Barnett, W. A. 1995. Exact aggregation under risk. In W. A. Barnett, M. Salles, H. Moulin, and N. Schofield, eds., *Social Choice, Welfare and Ethics*. Cambridge: Cambridge University Press. Reprinted in W. A. Barnett and A. Serletis, eds. (2000), *The Theory of Monetary Aggregation*. Amsterdam: North Holland, pp. 195–216.

Barnett, W. A. 1997. Which road leads to stable money demand? *Economic Journal* 107: 1171–85. Reprinted in W. A. Barnett and A. Serletis, eds. (2000), *The Theory of Monetary Aggregation*. Amsterdam: North Holland, pp. 577–92.

Barnett, W. A. 2003. Aggregation-theoretic monetary aggregation over the euro area when countries are heterogeneous. ECB working paper 260. European Central Bank, Frankfurt.

Barnett, W. A. 2007. Multilateral aggregation-theoretic monetary aggregation over heterogeneous countries. *Journal of Econometrics* 136: 457–82. Reprinted in W. A. Barnett and M. Chauvet, eds. (2011), *Financial Aggregation and Index Number Theory*. Singapore: World Scientific, pp. 167–206.

Barnett, W. A. 2009. Who's looking at the Fed's books? *New York Times*, October 22: A35.

Barnett, W. A. 2010. Audit the Federal Reserve? *Central Banking Journal* 20: 45–50.

Barnett, W. A., and M. Chauvet. 2011a. How better monetary statistics could have signaled the financial crisis. *Journal of Econometrics* 161: 6-23.

Barnett, W. A., and M. Chauvet. 2011b. *Financial Aggregation and Index Number Theory*. Singapore: World Scientific.

Barnett, W. A., and K. H. Choi. 2008. Operational identification of the complete class of superlative index numbers: An application of Galois theory. *Journal of Mathematical Economics* 44: 603–12.

Barnett, W. A., and E. A. Duzhak. 2008. Non-robust dynamic inferences from macroeconometric models: Bifurcation stratification of confidence regions. *Physica A* 387: 3817–25.

Barnett, W. A., and E. A. Duzhak. 2010. Empirical assessment of bifurcation regions within new Keynesian models. *Economic Theory* 45: 99–128.

Barnett, W. A., and P. A. Samuelson. 2007. *Inside the Economist's Mind*. Malden, MA: Wiley/ Blackwell.

Barnett, W. A., and A. Serletis. 1990. A dispersion-dependency diagnostic test for aggregation error: With applications to monetary economics and income distribution. *Journal of Econometrics* 43: 5–34. Reprinted in W. A. Barnett and A. Serletis, eds. (2000), *The Theory of Monetary Aggregation*. Amsterdam: North Holland, pp. 167–94.

Barnett, W. A., and A. Serletis, eds. 2000. *The Theory of Monetary Aggregation*. Amsterdam: Elsevier.

Barnett, W. A., and S. Wu. 2005. On user costs of risky monetary assets. *Annals of Finance* 1: 35–50. Reprinted in W. A. Barnett and M. Chauvet, eds. (2011), *Financial Aggregation and Index Number Theory*. Singapore: World Scientific, pp. 85–105.

Barnett, W. A., and G. Zhou. 1994. Partition of M2+ as a joint product: Commentary. *Federal Reserve Bank of St. Louis Review* 76: 53–62.

Barnett, W. A., U. Chae, and J. Keating. 2006. The discounted economic stock of money with VAR forecasting. *Annals of Finance* 2: 229–58. Reprinted in W. A. Barnett and M. Chauvet, eds. (2011), *Financial Aggregation and Index Number Theory*. Singapore: World Scientific, pp. 107–50.

Barnett, W. A., M. Chauvet, and H. L. R. Tierney. 2009. Measurement error in monetary aggregates: A Markov switching factor approach. *Macroeconomic Dynamics* 13: 381–412. Reprinted in W. A. Barnett and M. Chauvet, eds. (2010), *Financial Aggregation and Index Number Theory*. Singapore: World Scientific, pp. 207–49.

Barnett, W. A., W. E. Diewert, and A. Zellner. 2011. Introduction to "Measurement with Theory." *Journal of Econometrics* 161: 1–5.

Barnett, W., D. Fisher, and A. Serletis. 1992. Consumer theory and the demand for money. *Journal of Economic Literature* 30: 2086–2119. Reprinted in W. A. Barnett and A. Serletis, eds. (2000), *The Theory of Monetary Aggregation*. Amsterdam: North Holland, pp. 167–94.

Barnett, W. A., J. Geweke, and K. Shell, eds. 1989. *Economic Complexity: Chaos, Sunspots, Bubbles, and Nonlinearity: Proceedings of the Fourth International Symposium in Economic Theory and Econometrics*. Cambridge: Cambridge University Press.

Barnett, W. A., M. Hinich, and P. Yue. 1991. Monitoring monetary aggregates under risk aversion. In M. T. Belongia, ed., *Monetary Policy on the 75th Anniversary of the Federal Reserve System*. Boston: Kluwer Academic, pp. 189–222. Reprinted in W. A. Barnett and A. Serletis, eds. (2000), *The Theory of Monetary Aggregation*. Amsterdam: North Holland, pp. 217–44.

Barnett, W. A., M. Hinich, and P. Yue. 2000. The exact theoretical rational expectations monetary aggregate. *Macroeconomic Dynamics* 4: 197–221. Reprinted in W. A. Barnett and M. Chauvet, eds. (2010), *Financial Aggregation and Index Number Theory*. Singapore: World Scientific, pp. 53–84.

Barnett, W. A., Y. Liu, and M. Jensen. 1997. The CAPM risk adjustment for exact aggregation over financial assets. *Macroeconomic Dynamics* 1: 485–512. Reprinted in W. A. Barnett and A. Serletis, eds. (2000), *The Theory of Monetary Aggregation*. Amsterdam: North Holland, pp. 245–95.

Barnett, W. A., E. K. Offenbacher, and P. A. Spindt. 1984. The new Divisia monetary aggregates. *Journal of Political Economy* 92: 1049–85. Reprinted in W. A. Barnett and A. Serletis, eds. (2000), *The Theory of Monetary Aggregation*. Amsterdam: North Holland, pp. 360–88.

Barnett, W. A., A. Serletis, and D. Serletis. 2006. Nonlinear and complex dynamics in real systems. *International Journal of Nonlinear Sciences and Numerical Simulation* 7: 191–96.

Barnett, W. A., A. R. Gallant, M. J. Hinich, J. A. Jungeilges, D. T. Kaplan, and M. J. Jensen. 1997. A single-blind controlled competition among tests for nonlinearity and chaos. *Journal of Econometrics* 82: 157–92.

Batchelor, R. 1988. A monetary services index. *Economic Affairs* 8: 17–20.

Belongia, M. 1995. Weighted monetary aggregates: A historical survey. *Journal of International and Comparative Economics* 4: 87–114.

Belongia, M. 1996. Measurement matters: Recent results from monetary economics reexamined. *Journal of Political Economy* 104: 1065–83.

Belongia, M. T. 2000. Consequences of money stock mismeasurement: Evidence from three countries. In *Divisia Monetary Aggregates: Theory and Practice*, ed. M. T. Belongia and J. E. Binner, 293–312. London: Macmillan.

Belongia, M. 2009. Reforming the Fed: What would real change look like? MPRA paper 18977. Munich Personal RePEc Archive.

Belongia, M., and J. Binner. 2000. *Divisia Monetary Aggregates: Theory and Practice*. New York: Palgrave.

Belongia, M. T., and J. A. Chalfant. 1989. The changing empirical definition of money: Some estimates from a model of the demand for money substitutes. *Journal of Political Economy* 97: 387–97.

Belongia, M., and A. Chrystal. 1991. An admissible monetary aggregate for the United Kingdom. *Review of Economics and Statistics* 73: 497–503.

Belongia, M., and P. Ireland. 2006. The own-price of money and the channels of monetary transmission. *Journal of Money, Credit and Banking* 38: 429–45.

Belongia, M., and P. Ireland. 2010. The Barnett critique after three decades: A new Keynesian analysis. *Journal of Econometrics*, forthcoming.

Beyer, A., J. A. Doornik, and D. F. Hendry. 2001. Constructing historical euro-zone data. *Economic Journal* 111: 308–27.

Binner, J. M., and A. M. Gazely. 1999. A neural network approach to inflation forecasting: The case of Italy. *Global Business and Economics Review* 1:76–92.

Binner, J. M., A. M. Gazely, S.-H. Chen, and B.-T. Chie. 2004. Financial innovation and Divisia money in Taiwan: Comparative evidence from neural network and vector error-correction forecasting models. *Contemporary Economic Policy* 22:213–224.

Blackorby, C., D. Primont, and R. R. Russell. 1978. *Duality, Separability, and Functional Structure*. Amsterdam: North Holland.

Blanchard, O. J., and S. Fischer. 1989. *Lectures on Macroeconomics*. Cambridge: MIT Press.

Bliss, C. J. 1975. *Capital Theory and the Distribution of Income*. Amsterdam: North Holland.

Breeden, D., M. Gibbons, and R. Litzenberger. 1989. Empirical tests of the consumption CAPM. *Journal of Finance* 44: 231–62.

Bremmer, R. P. 2004. *Chairman of the Fed: William McChesney Martin and the Creation of the Modern American Financial System*. New Haven: Yale University Press.

Bullard, J. B. 2009. Three funerals and a wedding. *Federal Reserve Bank of St. Louis Review* 91: 1–12.

Caballero, R. J. 2010. Macroeconomics after the crisis: Time to deal with the pretense-of-knowledge syndrome. *Journal of Economic Perspectives* 24: 85–102.

Campbell, J. Y. 1996. Understanding risk and return. *Journal of Political Economy* 104: 298–345.

Campbell, J. Y., and J. H. Cochrane. 1999. By force of habit: A consumption-based explanation of aggregate stock market behavior. *Journal of Political Economy* 107: 205–51.

Cass, D., and K. Shell. 1983. Do sunspots matter? *Journal of Political Economy* 91: 193–227.

Caves, D. W., L. R. Christensen, and W. E. Diewert. 1982a. The economic theory of index numbers and the measurement of input, output, and productivity. *Econometrica* 50: 1392–1414.

Caves, D. W., L. R. Christensen, and W. E. Diewert. 1982b. Multilateral comparisons of output, input, and productivity using superlative index numbers. *Economic Journal* 92: 73–86.

Calik, S., and S. Uzun. 2009. Comparison of simple sum and Divisia monetary aggregates using panel data analysis. *International Journal of Social Sciences and Humanity Studies* 1:1–13.

Chari, V. V., L. Christiano, and P. J. Kehoe. 2008. Facts and myths about the financial crisis of 2008. Federal Reserve Bank of Minneapolis working paper 666. Minneapolis.

Chauvet, M. 1998. An econometric characterization of business cycle dynamics with factor structure and regime switches. *International Economic Review* 39: 969–96.

Chauvet, M. 2001. A monthly indicator of Brazilian GDP. *Brazilian Review of Econometrics* 21: 1–15.

Chen, N. F., R. Roll, and S. Ross. 1986. Economic forces and the stock market. *Journal of Business* 29: 383–403.

Chetty, K. V. 1969. On measuring the nearness of near-moneys. *American Economic Review* 59: 270–81.

Christensen, L. R., D. W. Jorgenson, and L. J. Lau. 1971. Conjugate duality and the transcendental logarithmic production function. *Econometrica* 39: 255–56.

Christensen, L. R., D. W. Jorgenson, and L. J. Lau. 1973. Transcendental logarithmic production frontiers. *Review of Economics and Statistics* 55: 28–45.

Christensen, L. R., D. W. Jorgenson, and L. J. Lau. 1975. Transcendental logarithmic utility functions. *American Economic Review* 65: 367–83.

Chrystal, A., and R. MacDonald. 1994. Empirical evidence on the recent behaviour and usefulness of simple-sum and weighted measures of the money stock. *Federal Reserve Bank of St. Louis Review* 76: 73–109.

Cieśla, N. 1999. Konstrukcja pieniężnych agregatów Divisia w warunkac Polskich. Materialy i Studia nr 89, NBP, Warszawa.

Clements, K. W., and H. Y. Izan. 1984. The measurement of inflation: A stochastic approach. *Journal of Business and Economic Statistics* 5: 339–50.

Cochrane, J. H. 2000. *Asset Pricing*. Princeton: Princeton University Press.

Cochrane, J. H. 2007. Inflation determination with Taylor rules: A critical review. NBER working paper 13409. Cambridge, MA.

Cockerline, J., and J. Murray. 1981. A comparison of alternative methods for monetary aggregation: Some preliminary evidence. Technical report 28. Bank of Canada, Ottawa.

Coen, R. M., and B. G. Hickman. 1970. Constrained joint estimation of factor demand and production functions. *Review of Economics and Statistics* 52: 287–300.

Collins, S., and C. L. Edwards. 1994. An alternative monetary aggregate: M2 plus household holdings of bond and equity mutual funds. *Federal Reserve Bank of St. Louis Review* 76: 7–29.

Dahalan, J., S. C. Sharma, and K. Sylwester. 2005. Divisia monetary aggregates and money demand for Malaysia. *Journal of Asian Economics* 15:1137–1153.

Davoudi, P., and Z. Zarepour. 2007. The role of definition of money in the stability of the Iranian demand for money. *Iranian Economic Research* 29:47–74.

Debreu, G. 1959. *Theory of Value*. New Haven: Yale University Press.

Deaton, A., and J. N. Muellbauer. 1980. *Economics and Consumer Behavior*. Cambridge: Cambridge University Press.

Diewert, W. E. 1976. Exact and superlative index numbers. *Journal of Econometrics* 4: 115–45.

Diewert, W. E. 1978. Superlative index numbers and consistency in aggregation. *Econometrica* 46: 883–900.

Diewert, W. E. 1980a. Aggregation problems in the measurement of capital. In D. Usher, ed., *The Measurement of Capital*. Chicago: University of Chicago Press/NBER, pp. 433–538.

Diewert, W. E. 1980b. Capital and the theory of productivity measurement. *American Economic Review* 70: 260–67.

Diewert, W. E. 1980c. Reply. In D. Usher, ed., *The Measurement of Capital.* Chicago: University of Chicago Press/NBER, p. 538.

Diewert, W. E. 1981a. The economic theory of index numbers: A survey. In A. Deaton, ed., *Essays in the Theory and Measurement of Consumer Behaviour in Honour of Sir Richard Stone.* Cambridge: Cambridge University Press, pp. 163–208.

Divino, J. A. 1997. An analysis of the money demand using Divisia monetary aggregates and Box–Cox transformation. *Revista Nova Economia.* Belo Horizonte, FACE/UFMG 7: 181–246.

Divino, J. A. 2000. Weighted monetary aggregation: An analysis of causality. *Economia Aplicada* 4:723–742.

Divisia, F. 1925. L'indice monétaire et la théorie de la monnaie. *Revue d'Economie Politique* 39: 842–64.

Divisia, F. 1926a. L'indice monétaire et la théorie de la monnaie. *Revue d'Economie Politique* 39: 980–1008.

Divisia, F. 1926b. *L'Indice monétaire et la théorie de la monnaie.* Paris: Sirey.

Divisia, F. 1928. *Économique rationnelle.* Paris: Doin.

Divisia, F. 1950. *Exposés d'économique.* Paris: Dunod.

Divisia, F. 1962. *Traitement économétrique de la monnaie, l'intérêt, l'emploi.* Paris: Dunod.

Donovan, D. 1978. Modeling the demand for liquid assets: An application to Canada. *IMF Staff Papers* 25: 676–704.

Drake, L. 1992. The substitutability of financial assets in the U. K. and the implication for monetary aggregation. *Manchester School of Economic and Social Studies* 60: 221–48.

Drake, L., A. Mullineux, and J. Agung. 1997. One Divisia money for Europe? *Applied Economics* 29: 775–86.

Driscoll, M. J., J. L. Ford, A. W. Mullineux, and W. Kohler. 1985. Monetary aggregates, their information content and their aggregation error: Some preliminary findings for Austria, 1965–1980. *Empirical Economics* 10:13–25.

Easterly, M., M. Paolo, and K. Schmidt-Hebbel. 1995. Money demand and seigniorage-maximizing inflation. *Journal of Money, Credit and Banking* 27: 583–603.

Fama, E. F., and K. French. 1992. The cross-section of expected stock returns. *Journal of Finance* 47: 427–65.

Fase, M. M. G. 1985. Monetary control, the Dutch experience: Some reflections on the liquidity ratio. In C. van Ewijk and J. J. Klant, eds., *Monetary Conditions for Economic Recovery.* Dordrecht: Martinus Nijhoff, pp. 95–125.

Fase, M. M. G. 2000. Divisia aggregates and the demand for money in core EMU. In M. T. Belongia and J. E. Binner, eds., *Divisia Monetary Aggregates: Theory and Practice.* London: Macmillan, pp. 138–69.

Fase, M. M. G., and C. C. A. Winder. 1994. *Money Demand within EMU: An Analysis with the Divisia Measure.* Amsterdam: De Nederlandsche BankNV, pp. 25–55.

Fayyad, S. K. 1986. Monetary asset component grouping and aggregation: An inquiry into the definition of money. PhD thesis. University of Texas at Austin.

Feenstra, R. C. 1986. Functional equivalence between liquidity costs and the utility of money. *Journal of Monetary Economics* 17: 271–91.

Fisher, I. 1922. *The Making of Index Numbers: A Study of Their Varieties, Tests, and Reliability*. Boston: Houghton Mifflin.

Fisher, F. M., and K. Shell. 1972. *The Economic Theory of Price Indices*. New York: Academic Press.

Fisher, F. M., and K. Shell. 1998. *Economic Analysis of Production Price Indexes*. Cambridge: Cambridge University Press.

Friedman, M. 1968. The role of monetary policy. *American Economic Review* 58: 1–17.

Friedman, M. 1994. *Money Mischief: Episodes in Monetary History*. Boston: Houghton Mifflin Harcourt.

Friedman, M., and A. J. Schwartz. 1970. *Monetary Statistics of the United States: Estimates, Sources, Methods, and Data*. Columbia University Press/NBER. New York.

Fuss, M. A. 1977. The demand for energy to Canadian manufacturing. *Journal of Econometrics* 5: 89–116.

Gaab, W. 1996. On the demand for Divisia and simple-sum M3 in Germany. In *Financial Innovation, Banking and Monetary Aggregates*, ed. A. Mullineux, 160–186. Cheltenham: Elgar.

Galbraith, J. K. [1955] 1961. *The Great Crash: 1929*. Boston: Houghton Mifflin.

Ganev, G. Y. 1997. Monetary aggregates in a transition economy: The case of Bulgaria, 1991–1997. PhD thesis. Department of Economics, Washington University, Saint Louis.

Gay, D. E. R. 2008. Divisia, François Jean Marie (1889–1964). In S. N. Durlauf and L. E. Blume, eds., *The New Palgrave Dictionary of Economics Online*. 2nd ed. Basingstoke: Palgrave Macmillan. <http://www.dictionaryofeconomics.com.www2.lib.ku.edu:2048/article?id=pde2008_D000175> doi:10.1057/9780230226203.0399.

Gilbert, R. A. 1994. A case study in monetary control: 1980–82. *Federal Reserve Bank of St. Louis Review* 76: 35–58.

Goldfeld, S. M. 1973. The demand for money revisited. *Brookings Papers on Economic Activity* 3: 577–638.

Gorman, W. M. 1953. Community preference fields. *Econometrica* 21: 63–80.

Greidanus, T. 1932. *The Value of Money*. London: King and Son.

Habibullah, M. S. 1999. *Divisia Monetary Aggregates and Economic Activities in Asian Developing Economics.*, 67–111. Aldershot: Ashgate Publishing.

Hall, R., and D. Jorgenson. 1967. Tax policy and investment behavior. *American Economic Review* 57: 391–414.

Hahm, J. H., and J. T. Kim. 2000. The signals from Divisia money in a rapidly growing economy. In *Divisia Monetary Aggregates: Theory and Practice*, ed. M. T. Belongia and J. E. Binner, 200–226. London: Macmillan.

Hancock, D. 1985. The financial firm: Production with monetary and non-monetary goods. *Journal of Political Economy* 93: 859–80.

Hancock, D. 1986. A model of the financial firm with imperfect asset and deposit elasticities. *Journal of Banking and Finance* 10: 37–54.

Hancock, D. 1991. *A Theory of Production for the Financial Firm*. Norwell, MA: Kluwer Academic.

Hancock, M. 2005. Divisia money. *Bank of England Quarterly Bulletin* 45:39–46.

Hanke, S., and M. Sekerke. 2002. A shroud of secrecy. *Central Banking Journal* 13:131–135.

Herrmann, J., J.-E. Reimers, and K.-H. Toedter. 2000. Weighted monetary aggregates for Germany. In *Divisia Monetary Aggregates: Theory and Practice*, ed. M. T. Belongia and J. E. Binner, 79–100. London: Macmillan.

Hicks, J. R. 1946. *Value and Capital*. Oxford: Clarendon Press.

Hoa, T. V. 1985. A Divisia system approach to modeling monetary aggregates. *Economics Letters* 17: 365–68.

Hueng, C. J. 1998. The demand for money in an open economy: Some evidence for Canada. *North American Journal of Economics and Finance* 9:15–31.

Hulten, C. 1973. Divisia index numbers. *Econometrica* 63: 1017–26.

Hutt, W. H. 1963. *Keynesianism: Retrospect and Prospect*. Chicago: Regnery.

Ingersoll, J. E. 1987. *Theory of Financial Decision Making*. Totowa, NJ: Rowman and Littlefield.

Ishida, K. 1984. Divisia monetary aggregates and the demand for money: A Japanese case. *Bank of Japan Monetary and Economic Studies* 2: 49–80.

Jha, R., and I. S. Longjam. 1999. Will the right monetary aggregate for India please stand up? *Economic and Political Weekly* 34:631–40.

Jones, B., D. Dutkowsky, and T. Elger. 2005. Sweep programs and optimal monetary aggregation. *Journal of Banking & Finance* 29: 483–508.

Jorgenson, D. 1963. Capital theory and investment behavior. *American Economic Review* 53: 247–59.

Jorgenson, D. 1967. The theory of investment behavior. In R. Ferber, ed., *Determinants of Investment Behavior*. New York: Columbia University Press, pp. 129–56.

Keynes, J. M. 1963. *The General Theory of Employment*: Interest, and Money. New York: Harcourt Brace.

Kloek, T. 1967. On quadratic approximations of cost of living and real income index numbers. Report 6710. Econometric Institute, Netherlands School of Economics, Rotterdam.

Kluza, S. 2001. *Zastosowanie indeksów Divisia w polsce. Rozprawa doctorska*. Warszawa: Kolegium Analiz Ekonomicznych, Szkola Glówna Handlowa.

Kocherlakota, N. 1996. The equity premium: It's still a puzzle. *Journal of Economic Literature* 34: 43–71.

Kocherlakota, N. 2010. Modern macroeconomic models as tools for economic policy. *The Region*, 5–21.

Konüs, A. A. 1924. The problem of the true index of the cost-of-living (in Russian). *The Economic Bulletin of the Institute of Economic Cojuncture*, Moscow, no. 9–10: 64–71. English translation: 1939. *Econometrica* 7: 10–29.

Kunter, K. 1993. Türkiye'deki parasal büyüklükler için indeks ve bilesim teorisinin bir uygulamasi: Divisia ve Fisher indeksi, CBRT discussion Papers. www.tcmb.gov.tr/research/discus/9304tur.pdf.

Kydland, F. E., and E. C. Prescott. 1982. Time to build and aggregate fluctuations. *Econometrica* 51: 1345–70.

La Cour, L. F. 2006. The problem of measuring "money": Results from an analysis of Divisia monetary aggregates for Denmark. In *Money, Measurement, and Computation*, ed. M. T. Belongia and J. E. Binner, 185–210. New York: Palgrave Macmillan.

Lamont, O. 2000. Economic tracking portfolio. *Journal of Econometrics* 105: 161–84.

Lettau, M., and S. Ludvigson. 2001. Resurrecting the (C)CAPM: A cross-sectional test when risk premia are time-varying. *Journal of Political Economy* 109: 1238–87.

Lintner, J. 1965. The valuation of risky assets and the selection of risky investments in stock portfolios and capital budgets. *Review of Economics and Statistics* 47: 13–37.

Longworth, D., and J. Atta-Mensah. 1994. The Canadian experience with weighted monetary aggregates. Working paper. Bank of Canada.

Lucas, R. E. 1976. Econometric policy evaluation: A critique. *Carnegie-Rochester Conference Series on Public Policy* 1: 19–46.

Lucas, R. E. 1981. *Studies in Business Cycle Theory*. Cambridge: MIT Press.

Lucas, R. E. 1987. *Models of Business Cycles*. New York: Basil Blackwell.

Lucas, R. E. 2000. Inflation and welfare. *Econometrica* 68: 247–74.

Lucas, R. E. 2003. Macroeconomic priorities. *American Economic Review* 93: 1–14.

Lemesle, L. L. V. 1998. François Divisia, a pioneer responsible for the integration of mathematical method into French economics. In W. J. Samuels, ed., *European Economists of the Early 20th Century*. Cheltenham: Elgar, pp. 81–93.

Malmquist, S. 1953. Index numbers and indifference surfaces. *Tradajos de Estatistica* 4: 209–41.

Marshall, D. 1997. Comments on CAPM risk adjustment for exact aggregation over financial assets. *Macroeconomic Dynamics* 1: 513–23.

McGrattan, E. R., and E. C. Prescott. 2000. Is the stock market overvalued? *Federal Reserve Bank of Minneapolis Quarterly Review* 24: 20–40.

Mehra, R., and E. C. Prescott. 1985. The equity premium: A puzzle. *Journal of Monetary Economics* 15: 145–61.

Meltzer, A. 2002. *A History of the Federal Reserve*, vol. 1. Chicago: University of Chicago Press.

Meltzer, A. 2010. *A History of the Federal Reserve*, vol. 2. Chicago: University of Chicago Press.

Moorsteen, R. H. 1961. On measuring productive potential and relative efficiency. *Quarterly Journal of Economics* 75: 451–67.

Morgenstern, O. 1965. *On the Accuracy of Economic Observations*, 2nd ed. Princeton: Princeton University Press.

Mullineux, A., ed. 1996. *Financial Innovation, Banking, and Monetary Aggregat.* Cheltenham: Elgar.

Neto, F. A. F., and J. Albuquerque. 2002. *Indicadores derivados de agregados monetários. Trabalhos para Discussão 47.* Banco Central do Brasil.

Ohta, M. 1974. A note on the duality between production and cost functions: Rate of returns to scale and rate of technical progress. *Economic Studies Quarterly* 25: 63–65.

Orphanides, A. 2001. Monetary policy rules based on real-time data. *American Economic Review* 91: 964–85.

Orphanides, A., B. Reid, and D. H. Small. 1994. The empirical properties of a monetary aggregate that adds bond and stock funds to M2. *Federal Reserve Bank of St. Louis Review* 76: 31–51.

Patrick, S. C. 1993. *Reform of the Federal Reserve System in the Early 1930's: The Politics of Money and Banking.* New York: Garland.

Phelps, E. S. 1970. The new microeconomics in employment and inflation theory. In E. S. Phelps, ed., *Microeconomic Foundations of Employment and Inflation Theory.* New York: Norton.

Phlips, L., and F. Spinnewyn. 1982. Rationality versus myopia in dynamic demand systems. In R. L. Basmann and G. F. Rhodes, eds., *Advances in Econometrics.* Greenwich, CT: JAI Press, pp. 3–33.

Poole, W. 1979. Monetary policy: Eight years of progress? *Journal of Finance* 34: 473–84.

Poterba, J. M., and J. J. Rotemberg. 1987. Money in the utility function: An empiricial implementation. In W. A. Barnett and K. J. Singleton, eds., *New Approaches to Monetary Economics.* Cambridge: Cambridge University Press, pp. 219–40.

Quirk, J. D., and R. Saposnik. 1968. *Introduction to General Equilibrium Theory and Welfare Economics.* New York: McGraw-Hill.

Rayton, B. A., and K. Pavlyk. 2010. On the recent divergence between measures of the money supply in the UK. *Economics Letters* 108: 159–62.

Reimers, H. E. 2002. Analysing Divisia aggregates for the euro area. Discussion paper 13/02. Economic Research Centre of the Deutsche Bundesbank, Frankfurt.

Robb, G. 2009. Fed's Bullard argues for return to setting monetary targets. *Market Watch,* www.marketwatch.com (accessed February 17, 2009).

Rotemberg, J. J. 1991. Commentary: Monetary aggregates and their uses. In M. T. Belongia, ed., *Monetary Policy on the 75th Anniversary of the Federal Reserve System.* Boston: Kluwer Academic, pp. 232–44.

Rotemberg, J. J., and J. Poterba. 1995. Money, output, and prices: Evidence from a new monetary aggregate. *Journal of Business and Economic Statistics* 12: 67–83.

Roy, R. 1964. Francois Divisia, 1889–1964. *Econometrica* 33: 635–40.

Rubinstein, M. 1976. The valuation of uncertain income streams and the pricing of options. *Bell Journal of Economics* 7: 407–25.

Samuelson, P. A. 1947. *Foundations of Economic Analysis.* Cambridge: Harvard University Press.

Samuelson, P. A., and R. Sato. 1984. Unattainability of integrability and definiteness conditions in the general case of demand for money and goods. *American Economic Review* 74: 588–604.

Sato, K. 1975. *Production Functions and Aggregation*. Amsterdam: North Holland.

Schunk, D. 2001. The relative forecasting performance of the Divisia and simple sum monetary aggregates. *Journal of Money, Credit and Banking* 33: 272–83.

Serletis, A. 1991. The demand for Divisia money in the United States: A dynamic flexible demand system. *Journal of Money, Credit and Banking* 23: 35–52.

Serletis, A. 2006. *Money and the Economy*. Singapore: World Scientific.

Serletis, A. 2007. *The Demand for Money: Theoretical and Empirical Approaches*. Berlin: Springer.

Serletis, A., and T. E. Molik. 2000. Monetary aggregation and monetary policy. In *Money, Monetary Policy and Transmission Mechanisms*. Bank of Canada, pp. 103–35.

Serletis, A., and A. Shahmoradi. 2007. Flexible functional forms, curvature conditions, and the demand for assets. *Macroeconomic Dynamics* 11: 455–86.

Shannon, C. E. 1951. Prediction and entropy of printed English. *Bell System Technical Journal* 30: 50–64.

Shaplen, R. 1960. *Kreuger Genius and Swinder*. New York: Knopf.

Sharpe, W. F. 1964. Capital asset prices: A theory of market equilibrium under conditions of risk. *Journal of Finance* 19: 425–42.

Shephard, R. W. 1970. *Theory of Cost and Production Functions*. Princeton: Princeton University Press.

Shih, J. C. 2000. Divisia monetary aggregates for Taiwan. In *Divisia Monetary Aggregates: Theory and Practice*, ed. M. T. Belongia and J. E. Binner, 227–248. London: Macmillan.

Shiller, R. J. 2000. *Irrational Exuberance*. Princeton: Princeton University Press.

Shiller, R. J. 2005. *Irrational Exuberance*, 2nd ed. Princeton: Princeton University Press.

Sims, C. A. 1969. Theoetical basis for a double deflated index of real value added. *Review of Economics and Statistics* 51: 470–71.

Spindt, P. A. 1985. The rates of turnover of money goods under efficient monetary trade: Implications for monetary aggregation. *Economics Letters* 17: 141–43.

Sriram, S. S. 2002. Determinants and stability of demand for M2 in Malaysia. *Journal of Asian Economics* 13:337–356.

Stein, C. 1973. Estimation of the mean of a multivariate normal distribution. *Proceedings of the Prague Symposium on Asymptotic Statistics*, September.

Stracca, L. 2001. Does liquidity matter: Properties of a synthetic Divisia monetary aggregate in the euro area. ECB working paper 79. European Central Bank, Frankfurt.

Swamy, P. A. V. B., and P. Tinsley. 1980. Linear prediction and estimation methods for regression models with stationary stochastic coefficients. *Journal of Econometrics* 12: 103–42.

Samuelson, P. A., and S. Swamy. 1974. Invariant economic index numbers and canonical duality: Survey and synthesis. *American Economic Review* 64: 566–93.

Spencer, P. 1997. Monetary integration and currency substitution in the EMS: The case of a European monetary aggregate. *European Economic Review* 41: 1403–19.

Swofford, J. L. 2000. Microeconomic foundations of an optimal currency area. *Review of Financial Economics* 9: 121–28.

Tariq, S. M., and K. Matthews. 1997. The demand for simple-sum and Divisia monetary aggregates for Pakistan: A cointegration approach. *Pakistan Development Review* 3:275–291.

Taylor, J. B. 1993. Discretion versus policy rules in practice. *Carnegie-Rochester Conference Series on Public Policy* 39: 195–214.

Tett, G. 2009. *Fool's Gold: How the Bold Dream of a Small Tribe at J.P. Morgan Was Corrupted by Wall Street Greed and Unleashed a Catastrophe*. New York: Free Press.

Theil, H. 1967. *Economics and Information Theory*. Amsterdam: North Holland.

Theil, H. 1971. *Principles of Econometrics*. New York: Wiley.

Thornton, D. L., and P. Yue. 1992. An extended series of Divisia monetary aggregates. *Federal Reserve Bank of St. Louis Review* 74: 35–52.

Toma, E. F., and M. Toma. 1985. Research activities and budget allocations among Federal Reserve Banks. *Public Choice* 45: 175–91.

Törnqvist, L. 1936. The Bank of Finland's Consumption Price Index. *Bank of Finland Review* 10: 1–8.

Usher, D. 1980. Introduction. In D. Usher, ed., *The Measurement of Capital*. Chicago: University of Chicago Press/NBER, pp. 1–21.

Vartia, Y. O. 1976. Ideal log change index numbers. *Scandinavian Journal of Statistics* 3: 121–26.

Wesche, K. 1997. The demand for Divisia money in a core monetary union. *Federal Reserve Bank of St. Louis Review* 7: 51–60.

White, L. H. 2005. The Federal Reserve System's influence on research in monetary economics. *Econ Journal Watch* 2: 325–54.

Woodford, M. 2003. *Interest and Prices: Foundations of a Theory of Monetary Policy*. Princeton: Princeton University Press.

Woodward, B. 2001. *Maestro: Greenspan's Fed and the American Boom*. New York: Simon and Schuster.

Wu, C. S., J. L. Lin, G. C. Tiao, and D. D. Cho. 2005. Is money demand in Taiwan stable? *Economic Modelling* 22:327–346.

Yu, Q., and A. K. Tsui. 2000. Monetary services and money demand in China. *China Economic Review* 11: 134–48.

Yue, P., and R. Fluri. 1991. Divisia monetary services indexes for Switzerland: Are they useful for monetary targeting? *Federal Reserve Bank of St. Louis Review* 73: 19–33.

Index

Advance Praise for

Getting It Wrong
How Faulty Monetary Statistics Undermine the Fed, the Financial System, and the Economy
By William A. Barnett

Getting It Wrong is a magisterial treatment on the measurement of monetary aggregates by the world's foremost authority. Barnett informs us about how to get the measurements right. He also shows us how the Federal Reserve gets them wrong. Indeed, if Paul Volcker's dashboard would have displayed Barnett's monetary metrics, the severe 1981–82 recession might never have occurred. Alas, the Fed's money supply gauges remain in need of an overhaul by Barnett, a monetary master craftsman.
—Steve H. Hanke, Professor of Applied Economics, Johns Hopkins University, and *Forbes* magazine columnist

You would think that by now so much has been written about the causes of the 2007–08 financial crisis that nothing else needs to be said. This book persuasively explains why any such assumption would be wrong. It turns out that mis-measured money is another culprit that has not been given its due. Professor Barnett, in this remarkable book, corrects this oversight. Economists, public policy makers, and informed students of monetary policy will never think about the subject the same way after reading this pathbreaking book.
—Robert E. Litan, Kauffman Foundation Vice President for Research and Policy and Brookings Institution Senior Fellow

Getting It Wrong gives masterful insights into causes of the financial crisis beyond simplistic notions of "greed" or "failure of theory." This book shows how faulty measures led to incorrect risk assessments and failure of policy makers, including the Fed. Using flawed gauges, policy makers promoted notions of a "Great Moderation" with reduced systemic risks and thereby ended up steering markets to crisis. William Barnett, a pioneer in economic measurement theory and practice, shows us how to do it right.
—Jeffrey M. Wrase, Professional Congressional Staff Member

This book is a tour de force. Barnett argues that theoreticians have provided the tools for practitioners to deliver sound macroeconomic policies. The problem is that the Fed is not producing data based on best-practice principles, thereby distorting the information set available to practitioners and leading to misguided policies, misperceptions about systemic risk, and the crisis that erupted in 2008. Barnett navigates effortlessly through the interconnections between theory and policy. The result is a compelling and fascinating study of "what went wrong," and the making of a modern classic in economics.
—George S. Tavlas, Director General, Bank of Greece; Alternate Member, ECB Governing Council; and Editor, *Open Economies Review*

In this masterful book, William Barnett provides a compelling explanation of what went wrong in the years leading up to the worst financial crisis since the Great Depression, as well as a broader history of the last half-century of Federal Reserve policy-making. He presents clear and intuitive arguments to support the message that runs through his most important scholarly work—that measures of the money supply, when properly constructed, accurately and reliably describe what monetary policy is actually doing—using a separate section to fill in the details for more technically inclined readers.
—Peter Ireland, Murray and Monti Professor of Economics, Boston College

This riveting read from William Barnett combines detailed and very deep knowledge of monetary history and precise economic theory, to provide a compelling personal view of the crisis in both the financial markets and in macroeconomic/monetary policy. Barnett is the leader in devising monetary aggregates, and he makes a strong case against alternative "simple-sum" aggregators that the Fed and others employ. His attribution of partial blame to bad data and bad aggregates for the "Great Recession" is novel, has merit, and is strongly argued. Some may argue that this too is a "symptom" rather than a cause, of recurring "cycles" in our type of economy, but Barnett is able to masterfully draw on his vast knowledge of many fields and his unusual command of current cultural and media influences to infuse his discussion of very deep theoretical and policy debates, making the book very readable and useful to noneconomists.
—Esfandiar Maasoumi, Arts and Sciences Distinguished Professor, Emory University, and Editor of *Econometric Reviews*

Whether you are a Wall Street professional, an academic economist, or simply interested in the Fed, *Getting It Wrong* is essential. William Barnett weaves personal vignettes into seminal monetary events, creating a riveting read. For the quant, Barnett—an eminent economic scientist—details his pathbreaking advances in monetary and financial measurement. With interest rates near record lows, Barnett's monetary theory and tools are needed more than ever for officials, investors, and the public.
—Lawrence Goodman, President, Center for Financial Stability, Inc.